SECOND EDITION

SOCIAL POLICY FOR CHILDREN AND FAMILIES

SECOND EDITION

SOCIAL POLICY FOR CHILDREN AND FAMILIES

A Risk and Resilience Perspective

Jeffrey M. Jenson
University of Denver

Mark W. Fraser
University of North Carolina at Chapel Hill

Los Angeles | London | New Delhi
Singapore | Washington DC

For information:

SAGE Publications, Inc.
2455 Teller Road
Thousand Oaks,
    California 91320
E-mail: order@sagepub.com

SAGE Publications Ltd.
1 Oliver's Yard
55 City Road
London EC1Y 1SP
United Kingdom

SAGE Publications India Pvt. Ltd.
B 1/I 1 Mohan Cooperative
    Industrial Area
Mathura Road, New Delhi 110 044
India

SAGE Publications Asia-Pacific Pte. Ltd.
33 Pekin Street #02-01
Far East Square
Singapore 048763

Printed in the United States of America

Library of Congress Cataloging-in-Publication Data

Social policy for children and families: a risk and resilience perspective /
editors Jeffrey M. Jenson, Mark W. Fraser. — 2nd ed.
    p. cm.
Rev. ed. of: Social policy for children & families: a risk and resilience perspective. 2006.
Includes bibliographical references and index.
ISBN 978-1-4129-8139-2 (pbk.)
    1. Children—Government policy—United States. 2. Child welfare—United States.
3. Youth—Government policy—United States. 4. Family policy—United States.
5. Developmental psychology. 6. Child development. I. Jenson, Jeffrey M. II. Fraser,
Mark W., 1946- III. Social policy for children & families.

HV741.S623 2011
362.820973—dc22   2010026685

This book is printed on acid-free paper.

    12   13   14   15   10   9   8   7   6   5   4   3

Acquisitions Editor:	Kassie Graves
Editorial Assistant:	Veronica K. Novak
Production Editor:	Libby Larson
Permissions Editor:	Adele Hutchinson
Copy Editor:	Jacqueline Tasch
Typesetter:	C&M Digitals (P) Ltd.
Proofreader:	Jenifer Kooiman
Indexer:	Rick Hurd
Cover Designer:	Gail Buschman
Marketing Manager:	Stephanie Adams

Contents

Foreword to the First Edition

Many young people in the United States grow up in circumstances that place them at risk for school failure, delinquency, substance abuse, and other social problems. Some children are born with disabilities that condition their capacity to learn. Others are raised in dangerous environments characterized by unsanitary conditions or are exposed to toxic substances that lead to developmental delays and learning problems in school. A significant number of American children and youth live in unsafe neighborhoods or neglectful families. Sadly, many of these children develop disruptive behaviors that alienate them from peers and teachers as they begin their formal education.

In most cases, parents find ways to offset biological and environmental risk by providing the social, emotional, and financial supports that are necessary to raise a healthy child or adolescent. However, despite their best efforts, some parents find it impossible to create the opportunities and environmental conditions that help their children succeed at school and in the community. The result is seen in a young person's decision to drop out of school, use illicit drugs, or participate in any number of anti-social behaviors as an adolescent or young adult. Lack of opportunities and environmental supports also contributes to childhood depression and eating disorders and may increase the likelihood that some youth will leave home to test their independence or escape abusive circumstances by living on the street or with friends. Such children and youth are often referred to public programs and become the concern of elected officials, policymakers, and practitioners.

How should we help? Finding effective solutions to the complex problems facing American children, youth, and families is one of our nation's foremost public policy challenges. Child and family policies have vacillated widely over time, depending on prevailing philosophical beliefs about the most effective way to help vulnerable children, youth, and families. Resultant programs and interventions for children and families have been plagued by inconsistency and by a fragmented service delivery system that often fails to consider the multiple needs of young people and their parents. In some cases, bureaucratic obstacles have worked to reduce innovations in policy or program responses.

Child, youth, and family policies are implemented in the nation's welfare, health, mental health, child welfare, juvenile justice, substance abuse, and education systems. Each of these systems is large and complex, and each operates in partial isolation from the other. My experience in the U.S. Congress reveals a need for fresh thinking about the individual and social problems facing American children and families. New frameworks are necessary to help elected officials and policymakers design and deliver integrated policies and programs across all systems of care for children, youth, and families.

In this book, Jeffrey M. Jenson and Mark W. Fraser outline a risk and resilience framework that offers promise for innovations in policies targeting vulnerable families and children. The model is based on knowledge gained from studying the risk and protective factors associated with the onset and persistence of such problems as delinquency and substance abuse. It suggests that policies and programs targeting known causes and correlates of child and adolescent problems are most likely to be successful in preventing problem behaviors and supporting children and families.

Jenson and Fraser have asked an impressive group of scholars to apply this framework to the design of social policies in income maintenance, child welfare, education, mental health, health, developmental disabilities, substance abuse, and juvenile justice. Each chapter author has addressed the issue of policy and service integration across different systems of care. Case examples are used to illustrate innovative approaches and to illustrate ways that service integration might be achieved. Borrowing from ecological theorists, Jenson, Fraser, and colleagues emphasize the importance of designing policies that address social and health problems at the individual, family, community, and state levels. The result is a book filled with promising ideas about the best ways to deliver a more comprehensive attack on the multiple problems facing young people.

The ideas expressed in this book represent an important shift in thinking about conventional policy development processes. A risk and resilience perspective—combined with principles emphasizing the integration of policy across different care systems—is a logical progression in the process of creating policies for children, youth, and families. Elected officials and policymakers would do well to read and apply the principles expressed in this book to the problems faced by American families.

—Mark Udall
U.S. Senator, Colorado

Foreword to the Second Edition

The message of this book is clear and compelling. Government policy affecting children and adolescents should be guided by recent advances in prevention science. Specifically, public policy should seek to address and reduce factors in children's lives that research has shown increase risk for later mental, emotional, and behavioral problems while simultaneously seeking to strengthen factors found through research to promote prosocial and healthy development and protect against risk. Jenson and Fraser and their colleagues show convincingly that in virtually every publicly funded social service system established to improve outcomes for children, a risk and protection-focused approach to designing policy would likely prevent later more serious and costly problems for children, their families, and their communities. These authors understand the contribution of evidence-based practice and seek to extend the use of intervention research to guide policy through the rigorous testing of preventive, early intervention, and treatment interventions. They suggest that future policy in the eight substantive areas addressed here should involve the selection, widespread application and faithful installation of interventions shown to effectively reduce risk, enhance protection and/or resilience, and prevent later health, mental health, emotional, or behavioral problems.

As noted by Jenson and Fraser in the final chapter, one of the striking things in reading this book is the degree to which outcomes in the income maintenance, child welfare, education, mental health, health, disabilities, drug prevention and treatment, and juvenile justice systems are predicted by common risk and protective factors. The same factors in communities, families, and individuals appear to predict diverse outcomes addressed in our current "system of services" by entirely different social service and educational bureaucracies. In fact, these diverse outcomes often co occur: mental health problems among juvenile offenders, alcohol and drug misuse among abused children, educational failure in late elementary grades followed by minor delinquency, alcohol and drug use, more serious crime, and early sexual risk-taking. It is often a struggle to find effective interventions for those with co-occurring problems. But Jenson and Fraser rightly point out that the greatest opportunity for progress would be for these diverse social service and educational bureaucracies to focus on identifying and reducing those common or shared risk factors affecting the youthful populations from which their students and clients are drawn.

To illustrate, evidence indicates that when adult caretakers fail to set clear expectations for children's behavior, fail to monitor children in developmentally appropriate ways, and are inconsistent or excessively severe in discipline, their children are at greater risk for drug abuse, early sexual behavior, delinquent behavior, and depression. Workshops for parents and families that teach good family management skills in 10 to 14 hours of total contact time during early adolescence have been shown to significantly reduce the future drug and alcohol use, delinquent behavior, and depressive symptoms of children (Mason et al., 2003, 2007, 2009). But I am aware of few communities in which the schools, primary health care providers, drug and alcohol abuse prevention and treatment agencies, children's mental health agencies, and juvenile justice system have teamed up to saturate a community with tested and effective parenting and family workshops for parents of children ages 10 to 14. I am convinced that, in the long run, doing so would reduce the need for intervention specialists in schools, adolescent drug treatment programs, juvenile detention beds, and mental health treatment services in communities. It is time that policy for children and families is guided by advances in scientific knowledge of what promotes successful child and adolescent development.

Jenson and Fraser's suggestions in the final chapter provide a concise yet general guide to development of policy for children and families across diverse agencies. They suggest a reasonable and feasible set of steps for moving forward toward a knowledge-driven approach to the development of a system of care involving the diverse stakeholder groups and agencies concerned with improving the well-being of children. Currently, in spite of the growing evidence on the effectiveness of preventive interventions, most

resources in most public social service agencies go to treatment of identified problems rather than to prevention. As Jenson and Fraser note, it is
time for policymakers to seriously consider and address the data presented in this book on the common risk factors for and shared protective
factors that inhibit diverse mental, emotional, and behavioral problems
through the development of systems of care that include evidence-based
preventive services as well as intervention and treatment services. Perhaps,
it is also time to create an overarching agency charged with promoting the
positive cognitive, social, and emotional development of all children
through the systematic assessment of risk and protective factors affecting
young people and the systematic selection, installation, and rigorous
implementation of tested and effective programs that address those risk
and protective factors to promote successful development in the multiple
domains of a child's life. This book shows the way forward.

J. David Hawkins, Ph.D.

Endowed Professor of Prevention

Social Development Research Group

School of Social Work

University of Washington

References

Mason, W. A., Kosterman, R., Haggerty, K. P., Hawkins, J. D., Redmond, C., Spoth, R. L.,
    & Shin, C. (2009). Gender moderation and social developmental mediation of
    the effect of a family-focused substance use preventive intervention on young
    adult alcohol abuse. *Addictive Behaviors, 34,* 599–605. doi: 10.1016/j.addbeh
    .2009.03.032

Mason, W. A., Kosterman, R., Hawkins, J. D., Haggerty, K. P., & Spoth, R. L. (2003).
    Reducing adolescents' growth in substance use and delinquency: Randomized
    trial effects of a preventive parent-training intervention. *Prevention Science, 4,*
    203–212. doi: 10.1023/A:1024653923780

Mason, W. A., Kosterman, R., Hawkins, J. D., Haggerty, K. P., Spoth, R. L., &
    Redmond, C. (2007). Influence of a family-focused substance use preventive
    intervention on growth in adolescent depressive symptoms. *Journal of
    Research on Adolescence, 17,* 541–564. doi: 10.1111/j.1532-7795.2007.00531.x

Acknowledgments

The ideas expressed in this volume address many of the most pressing problems confronting children, youth, and families in American society. We thank each of the chapter authors for the careful and rigorous thought they devoted to advancing new and innovative approaches to public policy. A book such as this owes a great debt to many people behind the scenes. Thanks to Diane Wyant of the University of North Carolina at Chapel Hill and Jenifer Rinner of the University of Denver for administrative and technical support in manuscript preparation. Finally, special thanks to Mary, Nils, and Anna Jenson and to Mary, Alex, and Katy Fraser for the daily reminders of what it means to be a family.

—Jeffrey M. Jenson

—Mark W. Fraser

Introduction

Much has been written about risk and protective factors associated with social and health problems. Begun some 35 years ago, research to trace the causes of problem behavior in young people has led to a new understanding of the individual, interpersonal, and environmental factors that affect developmental outcomes. In recent years, attention has also been directed to increasing our understanding of the concept of resilience, which is commonly thought of as a child's capacity to overcome adverse life conditions (Fraser, Kirby, & Smokowski, 2004). Knowledge of these characteristics has been widely used to improve the efficacy of prevention and treatment programs for vulnerable children and families (Catalano, 2007; Jenson, in press; Woolf, 2008).

In the first edition of this book, we argued that the principles of risk, protection, and resilience held great promise for the design of social policies and the delivery of social programs for children and families. We also noted that knowledge gained from longitudinal investigations of risk, protection, and resilience in children and youth was rarely applied to social policy. We still have much to learn about the etiological processes of risk and resilience and about the application of these principles to social interventions and programs. However, considerable progress in understanding principles of risk, protection, and resilience has been made since the publication of the first edition. Equally important, advances in prevention science—where research-based knowledge is used to design prevention interventions—are beginning to influence new social policies. Innovative policies and programs based on risk and resilience are evident in each of the chapters in this edition. Clearly, a dramatic example of change and innovation lies in health care reform, exemplified by the recent passage of the Patient Protection and

Affordable Care Act (P. L. 11–148). This legislation and other new policies affecting the nation's children and families are reviewed in this edition. We hope that this book will help students, practitioners, policymakers, and researchers apply principles of risk and resilience to the design of social and health policies.

Organization of the Book

The core section of the book is formed by eight chapters devoted to anti-poverty, child welfare, education, mental health, health, developmental disabilities, substance abuse, and juvenile justice policies. Chapter authors identify key policies in their respective areas and evaluate the extent to which the principles of risk, protection, and resilience can be used to improve existing programs and services. Recommended readings, questions for discussion, and Web-based resources are provided for each of the core chapters. In this regard, authors follow a similar outline in which they

- trace the purpose of social policy in a substantive area;
- describe the incidence and prevalence of problems;
- articulate common risk and protective factors associated with the onset or persistence of the relevant problem behavior;
- identify historical and current policies that have been developed to address these problems;
- evaluate the extent to which policies have been based on the principles of risk, protection, and resilience;
- identify strategies for incorporating elements of risk, protection, and resilience in new policy directives; and
- discuss ways of integrating social policy for children, youth, and families across policy and service domains.

New to this edition, Trina Williams Shanks and Sandra Danziger identify critical approaches to combating poverty in Chapter 2. Past and current income maintenance policies are reviewed in the context of risk, protection, and resilience. Williams Shanks and Danziger describe several innovative programs to illustrate the promise of recent policy approaches to reducing poverty and social disadvantage.

Peter Pecora and Markell Harrison-Jackson examine child welfare policies and programs aimed at children, youth, and families in Chapter 3. In describing a key service domain for children, youth, and families, Pecora and Harrison-Jackson trace the history and evolution of American child welfare policy and offer suggestions about ways to incorporate principles of risk, protection, and resilience in a key service domain.

Public schools touch the lives of a majority of American children and families. Changes in educational policy and practice made since the publication of the first edition of this book are having a profound effect on teachers, parents, and children and youth in elementary, middle, and high schools. In Chapter 4, Andy Frey, Hill Walker, and Armon Perry update their discussion of the landmark No Child Left Behind Act and its sweeping implications for the character of public education across the country. They note that educational reform is closely linked to political ideology and societal values pertaining to educational access and opportunity. Frey, Walker, and Perry conclude by offering an agenda for reform.

In Chapter 5, Mary Fraser reviews the effectiveness of mental health policies for children, youth, and families. Key among the promising policy and program directives she identifies is the *system of care* (SOC) approach. Fraser notes the frequency of co-occurring problems among youth and suggests making the integration of mental health, juvenile justice, and substance abuse policies a public policy priority.

Kathleen Rounds, Guadalupe Huitron, and Thomas Ormsby trace the development of key U.S. public health policies in Chapter 6. They highlight recent changes reflected in the passage of the Patient Protection and Affordable Care Act (P. L. 11–148) and assess the potential impact of those changes on children and families. Recommendations for integrated health policy based on risk, protection, and resilience are offered.

In recent years, recognizing and understanding developmental disabilities commonly found among children and youth has become a focus of policy debate. In Chapter 7, Susan Parish, Alison Saville, and Jamie Swaine discuss changes in policy for children with developmental disabilities in the past several decades. Using a risk and protective factor perspective, they offer recommendations for improving service delivery to children and youth with developmental disabilities.

In Chapter 8 Jeffrey Jenson, Elizabeth Anthony, and Matthew Howard review recent trends in the prevalence, etiology, prevention, and treatment of adolescent substance abuse. They trace the origins of policies aimed at young substance abusers and comment on the relative effectiveness of alternate policy approaches. Jenson and colleagues conclude that principles of risk, protection, and resilience have been influential in improving the efficacy of prevention and treatment programs for young people and reflect on the implications of these findings for substance abuse policy.

In Chapter 9 William Barton traces major changes in juvenile justice policy since the creation of the juvenile court. He identifies the tension found in public policy between competing program goals of rehabilitation and punishment. Barton concludes with cautious optimism about the application of public health principles to juvenile justice policies and programs.

In the final chapter of the book, we expand on our framework for using principles of risk, protection, and resilience to develop more fully integrated policies for children, youth, and families. We argue that integration of policy and programs across service domains should be a goal of future policy directives targeting children, youth, and families. Considerations are given to developmental processes of children and youth in the design of this framework. Recommendations for ways to advance a public health framework based on risk, protection, and resilience in policy design, implementation, and evaluation are offered.

Summary

We hope the framework described in this book stimulates innovative ideas about the design of policies for vulnerable children and families. Principles of risk, protection, and resilience—too often ignored in policy discussions— hold great promise for improving the efficacy of social policies. By increasing the precision with which we address risk and promote protection, policies in fields ranging from child welfare to substance abuse are more likely to produce services and programs that effectively help children and families prevail over adversities.

References

Catalano, R. F. (2007). Prevention is a sound public and private investment. *Criminology and Public Policy, 6*, 377–398. doi: 10.1111/j.1745-9133.2007.00443.xx

Fraser, M. W., Kirby, L. D., & Smokowski, P. R. (2004). Risk and resilience in childhood. In M. W. Fraser (Ed.), *Risk and resilience in childhood: An ecological perspective* (2nd ed., pp. 13–66). Washington, DC: NASW Press.

Jenson, J. M. (in press). Advances in preventing childhood and adolescent problem behavior. *Research on Social Work Practice.*

Woolf, S. H. (2008). The power of prevention and what it requires. *Journal of the American Medical Association, 299*, 2437–2439. doi:10.1001/jama.299.20.2437

1

A Risk and Resilience Framework for Child, Youth, and Family Policy

Jeffrey M. Jenson

Mark W. Fraser

During the past century, social policies and programs for American children, youth, and families have undergone frequent shifts in philosophy and direction. Many policy frameworks, such as selective eligibility, universal prevention, rehabilitation, and punishment, have contributed to the conceptual bases for services, programs, and interventions designed for young people. However, the most consistent characteristic of American social policy for children and families may be the sheer inconsistency of efforts aimed at helping the nation's most vulnerable populations.

Recent advances in understanding the developmental processes associated with the onset and persistence of childhood and adolescent problems warrant new thinking about policies and programs. Since the first edition of this book was published in 2006, we have learned more about why some children and adolescents develop social and health problems, and—in the case of such problems as sexually transmitted diseases, drug use, and delinquency—why some youths make choices that lead to poor outcomes at home and in school and the community. Unfortunately, this knowledge is not yet systematically applied to policy or program design, which results in poorly specified, inadequately integrated, and wastefully duplicated services for children and families. The motivation for this volume comes from the growing recognition that knowledge gained from understanding the developmental trajectories of children who experience social and health problems must be used to craft more effective policies and programs.

Coming of Age in America

Children, youth, and families face enormous challenges in American society. At no time in the country's history have young people and their parents been confronted simultaneously by such a wide array of positive and negative influences and opportunities. Most children and youth become healthy adults who participate in positive—or prosocial—activities guided by interests that lead to meaningful and fulfilling lives. However, for some American children and youth, the path to adulthood is a journey filled with risk and uncertainty. Because of the adversities these young people face, the prospect of a successful future is often bleak.

If we were to draw a picture depicting the current health of America's children and youth, it would be a portrait of contrasts. On a positive note, young people between 15 and 25 years old are volunteering and becoming more involved in social causes than in the past (Center for Information and Research on Civic Learning and Engagement, 2010). In addition, the prevalence of some problem behavior—most notably violent offending—has decreased considerably in recent years. For example, following a period of rapid increase between the late 1980s and 1995, the violent juvenile crime rate returned to its pre-1988 level and has remained relatively stable since 1996 (Puzzanchera, 2009).

Juxtaposed against this promising news are the disturbing accounts of school shootings, persistently high rates of school dropout and drug use, and increases in childhood poverty (for reviews of school shootings, see Vossekuil, Fein, Reddy, Borum, & Modzeleski, 2002; Wike & Fraser, 2009). Nearly 38% of public schools in the United States reported at least one violent incident to police in the 2005–2006 school year (U.S. Department of Education, 2007). Sporadic acts of school violence have occurred in virtually every region of the country in the decade following the 1999 shootings at

Columbine High School in Colorado (Centers for Disease Control and Prevention, 2008a).

Academic failure and school dropout have become profound social problems. About 6% of all youth between the ages of 16 and 19 years old dropped out of school in 2008. Particularly troubling is evidence indicating that youth of color drop out of school at much higher rates than Caucasian students. In 2008, 11% of Latino, 13% of American Indian, and 8% of African American students dropped out of school as compared to only 5% of Caucasian youth (Annie E. Casey Foundation, 2010). As the world moves to greater globalization of markets and demands a more educated workforce, these young people face lives of limited opportunities and high unemployment, which brings consequential high societal costs.

Drug use among American youth also imposes considerable individual and societal costs on the nation. In 2009, nearly 47% of the nation's senior high school students reported lifetime use of any illicit drug, and 24% indicated they had used an illicit drug other than marijuana (Johnston, O'Malley, & Bachman, 2010). Despite a recent leveling in drug use trends, more than 19% of eighth-grade students reported lifetime use of any illicit drug in 2009. Particularly worrisome is evidence indicating that 7% of the nation's high school seniors have tried dangerous drugs such as ecstasy (Johnston et al., 2010). These unacceptably high rates of drug use among children and youth are the focus of multifaceted policy and practice efforts at the federal, state, and local levels.

Poverty is related to many social and health problems. Nearly 18% of U.S. children younger than 18 years old live in poverty, which significantly affects individuals, families, and communities (Annie E. Casey Foundation, 2010). In the United States, children are more likely than all other age groups to be poor (Cauce, Stewart, Rodriguez, Cochran, & Ginzler, 2003), and children of color are disproportionately represented in poverty. Among all U.S. children younger than 18 years, 34% of African Americans, 31% of American Indians, and 28% of Latino children were poor in 2007. Those rates are more than double the rates for Asian and Pacific Islanders (12%) and non-Latino Caucasians (11%) living in poverty (Annie E. Casey Foundation, 2010). These statistics are important because living in poverty has both short- and long-term effects. Poverty has negative effects on several key outcomes during childhood and adolescence, including school achievement and delinquency (Brooks-Gunn & Duncan, 1997; Hannon, 2003). Poverty is also associated with adverse consequences during adulthood and later stages of life (McCord, 1997). The social and environmental conditions created by poverty give rise to a variety of public health problems that require well-reasoned evidence-based policy and program responses.

Policy and Program Responses to Childhood and Adolescent Problems

Experts from the fields of criminology, education, medicine, psychology, public health, social work, and sociology agree no single pathway leads to school failure, drug use, delinquency, and other problems. Rather, it is the accumulation of risk—the sheer number of adversities and traumas confronted by children and families—that seems to disrupt normal developmental trajectories (Rutter, 2001). In the mid-1970s, Jessor and Jessor (1977) asserted that a small group of youth simultaneously engaged in a variety of dangerous and costly problem behaviors; that assertion has been well supported by the research evidence over the past three decades. Indeed, the same academically marginalized youths who are involved in drug use may also be the youths at risk of sexually transmitted diseases and violent victimization from family members or partners. Despite the fact that we know far more about these high-risk youths, their friends, and their families (e.g., Elliott, Huizinga, & Menard, 1989; Huizinga, Loeber, & Thornberry, 1994; Loeber, Farrington, Stouthamer-Loeber, & Van Kammen, 1998; Robins & McEvoy, 1990; White, Loeber, Stouthamer-Loeber, & Farrington, 1999), we have seen few innovative policy strategies introduced to reduce the number of children and adolescents who experience these problems. A looming challenge for both advocates and experts is to find ways to incorporate and translate new knowledge (i.e., the product of research) into public policies and programs.

One barrier to the efficient translation of research knowledge to practice is that current social policies and programs intended to meet the needs of U.S. children, youth, and families are highly fragmented. Many policies aimed at improving conditions for vulnerable and high-risk populations have failed to consider the number, nature, or severity of problems experienced by American families. Other policies and resultant programs are duplicated among agencies, leading to a host of eligibility and implementation conflicts in child welfare, developmental disabilities, mental health, substance abuse, education, and juvenile justice services.

Moreover, the application of theoretical and empirical evidence to the design of social policies and programs aimed at improving the lives of children, youth, and families is limited. Social policy is often hurriedly created in the context of galvanizing community events—such as the rush of safety policies implemented in the aftermath of the campus shootings at Virginia Tech in 2007—or trends that have attracted public attention and compelled legislation. In some cases, policies developed in reaction to specific events lead to decisions that fail to account adequately for unforeseen or unintended long-term consequences. A case in point is that of the extensive juvenile justice reforms implemented across the country in the early to mid-1990s. Faced with increased rates of gang activity and violent youth crime, nearly all states enacted reforms emphasizing strict sanctions and punishments for young offenders. Many of these reforms—most notably boot camp programs and the extensive use of judicial waivers for serious offenders (i.e., where some juvenile offenders were prosecuted in criminal courts and exposed to adult rather than juvenile sanctions)—subsequently produced mixed or ineffective results (Jenson, Potter, & Howard, 2001).

Over the past several decades, we have learned much about the causes and progression of child and adolescent problems. However, advances in understanding the life-course development of problem behaviors among children and youth have primarily been used to enhance prevention and treatment strategies rather than to inform theory development (Biglan, Brennan, Foster, & Holder, 2004). Aside from Bronfenbrenner's (1979, 1986) ecological perspective, the field lacks conceptual models that inform the design and direction of social policies for children, youth, and families. In this book, we argue that a public health framework—rooted in ecological theory and based on principles of risk and resilience—is defining a new and useful conceptual model for the design of social policy across the substantive areas of child welfare, education, income assistance, mental health, health, developmental disabilities, substance use, and juvenile justice.

Public Health Frameworks for Social Policy

In the field of prevention science, public health frameworks for understanding and preventing childhood and adolescent problems have become widely used to promote positive youth outcomes (Biglan et al., 2004; Hawkins, 2006; Hawkins, Catalano, & Miller, 1992; Jenson, in press). When designing or selecting interventions to ameliorate youth problems, social scientists give first consideration to the presence or absence of risk and protective factors affecting youth outcomes. Another concept closely related to those of risk and protection is the concept of resilience, which is the ability to overcome adverse conditions and to function normatively in the face of risk. A public health perspective guiding policy development aimed at children, youth, and families must incorporate these key concepts of risk, protection, and resilience.

Risk and Protection

Risk factors are individual, school, peer, family, and community influences that increase the likelihood that a child will experience a social or health problem. Although the idea of identifying risk factors to better understand childhood and adolescent problems has gained widespread acceptance in the prevention field (Catalano, 2007; Jenson, 2006; Romer, 2003; Woolf, 2008), its origins are relatively recent. The early work on identifying risk factors dates to the 1970s, when researchers began placing greater importance on understanding the individual, family, and community correlates of mental illness (Rutter, 1979, 1987). Stimulated in part by advances in research design and statistical analysis (e.g., the development of path analysis and structural equation modeling), a new emphasis on modeling underlying causes led investigators to identify specific factors that were consistently associated with the occurrence of delinquency, drug use, suicide, school dropout, and other problems. This approach, adapted from public health efforts to identify risk factors associated with problems such as smoking and heart disease, led to the use of "risk-based" strategies to prevent childhood and adolescent problems (Hawkins, Catalano, & Miller, 1992).

Risk Factors

The earliest risk factor models were primarily lists of the correlates of adolescent problems (e.g., Garmezy, 1971). These models were drawn from previous research that identified risk factors for adolescent problem behaviors such as substance abuse and delinquency (e.g., Hawkins, Jenson, Catalano, & Lishner, 1988). These early models often failed to consider the temporal relationship of risk factors to the occurrence of specific behaviors or to examine the additive and interactive effects of risk factors. However, recent reviews of risk factors for adolescent problem behaviors have improved on earlier efforts by limiting their selection of studies to those in which the risk factor clearly preceded a problem behavior (e.g., Fraser, Kirby, & Smokowski, 2004; Fraser & Terzian, 2005; Herrenkohl, Chung, & Catalano, 2004). In addition, longitudinal studies have been conducted to better understand the processes by which risk factors influence behavior over the course of childhood and adolescence (e.g., Hawkins, Kosterman, Catalano, Hill, & Abbott, 2005; Loeber et al., 1998; Spoth, Redmond, & Shin, 1998). In this book, we adopt Fraser and Terzian's (2005) definition of a risk factor: "Broadly defined, the term *risk factor* relates to any event, condition, or experience that increases the probability that a problem will be formed, maintained, or exacerbated" (p. 5).

This definition recognizes that the presence of one or more risk factors in a person's life has the potential to increase the likelihood that a problem behavior will occur at a later point in time. However, the presence of a risk factor does not ensure or guarantee that a specific outcome, such as school failure, will inevitably occur. Rather, the presence of a risk factor suggests an increased chance or probability that such a problem might develop. Table 1.1 presents common risk factors for childhood and adolescent problems arranged by level of influence. These and other factors are discussed in relation to specific topics presented in Chapter 2 through Chapter 9. In addition, the discussions address protective factors, which are closely related to risk factors. *Protective factors* are those influences, characteristics, and conditions that buffer or mitigate a person's exposure to risk.

Protective Factors

Researchers began to notice that some apparently high-risk youths did not engage in problem behaviors. Studies showed that these youths were protected from risk. That is, they seemed to have personal resources that helped them prevail over adversities. These resources came to be called *protective factors*. Still today, there is ongoing debate about the exact definition of *protection* as well as how to put knowledge about protective factors into practice (Fraser et al., 2004; Rossa, 2002). Most investigators agree that protective factors are attributes or characteristics that lower the probability of an undesirable outcome (Benard, 2004; Rutter, 1987; Werner & Smith, 1992). However, whether protective factors are independent of risk factors remains in contention.

The knowledge base associated with the concept of protection emerged in the 1980s, when investigators such as Rutter (1979) and Werner and Smith (1982) observed that certain positive attributes appeared to operate in the presence of risk or adversity. However, the exact definition of a protective factor quickly became a topic of debate. Most of this debate has centered on the confusion created when risk and protective factors are thought of as opposite ends of a single continuum (Pollard, Hawkins, & Arthur, 1999). For example, researchers have often identified consistent family management practices as important

Table 1.1   Common Risk Factors for Childhood and Adolescent Problems by Level of Influence[a]

Environmental Factors

Laws and norms favorable to antisocial behavior

Poverty and economic deprivation

Low economic opportunity

Neighborhood disorganization

Low neighborhood attachment

Interpersonal and Social Factors

Family communication and conflict

Poor parent–child bonding

Poor family management practices

Family alcohol and drug use

School failure

Low commitment to school

Rejection by conforming peer groups

Association with antisocial peers

Individual Factors

Family history of alcoholism

Sensation-seeking orientation

Poor impulse control

Attention deficits

Hyperactivity

a. Adapted from Fraser et al. (2004); Jenson and Howard (1999); and Hawkins et al. (1998).

in producing positive outcomes in children, whereas a style of inconsistent family management is construed as a factor leading to poor outcomes. In some studies consistent family management is identified as a protective factor, and inconsistent family management is seen as a risk factor. Using risk and protection in this manner establishes the two concepts as polar opposites, with one pole representing positive outcomes and the other pole representing negative outcomes. Therein lies the ongoing debate among social scientists, which can be briefly summarized as two questions:

1. Do risk and protective factors represent measurable levels of an attribute or characteristic that has two poles along a single continuum?

2. Are risk and protective factors separate and independent constructs?

Our concept of protection holds that protective factors operate as a buffering agent to moderate exposure to risk. We offer the following definition from Fraser and Terzian (2005): "protective factors [are] resources—individual or environmental—that minimize the impact of risk" (p. 12).

This definition is important because it views protective factors as individual characteristics and environmental conditions, and it emphasizes that those conditions or characteristics interact with specific risk factors present in either the child or the child's environment. We argue that protective factors operate in three ways, by serving to

- reduce or buffer the impact of risk in a child's life,
- interrupt a chain of risk factors that may be present in a young person's life (e.g., disrupt a potential chain of risk that begins with peer rejection and leads to involvement with antisocial peers and then to delinquency), and
- prevent or block the onset of a risk factor. (Fraser & Terzian, 2005)

Table 1.2 shows common protective factors discussed by authors in subsequent chapters.

Resilience: When a Child Prevails Over Adversity

Resilience is characterized by successful adaptation in the presence of risk or adversity (Garmezy, 1986; Luthar, 2003; Olsson, Bond, Burns, Vella-Brodrick, & Sawyer, 2003). Fortunately, we have numerous examples of young people and adults who have "overcome the odds" of the negative effects of risks identified in areas of child welfare (Festinger, 1984), juvenile justice (Vigil, 1990), and substance abuse (Werner & Smith, 2001). Rather than a single influence or factor, we conceptualize resilience as the outcome of a process that takes into account both the level of risk exposure and the presence of protective factors. When exposure to risk is high, evidence suggests that most children and adolescents experience some type of problem or developmental difficulty (Cicchetti & Rogosch, 1997). In circumstances when the risk level is high, protective factors exert their influence on developmental outcomes; however, in circumstances in which the risk level is low, protective factors are more likely to have a neutral or relatively benign effect (Fraser, Richman, & Galinsky, 1999).

Sameroff and his colleagues (Sameroff, 1999; Sameroff & Fiese, 2000; Sameroff & Gutman, 2004) have used the phrase *promotive factor* to refer to attributes or characteristics that have positive effects on people's lives, irrespective of the level of risk exposure. These researchers have argued that promotive factors (e.g., high intelligence) have direct effects on child and adolescent outcomes. Tests of the direct impact of promotive effects have been relatively limited to date (Sameroff, Bartko, Baldwin, Baldwin, & Siefer, 1999).

Table 1.2   Common Protective Factors for Childhood and Adolescent Problems by Level of Influence[a]

Environmental Factors

　Opportunities for education, employment, and other pro-social activities

　Caring relationships with adults or extended family members

　Social support from non-family members

Interpersonal and Social Factors

　Attachment to parents

　Caring relationships with siblings

　Low parental conflict

　High levels of commitment to school

　Involvement in conventional activities

　Belief in pro-social norms and values

Individual Factors

　Social and problem-solving skills

　Positive attitude

　Temperament

　High intelligence

　Low childhood stress

a. Adapted from Fraser et al. (2004); Jenson and Howard (1999); and Hawkins et al. (1998).

Increasingly, experts are viewing resilience as the outcome of an interactive process involving risk, protection, and promotion. Thus, *adaptation,* which is expressed through individual behavior, is interpreted as an interactive product involving the presence or absence of specific risk; level of exposure to risk; and the strength of the specific risk, protective, and promotive factors present in a child's life.

Applying Principles of Risk and Resilience to Social Policy

Applications of public health principles have primarily been used to develop prevention interventions in school and community settings (Cicchetti, Rappaport, Sandler, & Weissberg, 2000; Luthar & Cicchetti, 2000; Marsten, 2001). The results have been impressive. Recent research has identified a number of efficacious risk-oriented programs aimed at preventing child and adolescent problems such as substance abuse (Foxcroft, Ireland, Lister-Sharp, Lowe, & Breen, 2003; Gottfredson & Wilson, 2003) and delinquency (Catalano, Loeber, & McKinney, 1999; Limbos et al., 2007; Wilson & Lipsey, 2007). Research and governmental entities, which are concerned with improving the dissemination of effective programs, have made lists of effective interventions available to practitioners, educators, and the general public (Campbell Collaboration Library, 2010; Center for the Study and Prevention of Violence, 2010; Substance Abuse and Mental Health Administration, 2010). Prevention and treatment strategies using a risk and protective perspective are now widely recognized by public and private entities (at both the state and federal level) as the dominant approach to preventing and treating childhood and adolescent problems (Center for the Study and Prevention of Violence, 2010; Centers for Disease Control and Prevention, 2008b; National Institute on Drug Abuse, 1997; Schinke, Brounstein, & Gardner, 2002).

A logical next step in the application of the risk and resilience model requires extending the framework to the development of a broader cross-section of programs and public policies (Fraser & Galinsky, 2004). To date, only a few examples of this process exist. Investigators in the public health field have applied principles of risk, protection, and resilience to their design of prevention strategies targeting risk factors for AIDS. Evidence suggests that the implementation of this approach has led to reductions in the spread of AIDS in many parts of the world (Sorenson, Masson, & Perlman, 2002).

A second example of using a public health framework to affect program and policy change comes from innovations in substance abuse prevention. Hawkins, Catalano, and Associates (1992) created the *Communities That Care* (CTC) program, which is a theoretically based prevention process designed to help community leaders develop and implement effective substance abuse prevention programs. The CTC program is based on the social development model (SDM), which is a general theory of human behavior that integrates perspectives from social control theory (Hirschi, 1969), social learning theory (Bandura, 1989), and differential association theory (Matsueda, 1982; Sutherland, 1973). SDM specifies the mechanisms and causal pathways by which risk and protective factors interact in the etiology of various behaviors, including adolescent drug use (Catalano & Hawkins, 1996). The SDM proposes that four protective factors inhibit the development of antisocial behaviors in children: (1) *bonding*, defined as attachment and commitment to family, school, and positive peers (Garmezy, 1986); (2) *belief in the shared values or norms* of these social units; (3) *external constraints* such as clear, consistent standards against drug use (Hansen, Malotte, & Fileding, 1988; Scheier & Botvin, 1998); and (4) *social, cognitive, and emotional skills* that provide protective tools for children to solve problems (Rutter, 1987), to perform in social situations (Werner & Smith, 1982), and to resist influences and impulses to violate their norms for behavior (Hansen et al., 1987).

In the CTC model, communities form coalitions to engage in systematic prevention planning, which requires them to identify risk and protective factors for adolescent problems that are prevalent in their localities. Following the assessment of such factors, communities are encouraged to select prevention strategies based on available empirical evidence (Hawkins et al., 2008). Recent findings from the Community Youth Development Study, which is a longitudinal, randomized trial that uses principles of CTC, have revealed significantly lower rates of delinquency and drug use among students in experimental communities compared to control communities (Hawkins et al., 2008). These groundbreaking findings suggest that well-organized and well-implemented community planning efforts that focus on risk and protection can lead to positive outcomes for young people (Hawkins, Catalano, Kosterman, Abbott, & Hill, 1999). Although the CTC model falls short of satisfying the criteria for a formal policy, it successfully initiates a process whereby knowledge of risk and protective factors becomes an integral part of program design. As implied in the preceding examples, applying principles of risk and resilience to policy design requires an understanding of the developmental trajectories associated with the onset or persistence of child and adolescent problems. Figure 1.1 illustrates the process involved in applying a public health perspective to policy and program design for children, youth, and families.

Two additional elements in the risk and resilience model, ecological theory and life course development, are outlined briefly in the next section.

Ecological Theory and Life Course Development

As we mentioned earlier, we use an ecological perspective to provide a context for thinking about principles of risk, protection, and resilience over the course of child development. The ecological perspective is well known and widely applied in education, practice, and research across many disciplines and professions (Bronfenbrenner, 1979, 1986; Germain, 1991; Fraser, 2004). Ecological theory posits that development is deeply affected by interactions between the biological and psychological characteristics of the individual child and conditions in his or her environment.

Figure 1.1   A Risk and Resilience Framework for Child, Youth, and Family Policy

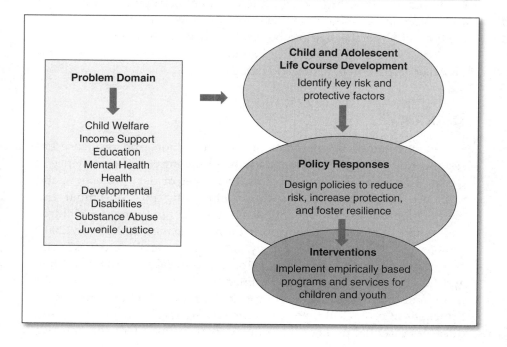

Environmental conditions are usually described as family, peer, school, and community influences (Bronfenbrenner, 1979, 1986). An ecological perspective holds that child development is a product of transactions between an organism and the context. In the vernacular of practice, child development is influenced by events that occur in the lives of young people within their family, peer, school, and community settings.

We believe social policies for children, youth, and families must be framed in an ecological perspective that considers the influence of the context. For example, a child referred to the juvenile justice system is also a child who lives within some type of family unit, attends a local school, and has a network of peers. Evidence indicates that both unique and interrelated risk and protective factors increase or decrease the likelihood of problem behavior within each of these domains (Fraser, 2004; Herrenkohl, Aisenberg, Williams, & Jenson, 2011; Jenson & Howard, 1999). Therefore, social policies are most likely to be effective when they address the myriad influences that lead to and may sustain problem behavior for young people. In earlier work, we discussed risk and protective factors in the context of the ecological perspective as a way to explain the onset and prevention of childhood and adolescent problems (Fraser, 2004; Jenson, 2004). However, the knowledge of such factors has seldom been used as a lens through which to examine social policy for children, youth, and families. Our intention is to show how principles contained in the ecological perspective can be used to create integrated policies that may cut across traditional policy boundaries found within care systems for American children, youth, and families.

Summary

Knowledge gained from studies of risk, protection, and resilience has significantly affected our understanding of the onset and persistence of childhood and adolescent problems. Principles of risk, protection, and resilience have also been helpful in improving the conceptual and methodological rigor of prevention and treatment programs for children and youth (Kaftarian, Robinson, Compton, Davis, & Volkow, 2004; Limbos et al., 2007; Wilson & Lipsey, 2007). However, to date these principles have not been systematically applied to social policies for children and families. This chapter has outlined a public health framework for child and family policy based on risk, protection, and resilience. Principles of ecological theory and life course development were introduced as essential parts of the framework. In subsequent chapters, we more fully examine the utility of a public health framework for child and family policy.

References

Annie E. Casey Foundation. (2010). *Kids count data center.* Retrieved from http://www.kidscount.org/datacenter/

Bandura, A. (1989). Human agency in social cognitive theory. *American Psychologist, 14*, 1175–1184. doi:10.1037/0003–066X.44.9.1175

Benard, B. (2004). *Resiliency: What we have learned.* San Francisco: WestEd.

Biglan, A., Brennan, P. A., Foster, S. L., & Holder, H. D. (2004). *Helping adolescents at risk. Prevention of multiple problem behaviors.* New York: Guilford Press.

Bronfenbrenner, U. (1979). *The ecology of human development: Experiments by nature and design.* Cambridge, MA: Harvard University Press.

Bronfenbrenner, U. (1986). Ecology of the family as a context to human development: Research perspectives. *Development Psychology, 22*, 723–742. doi:10.1037/0012–1649.22.6.723

Brooks-Gunn, J., & Duncan, G. J. (1997). The effects of poverty on children. *Future of Children, 7*, 55–71. doi:10.2307/1602387

Campbell Collaboration Library. (2010). [Database]. Retrieved from http://www.campbellcollaboration.org/

Catalano, R. F. (2007). Prevention is a sound public and private investment. *Criminology and Public Policy, 6*, 377–398. doi: 10.1111/j.1745-9133.2007.00443.x

Catalano, R. F., & Hawkins, J. D. (1996). The social development model: A theory of antisocial behavior. In J. D. Hawkins (Ed.), *Delinquency and crime: Current theories* (pp. 149–197). New York: Cambridge University Press.

Catalano, R. F., Loeber, R., & McKinney, K. (1999). *School and community interventions to prevent serious and violent offending* (NCJ 177624). Washington, DC: Office of Juvenile Justice and Delinquency Prevention, U.S. Department of Justice. Retrieved from http://www.ncjrs.gov/pdffiles1/ojjdp/177624.pdf

Cauce, A. M., Stewart, A., Rodriguez, M. D., Cochran, B., & Ginzler, J. (2003). Overcoming the odds? Adolescent development in the context of urban poverty. In S. S. Luthar (Ed.), *Resilience and vulnerability: Adaptation in the context of childhood adversities* (pp. 343–363). Cambridge, UK: Cambridge University Press. doi:10.1017/CBO9780511615788.016

Center for Information and Research on Civic Learning and Engagement. (2010). Volunteering and community service. Retrieved from http://www.civicyouth.org/?page_id=237

Center for the Study and Prevention of Violence. (2010). *Blueprints for violence prevention.* Retrieved from http://www.colorado.edu/cspv/blueprints/index.html

Centers for Disease Control and Prevention. (2008a). *School-associated student homicides-United States, 1992–2006.* Washington, DC: Author.

Centers for Disease Control and Prevention. (2008b). *Understanding youth violence. Fact sheet.* Atlanta, GA: Author. http://www.cdc.gov/ncipc/pub-res/YVFactSheet.pdf

Cicchetti, D., Rappaport, J., Sandler, L., & Weissberg, R. P. (Eds.). (2000). *The promotion of wellness in children and adolescents.* Washington, DC: Child Welfare League of America.

Cicchetti, D., & Rogosch, F. A. (1997). The role of self-organization in the promotion of resilience in maltreated children. *Development and Psychopathology, 9,* 787–815. doi:10.1017/S0954579497001442

Elliott, D. S., Huizinga, D., & Menard, S. (1989). *Multiple problem youth: Delinquency, substance use, and mental health problems.* New York: Springer-Verlag.

Festinger, T. (1984). *No one ever asked us: A postscript to the foster care system.* New York: Columbia University Press.

Foxcroft, D. R., Ireland, D., Lister-Sharp, D. J., Lowe, G., & Breen, R. (2003). Longer term primary prevention for alcohol misuse in young people: A systematic review. *Addiction, 98,* 397–411. doi:10.1046/j.1360–0443.2003.00355.x

Fraser, M. W. (2004). The ecology of childhood: A multisystems perspective. In M. W. Fraser (Ed.), *Risk and resilience in childhood: An ecological perspective* (2nd ed., pp. 1–12). Washington, DC: NASW Press.

Fraser, M. W., & Galinsky, M. J. (2004). Risk and resilience in childhood: Toward an evidence-based model of practice. In M. W. Fraser (Ed.), *Risk and resilience in childhood: An ecological perspective* (2nd ed., pp. 385–402). Washington, DC: NASW Press.

Fraser, M. W., Kirby, L. D., & Smokowski, P. R. (2004). Risk and resilience in childhood. In M. W. Fraser (Ed.), *Risk and resilience in childhood: An ecological perspective* (2nd ed., pp. 13–66). Washington, DC: NASW Press.

Fraser, M. W., Richman, J. M., & Galinsky, M. J. (1999). Risk, protection, and resilience: Towards a conceptual framework for social work practice. *Social Work Research, 23,* 131–144.

Fraser, M. W., & Terzian, M. A. (2005). Risk and resilience in child development: Practice principles and strategies. In G. P. Mallon & P. McCartt Hess (Eds.), *Handbook of children, youth, and family services: Practice, policies, and programs* (pp. 55–71). New York: Columbia University Press.

Garmezy, N. (1971). Vulnerability research and the issue of primary prevention. *American Journal of Orthopsychiatry, 41,* 101–116.

Garmezy, N. (1986). On measures, methods, and models. *Journal of the American Academy of Child and Adolescent Psychiatry, 25,* 727–729. doi:10.1016/S0002–7138(09)60303–4

Germain, C. B. (1991). *Human behavior in the social environment: An ecological view.* New York: Columbia University Press.

Gottfredson, D. C., & Wilson, D. B. (2003). Characteristics of effective school-based substance abuse prevention. *Prevention Science, 4,* 27–38. doi:10.1023/A:1021782710278

Hannon, L. (2003). Poverty, delinquency, and educational attainment: Cumulative disadvantage or disadvantage saturation? *Sociological Inquiry, 73*, 576–594. doi:10.1111/1475–682X.00072

Hansen, W. B., Graham, J. W., Sobel, J. L., Shelton, D. R., Flay, B. R., & Johnson, C. A. (1987). The consistency of peer and parent influences on tobacco, alcohol, and marijuana use among young adolescents. *Journal of Behavioral Medicine, 10*, 559–579. doi:10.1007/BF00846655

Hansen, W. B., Malotte, C. K., & Fileding, J. E. (1988). Evaluation of a tobacco and alcohol abuse prevention curriculum for adolescents. *Health Education Quarterly, 15*, 93–114.

Hawkins, J. D. (2006). Science, social work, prevention: Finding the intersection. *Social Work Research, 30*, 137–152.

Hawkins, J. D., Brown, E. C., Oesterle, S., Arthur, M. W., Abbot, R. D., & Catalano, R. F. (2008). Early effects of Communities that Care on targeted risks and initiation of delinquent behavior and substance use. *Journal of Adolescent Health, 43*, 15–22. doi:10.1016/j.jadohealth.2008.01.022

Hawkins, J. D., Catalano, R. F., & Associates. (1992). *Communities that care: Actions for drug abuse prevention.* San Francisco: Jossey-Bass.

Hawkins, J. D., Catalano, R. F., Kosterman, R., Abbott, R., & Hill, K. G. (1999). Preventing adolescent health-risk behaviors by strengthening protection during childhood. *Archives of Pediatrics and Adolescent Medicine, 153*, 226–234.

Hawkins, J. D., Catalano, R. F., & Miller, J. Y. (1992). Risk and protective factors for alcohol and other drug problems in adolescence and early adulthood: Implications for substance abuse prevention. *Psychological Bulletin, 112*, 64–105. doi:10.1037/0033–2909.112.1.64

Hawkins, J. D., Jenson, J. M., Catalano, R. F., & Lishner, D. L. (1988). Delinquency and drug abuse: Implications for social services. *Social Service Review, 62*, 258–284. doi:10.1086/644546

Hawkins, J. D., Kosterman, R. Catalano, R. F., Hill, K. G., & Abbott, R. D. (2005). Promoting positive adult functioning through social development intervention in childhood: Long-term effects from the Seattle Social Development Project. *Archives of Pediatrics and Adolescent Medicine, 159*, 25–31. doi:10.1001/archpedi.159.1.25

Herrenkohl, T. I., Aisenberg, E., Williams, J. H., & Jenson, J. M. (2011). *Violence in context: Current evidence on risk, protection, and prevention.* New York: Oxford University Press.

Herrenkohl, T. I., Chung, I. J., & Catalano, R. F. (2004). Review of research on predictors of youth violence and school-based and community-based prevention approaches. In P. Allen-Meares and M.W. Fraser (eds.), *Intervention with children and adolescents: An interdisciplinary perspective* (pp. 449–476). Boston: Pearson Education.

Hirschi, T. (1969). *Causes of delinquency.* Berkeley: University of California Press.

Huizinga, D., Loeber, R., & Thornberry, T. P. (1994). *Urban delinquency and substance abuse: Initial findings* (Research Summary Series, NCJ 143454).

Washington, DC: U.S. Department of Justice, Office of Juvenile Justice and Delinquency Prevention.

Jenson, J. M. (2004). Risk and protective factors for alcohol and other drug use in adolescence. In M. W. Fraser (Ed.), *Risk and resiliency in childhood: An ecological perspective* (2nd ed., pp. 183–208). Washington, DC: NASW Press.

Jenson, J. M. (2006). Advances and challenges in preventing childhood and adolescent problem behavior. *Social Work Research, 30,* 131–134.

Jenson, J. M. (in press). Advances in preventing childhood and adolescent problem behavior. *Research on Social Work Practice.*

Jenson, J. M., & Howard, M. O. (1999). *Youth violence. Current research and recent practice innovations.* Washington, DC: NASW.

Jenson, J. M., Potter, C. C., & Howard, M. O. (2001). American juvenile justice: Recent trends and issues in youth offending. *Social Policy and Administration, 35,* 48–68. doi:10.1111/1467–9515.00219

Jessor, R., & Jessor, S. L. (1977). *Problem behavior and psychosocial development: A longitudinal study of youth.* New York: Academic Press.

Johnston, L. D., O'Malley, P. M., & Bachman, J. G. (2010). *Drug use, drinking, and smoking: National survey results from high school, college, and young adult populations.* Washington, DC: Government Printing Office.

Kaftarian, S., Robinson, E., Compton, W., Davis, B. W., & Volkow, N. (2004). Blending prevention research and practice in schools: Critical issues and suggestions. *Prevention Science, 5,* 1–3. doi:10.1023/B:PREV.0000013975.74774.bc

Limbos, M. A., Chan, L. S., Warf, C., Schneir, A., Iverson, E., Shekelle, P., & Kipke, M. D. (2007). Effectiveness of interventions to prevent youth violence. A systematic review. *American Journal of Preventive Medicine, 33,* 65–74.

Loeber, R., Farrington, D. P., Stouthamer-Loeber, M., & Van Kammen, W. B. (1998). *Antisocial behavior and mental health problems.* Mahwah, NJ: Lawrence Erlbaum.

Luthar, S. S. (2003). *Resilience and vulnerability: Adaptation in the context of childhood adversities.* Cambridge, UK: Cambridge University Press. doi:10.1017/CB09780511615788

Luthar, S. S., & Cicchetti, D. (2000). The construct of resilience: Implications for interventions and social policies. *Development and Psychopathology, 12,* 857–885. doi:10.1017/S0954579400004156

Marsten, A. S. (2001). Ordinary magic: Resilience processes in development. *American Psychologist, 56,* 227–238. doi:10.1037/0003–066X.56.3.227

Matsueda, R. L. (1982). Testing control theory and differential association: A causal modeling approach. *American Sociological Review, 47,* 489–504. doi:10.2307/2095194

McCord, J. (1997). *Violence and childhood in the innercity.* Cambridge, UK: Cambridge University Press.

National Institute on Drug Abuse. (1997). *Preventing drug use among children and adolescents: A research guide to what works* (NIH Publication Number 97–4212). Bethesda, MD: National Institutes of Health.

Olsson, C. A., Bond, L., Burns, J. M., Vella-Brodrick, D. A., & Sawyer, S. M. (2003). Adolescent resilience: A concept analysis. *Journal of Adolescence, 26,* 1–11.

Pollard, J. A., Hawkins, J. D., & Arthur, M. W. (1999). Risk and protection: Are both necessary to understand diverse behavioral outcomes in adolescence? *Social Work Research, 23,* 145–158.

Puzzanchera, C. (2009). *Juvenile arrests, 2008* (NCJ 227489): Washington DC: U.S. Department of Justice, Office of Juvenile Justice and Delinquency Prevention. Retrieved from http://www.ncjrs.gov/pdffiles1/ojjdp/228479.pdf

Robins, L. N., & McEvoy, L. (1990). Conduct problems as predictors of substance abuse. In L. N. Robins & M. Rutter (Eds.), *Straight and devious pathways from childhood to adulthood* (pp. 182–204). Cambridge, UK: Cambridge University Press.

Romer, D. (2003). Prospects for an integrated approach to adolescent risk reduction. In D. Romer (Ed.), *Reducing adolescent risk: Toward an integrated approach* (pp. 1–9). Thousand Oaks, CA: Sage.

Rossa, M. W. (2002). Some thoughts about resilience versus positive development, main effects, versus interaction effects and the value of resilience. *Child Development, 71,* 567–569. doi:10.1111/1467–8624.00166

Rutter, M. (1979). Protective factors in children's responses to stress and disadvantage. In M. W. Kent & J. E. Rolf (Eds.), *Primary prevention of psychopathology: Vol. 3. Social competence in children* (pp. 49–74). Lebanon, NH: University Press of New England.

Rutter, M. (1987). Psychosocial resilience and protective mechanisms. *American Journal of Orthopsychiatry, 57,* 316–331.

Rutter, M. (2001). Psychosocial adversity: Risk, resilience, and recovery. In J. M. Richman & M. W. Fraser (Eds.), *The context of youth violence: Resilience, risk, and protection* (pp. 13–41). Westport, CT: Praeger.

Sameroff, A. J. (1999). Ecological perspectives on developmental risk. In J. D. Osofsky & H. E. Fitzgerald (Eds.), *WAIMH handbook of infant mental health: Vol. 4. Infant mental health groups at risk* (pp. 223–248). New York: Wiley.

Sameroff, A. J., Bartko, W. T., Baldwin, A., Baldwin, C., & Siefer, R. (1999). Family and social influences on the development of child competence. In M. Lewis & C. Feiring (Eds.), *Families, risk, and competence* (pp. 161–186). Mahwah, NJ: Lawrence Erlbaum.

Sameroff, A. J., & Fiese, B. H. (2000). Transactional regulation: The developmental ecology of early intervention. In J. P. Shonkoff & S. J. Meisels (Eds.), *Handbook of early childhood intervention* (2nd ed., pp. 135–159). New York: Cambridge University Press.

Sameroff, A. J., & Gutman, L. M. (2004). Contributions of risk research to the design of successful interventions. In P. Allen-Meares & M. W. Fraser (Eds.), *Intervention with children and adolescents: An interdisciplinary approach* (pp. 9–26). Boston: Allyn & Bacon.

Scheier, L. M., & Botvin, G. J. (1998). Relations of social skills, personal competence, and adolescent drug use: A developmental exploratory study. *Journal of Early Adolescence, 18,* 77–114. doi:10.1177/0272431698018001004

Schinke, S., Brounstein, P., & Gardner, S. (2002). *Science-based prevention programs and principles, 2002* (DHHS Pub No. SMA 03–3764). Rockville, MD: Substance Abuse and Mental Health Services Administration.

Sorenson, J. L., Masson, C. L., & Perlman, D. C. (2002). HIV/Hepatitis prevention in drug abuse treatment programs: Guidance from research. *NIDA Science and Practice Perspectives, 1,* 4–12. Washington, DC: National Institute on Drug Abuse. Retrieved from http://www.drugabuse.gov/pdf/perspectives/v011n01/02perspectives-hivhep.pdf

Spoth, R., Redmond, C., & Shin, C. (1998). Direct and indirect latent variable parenting outcomes of two universal family-focused preventive interventions: Extending a public-health oriented research base. *Journal of Consulting and Clinical Psychology, 66,* 385–399. doi:10.1037/0022–006X.66.2.385

Substance Abuse and Mental Health Administration. (2010). *National registry of effective programs.* Retrieved from http://www.nrepp.samhsa.gov/

Sutherland, E. H. (1973). Development of the theory [Private paper published posthumously]. In K. Schuessler (Ed.), *Edwin Sutherland on analyzing crime* (pp. 13–29). Chicago: University of Chicago Press.

U.S. Department of Education. (2007). *Indicators of school crime and safety 2007* (NCES 2008–021). Washington, DC: Author.

Vigil, J. D. (1990). Cholos and gangs: Culture change and street youth in Los Angeles. In R. Huff (Ed.), *Gangs in America: Diffusion, diversity, and public policy* (pp. 142–162). Thousand Oaks, CA: Sage.

Vossekuil, B., Fein, R. A., Reddy, M., Borum, R., & Modzeleski, W. (2002). *The final report and findings of the Safe School Initiative: Implications for the prevention of school attacks in the United States.* Washington, DC: U.S. Secret Service and U.S. Department of Education.

Werner, E. E., & Smith, R. S. (1982). *Vulnerable but invincible: A longitudinal study of resilient children and youth.* New York: Adams, Bannister, & Cox.

Werner, E. E., & Smith, R. S. (1992). *Overcoming the odds: High risk children from birth to adulthood.* New York: Cornell University Press.

Werner, E. E., & Smith, R. S. (2001). *Journeys from childhood to the midlife: Risk, resilience, and recovery.* New York: Cornell University Press.

White, H. R., Loeber, R., Stouthamer-Loeber, M., & Farrington, D. P. (1999). Developmental associations between substance use and violence. *Development and Psychopathology, 11,* 785–803. doi:10.1017/S0954579499002321

Wike, T. L., & Fraser, M. W. (2009). School shootings: Making sense of the senseless. *Aggression and Violent Behavior, 14,* 162–169. doi: 10.1010/j.avb.2009.01.005

Wilson, S. J., & Lipsey, M. W. (2007). School-based interventions for aggressive and disruptive behavior: Update of a meta-analysis. *American Journal of Preventive Medicine, 33,* S130–S143. doi:10.1016/j.amepre.2007.04.011

Woolf, S. H. (2008). The power of prevention and what it requires. *Journal of the American Medical Association, 299,* 2437–2439. doi:10.1001/jama.299.20.2437

2

Anti-Poverty Policies and Programs for Children and Families

Trina R. Williams Shanks

Sandra K. Danziger

Poverty is acknowledged as a risk factor for many problems experienced by children and youth. Evidence from various disciplines indicates that children growing up in low-income households experience social and health conditions that place them at risk for later academic, employment, and behavioral problems (Conley, 1999; Davis-Kean, 2005; Duncan & Brooks-Gunn, 1997; Guo & Harris, 2000; McLoyd, 1998; Sampson, Morenoff, & Gannon-Rowley, 2002; Williams Shanks, Kim, Loke, & Destin, 2010). Indeed, the detrimental influence of poverty is apparent in all of the substantive policy areas discussed in this book.

AUTHORS' NOTE: The authors would like to thank Megan Gilster for her diligent research assistance in preparing this chapter.

Children are poor because they reside in households and/or communities that are poor. Thus, a principal goal of anti-poverty policies is to break the link between poor resources of parents or caregivers and adverse child outcomes. To achieve this goal, some anti-poverty policies and programs provide material support to parents. Other anti-poverty initiatives offer resources and opportunities directly to children. Evidence suggests that the specific targets of social policy should not be an "either-or" proposition or strategy. That is, studies show that it is important to both support low-income parents and promote child well-being (Waldfogel, 2006; Waters Boots, Macomber, & Danziger, 2008).

In this chapter, we examine risk and protective factors associated with childhood and adolescent poverty. Major income assistance and income maintenance policies for children and families are reviewed. Trends in anti-poverty policy are noted; particular emphasis is paid to the Personal Responsibility and Work Opportunity Reconciliation Act of 1996. We conclude with a brief discussion of how American social policies aimed at ameliorating childhood poverty compare to approaches in other industrialized countries. Finally, policy and program directives that may help improve the integration of services and promote positive outcomes for children and families are identified.

Prevalence and Trends in Poverty

The debate about the best way to measure poverty is long and ongoing (Blank, 2008; Couch & Pirog, 2010). To bring some unity to the study of poverty, the U.S. Census Bureau in the 1960s established income thresholds to determine whether a household is officially poor. These thresholds are updated annually. As shown in Figure 2.1, child poverty rates reached a low during the 1960s. Since the 1970s, child poverty rates have fluctuated with periodic increases and decreases in the last three decades. Nearly 23% of all children under the age of 18 lived in poverty in 1993. Poverty rates declined between 1993 and 2002 but have increased slightly in the past several years. About 19% of children lived in poverty in 2008.

However, the average poverty rate hides considerable variation by race and ethnicity. Black and Hispanic children are twice as likely to be poor compared with Asian and White children. As shown in Figure 2.2, children residing in female-headed households experience poverty at four times the rate of all other households.

Figure 2.1   Child Poverty Rates in the United States by Race and Ethnicity, 1960–2009

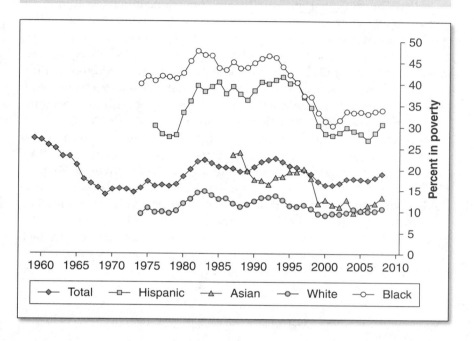

Figure 2.2   Child Poverty Rates by Household Type, 1960–2009

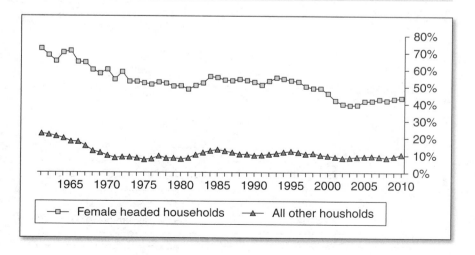

In spite of the widespread use of the Census Bureau definition, the measurement of poverty continues to be debated. Critics charge that the majority of surveys that measure income flows into a household miss an important aspect of a household's financial situation because they fail to consider family assets. For example, a family with housing equity, savings, and investments is in a better situation and has more favorable long-term prospects than a family of equal income but no assets. Although there is no official means to assess assets, researchers have developed ways to calculate it by using household net worth (Brandolini, Magri, & Smeeding, 2010; Haveman & Wolff, 2004; Shapiro, Oliver, & Meschede, 2009)

Data reflecting household net worth reveal that racial and ethnic disparities in assets are even greater than disparities in income (Lui, Robles, Leondar-Wright, Brewer, & Adamson, 2006; Oliver & Shapiro, 1995; Shapiro, 2004). As shown in Figure 2.3, Black and Hispanic households own between an eighth and a tenth, respectively, of the median net worth of White households. Furthermore, as depicted in Figure 2.4, households with children are most likely to be asset poor. In fact, female-headed households with children had asset poverty rates as high as 70% in 2001.

Figure 2.3   Median Household Net Worth by Race and Ethnicity, 1983–2007

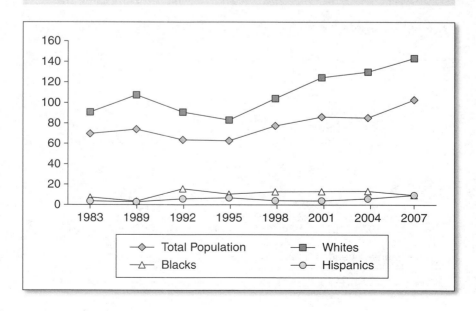

Figure 2.4   Liquid Asset Poverty Rate by Household Type (for household heads under age 65)

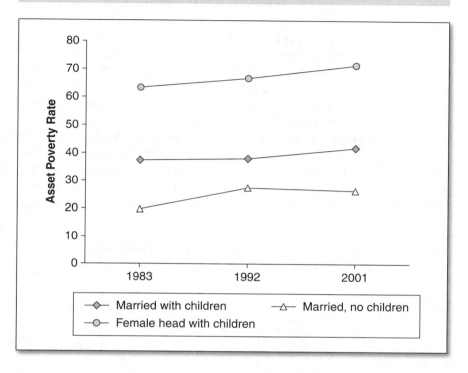

Poverty is also viewed commonly at the neighborhood or community level. Neighborhood poverty refers to the spatial concentration of poor households in neighborhoods, which are measured by census tracts. Generally, a poor neighborhood is one in which 20% to 40% of residents live below the poverty line. The concentration of the poor in metropolitan areas of the United States increased dramatically between 1970 and 1990. As shown in Figure 2.5, the number of people living in poor neighborhoods and the number of poor neighborhoods nearly doubled during this time (Jargowsky, 1997).

It appears that two main macroeconomic changes contributed to the shifting spatial distribution of poor families. First, a decline in manufacturing markets negatively impacted inner cities and resulted in an increase in urban poverty rates. Second, factors such as discrimination in the housing and lending markets and rapid suburban development increased racial and socioeconomic segregation such that inner-city neighborhoods became predominantly Black and poor (Jargowsky, 1997; Massey & Denton, 1993). The 1990s were also characterized by an increase in the suburbanization of neighborhood poverty. That is, although poverty declined in all other areas, rates of suburban poverty experienced almost no change (Jargowsky, 2003; Kingsley & Pettit, 2007).

The decline in neighborhood poverty between 1990 and 2000 may be explained by neighborhood fluctuations in moderate, high, and extreme poverty rates (Kingsley & Pettit, 2007) and by decreases in overall poverty caused by the improving economy of the late 1990s (Jargowsky, 2003). Figure 2.5 also shows that the percentage of the population in high-poverty neighborhoods has declined in the past decade. However, the number of poor census tracts in 2000 still exceeds the number in 1980. Recent evidence suggests that the economic decline since 2000 has led to a new increase in poverty—both nationally and in isolated neighborhood settings. Suburban poverty has continued to grow, especially in western

Figure 2.5   Number of Poor Census Tracts and Percent of Population Living in Poor Tracts

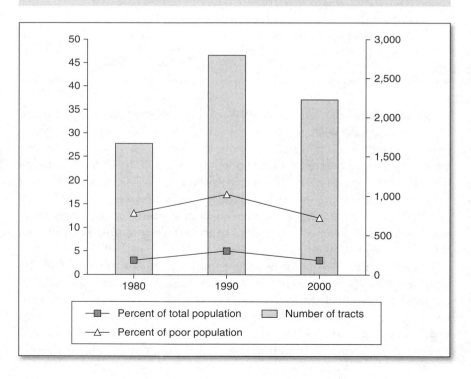

and Sun Belt states (Kneebone, 2009), and neighborhood poverty has also increased in midwestern cities and suburbs in recent years (Kneebone & Garr, 2010).

Neighborhood poverty is experienced at much higher rates among people of color; this disparity is most evident among children (Jargowsky, 2003; Sharkey, 2009). Only 1% of White children born between 1955 and 1970 lived in poor neighborhoods whereas 29% of Black children born during this time lived in poor neighborhoods at some point in their childhood. About 31% of Black children born between 1985 and 2000 experienced neighborhood poverty (Sharkey). Inequality and poverty in neighborhood contexts for children expose them to serious risks that often compromise normal and healthy development.

Poverty, Risk, and Protection

Poverty stems from interpersonal, social, and environmental factors that occur at all levels of a child's life (Bronfenbrenner, 1979). In Figure 2.6, we depict the increasingly wide spheres of influence related to the onset, persistence, and consequences of poverty. Clearly, efforts to prevent or reduce poverty should include state and federal policies and programs that target each of these levels. We discuss interpersonal, social, and environmental risk and protective factors associated with poverty in the following section.

Interpersonal and Social Risk Factors

Material hardships such as food insufficiency, unstable housing, and lack of basic health care are consistently associated with poverty. Material hardship is particularly important because it adversely affects many aspects of child development. In 1999, findings from a national sample of children revealed that 23% of families below the federal poverty level had experienced *food insecurity* (they were unable to afford balanced meals, cut the size of meals, or had too little money for food) in the past year (Gershoff, 2003). A 2006 survey revealed that 25% of children in families with income below the poverty level had experienced food insecurity in the past year (Nord, 2009). Qualitative researchers have detailed the many stressors and negative outcomes experienced by children residing in low-income families that are trying to meet basic needs (Edin & Lein, 1998; Newman, 1999). Parenting practices and behaviors created as a result of economic strain and

Figure 2.6 Circles of Influence on Childhood Family Poverty

- Child
- Family
- Home
- Community
- Locality
- Institutions
- Policies

NOTE. Adapted from Bronfenbrenner (1979).

material hardship also indirectly affect children. Conger and colleagues (1991) have proposed a family process model that considers the influence of a family's economic problems and parental depression on child and youth development. In this model, a mother's and father's depression is hypothesized to increase marriage hostility and decrease nurturing and involved parenting (Conger et al., 1991; Conger et al., 2002). Studies have also found that material hardship and financial stress are related to low self-esteem, less sense of control over one's life, and feelings of helplessness among parents, which in turn adversely affects their ability to use effective parenting skills (Bradley & Corwyn, 2002; Conger & Donnellan, 2007; Gershoff, Aber, Raver, & Lennon, 2007; McLoyd, 1990, 1998).

Parent and family investment in children's education and development—including educational materials in the home, engagement with school, and facilitation of extracurricular activities—is another way in which poverty influences child development. Mayer (1997) found that parental education, attitudes, and behaviors were more important in explaining child outcomes than income, once basic material needs are met (Mayer, 1997). Cognitive stimulation in the home both in terms of the availability of learning materials and parental teaching and conversations is correlated with household income and is predictive of positive educational outcomes and fewer behavior problems (Bradley & Corwyn, 2002, 2003; Guo & Harris, 2000; Shonkoff & Phillips, 2000). A positive home environment is especially important for children's academic growth during the summer, when school resources are not available (Downey, von Hippel, & Broh, 2004; Entwisle & Alexander, 1992). Clearly, poor parents often lack the resources, skills, and opportunities to help their children succeed in school.

Recent findings from investigators interested in promoting asset-based policies suggest that a family's assets offer protection for children, particularly those residing in low-income households (Williams Shanks et al., 2010). Assets appear to operate as an important protective factor in relation to standardized test scores, school performance, and certain types of antisocial conduct and behavior problems (Conley, 1999; Orr, 2003; Williams Shanks, 2007). Equally important, studies have found positive relationships between household assets and children's academic outcomes across racial groups (Williams Shanks & Destin, 2009) and among female-headed households (Zhan, 2006; Zhan & Sherraden, 2003).

Environmental Risks

Wilson (1987, 2009) has suggested that concentrated neighborhood poverty isolates poor residents and limits their exposure to positive role models, employment networks, and community resources. A large body of research has examined the direct and indirect effects of neighborhood poverty on various child and adolescent outcomes (Harding, 2003; Hart, Atkins, & Matsuba, 2008; Kling, Ludwig, & Katz, 2005; Leventhal & Brooks-Gunn, 2000; Pachter, Auinger, Palmer, & Weitzman, 2006). Many investigators have emphasized the significant and adverse effect of limited local resources and opportunities on children's development. Poor neighborhoods tend to lack quality institutions and social services (Leventhal & Brooks-Gunn, 2000; Sampson et al., 2002). Children growing up in poor neighborhoods witness frequent acts of violence and experience considerable chaos, disorder, and isolation.

In such communities, parents' stress levels as they struggle to cope with limited resources may negatively affect developmental outcomes (Klebenov, Brooks-Gunn, & Duncan, 1994; Kohen, Leventhal, Dahinten, & McIntosh, 2008; McLoyd, 1998).

In sum, children and families living in poor neighborhoods are doubly disadvantaged by frequent exposure to numerous interpersonal, social, and environmental risk factors. These factors interact in complex ways and lead to a number of adverse outcomes for children. Youth exposed to neighborhood and household poverty encounter negative influences and antisocial environments that place them at risk for a number of adverse individual and social outcomes. These risks are particularly influential during early childhood (Shonkoff & Phillips, 2000). Policies and programs such as asset building and income support, which target the upstream economic strain of poverty, along with initiatives to enhance parenting skills and home environments, which intervene in the down-stream processes of social disadvantage, are necessary to set a course for children to escape poverty. While it is important that interventions take place during early childhood, it is also crucial to develop and sustain policies and programs aimed at reducing risk and fostering resilience across the life course.

Anti-Poverty Policies and Programs

The United States has never instituted a comprehensive federal response to child poverty. In fact, no federal role in cash aid to poor children and families existed prior to 1935; only assistance from state, local, and private charities was available. Even today, with an array of federal anti-poverty programs, no policy or program reaches everyone who is eligible.

The first federal welfare program, Aid to Dependent Children, was part of the 1935 Social Security Act. The name of the program changed at mid-century to Aid to Families with Dependent Children (AFDC). The text box in this chapter summarizes changes in this program over time (Danziger, 2010). Table 2.1 provides an overview of some of the other major federal programs that offer support for basic needs of low-income children; funding levels for major anti-poverty programs between 1960 and 2009 are shown in Figure 2.7. Although critically important to child well-being, we exclude health insurance, medical care, and educational programs because these topics are covered in other chapters.

Table 2.1 Characteristics of Current Federal Anti-Poverty Programs

Program	When Began	Participation (FY 2009)	Percentage of Eligible Served[a]	Eligibility	Purpose (and site for further information)	Discretionary/ Entitlement
Subsidized Housing	1937	2.34 million families	9%[b]	Very low income families. Income limits vary from Housing Authority Area.	Subsidized housing units located in buildings that are publicly managed (i.e., public housing) or privately owned and managed under government contracts. http://portal.hud.gov/portal/page/portal/HUD/topics/rental_assistance/phprog	Discretionary
Supplemental Nutrition Assistance Program (SNAP)	1964	33.70 million people	66%	Gross monthly income < 130% Federal Poverty level (FPL). Net monthly income < 100% FPL.	Provides poor families with assistance purchasing food they need. http://www.fns.usda.gov/snap	Entitlement
Women, Infants, and Children (WIC)	1972	9.10 million women and children	59%	States set income eligibility (between 185% and 100% FPL) and nutrition risk eligibility.	Provides food, health care referrals, and nutrition education for low-income pregnant and postpartum women and to infants and children up to age five. http://www.fns.usda.gov/wic	Discretionary

(Continued)

Table 2.1 (Continued)

Program	When Began	Participation (FY 2009)	Percentage of Eligible Served[a]	Eligibility	Purpose (and site for further information)	Discretionary/ Entitlement
Supplemental Security Income (SSI)	1974	7.52 million people (in 2008)	68%	Age 65 or older, or blind, or disabled and limited income and resources (e.g., monthly income < $674 and resources < $2,000 for a single person).	Income assistance for aged, blind, and disabled people, who have little or no income. http://www.socialsecurity.gov/ssi	Entitlement
Section 8	1974	1.97 million families	15%[b]	Household income up to 80% of the area median.	A housing vouchers program that allows participants to rent privately owned residences from participating owners. Renters pay 30% of family income toward housing costs. http://portal.hud.gov/portal/page/portal/HUD/topics/rental_assistance http://portal.hud.gov/portal/page/portal/HUD/topics/housing_choice_voucher_program_section_8	Discretionary

Program	When Began	Participation (FY 2009)	Percentage of Eligible Served[a]	Eligibility	Purpose (and site for further information)	Discretionary/ Entitlement
Earned Income Tax Credit (EITC)	1975	24.58 million households (in 2007)	86%	Income limits based on family size (e.g., <$48,279 for married filing jointly with 3+ children).	A refundable tax credit to low-income workers (especially targeted at those with qualifying, dependent children). http://www.eitc .irs.gov	Entitlement
Hope VI	1993	See subsidized housing.	See subsidized housing.	Current residents of public housing are affected/new housing is open to those residents, other low income, and moderate income families.	Redevelopment of large-scale public housing sites to create mixed income housing in order to de-concentrate poverty._http://www.hud .gov/hopevi	Discretionary
Child Care and Development Block Grant (CCDBG)	1996	1.71 million children in .99 million families (in 2007)[c]	20%[d]	States determine income and work status eligibility.	Child care vouchers provided to families who choose the type of care (including formal care centers, family care homes, relative care, and care by nonrelatives).	Discretionary

(Continued)

Table 2.1 (Continued)

Program	When Began	Participation (FY 2009)	Percentage of Eligible Served[a]	Eligibility	Purpose (and site for further information)	Discretionary/ Entitlement
Temporary Assistance to Needy Families (TANF)	1996	4.03 million people	40%	States determine eligibility of families with children.	Cash assistance with a work requirement. Five-year limited term of lifetime federal assistance.	Discretionary
Workforce Investment (WIA)	1998	1.23 million exiters (in 2008)[e]	Not Available	Adults, dislocated workers, and youth aged 14 to 21 who face employment challenges and are primarily low income.	Job search and placement assistance and labor market information ("core" services) then career counseling and assessment ("intensive" services) before job training or education. http://www .doleta.gov/programs/	Discretionary

a. Source for participation rates if not otherwise noted: Waters Boots (2010).

b. U.S. House of Representatives (2008).

c. National Association of Child Care Resource and Referral Agencies (2010).

d. Social Policy Research Associates (2010).

e. Turner and Kingsley (2008).

The food stamp program became the Supplemental Nutrition Assistance Program (SNAP) program in 2008 (H.R. 2419, the Food, Conservation, and Energy Act of 2008). SNAP provides food assistance in the form of electronic benefit transfer (EBT) cards, which function like debit cards at retail grocery stores. SNAP program participation increased to an estimated 11% of U.S. households in 2009 (U.S. Department of Agriculture, 2010a). The rise in program participation is associated with the deep recession and rise in unemployment and poverty. A federal entitlement program, SNAP is open to anyone who is income eligible and helps ease the family budget by covering food costs. The average household benefit in 2008 was $222 (Food and Nutrition Service, 2009). The maximum benefit for a family of four in 2010 is $668. As shown in Figure 2.7, participation rates for SNAP are quite high. However, only 37.9% of low-income (< 185% poverty level) children experiencing food insecurity receive SNAP. Similarly, the Special Supplemental Nutrition Program for Women, Infants, and Children (WIC) is a federal food support program for low-income pregnant and postpartum women and their young children (U.S. Department of Agriculture, 2010b). However, states administer WIC and set the eligibility requirements, and its funding is through the mechanism of a limited block grant to states rather than an open-ended entitlement.

An increasingly important addition to anti-poverty efforts is the Earned Income Tax Credit (EITC), a refundable tax credit to low-income workers and their families. In 2008, more than 24 million families received income support through the federal EITC for a total of $50 billion in aid. It is estimated that the program lifts 2.5 million children with working parents out of poverty each year (U.S. Department of the Treasury, 2010). For most individuals filing without children, the maximum benefit in 2009 is $457, but for a single person with two dependent children, the maximum benefit is $5,028. The maximum allowable income to receive any benefit is just above $48,000 (married filing jointly with three or more children), which is more than 200% of the federal poverty line. Some states and localities also have tax credits for working low-income families that supplement this program (Purmort, 2010). As Figure 2.7 shows, the number of households that receive the EITC began to exceed Temporary Assistance for Needy Families (TANF) participation in the early 1990s when EITC federal policy expanded. EITC has now outstripped TANF as a source of income support.

The 1996 Personal Responsibility and Work Opportunity Reconciliation Act (PRWORA) expanded and consolidated federal funding for child care

Figure 2.7   Federal Anti-Poverty Program Participation, 1960 to 2009

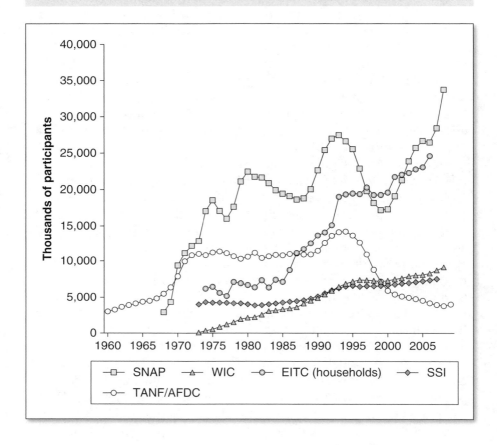

for employed parents into the Child Care and Development Block Grant (CCDBG). Under this act, states are provided flexibility in determining income and work eligibility, structuring the voucher program, and determining which types and standards of care will be reimbursed at what rates. There is consistent evidence that subsidies facilitate employment of low-income and welfare recipient families (Blau & Tekin, 2007; Danziger, Ananat, & Browning, 2004; Bainbridge, Meyers, & Waldfogel, 2003; Meyers, Heintze, & Wolf, 2002; Press, Fagan, & Laughlin, 2006). Between 1997 and 2006, public funding more than doubled from $3.7 billion to $9 billion (U.S. House of Representatives, 2008). The American Recovery and

Reinvestment Act of 2009 also expanded funds for child care subsidies and for quality improvements in child care services. Although the majority of low-income families rely on child care that is developmentally inadequate or minimally adequate (Levine Coley, Li-Grining, & Chase-Lansdale, 2006), it is unclear whether subsidy receipt leads to higher quality care (Antle et al., 2008). Subsidies could be structured to promote use of higher quality of care, but a high priority issue is access—only 20% of those eligible receive assistance with child care.

The 1996 Welfare Reform: AFDC Becomes TANF

Several welfare policy changes in the 1980s paved the way for welfare reform in 1996 (Danziger & Danziger, 2009). The 1981 Omnibus Reconciliation Act signed into law by President Ronald Reagan represented the first reduction in cash welfare in decades. The welfare rolls fell by about 14%, and work incentive provisions were eliminated. The Family Support Act of 1988 increased work requirements for welfare recipients but also initiated transitional assistance for child care and Medicaid for families leaving welfare for work. Throughout the 1980s and early 1990s, the federal government granted many waivers, which allowed the states to experiment with welfare-to-work programs. This led to increased state control over program administration (Heclo, 2001).

The PRWORA (Public Law No. 104–93) signed by President Bill Clinton in August 1996 ended AFDC's 60-year history and resulted in major changes in the structure of the program and its diminished role as a resource for the poor. Compared to Aid to Families with Dependent Children (AFDC), the Temporary Assistance for Needy Families (TANF) plays a smaller role as a resource for families.

Several rules reduced participation in TANF. A federal lifetime time limit for benefit receipt was imposed. States were required to institute mandatory work rules and to achieve specified rates of participation in work requirements. States were also required to impose sanctions in the form of benefit reduction or case closure to families that did not comply with the new requirements. States could implement diversion programs to deter or deflect applicants from entering the program (e.g., providing a one-time lump sum payment to families who agreed not to seek cash benefits for a set period of time). Furthermore, the federal legislation made eligibility for benefits contingent on a number of conditions and allowed states to add further contingencies. TANF disallowed

(Continued)

(Continued)

parents who had a drug felony conviction. Teen parents under the age of 18 were required to live with an adult and attend school as a condition of receiving benefits. New legal immigrants were not allowed to receive means-tested public benefits, including TANF, for the first 5 years after entry (Fix, 2006).

The wide discretion allowed in the federal legislation has led some analysts to suggest that welfare is now more of a state than a federal policy and that there are now 50 different welfare programs. Rowe and Giannarelli (2006) have observed that "virtually any statement about welfare is no longer universally true across the country" (p. 1). For example, as of 2003, southern states paid a maximum benefit of less than $300 per month to a family of three whereas six states paid more than $600 to such families with no other income. Many states had no diversion policies but 19 states permitted a diversion payment of more than $1,000 to a family of three. While 35 states imposed the federal time limit of 60 months, 8 states had shorter time limits, from 21 to 48 months, and 6 states had set no time limits to cash welfare (these states use state funds to pay benefits after 60 months; Rowe & Giannarelli, 2006).

The clearest result of welfare reform is the dramatic nationwide decline in reliance on cash assistance, while participation in other anti-poverty programs has grown, shown in Figure 2.7 (Danziger, 2010). Welfare caseloads have fallen precipitously since the mid-1990s and did not increase during the "great recession" that began in December 2007. The failure of the welfare system to respond to increased poverty during the recession raises concern for how single mothers and their children will fare in the coming years.

The Effects of the 1996 Welfare Reform on Child Outcomes

Neither the critics' dire predictions of increased child poverty, nor the proponents' rosy forecasts that children would directly benefit from seeing their mothers take jobs, came true. Millions of destitute children were not put out on the streets in the first decade following welfare reform. On the other hand, child and family troubles did not melt away when mothers entered the workforce. Studies are not finding that welfare leavers' stress levels and mental health status have improved as they exit the rolls, which suggests that children's lives are also not improving as a result of welfare reform.

The Three-City Study (Chase-Lansdale et al., 2003) analyzed early child and young adolescent cognitive, psychological, and behavioral outcomes and the effects of mothers' transitions in and out of work and welfare. Neither gains nor losses in employment nor exits nor returns to welfare (compared with no changes in mother's work/welfare status) affected five measures of preschoolers' well-being. Results for the 10- to 14-year-olds were mixed. For example, mental health improved among adolescents whose mothers had gains in employment. Entry into employment resulted in income gains in every model; it reduced time spent with young children, but not with older children.

Many studies suggest that the transition from welfare to work itself may not directly affect child behavioral outcomes but may operate through mediators such as parental stress and the family's experiences of economic hardship (Slack, Magnuson, & Berger, 2007). In several studies, mother's stress and hardship remained high regardless of employment and welfare status, indicating that increased employment may improve income but not other dimensions of well-being. Because mother's well-being is directly predictive of child behavior problems, these indicators improve or decline together (e.g., Kalil & Dunifon, 2007). A study of Michigan families found that mothers whose jobs were unstable, who worked full time with low pay, or who were in jobs with irregular, fluctuating schedules had young children whose behavior and academic achievement were adversely affected (Johnson, Kalil, & Dunifon, 2010). A study of mothers in six cities found that mothers whose cash benefits were terminated or reduced compared with those with no change in benefits had greater odds of child hospitalization, of being food insecure, and of having children admitted to the hospital after being seen in emergency care (Cook et al., 2002).

High levels of family economic distress and vulnerability compromise child well-being. Welfare agencies that restrict entry, push welfare exits, and offer only a work-first message exacerbate rather than help the situation of many poor families. The recent recession could bring harsher indictments of the effects of welfare reform as the number of vulnerable families with access to neither work nor cash assistance grew as employment and earnings fell.

Supplemental Security Income (SSI) is a program of the Social Security Administration. Unlike retirement income from social security, which is funded by social security taxes, SSI is funded by general federal tax revenues. Families with children who have a disability are eligible to receive SSI support; 15.7% of recipients were under 18 in 2010 (Social Security Administration, 2010). Eligibility requirements were made more stringent with the passing of PRWORA in 1996. The average monthly benefit for a child (recipient under age 18) is $597 in 2010 (Social Security Administration). Although a relatively high rate of those who qualify are served, many people who are unemployed for long periods due to illness or disability experience long delays in the application and review process (U.S. General Accounting Office, 2009).

The federal government also supports the employment of youth and adults through training and education programs designed to ensure that participants are job-ready. Although job-training programs were originally designed to assist dislocated workers, they became a part of federal anti-poverty strategies by the 1960s (LaLonde, 1995). Just as PRWORA shifted the focus of welfare toward "work first," the approach of job-training programs has also shifted toward employment. The Workforce Investment Act of 1998 (WIA) was enacted to replace the Job Training Partnership Act (JTPA), with an emphasis on job placement before training or education (Holzer, 2008). With the changes from JTPA to WIA, substantially fewer low-income youth and adults received training. About 95% of program leavers reported receiving training in JTPA, compared with 68.4% of exiters from WIA in 2003 (Frank & Minoff, 2005).

Federal housing assistance is funded through the U.S. Department of Housing and Urban Development (HUD) and administered by local housing authorities. It takes two main forms: Section 8 housing vouchers for private units and subsidized public housing units. Both programs serve a small fraction of low-income renters and have long waiting lists of families that apply for assistance. Only half of those served, 2.6 million, are families with children. Moreover, 5.6 million eligible households with children experience serious housing needs (Turner & Kingsley, 2008). The character of public housing in the United States has been changing in the last 20 years due to efforts like Moving to Opportunity (MTO) and Hope VI. These initiatives attempt to disperse concentrated neighborhood poverty. Although the goal of the program was to improve outcomes for individuals, the development of new mixed income housing units decreased the amount of housing generally available to poor residents (Sharkey, 2009). Once again, access has been a key concern, with few eligible households receiving needed assistance.

Another way to think about the degree to which social policy assists children and families is to compare child poverty in the United States to other industrialized countries. The U.S. child poverty rate is more than

4 times higher than rates in such European countries as Sweden, Norway, Finland, and Denmark (Lindsey, 2004; Rainwater & Smeeding, 2003a, 2003b). The low child poverty rates in these nations are realized not because earnings are higher but because a large proportion of children are being lifted from poverty through government intervention (Rainwater & Smeeding, 2003a). The child poverty reduction from governmental programs and income transfers in the United States is less than 25% compared with more than 75% in Sweden and Norway (Lindsey, 2004; Rainwater & Smeeding, 2003a, 2003b).

In sum, a variety of anti-poverty programs provide assistance through cash, food support, tax credits, child care, workforce development, and housing. Yet, with all these programs, few focus on low-income households with children. In some cases, mothers with work requirements may be able to increase earnings through employment but subsequently risk losing eligibility for other forms of assistance, and this may provide little aggregate benefit in terms of poverty status (Currie, 2006). And, when parents are required to work outside the home, parental psychosocial well-being may not improve, and children may actually receive less attention. Indeed, there could be an increase in the number of unsupervised, latchkey children and little reduction in family poverty. There are many gaps in the existing safety net, particularly when viewed from the broader goal of improving outcomes for children and youth.

Using Knowledge of Risk, Protection, and Resilience to Achieve Service Integration

In recent years, investigators and policy officials have begun to promote positive social development as a means to ameliorate childhood poverty. Such a focus represents an alternative to emphasizing the relationship between poverty and adverse child outcomes in policies and programs. Sen (1993, 1999) suggests that a person's functional capabilities and the freedom to attain what is valued for one's own welfare should form the basis of anti-poverty policies and programs. In a similar vein, Sherraden (1991) argues that income support policies provide an important safety net but are insufficient for long-term growth and development. He suggests that helping low-income households build tangible financial assets can lead to positive changes in self-efficacy and civic participation and to improvements in child well-being (Sherraden, 2005). Sherraden's work

indicates that accumulated resources in the form of saving accounts promote investment for long-term security either by increasing human capital or by anticipating future circumstances (e.g., expanding a business or
planning for retirement).

Integrated and systems-level approaches represent another important
approach to preventing and ameliorating childhood poverty. Systems-
level approaches focus on better coordination across service sectors. Thus,
rather than creating public policies composed of separate streams of
money to address particular needs or problems, a systems approach
argues for a comprehensive community change strategy that addresses
the full array of problems facing families. One cross-system policy and
program example that has received considerable attention recently is the
Harlem Children's Zone (HCZ) in New York City (Tough, 2008). In the
HCZ, Geoffrey Canada and colleagues have developed an array of community programs and educational innovations (including two charter
schools) in a 97-block area of Harlem. Services are designed to support
children and families in a metaphorical "conveyor belt" from birth to college (Tough). Specific interventions include parenting classes in *Baby
College*, pre-kindergarten instruction in *Harlem Gems*, and an array of
afterschool, health, college preparatory, employment training, and substance abuse programs and services. Initial evidence shows that children
in the HCZ schools have better attendance, more time in classroom
instruction, and better achievement scores in math and English than those
who are not enrolled (Dobbie & Fryer, 2009; Tough). Although it is hard to
disentangle school and community effects, HCZ intentionally bundled a
high-quality school experience with complementary wrap-around services to improve achievement and reduce gaps that have traditionally
existed between low-income minority children and their better-off peers
(Dobbie & Fryer).

Others have created and supported similar comprehensive community-
building strategies. For example, the Annie E. Casey Foundation has
funded a series of neighborhood change initiatives aimed at childhood
poverty, including the Rebuilding Communities and Making Connections
programs (Annie E. Casey Foundation, 2010). The Skillman Foundation
has launched comprehensive community-building initiatives in six local
neighborhoods in Detroit through its Good Neighborhoods initiative
(Skillman Foundation, 2010). Efforts to assess and evaluate these long-
term comprehensive change projects face major research challenges
(Kubisch et al., 2002; Stone, 1996). Although much has been learned, no

clear blueprint for how to successfully make low-income communities safe and healthy places for children has emerged.

Another promising approach to promoting positive development among low-income youth uses an asset-building strategy to establish a child development account (CDA) system (Goldberg, 2005; Williams Shanks et al., 2010). The vision is that every child from birth gets a subsidized account in her or his own name with an initial deposit that also matches additional savings. The deposit is intended to provide a foundation for family financial literacy and tangible resources that can be invested in a child's future. A primary use of the account is to save for college or postsecondary education. However, money can also be used for other purposes in early adulthood. The purpose of this strategy is provide young people with resources to support whatever choices they think will help them build personal capabilities and get started in life, regardless of their parents' financial situation. An example of this approach, the Saving for Education, Entrepreneurship, and Downpayment (SEED) initiative, is currently being tested in the United States (Center for Social Development, 2010).

The concept of children's development accounts has already been established as policy internationally. In the United Kingdom, the Child Trust Fund (CTF) provides a certificate for at least £250 to the parents of every baby born in the country, with additional funds offered to the parents of low-income children (Child Trust Fund, 2010). Parents use these certificates to open an account on their child's behalf, which can grow tax-exempt until the child reaches age 18. The UK government imposes no restrictions on use once a child reaches 18 but plans to offer financial information and counseling within schools as part of its national education curriculum. When the program launched in 2005, it opened 3 million CTFs. In 2007, about one quarter of these accounts received additional contributions beyond the initial government deposit (Bennett, Chávez Quezada, Lawton, & Perun, 2008).

Singapore has introduced child development accounts that can be used for preschool and other education- or health-related expenses from birth to age 6 (Loke & Sherraden, 2007). The government has also created the Post-Secondary Education Account (PSEA) to cover approved education-related expenses between the ages of 7 and 20. Unused balances from the child accounts can roll over to a child's PSEA, and unused balances from PSEAs can be rolled over to the adult child's Central Provident Fund. Thus, Singapore essentially has a lifelong system of accounts to help its citizens build assets and meet personal and financial goals (Loke & Cramer, 2009). These examples may provide important lessons to policy-makers in the United States.

Summary

This chapter has provided evidence that income poverty, asset poverty, and neighborhood poverty, alone and in combination, are associated with pro-found disadvantages for children and families. From our review, it is also apparent that existing anti-poverty policies and programs in the United States, although providing crucial supports to many, are not sufficient to lift large numbers of children out of poverty or greatly shift developmental outcomes for poor children. However, if the will and resources to make sys-temic change could be found, a variety of programs, including comprehen-sive community change strategies and asset building, are showing promise.

To realize long-term success in breaking the link between household poverty and child well-being, a few observations can be made. A "family security approach"—like that called for by Waters Boots, Macomber, and Danziger (2008)—is crucial, in that multiple generations and multiple levels of influence must be targeted concomitantly. No single program is likely to be enough. And although the most concrete issue for a family may be insufficient income, "fixing" income support policies alone might not take us far enough along in a risk and protection framework. Families with children, especially those headed by young single women, could undoubtedly use better-designed cash and financial help with housing, child care, food, and job training to make ends meet. However, to prevent a lifetime of poverty and dead-end jobs, a host of other resources—education, parenting support, services to provide their children a nurturing home environment, and high-quality early child care—are needed. Given that families often experience spells in and out of poverty throughout the life course, it would be strategic to assist parents of young children to increase their educational attainment and plan a better life for themselves and for their children. Work-related participation requirements might be part of a broader goal to improve long-term outcomes for entire families.

Finally, American anti-poverty policies and programs have failed to reduce racial and ethnic inequities in income, wealth, and neighborhood poverty. Income and, indeed, health disparities by race and ethnicity have not narrowed over time (see Chapter 6). This warrants targeted supports and interventions for diverse communities at highest risk, particularly

Hispanic-origin and Black families. Benchmarks for a successful policy approach would be both improved outcomes for poor children and decline in racial or ethnic disparities.

QUESTIONS FOR DISCUSSION

1. What risk and protective factors are associated with poverty?

2. Some experts point to income inequality itself as a cause of poor child developmental outcomes. What are the relative advantages and potential disadvantages of focusing policy attention on reducing poverty (i.e., income inequality) versus assisting children and families in need?

3. How do current public assistance programs target supports for low-income families with children? What are their limitations from a risk and resilience framework?

4. What new system-level approaches have been developed to prevent or reduce poverty? How do these approaches aim to break the link between poverty and child well-being?

5. How much can government and community-based partners do for families in need? What is the role of personal, parental, and community responsibility in anti-poverty policies and programs?

References

Annie E. Casey Foundation. (2010). *Helping vulnerable kids and families succeed.* Retrieved from http://www.aecf.org

Antle, B., Frey, A., Barbee, A., Frey, S., Grisham-Brown, J., & Cox, M. (2008). Child care subsidy and program quality revisited. *Early Education and Development, 19,* 560–573.

Bainbridge, J., Meyers, M. K., & Waldfogel, J. (2003). Child care policy reform and the employment of single mothers. *Social Science Quarterly, 84,* 771–791. doi:10.1046/j.0038–4941.2003.08404002.x

Bennett, J., Chávez Quezada, E., Lawton, K., & Perun, P. (2008). *The U.K. Child Trust Fund: A successful launch.* London: Institute for Public Policy Research and Aspen Institute.

Blank, R. M. (2008). Presidential address: How to improve poverty measurement in the United States. *Journal of Policy Analysis and Management, 27,* 233–254. doi:10.1002/pam.20323

Blau, D., & Tekin, E. (2007). The determinants and consequences of child care subsidies for single mothers in the USA. *Journal of Population Economics, 20,* 719–741. doi:10.1007/s00148–005–0022–2

Bradley, R. H., & Corwyn, R. F. (2002). Socioeconomic status and child development. *Annual Review of Psychology, 53,* 371–399. doi:10.1146/annurev.psych.53.100901 .135233

Bradley, R. H., & Corwyn, R. F. (2003). Age and ethnic variations in family process mediators of SES. In M. H. Bornstein & R. H. Bradley (Eds.), *Socioeconomic status, parenting, and child development* (pp. 161–188). New York: Lawrence Erlbaum.

Brandolini, A., Magri, S., & Smeeding, T. M. (2010). Asset-based measurement of poverty. *Journal of Policy Analysis and Management, 29*(2), 267–284. doi:10.1002/pam.20491

Bronfenbrenner, U. (1979). *The ecology of human development.* Cambridge, MA: Harvard University Press.

Center for Social Development, Washington University in St. Louis. (2010). *Saving for Education, Entrepreneurship, and Downpayment national initiative.* Retrieved from http://csd.wustl.edu/AssetBuilding/SEED

Chase-Lansdale, P. L., Moffitt, R., Lohman, B., Cherlin, A., Coley, R. et al. (2003). Mothers' transitions from welfare to work and the well-being of preschoolers and adolescents. *Science, 299,* 1548.

Child Trust Fund. (2010). *About the Child Trust Fund.* Retrieved from http://www.childtrustfund.gov.uk

Conger, R. D., & Donnellan, M. B. (2007). An interactionist perspective on the socioeconomic context of human development. *Annual Review of Psychology, 58,* 175–199. doi:10.1146/annurev.psych.58.110405.085551

Conger, R. D., Lorenz, F. O., Elder, G. H., Jr., Melby, J. N., Simons, R. L., & Conger, K. J. (1991). A process model of family economic pressure and early adolescent alcohol use. *The Journal of Early Adolescence, 11*(4), 430–449. doi:10.1177/0272431691114003

Conger, R. D., Wallace, L. E., Sun, Y., Simons, R. L., McLoyd, V. C., & Brody, G. H. (2002). Economic pressure in African American families: A replication and extension of the family stress model. *Developmental Psychology, 38*(2), 179–193. doi:10.1037/0012-1649.38.2.179

Conley, D. (1999). *Being Black, living in the red: Race, wealth, and social policy in America.* Berkeley: University of California Press.

Cook, J. T., Frank, D. A., Berkowitz, C., Black, M. M., Casey, P. H., Cutts, D. B., Meyers, A. F., Zaldivar, N., Skalicky, A., Levenson, S., & Heeren, T. (2002). Welfare reform and the health of young children: A sentinel survey in 6 U.S. cities. *Archives of Pediatrics & Adolescent Medicine, 156,* 678–684.

Couch, K. A., & Pirog, M. A. (2010). Poverty measurement in the U.S., Europe, and developing countries. *Journal of Policy Analysis and Management, 29*(2), 217–226. doi:10.1002/pam.20488

Currie, J. M. (2006). *The invisible safety net: Protecting the nation's poor children and families.* Princeton, NJ: Princeton Univ. Press.

Danziger, S., & Danziger, S. K. (2009). The U.S. social safety net and poverty: Lessons learned and promising approaches. In M. J. Bane & R. Zenteno (Eds.), *Poverty and poverty alleviation strategies in North America* (pp. 233–241). Cambridge, MA: Harvard University Press.

Danziger, S. K. (2010). The decline of cash welfare and implications for social policy and poverty. *Annual Review of Sociology, 36,* 523–545. doi:10.1146/annurev.soc .012809.102644

Danziger, S. K., Ananat, E., & Browning, K. (2004). Child care subsidies and the transition from welfare to work. *Family Relation, 53,* 219–228.

Davis-Kean, P. E. (2005). The influence of parent education and family income on child achievement: The indirect role of parental expectations and the home environment. *Journal of Family Psychology, 19*(2), 294–304. doi:10.1037/ 0893–3200.19.2.294

Dobbie, W., & Fryer, R. G. (2009). *Are high quality schools enough to close the achievement gap? Evidence from a social experiment in Harlem* (NBER Working Paper 15473). Cambridge, MA: National Bureau of Economic Research.

Downey, D. B., von Hippel, P. T., & Broh, B. A. (2004). Are schools the great equalizer? Cognitive inequality during the summer months and the school year. *American Sociological Review, 69*(5), 613–635. doi:10.1177/000312240406900501

Duncan, G. J., & Brooks-Gunn, J. (Eds.). (1997). *Consequences of growing up poor.* New York: Russell Sage Foundation.

Edin, K., & Lein, L. (1998). The private safety net: The role of charitable organizations in the lives of the poor. *Housing Policy Debate, 9*(3), 541–573.

Entwisle, D. R., & Alexander, K. L. (1992). Summer setback: Race, poverty, school composition, and mathematics achievement in the first two years of school. *American Sociological Review, 57*(1), 72–84. doi:10.2307/2096145

Fix, M. (2006). *Immigrants' costs and contributions: The effects of reform.* Washington, DC: Migration Policy Institute.

Food and Nutrition Service. (2009). *Characteristics of supplementary assistance program households: Fiscal year 2008* (No. SNAP-09-CHAR). Washington, DC: United States Department of Agriculture.

Frank, A., & Minoff, E. (2005, December 14). *Declining share of adults receiving training under WIA are low-income or disadvantaged.* Washington, DC: Center for Law and Social Policy.

Gershoff, E. T. (2003). *Low income and hardship among America's kindergarteners in living at the edge* (Research Brief No. 3). New York: National Center for Children in Poverty.

Gershoff, E. T., Aber, J. L., Raver, C. C., & Lennon, M. C. (2007). Income is not enough: Incorporating material hardship into models of income associations with parenting and child development. *Child Development, 78,* 70–95. doi:10.1111/j.1467–8624.2007.00986.x

Goldberg, F. (2005). The universal piggy bank: Designing and implementing a system of savings accounts for children. In M. Sherraden (Ed.), *Inclusion in the American dream* (pp. 303–322). Oxford, UK: Oxford University Press.

Guo, G., & Harris, K. M. (2000). The mechanisms mediating the effects of poverty on children's intellectual development. *Demography, 37*(4), 431–447. doi:10.1353/ dem.2000.0005

Harding, D. J. (2003). Counterfactual models of neighborhood effects: The effect of neighborhood poverty on dropping out and teenage pregnancy. *American Journal of Sociology, 109*(3), 676–719. doi:10.1086/379217

Hart, D., Atkins, R., & Matsuba, M. K. (2008). The association of neighborhood poverty with personality change in childhood. *Journal of Personality and Social Psychology, 94,* 1048–1061.

Haveman, R. H., & Wolff, E. N. (2004). The concept and measurement of asset poverty: Levels, trends and composition for the U.S., 1983–2001. *Journal of Economic Inequality, 2,* 145–169. doi:10.1007/s10888–005–4387-y

Heclo, H. (2001). The politics of welfare reform. In R. Blank & R. Haskins (Eds.), *The new world of welfare* (pp. 169–200). Washington, DC: The Brookings Institution.

Holzer, H. J. (2008). *Workforce development and the disadvantaged: New directions for 2009 and beyond* (Brief No. 7). Washington, DC: The Urban Institute.

Jargowsky, P. A. (1997). *Poverty and place: Ghettos, barrios, and the American city.* New York: Russell Sage Foundation.

Jargowsky, P. A. (2003). *Stunning progress, hidden problems: The dramatic decline in concentrated poverty in the 1990s.* Washington, DC: The Brookings Institution.

Johnson, R. C., Kalil, A., & Dunifon, R. (2010). *Leaving welfare for work: How welfare reform has affected the well-being of children.* Kalamazoo, MI: W.E. Upjohn Institute for Employment Research.

Kalil, A., & Dunifon, R. (2007). Maternal work and welfare use and child well-being: Evidence from 6 years of data from the women's employment study. *Children and Youth Services Review, 29,* 742–761.

Kingsley, G. T., & Pettit, K. L. S. (2007). *Concentrated poverty: Dynamics of change* (Neighborhood Change in Urban America No. 5). Washington, DC: Urban Institute.

Klebanov, P. K., Brooks-Gunn, J., & Duncan, G. J. (1994). Does neighborhood and family poverty affect mothers' parenting, mental health, and social support? *Journal of Marriage and Family, 56*(2), 441–455. doi:10.2307/353111

Kling, J. R., Ludwig, J., & Katz, L. F. (2005). Neighborhood effects on crime for female and male youth: Evidence from a randomized housing voucher experiment. *Quarterly Journal of Economics, 120,* 87–130.

Kneebone, E. (2009). *The suburbanization of American poverty* (Metropolitan Opportunity Series No. 2). Washington, DC: The Brookings Institution.

Kneebone, E., & Garr, E. (2010). *The suburbanization of poverty: Trends in metropolitan America, 2000 to 2008* (Metropolitan Opportunity Series No. 3). Washington, DC: The Brookings Institution.

Kohen, D. E., Leventhal, T., Dahinten, V. S., & McIntosh, C. N. (2008). Neighborhood disadvantage: Pathways of effects for young children. *Child Development, 79*(1), 156–169. doi:10.1111/j.1467–8624.2007.01117.x

Kubisch, A. C., Auspos, P., Brown, P., Chaskin, R., Fulbright-Anderson, K., & Hamilton, R. (2002). *Voices from the field II: Reflections on comprehensive community change.* Washington, DC: Aspen Institute.

LaLonde, R. J. (1995). The promise of public sector–sponsored training programs. *The Journal of Economic Perspectives, 9*(2), 149–168.

Leventhal, T., & Brooks-Gunn, J. (2000). The neighborhoods they live in: The effects of neighborhood residence on child and adolescent outcomes. *Psychological Bulletin, 126*(2), 309–337. doi:10.1037/0033–2909.126.2.309

Levine Coley, R., Li-Grining, C. P., & Chase-Lansdale, P. L. (2006). Low-income families' child care experiences: Meeting the needs of children and families. In N. J. Cabrera, R. Hutchens, & H. E. Peters (Eds.), *From welfare to child care* (pp. 149–170). Mahwah, NJ: Lawrence Erlbaum.

Lindsey, D. (2004). *The welfare of children.* New York: Oxford University Press.

Loke, V., & Cramer, R. (2009). *Singapore's Central Provident Fund: A national policy of life-long asset accounts.* Washington, DC: New America Foundation.

Loke, V., & Sherraden, M. (2007). *Building children's assets in Singapore: The Post-Secondary Education Account policy* (CSD Policy Brief 07–36). St. Louis, MO: Center for Social Development.

Lui, M., Robles, B., Leondar-Wright, B., Brewer, R., & Adamson, R. (2006). *The color of wealth: The story behind the U.S. racial wealth divide.* New York: New Press.

Massey, D. S., & Denton, N. A. (1993). *American apartheid: Segregation and the making of the underclass.* Cambridge, MA: Harvard University Press.

Mayer, S. E. (1997). *What money can't buy: Family income and children's life chances.* Cambridge, MA: Harvard University Press.

McLoyd, V. C. (1990). The impact of economic hardship on Black families and children: Psychological distress, parenting, and socioemotional development. *Child Development, 61,* 311–346. doi:10.2307/1131096

McLoyd, V. C. (1998). Socioeconomic disadvantage and child development. *American Psychologist, 53,* 185–204. doi:10.1037/0003–066X.53.2.185

Meyers, M. K., Heintze, T., & Wolf, D. A. (2002). Child care subsidies and the employment of welfare recipients. *Demography, 39,* 165–179. doi:10.1353/dem.2002.0008

National Association of Child Care Resource and Referral Agencies. (2010). *Average monthly number of children served.* Retrieved from http://www.naccrra.org/randd/ccdbg-tanf/avg-monthly-number-of-children-served

Newman, K. S. (1999). *No shame in my game: The working poor in the inner city.* New York: Russell Sage Foundation.

Nord, M. (2009). *Food insecurity in households with children: Prevalence, severity, and household characteristics* (Economic Information Bulletin No. 56). Washington, DC: United States Department of Agriculture Economic Research Service.

Oliver, M. L., & Shapiro, T. M. (1995). *Black wealth/White wealth: A new perspective on racial inequality.* New York: Routledge.

Orr, A. (2003). Black–White differences in achievement: The importance of wealth. *Sociology of Education, 76*(4), 281–304.

Pachter, L. M., Auinger, P., Palmer, R., & Weitzman, M. (2006). Do parenting and the home environment, maternal depression, neighborhood, and chronic poverty affect child behavioral problems differently in different racial-ethnic groups? *Pediatrics, 117,* 1329–1338.

Press, J., Fagan, J., & Laughlin, L. (2006). Taking pressure off families: Child-care subsidies lessen mothers' work-hour problems. *Journal of Marriage and Family, 68,* 155–171. doi:10.1111/j.1741–3737.2006.00240.x

Purmort, J. (2010). *Making work supports work: A picture of low wage workers in America.* New York: National Center for Children in Poverty.

Rainwater, L., & Smeeding, T. M. (2003a). Doing poorly: U.S. child poverty in cross-national context. *Children, Youth and Environments, 13.* Retrieved from http://colorado.edu/journals/cye

Rainwater, L., & Smeeding, T. M. (2003b). *Poor kids in a rich country: America's children in comparative perspective.* New York: Russell Sage Foundation.

Rowe, G., & Giannarelli, L. (2006). *Getting on, staying on, and getting off welfare: The complexity of state- by-state policy choices.* Washington, DC: The Urban Institute.

Sampson, R. J., Morenoff, J. D., & Gannon-Rowley, T. (2002). Assessing "neighborhood effects": Social processes and new directions in research. *Annual Review of Sociology, 28,* 443–478. doi:10.1146/annurev.soc.28.110601.141114

Sen, A. (1993). Capability and well-being. In M. Nussbaum & A. Sen (Eds.), *The quality of life* (pp. 30–53). Oxford, UK: Clarendon Press. doi:10.1093/0198287976.003.0003

Sen, A. (1999). *Development as freedom.* New York: Knopf.

Shapiro, T. M. (2004). *The hidden cost of being African American: How wealth perpetuates inequality.* New York: Oxford University Press.

Shapiro, T. M., Oliver, M. L., & Meschede, T. (2009). *The Asset Security and Opportunity Index.* Waltham, MA: Brandeis University.

Sharkey, P. (2009). *Neighborhoods and the Black–White mobility gap.* Washington, DC: Pew Charitable Trusts.

Sherraden, M. (2005). Assets and public policy. In M. Sherraden (Ed.), *Inclusion in the American dream: Assets, poverty, and public policy* (pp. 3–19). Oxford, UK: Oxford University Press.

Sherraden, M. W. (1991). *Assets and the poor: A new American welfare policy.* Armonk, NY: M. E. Sharpe.

Shonkoff, J. P., & Phillips, D. A. (2000). *From neurons to neighborhoods: The science of early childhood development.* Washington, DC: National Academies Press.

Skillman Foundation (2010). *About the Skillman Foundation.* Retrieved from www.skillman.org

Slack, K. S., Magnuson, K. A., & Berger, L. A. (2007). Editorial: How are children and families faring a decade after welfare reform? Evidence from five non-experimental panel studies. *Children and Youth Services Review, 29,* 693–697.

Social Policy Research Associates. (2010). *PY 2008 WIASRD data book* (Project No. 1382). Washington, DC: U.S. Department of Labor, Office of Performance Technology, Employment and Training Administration.

Social Security Administration. (2010). *Monthly statistical snapshot, May 2010.* Retrieved from http://www.socialsecurity.gov/policy/docs/quickfacts/stat_snapshot/#table3

Stone, R. (1996). *Core issues in comprehensive community-building initiatives.* Chicago: Chapin Hall.

Tough, P. (2008). *Whatever it takes: Geoffrey Canada's quest to change Harlem and America.* New York: Houghton Mifflin.

Turner, M. A., & Kingsley, G. T. (2008). *Federal programs for addressing low-income housing needs: A policy primer.* Washington, DC: The Urban Institute.

U.S. General Accounting Office. (2009). *Social Security Administration: Further actions needed to address disability claims and service delivery challenges* (GAO 09–511T). Washington, DC: U.S. Government Printing Office.

U.S. Department of Agriculture. (2010a). *Supplemental nutrition assistance program.* Retrieved from http://www.fns.usda.gov/snap

U.S. Department of Agriculture. (2010b). *Women, infants and children program.* Retrieved from http://www.fns.usda.gov/wic/

U.S. Department of the Treasury. (2010). *The earned income tax credit.* Retrieved from http://www.eitc.irs.gov

U.S. House of Representatives. (2008). Background material and data on the programs within the jurisdiction of the Committee on Ways and Means. *2008 Green Book.* Washington, DC: Government Printing Office. Retrieved from http://waysandmeans.house.gov/singlepages.aspx?NewsID=10490

Waldfogel, J. (2006). *What children need.* Cambridge MA: Harvard University Press.

Waters Boots, S. (2010). *Improving access to public benefits: Helping eligible individuals and families get the income supports they need.* Baltimore: The Ford Foundation, Open Society Institute, and Annie E. Casey Foundation.

Waters Boots, S., Macomber, J., & Danziger, A. (2008). *Family security: Supporting parents' employment and children's development* (New Safety Net Paper No. 3). Washington, DC: Urban Institute.

Williams Shanks, T. R. (2007). The impact of household wealth on child development. *Journal of Poverty, 11*(2), 93–116. doi:10.1300/J134v11n02_05

Williams Shanks, T. R., & Destin, M. (2009). Parental expectations and educational outcomes for young African American adults: Do household assets matter? *Journal of Race and Social Problems, 1*(1), 27–35. doi:10.1007/s12552-009-9001-7

Williams Shanks, T. R., Kim, Y., Loke, V., & Destin, M. (2010). Assets and child well-being in developed countries. *Children and Youth Services Review.* doi:10.1016/j.childyouth.2010.03.011

Wilson, W. J. (1987). *The truly disadvantaged: The inner city, the underclass, and public policy.* Chicago: University of Chicago Press.

Wilson, W. J. (2009). *More than just race: Being Black and poor in the inner city.* New York: W. W. Norton.

Zhan, M. (2006). Assets, parental expectations and involvement, and children's educational performance. *Children and Youth Services Review, 28*(8), 961–975. doi:10.1016/j.childyouth.2005.10.008

Zhan, M., & Sherraden, M. (2003). Assets, expectations, and children's educational achievement in female-headed households. *Social Service Review, 77*(2), 191–211. doi:10.1086/373905

Additional Reading

Bane, M. J., & & Zenteno, R. (Eds.). (2009). *Poverty and poverty alleviation strategies in North America*. Cambridge, MA: Harvard University Press.

Cancian, M., & Danziger, S. (Eds.). (2009). *Changing poverty*. New York: Russell Sage Foundation.

Currie, J. M. (2006). *The invisible safety net: Protecting the nation's poor children and families*. Princeton, NJ: Princeton University Press.

Lindsey, D. (2004). *The welfare of children*. New York: Oxford University Press.

Sherraden, M. (Ed.). (2005). *Inclusion in the American dream: Assets, poverty, and public policy*. Oxford, UK: Oxford University Press.

Tough, P. (2008). *Whatever it takes: Geoffrey Canada's quest to change Harlem and America*. New York: Houghton Mifflin.

Waldfogel, J. (2006). *What children need*. Cambridge MA: Harvard University Press.

Web-Based Resources

Center for Social Development, George Warren Brown School of Social Work, Washington University in St. Louis, http://csd.wustl.edu

Institute for Research on Poverty, University of Wisconsin–Madison, http://www.irp.wisc.edu/

National Center for Children in Poverty, http://www.nccp.org/

National Poverty Center, Gerald R. Ford School of Public Policy, University of Michigan, http://www.npc.umich.edu/

3

Child Welfare Policies and Programs

Peter J. Pecora

Markell Harrison-Jackson

Purpose and Overview of Child Welfare Policy

The child welfare system, which provides a variety of child and family social services, is overburdened. About 3.3 million referrals for alleged maltreatment were reported to U.S. child protection services in 2008 (U.S. Department of Health and Human Services [DHHS], 2010). Compared with 1990, this is a profound increase in the number of children being

AUTHORS' NOTE: This chapter draws from material in the third edition of *The Child Welfare Challenge*. We appreciate the advice from that textbook's co-authors, James Whittaker, Anthony Maluccio, Richard Barth, Diane DePanfilis, and Robert Plotnick. Special thanks to JooYuen Chang, Fran Gutterman, Adrienne Hahn, Martha Jenkins, Betsey Rosenbaum, Regina Schofield, and the legislative advocacy staff of the Child Welfare League of America for the policy briefs and position statements that informed the legislative policy section. Finally, foster care alumni, practitioners, and foster parents have taught us much about the real impacts of policy; we appreciate the time they have devoted to improving the child welfare system.

referred as victims of maltreatment.[1] Not withstanding these long-term increases, there is some evidence that both reporting and incidence rates of child maltreatment have decreased significantly over the past few years (Finkelhor & Jones, 2006; Sedlak et al., 2010; U.S. DHHS).

For the analyses included in a recent report from the National Center on Child Abuse and Neglect Data System, a perpetrator is the person who is responsible for the abuse or neglect of a child. In 2008, 80.1% of perpetrators of child maltreatment were parents, and another 6.5% were other relatives of the victim. Of the perpetrators who were parents, 90.9% were the biological parent of the victim. In terms of perpetrator gender and age, women are more likely than men to be perpetrators, accounting for 56.2% and 42.6% of perpetrators, respectively, and 75.2% of all perpetrators were younger than age 40. Of note is that of the perpetrators who were child day care providers, 21.2% committed sexual abuse (U.S. DHHS, 2010).

In the United States during 2008, about 463,000 children were in out-of-home protective placements in foster care and nonfamily settings, and 748,000 children were served by child welfare agencies[2] (see Table 3.1). Overall, the number of children in placement rose steadily between 1980 and 2000. However, the number of children in out-of-home care has slowly decreased since 2000, as a result of changes in public policies (U.S. DHHS, 2009b). This decline in out-of-home care is likely due also to decreases in the incidence rates of child maltreatment (Sedlak et al., 2010).

Child maltreatment is clearly a major social and health problem. The purpose of this chapter is to describe public policies in the field of child welfare. In this field, public policymakers, practitioners, and scholars are working to devise new ways to deal with maltreatment. Indeed, new resources and ideas are reshaping child welfare practices in many locales. Notably, agencies in Florida, Illinois, and New York City are making successful efforts to reduce children's lengths of stay in out-of-home care, to reduce the level of restrictiveness of child placements, and to increase the proportion of children placed with kin who are not blood relatives. In addition, the number of children being adopted or securing a permanent placement through guardianship has increased over the last two decades because some states have substantially decreased the time to adoption (Avery, 1998; U.S. DHHS, 2003a, 2009b).

These innovations may expand further with dramatic new initiatives designed to reduce time in care and increase permanency. These initiatives include child welfare demonstration waivers, expedited adoptive parent

Table 3.1   Children in America: Selected Facts and Figures

National Child Demographics	
Child population younger than age 18 years in 2007[a]	73,901,733
Racial/ethnic diversity of children younger than age 18 years in the United States:[b]	
White	56%
Black or African American	14%
American Indian & Alaska Native	1%
Asian	4%
Hispanic or Latino	22%
Native Hawaiian & Other Pacific Islander	< 1%
Two or more races	3%
Who Cared for America's Children?	
Estimated number of "stay-at-home" parents: 5.3 million mothers and 140,000 fathers[c]	~5.4 million
Percentage of children living with two parents varied by race and origin.[c]	
Asian children	85%
White non-Hispanic children	78%
Hispanic children	70%
Black children	38%
Importance of grandparents: Percentage of all children living in a household that included a grandparent. (Note that 23% of children living with a grandparent had no parent present.)[c]	9% (6.6 million)
The Most Vulnerable Children?	
Poverty rate for children and adults in 2008[d]	13.2%
13.2%	

(Continued)

Table 3.1 (Continued)

The Most Vulnerable Children?	
Number of people in poverty in 2008[d]	39.8 million
39.8 million	
Real median household income for families with and without children fell 3.6% between 2007 and 2008[d]	$50,303
National poverty rate for children younger than age 18 years in 2008[d]	19%
Referrals for possible child abuse or neglect in 2007[e]	3.2 million
3.2 million	
Children substantiated or indicated as abused or neglected in 2007[e]	794,000
Children who died as a result of abuse or neglect in 2007[e]	1,760
Children in foster care on September 30, 2008[f]	463,000
Children adopted from the public foster care system during the fiscal year ending September 30, 2008[f]	55,000
Children waiting to be adopted from the public foster care system as of September 30, 2008[f]	123,000

a. U.S. Census Bureau (2010).

b. The terms used to describe racial/ethnic groups are those used by the U.S. Census Bureau. Source: The Annie E. Casey Foundation, KIDS COUNT Data Center (July 2009) http://datacenter .kidscount.org/data/acrossstates/Rankings.aspx?ind=103. The racial diversity of children under age 18 in the United States changed significantly from 1990 to 2000. The percentage of White children has decreased from 74.9% to 68.6%; whereas the percentage of Hispanic children has increased from 12.2% to 17.1%. See http://www.naeyc.org/policy/advocacy/Childrenand FamiliesFacts#Diversity.

c. U.S. Census Bureau (2009a).

d. U.S. Census Bureau (2009b).

e. U.S. Department of Health and Human Services (DHHS; 2009a).

f. U.S. DHHS (2009b).

assessments, expedited approvals of subsidy applications, increased judicial personnel, and heightened attention by the agencies and courts to the need for more timely permanency planning. Although the child welfare system is burdened, professionals, families, and advocates across the country are experimenting with new policies and procedures designed to find safe and enduring living arrangements for children.

In this chapter, we review risk and protective factors related to the reasons that children and their families become involved in the child welfare system, as well as the major social policies that are directed toward these families. In addition, we examine the ways in which the concepts of risk and protection are implemented in those policies. Drawing from innovative projects and programs across the country, we conclude with a discussion of current policy issues and recommendations for improving child welfare services.

Mission and Goals of Child Welfare Services

Child maltreatment is a costly problem, with detrimental sequelae that follow the initial trauma of neglect or abuse and continue throughout development to adult emotional and physical adaptation. According to some research, foster care expenditures in the past decade for child maltreatment alone totaled $14.4 billion (Wang & Holton, 2008). Developmentally, maltreatment often results in delayed physical growth, neurological damage, and mental and emotional/psychological problems, such as violent behavior, depression, and posttraumatic stress disorder. Research shows that maltreatment is positively associated with a variety of social and health problems, including substance abuse, eating disorders, obesity, depression, suicide, and sexual promiscuity in transition to adulthood (e.g., Kendall-Tackett, 2003).

Historically, the mission of child welfare has been to respond to the needs of children reported to public child protection agencies. The foster care system is a coordinated set of services for children (infants to age 21 years, but often to 18 years, depending on each state's laws) and their families. If found to be victims of maltreatment, children and adolescents may be removed from the custody of biological parents and placed in a foster care home as either a short-term or permanent placement. Children taken into custody by child welfare agencies reside in a variety of placements, including emergency shelters, long-term foster care, preadoption care, respite care, therapeutic care, kinship-care group homes, and residential treatment facilities (Pecora et al., 2009).

Recently, a somewhat broader framework for child welfare has emerged, and in the interest of protecting and nurturing of children, greater emphasis is being placed on communities as a whole. Consistent with this expanded frame of reference, the child welfare system has increased its efforts to form collaborative community strategies aimed at preventing and responding to child abuse and neglect. Child welfare agencies have begun to look beyond the parent–child dyad and considering what is known about the interplay of risk and protective factors at the levels of the child, parent, family, neighborhood, and community. Although children have highly individual needs and characteristics, they are viewed as living in the context of a family structure. In turn, families are viewed as embedded in the context of a culture and a neighborhood. Finally, neighborhoods are seen as clustered in the context of social, economic, cultural, and political environments. Thus, as a field, child welfare has come to embrace a multisystem ecological perspective.

A child welfare system that fails to incorporate and draw on the richness and strength embodied in this contextual view of family life cannot effectively respond to the needs of vulnerable children and troubled families. Although agency mission statements provide the guiding structure for service, it is essential that key goals and outcomes are specified to embrace such functions as establishing strategic plans, using evidence-based programs, securing adequate funding, and implementing practice guidelines within a context that promotes child safety and supports families (American Humane Association, 1998).

A key issue affecting the field is the lack of common procedures for describing and classifying child maltreatment. The definitions of abuse and neglect vary across states. Researchers have tried to shed light on the problem, seeking data to define maltreatment in terms of severity, incidence, chronicity, extent, type, age of onset, and perpetrator (Barnett, Manly, & Cicchetti, 1993; Hanson, Smith, Saunders, Swenson, & Conrad, 1995; Pecora et al., 2010). Notwithstanding, the field lacks a common definition of child maltreatment. To be sure, there are similarities in states' definitions, so that researchers who collect data across states can develop commonalties among the different types of maltreatment (Pecora et al., 2009; U.S. DHHS, 2010). However, no single, comprehensive, definitive breakdown of maltreatment types and combinations of abuse unifies either research or public policy.

In short, the field of child welfare lacks a common nomenclature for describing and classifying a child's maltreatment experience. A substantial number of children and adolescents entering and exiting foster care placement are known to have emotional, psychological, and cognitive developmental delays as compared with their peers who are in non-foster care placements (Haskins, Wulczyn, & Webb, 2007; Stahmer et al., 2005;

Webb, Dowd, Jones-Harden, Landsverk, & Testa, 2010). Currently, however, no agreement exists across states on either the fundamental experiences that place children at risk or the procedures that should be used to assess incidents of maltreatment.

Key Goals and Outcomes for Child Welfare Services

In spite of foundational disagreements on the definition of maltreatment, the field of child welfare services is gaining clarity and consensus about its primary mission. A primary goal and two secondary goals for child welfare services have emerged with widespread support. First and foremost, the primary goal is to protect children from harm. The second goal is to preserve existing family units, which include both birth family and relative families as appropriate. The third goal is to promote children's development as adults who can live independently and contribute to their communities. This last goal may require a variety of permanency planning alternatives such as family reunification, placement with relatives, different forms of guardianship (depending on local law), adoption, and intentionally planned long-term foster care or kinship care with legal safeguards such as guardianship (Pecora et al., 2009; U.S. DHHS, 2003a).

Currently, a challenging and controversial issue facing the child welfare system is the disproportionate number of children of color in foster care placements. Of the 123,000 U.S. children awaiting adoption in 2008, nearly 30% (36,913) were Black and 21% (26,223) were Hispanic (U.S. DHHS, 2009b). In fact, 54% of the foster care population (292,692 children) is comprised of children of color (i.e., African American/Black, Latino/ Hispanic, Asian, and Native American/Indigenous), and some of these children will remain in foster care placements until they are emancipated at age 18 (U.S. DHHS, 2009b; Wulczyn, Hislop, & Chen, 2007). Furthermore, African American children currently represent 26% of the children placed in out-of-home care nationwide, which is a significantly higher percentage than the number of African American children in the general population (U.S. Government Accountability Office, 2007).

There is some debate in the field about making child safety a goal superior to family support. Indeed, many family advocates and some researchers have argued that without a simultaneous emphasis on child safety *and* family support, neither goal will be achieved in an equitable manner. Similarly, the capacity of the system to support families and promote positive developmental outcomes for children in custody has been the subject of much criticism and debate (Berrick, Needell,

Barth, & Johnson-Reid, 1998; Wulczyn et al., 2005). The key components of each of these major goals (also called *outcome domains*) are summarized next.

Safety of Children

Maltreatment has a detrimental impact on the cognitive, emotional, and physical development of children. Thus, a core goal for child welfare services is keeping children safe from child abuse and neglect. This goal includes children living with their birth families, children reunited with their families after a maltreatment event, and children placed in out-of-home care when parental custody has been terminated because of maltreatment. In terms of concrete outcomes, the public policies that support child welfare services are intended (a) to prevent children from being maltreated and (b) to keep families safely together, including families that may be functioning at a minimum standard of parenting. Child welfare workers operate on the philosophical basis that all children have a right to live in a safe environment that is free from abuse and neglect. For example, the focus of child protective services should be to deliver services that are preventive, nonpunitive, and geared toward parental rehabilitation through identification and treatment of the factors that underlie maltreatment.

At the most general level, there is consensus regarding the mission of child protective services: Such services are designed to protect children from maltreatment committed by their parents or other caretakers. However, in translating this broad mandate into policy and practice, the consensus breaks down in a variety of areas such as defining what constitutes child abuse or neglect, establishing standards for agency intervention, and specifying what constitutes a minimum standard of parenting (popularized by the question, "What is a good enough parent?"). In the face of this widespread disagreement, child welfare is a policy and practice area that is benefitting from recent research on risk and protective factors in child development.

Permanency: A Stable and Permanent Home

When the state steps in to protect an abused or neglected child, it is not enough to keep the child safe; the state must also consider the child's needs for permanent and stable family ties. In addition to protecting a child, the state should ensure that the child has the opportunity to be brought up by stable and legally secure permanent families, rather than in temporary foster care under the supervision of the state. This principle has been well established in federal law: first by the Adoption Assistance and Child Welfare Act of 1980, and then by the Adoption and Safe Families Act of 1997.

Child Well-Being: Meeting Developmental Needs

Achieving child well-being means not only that a child is safe from child abuse or neglect but also that a child's basic needs are being met and that the child is provided with the opportunity to grow and develop in an environment with consistent nurture, support, and stimulation. In this outcome domain, we include the need for children to develop a healthy sense of identity; an understanding of their ethnic heritage; and skills for coping with racism, sexism, homophobia, and other forms of discrimination that remain prevalent in our society. Although there are limits to what child welfare services can provide, the system should promote standards of parenting that, at a minimum, will provide a child with the developmental opportunities and emotional nurturance needed to grow into an adult who can live as independently as possible.

Family Well-Being: Strengthening the Capacity to Care

Family well-being means that families have the capacity to care for children and to fulfill children's basic developmental, health, educational, social, cultural, spiritual, and housing needs. Ensuring family well-being also implies that child welfare staff members have responsibility for locating these essential services and supports and for helping to sustain or promote parents in their child-rearing roles.

Each of these outcome domains is exemplified, albeit imperfectly, by federal outcome standards as shown in Table 3.2. A report from the U.S. General Accounting Office (2004) proposed the first set of federal outcomes set as benchmarks for the performance of state-level child welfare systems:

> It is against these benchmarks for statewide data indicators that a state is measured. Any state whose performance is found to fall short of substantial conformity (based upon data analysis and an on-site review of individual cases) is given an opportunity to develop and implement a plan to improve performance and avoid the withholding of federal funds. [The Adoption and Safe Families Act] also required HHS to prepare and submit to Congress an annual report on the performance of each state on each outcome measure. (McDonald, Salyers, & Shaver, 2004, p. 5)

Using these indicators during a child and family services review, a review team assesses a state's performance by collecting data on (a) seven outcomes in the domains of safety, permanency, and child and family well-being; and (b) seven systemic factors that affect outcomes for children and families.

To measure a state's achievement of the outcomes, the review team assesses items (via onsite review) or items and data indicators (via onsite review plus statewide assessment). To measure achievement of the systemic factors, the review team assesses items to determine whether the systemic factors are in place and functioning satisfactorily. The items or data indicators associated with the outcomes and systemic factors are listed in Table 3.2. The numerical performance standards can be found in Appendix H of the federal Child and Family Services Review manual: http://www .acf.hhs.gov/programs/cb/cwmonitoring/tools_guide/.

Across states, these review benchmarks and performance measurement methods have stimulated helpful introspection and discussion. However, many experts have continued to advocate for additional refinement (e.g., National Coalition for Child Protection Reform, 2008; Testa & Poertner, 2010; Wulczyn, Orlebeke, & Haight, 2009).

Theoretical Frameworks Underlying Child Welfare Policies and Programs

A number of theoretical orientations underpin the design of policies and programs in child welfare, including ecological models, child development theories, social learning and social support theories, and risk and protective factor frameworks.

Ecological Developmental Models

From an ecological and developmental perspective, the life course outcomes of children involved in the child welfare system are perceived as deriving from the complex interaction of life experiences with biological factors (e.g., genetic vulnerability for certain disorders) and a variety of environmental and psychological factors. The conditions that produce developmental outcomes include genetic and epigenetic factors[3] such as experiences of poverty, racism, and dangerous living environments as well as family-of-origin characteristics and functioning. In addition, other factors, such as family characteristics and functioning, child and family supports, and the quality and nature of services provided by various community

Table 3.2   National Child and Family Service Review Standards for Child Welfare: Nonsystemic Standards

Standard	Description
Safety	Safety Outcome 1: Children are protected from abuse and neglect. • Timeliness of initiating investigations of reports of child maltreatment (Item 1) • Repeat maltreatment (Item 2) • Absence of recurrence of maltreatment (data indicator) • Absence of maltreatment of children in foster care (data indicator)
	Safety Outcome 2: Children are safely maintained in their homes whenever possible and appropriate. • Services to family to protect child(ren) in home and prevent removal or re-entry into foster care (Item 3) • Risk assessment and safety management (Item 4)
Permanency	Permanency Outcome 1: Children have permanency and stability in their living situations. • Foster care re-entries (Item 5) • Stability of foster care placement (Item 6) • Permanency goal for child (Item 7) • Reunification, guardianship, or permanent placement with relatives (Item 8) • Adoption (Item 9) • Other planned permanent living arrangement (Item 10) • Timeliness and permanency of reunifications (Permanency Composite 1) • Timeliness of adoptions (Permanency Composite 2) • Achieving permanency for children in foster care (Permanency Composite 3) • Placement stability (Permanency Composite 4)
	Permanency Outcome 2: The continuity of family relationships and connections is preserved for children. • Proximity of foster care placement (Item 11) • Placement with siblings (Item 12) • Visiting with parents and siblings in foster care (Item 13) • Preserving connections (Item 14) • Relative placement (Item 15) • Relationship of child in care with parents (Item 16)

(Continued)

Table 3.2 (Continued)

Standard	Description
Child and Family Well-Being	Child and Family Well-Being Outcome 1: Families have enhanced capacity to provide for their children's needs. • Needs and services of child, parents, and foster parents (Item 17) • Child and family involvement in case planning (Item 18) • Caseworker visits with child (Item 19) • Caseworker visits with parent(s) (Item 20)
	Child and Family Well-Being Outcome 2: Children receive appropriate services to meet their educational needs. • Educational needs of the child (Item 21)
	Child and Family Well-Being Outcome 3: Children receive adequate services to meet their physical and mental health needs. • Physical health of the child (Item 22) • Mental/behavioral health of the child (Item 23)

SOURCES: U.S. Department of Health and Human Services, Administration for Children and Families, Administration on Children, Youth and Families, Children's Bureau. (2006). *Child and Family Services Reviews Procedures Manual.* (Working Draft.) Retrieved from http://www.acf.hhs.gov/programs/cb/cwmonitoring/tools_guide/proce_manual.htm

Appendix B: Index of Outcomes and Systemic Factors, and Associated Items and Data Indicators. Retrieved from http://www.acf.hhs.gov/programs/cb/cwmonitoring/tools_guide/procedures/appendixb.htm

Note that the CFSR assesses: (1) Statewide Information Systems; (2) Case Review Systems; (3) Quality Assurance Systems; (4) Staff and Provider Training; (5) Service Array and Resource Development; (6) Agency Responsiveness to the Community; and (7) Foster and Adoptive Parent Licensing, Recruitment, and Retention.

agencies, interact in various ways with the experiences of child maltreatment to produce outcomes (Cicchetti & Lynch, 1993; Fraser, 2004; O'Connell, Boat, & Warner, 2009).

The ecological perspective delineated by Cicchetti and Lynch (1993) suggested that the family is a powerful microsystem. In typical child development, the family confers protection, whereas in atypical child development—in families in which maltreatment occurs—the family confers risk. The ecological model proposed by Bronfenbrenner (1979, 1986, 2004) posits that individual development occurs and can be understood only within the context of the family and the larger social–environmental context in which the family is embedded. In this model, to understand child developmental outcomes, it is necessary to understand the interplay of factors at the individual, family, and environmental levels. The ecological perspective requires identifying and analyzing risk and protective factors at the level of the child, the level of his or her family, and the level of the broader society: Children's development is conceptualized as arising from the complex interplay of these interwoven circles of influence.

Developmental Theories and Perspectives

Five approaches related to child development theories are especially relevant to child welfare practice. First, attachment theory addresses relationships and traumas occurring prior to age 2 years (e.g., Ainsworth, 1989; Weinfield, Ogawa, & Sroufe, 1997). Second, trauma theory (Briere, 1992), as it relates to the effects of abuse and neglect, offers explanations for variations in the influence of abuse and recovery from abuse. Third, as discussed above, the ecological perspective offers useful concepts addressing the relative importance of individual, familial, and societal contexts (e.g., Bronfenbrenner & Morris, 1998; Garbarino, 1992; Pecora et al., 2009). Fourth, risk and protective factor frameworks have descriptive utility for explaining resilience in children and youth who recover from maltreatment and for identifying predictors of life course outcomes. Protective factors can be personal assets (e.g., social competence) and environmental resources (e.g., supportive parents or other relatives) that buffer or suppress risk (Catalano & Hawkins, 1996; Fraser, 2004; Rutter, 1989). Fifth, Erikson's (1985) stages or steps in child development are useful in understanding and predicting child adjustment sequelae, including how children might adjust to foster care (Downs & Pecora, 2004).

Social Learning and Social Support Theories

In addition, social learning theory is widely applied in child welfare practice. This theory emphasizes the reciprocal influences of the environment on the person and the person on the environment. Social learning theory holds that human behavior is learned within an interactive social context and conditioned by relationships with family members, peers, and other close associates. Based on social learning theory, Chamberlain (2003) and her colleagues have developed and implemented a promising program called Multidimensional Treatment Foster Care.

Introduced nearly 100 years ago, social support theory is one of the earliest frameworks for understanding social relations and human development. This theory integrates three aspects of human connectedness (the community, social networks, and bonding relationships) and articulates conditions under which children grow to be self-reliant adults (Caplan, 1974; Casey Family Programs, 2003a; Maluccio, Pine, & Tracy, 2002). The perspective stresses the value of providing consistent supports to children, birth parents, and foster families. In addition, social support theory postulates that lack of supportive social relationships can negatively affect children's mental health and other developmental outcomes (Caplan, 1974). Social support theory is often applied to placement disruptions and transition from foster care to young adulthood (e.g., Pecora et al., 2010; Ryan & Testa, 2004). On balance, studies suggest that social support reduces stress, buffers risk exposure, and promotes psychological adaptation (DePanfilis, 1996; Mann, 2003; McIntosh, 1991).

Risk, Protection, and Resilience in Child Welfare

A variety of biological, psychological, and environmental factors converge to create the conditions in which maltreatment occurs, and a somewhat similar set of factors influences a child's recovery from maltreatment. The application of a risk and resilience perspective to child welfare falls in two areas. The first has to do with factors that elevate the odds for maltreatment, and the second has to do with factors that promote recovery from the experience of maltreatment. As shown in Table 3.3, the factors correlated with maltreatment include poverty, parental substance abuse, parental mental illness, parental history of child maltreatment, social isolation, lack of employment resources in the community, and neighborhood gangs and crime (see Child Welfare Information Gateway, 2010). However, none of these factors alone is sufficient to produce maltreatment. Nevertheless, maltreatment becomes more likely as the number of risk factors increases. At the same time, we now know that a number of factors operate protectively and can reduce the likelihood of maltreatment in the presence of risk. These protective factors are also shown in Table 3.3.

The recent fourth National Incidence Study (NIS-4) updated the set of risk factors for child maltreatment in key areas:

- **Employment.** Compared to children with employed parents, those with no parent in the labor force had 2 to 3 times the rate of maltreatment overall.
- **Family structure and living arrangement.** Compared to children living with married biological parents, those children whose single parent had a

live-in partner had more than 8 times the rate of maltreatment overall, over 10 times the rate of abuse, and nearly 8 times the rate of neglect.[4]

- **Grandparents as caregivers.** Children cared for by a grandparent had lower rates of physical abuse compared to those with no identified grandparent caregiver.[5]
- **Socioeconomic status.** Children in low socioeconomic status households had significantly higher rates of maltreatment. They experienced some types of maltreatment at more than 5 times the rate of other children; they were more than 3 times as likely to be abused and about 7 times as likely to be neglected.[6]
- **Family size.** The general pattern was nonlinear: The incidence rates were highest for children in the largest families (those with four or more children), intermediate for singleton children (i.e., "only" children) and those in households with three children, and lowest among children in families with two children (See the NIS-4 report for more details.)
- **Child's age.** In most cases, 0- to 2-year-olds had significantly lower maltreatment rates than older children.[7]
- **County metropolitan status.** On balance, the incidence of maltreatment was higher in rural counties than in urban counties.
- **Perpetrator's relationship to the child.** Biological parents were the most closely related perpetrators, accounting for 71% of physically abused children and for 73% of emotionally abused children. The pattern was distinctly different for sexual abuse, with 42% of sexually abused children victimized by someone other than a parent (whether biological or nonbiological) or a parent's partner, whereas just over one third (36%) were sexually abused by a biological parent. In addition, severity of harm from physical abuse varied by the perpetrator's relationship to the child. A physically abused child was more likely to sustain a serious injury when the abuser was not a parent.
- **Perpetrator's alcohol use, drug use, and mental illness.** Alcohol use and drug use contributed approximately equally to maltreatment, each applying to 11% of the countable children, whereas mental illness was a factor in the maltreatment of 7% of the children. All three factors were more often involved in maltreatment when the perpetrator was a biological parent (Sedlak et al., 2010, pp. 14–15).

In cases involved with child welfare, indeed across all children, the NIS-4 and other data suggest that developmental outcomes are influenced by individual and environmental risk factors as well as by a host of cultural resources and practices that may both buffer against risk and promote recovery from negative life events. One of the most frequently discussed risk factors is poverty. Low-income families are less likely to have adequate food, safe housing, and prenatal or other medical care. Households that are living near or below the poverty line tend to have few social supports and experience more stress in child rearing, all of which can increase the risk of child maltreatment. Generally, poverty has a direct negative influence on maternal behavior and subsequently on the quality of parenting that children receive (Brooks-Gunn, Klebanov, & Liaw, 1995). For children, living in poverty is associated with a host of negative consequences, including poor physical health, diminished cognitive abilities, reduced educational attainment, increased emotional and behavioral problems, and higher risk of maltreatment (Brooks-Gunn & Duncan, 1997; Ridge, 2009; Sedlak et al., 2010).

The relationship of poverty to maltreatment and other negative child developmental outcomes appears mediated in part by stress. Using global data, Wilkinson and Pickett (2009) charted the level of health and social problems against the level of income inequality in 20 of the world's richest nations and in each state of the United States. They found that mental illness, drug and alcohol abuse, obesity, and teenage pregnancy were more common in states and countries with a big gap between the incomes of rich and poor households. Moreover, areas with a large income gap also had higher homicide rates, shorter life expectancies, and lower scores for children's educational performance and literacy. The Scandinavian countries and Japan consistently scored at the positive end of this spectrum, and these countries have the smallest differences between higher and lower incomes and the best record of psychosocial health. The countries with the widest gulf between rich and poor, and the highest incidence of health and social problems, were Britain, the United States, and Portugal.

The Wilkinson and Pickett (2009) data suggest that poverty creates not only physical hardship but also a stressful environment that exacerbates social and health problems. Commenting on Wilkinson and Pickett, Carey (2009) argued,

> It is not only the poor who suffer from the effects of inequality, but the majority of the population. For example, rates of mental illness are five times higher across the whole population in the most unequal than in the least unequal societies in their survey. One explanation . . . is that inequality increases stress right across society, not just among the least advantaged. Much research has been done on the stress hormone cortisol, which can be measured in saliva or blood, and it emerges that chronic stress affects the neural system and in turn the immune system. When stressed, we are more prone to depression and anxiety, and more likely to develop a host of bodily

ills including heart disease, obesity, drug addiction, liability to infection and rapid ageing. (p. 1)

Although it is far beyond the capacity of service providers to influence national income differentials, these data suggest that health promotion and child safety may be associated with poverty and stress. In seeking to reduce stress, researchers are increasingly looking at protective factors, including cultural rootedness and resources, which buffer against stress related to poverty and other adversities such as racial discrimination.

Consistent with this perspective, the American Psychological Association's Task Force on Resilience and Strength in Black Children and Adolescents (hereafter, APA Task Force) recently called for reframing research to better conceptualize adaptive and protective processes for African American children. With the intent of providing researchers, policymakers, educators, practitioners, and the public with a useful lens through which to view the design of services for African American youth, the report explored how themes of resilience cut across five widely accepted developmental domains of functioning:

- **Identity development.** A positive racial identity is essential to the well-being of African American youth. Children should be encouraged to develop a positive sense of self in a society that often devalues them through negative stereotypes.
- **Emotional development.** Coping with emotions effectively is directly related to self-esteem and better mental health. African American youth need to be made aware of how their emotional expressions resonate across all situations and circumstances.
- **Social development.** Family and community interaction are crucial to African American youths' social development. This interaction includes having access to high-quality child care, afterschool programs, and faith-based institutions.
- **Cognitive development.** African American youth must believe in their abilities in the classroom. Parents should avoid harsh parenting styles, and schools should continue to look at ways to infuse culturally relevant themes into the classroom as a way to improve academic performance.
- **Physical health and development.** Access to health care must be improved. A wide range of health conditions disproportionately affect African American youth, including obesity, poor oral health, asthma, violent injury, sickle-cell anemia, diabetes, and HIV/AIDS (APA Task Force, 2008).

In addition to African American youth and their families, immigrant families constitute an increasing part of the population served by child welfare. In designing more effective services for these children, data suggest that it is important to understand how the experiences of immigration, immigration stress, and acculturation affect family dynamics, strengths, and risk and protective factors (e.g., Dalla, Defrain, Johnson, & Abbott, 2009; De Anda, 2003).

In child welfare, protection has always been an element of services, but the literature on risk and resilience has given new meaning to protection. For many children, prevailing over the adversity of maltreatment involves strengthening protective processes in the family and community context. These strengthening efforts include building parental competence and teaching positive disciplinary approaches; enhancing the racial and ethnic identities of children; and engaging caregivers, advocates, peer networks, and extended family members in providing culturally anchored social support. Other critical protective characteristics involve inclusion of families in community activities and the availability of medical, educational, and financial resources that allow parents to provide appropriate care for their children.

Table 3.3   Common Risk Factors for Child Abuse and Neglect

Risk Factors	Protective Factors
Child Risk Factors	Child Protective Factors[a]
<ul><li>Premature birth, birth abnormalities, low birth weight, exposure to toxins *in utero*</li><li>Temperament: difficult or slow to warm up to others</li><li>Physical/cognitive/emotional disability, chronic or serious illness</li><li>Childhood trauma</li><li>Antisocial peer group</li><li>Age</li><li>Child aggression, behavior problems, attention deficits</li></ul>	<ul><li>Birth order—first born</li><li>Health status—healthy during infancy and childhood</li><li>Activity level—multiple interests and hobbies, participation, and competence</li><li>Disposition—good-natured, precocious, mature, inquisitive, willing to take risks, optimistic, hopeful, altruistic, personable, independent</li><li>Developmental milestones—meets or exceeds age-appropriate expectations</li><li>Self-concept—high self-esteem, internal locus of control, ability to give and receive love and affection</li></ul>

Risk Factors	Protective Factors
	• Perceptive—quickly assesses dangerous situations and avoids harm • Interpersonal skills—able to create, develop, nurture, and maintain supportive relationships with others; is assertive and articulate; has good social skills and can relate to both children and adults • Cognitive skills—able to focus on positive attributes and ignore negative • Intellectual abilities—high academic achievement
Parental/Family Risk Factors • External locus of control • Poor impulse control • Depression/anxiety • Low tolerance for frustration • Feelings of insecurity • Lack of trust • Insecure attachment with own parents • Childhood history of abuse • High parental conflict, including domestic violence • Family structure—single parent with lack of support, high number of children in household • Social isolation, lack of support	Parental/Family Protective Factors[b] • Structure—rules and household responsibilities for all members • Family Relational Factors—coherence and attachment, open exchange and expression of feelings and emotions • Parental Factors—supervision and monitoring of children, a strong bond to at least one parent figure, a warm and supportive relationship, abundant attention during the first year of life, parental agreement on family values and morals, emotional availability (parental accessibility and capacity for reading the emotional cues and meeting the emotional needs of the infant)
• Parental psychopathology • Substance abuse • Separation/divorce, especially high conflict divorce • Age • High general stress level • Poor parent–child interaction, negative attitudes and attributions about child's behavior • Inaccurate knowledge and expectations about child development	• Reciprocity–mutually satisfying relationships are built between an infant/young child and a parent • Family size—four or fewer children spaced at least w years apart • Socioeconomic status (SES)—middle- to upper-level SES • Extended family—nurturing relationships with substitute caregivers such as aunts, uncles, and grandparents • Other positive social network support

(Continued)

Table 3.3 (Continued)

Risk Factors	Protective Factors
• Mental health problems, including maternal depression • Cultural "mismatch" (i.e., when a parent has a perception of normative development that is incongruent with that of the broader society and its service providers)	
Community/Social/ Environmental Risk Factors • Low socioeconomic status of the neighborhood • Stressful life events • Lack of access to medical care, health insurance, adequate child care, and social services • Parental unemployment; homelessness • Social isolation/lack of social support • Exposure to racism/ discrimination	Community/Social/ Environmental Protective Factors[c] • Positive peer relationships • Extended family in close proximity • Schools—academic and extracurricular participation and achievements, close relationship with a teacher(s) • Reliance on informal network of family, friends, and community leaders for advice

SOURCE: This table is adapted from Coll and Magnuson (2000); Garbarino and Ganzel (2000); Hodges (1994); Osofsky and Thompson (2000); and U.S. Department of Health and Human Services (2003b).

a. Much of the research on protective factors has focused on individual traits. This category of protective factors refers to factors that are learned (self-care and interpersonal attributes) as well as factors for which the individual has no control (birth order, gender). (Garmezy, 1983, 1985; Rae-Grant, Thomas, Offord, & Boyle, 1989; Rutter, 1979, 1981, 1985, 1987, 1990; Werner, 1989).

b. Family characteristics also act as protective factors (Garmezy, 1983, 1985; Rae-Grant et al., 1989; Rutter, 1979, 1981, 1985, 1987, 1990; Werner, 1989).

c. Community characteristics include individuals and institutions that are external to the family and that provide educational, emotional, and general supportive ties with the family unit as a whole or with individual family members. (Garmezy, 1983, 1985; Rae-Grant et al., 1989; Rutter, 1979, 1981, 1985, 1987, 1990; Werner, 1989).

Although the available research on protective factors associated with child maltreatment is limited, this research has been informed by the larger body of literature on protective factors. Several studies have outlined factors that differentiate resilient children from those children who experience serious adjustment problems. Protective factors appear to fall into three general categories: individual characteristics, family characteristics, and the presence of supportive others (Garmezy, 1985; Rutter, 1990; Werner, 1989). Individual characteristics include attributes such as self-sufficiency, high self-esteem, and altruism. Family characteristics include supportive relationships with adult family members, harmonious family relationships, expressions of warmth between family members, and the ability to mobilize supports in times of stress. Finally, community supports refer to supportive relationships with people or organizations that are external to the family. These external supports provide positive and supportive feedback to the child and act to reinforce and reward the child's positive coping abilities (Hodges, 1994).

Race, Ethnicity, Income, and Maltreatment

Poverty and race/ethnicity are related in the United States, and both are correlated with maltreatment. Indeed, the racial and ethnic distribution of perpetrators is similar to the race and ethnicity of victims. During 2008, nearly one half (47.8%) of perpetrators were White, 19.6% were African American, and 19.5% were Hispanic. These proportions have changed little in recent years (U.S. DHHS, 2010, p. 65).

Unlike previous National Incidence Studies, the NIS-4 identified racial/ethnicity differences in the incidence of maltreatment:

> In nearly all cases, the rates of maltreatment for Black children were significantly higher than those for White and Hispanic children. These differences occurred under both definitional standards in rates of overall maltreatment, overall abuse, overall neglect, and physical abuse and for children with serious or moderate harm from their maltreatment. They also occurred in the incidence of Harm Standard sexual abuse, in the incidence of children who were inferred to be harmed by Harm Standard maltreatment, and in Endangerment Standard rates for physical neglect, emotional maltreatment, and children who were endangered but not demonstrably harmed by their maltreatment. . . .
>
> In part, the emergence of race/ethnicity differences in the NIS-4 may stem from the greater precision of the NIS-4 estimates. . . . Differences are also consistent with changes in maltreatment rates since the NIS-3. While general declines in rates of maltreatment were noted since the NIS-3, these declines did not occur equally for all races and ethnicities. Rather . . . rates of maltreatment for White children declined more than the rates for Black and Hispanic children in the incidence of abuse, physical abuse, and children seriously harmed by maltreatment. For Harm Standard emotional neglect, maltreatment rates for White children declined while rates for Black and

Hispanic children increased. For Endangerment Standard emotional neglect, rates for White children increased less than the rates for Black and Hispanic children. (Sedlak et al., 2010, pp. 9–10)

Although the literature is sparse, differences by race and ethnicity should be understood in the context of other known risk factors, especially poverty. The NIS-4 also found significant differences in child abuse rates based on socioeconomic factors. Poor children were 3 times more likely than other children to experience abuse (Crary, 2010). When income was controlled in analyses, the differences found in maltreatment rates between White and Black children in low-income families were negligible. In fact, larger differences were observed in the "not low income" classification, in which higher rates were observed for African American families as compared to White families.

The preceding discussion offers a brief overview of the individual, family, and community risk and protective factors related to child abuse and neglect. We have placed emphasis on protective factors because they serve to buffer stress for some children and provide important clues for how to strengthen child welfare services. Given differences in family structure, child-rearing practices, and relationship to community, the degree to which these factors are moderated by race and ethnicity is unclear. This is the subject of much current research. Certainly, some of the protective factors associated with, for example, socioeconomic status and academic success are universal. However, other factors may be conditioned on or differentially more important among African American, Latino, and other children with strong racial, ethnic, or religious backgrounds. From Hodges (1994), these protective factors include:

- Active extended family—fictive or blood relatives who are active in the child's life; provides material resources, child care, supervision, parenting, and emotional support to the child (Wilson, 1984).
- Faith-based affiliation—belongs to and actively participates in a group religious experience (Werner, 1989).
- Strong racial identity—exhibits racial pride, strongly identifies with ethnic group through clubs, organizations, political, and social-change movements.
- Close attachment to the ethnic community—resides in the ethnic community, easy access to ethnic resources, including social services, merchants, media (newspaper), and demonstrates a commitment to the ethnic community.
- Dispositional attributes—activity level, sociability, average intelligence, competence in communication (oral and written), internal locus of control (Werner, 1989).

- Personal attributes—high self-esteem, academic achievement, assertiveness, quality of adjustment to single-parent household.
- Supportive family milieu—cohesiveness, extensive kinship network, nonconflictual relations.
- External support system—involvement of absent fathers, male role models, supportive social environments of various ethnic communities.

Risk, Resilience, and Protection in Child Welfare Policy[8]

Child welfare policy is slowly but steadily being shaped by research related to risk, resilience, and protection. Landmark books such as *Neurons to Neighborhoods* reinforce infant and young child stimulation principles outlined by earlier pioneers and make scientific knowledge accessible to a broad audience (Shonkoff & Phillips, 2000). Other child welfare researchers such as Berrick and colleagues (1998) and Maier (1978) have emphasized the importance of paying attention to child development fundamentals (e.g., attachment theory and social learning) in designing child welfare policy and programs. Advances in the treatment of child abuse and neglect have emphasized how children with varied psychological compositions and differing amounts of social support respond differently to various healing approaches (Briere, 1992; Cohen, Mannarino, Zhitova, & Capone, 2003). Ecological and diversity perspectives underscore the vital roles that broad community networks and environments play in services and healing. In addition, a recent Institute of Medicine report described a growing array of evidence-based programs for preventing emotional, behavioral, and substance abuse disorders in youth and young adults (O'Connell et al., 2009). We are making progress. Policy and program reforms include

- strategically focused family-centered services to strengthen parenting;
- child-centered early intervention and remedial services based on increased understanding of early brain development;
- attempts to embed substance abuse treatment services within child welfare and to strengthen linkages across service delivery systems such as mental health, education, and juvenile justice;
- use of least restrictive placement environments, which facilitated the closure of hundreds of residential institutions; and
- permanency planning for children to secure a stable family if birth parents are unable to provide care for the child; and

- aggressive permanency planning for older youth in foster care so they do not age out or emancipate from foster care without a legal guardian and a network of supportive relationships.

Three other significant transformations bear mentioning. First, leaders in child protective services, family support, and foster care have identified community collaborations as essential for effective services (Morgan, Spears, & Kaplan, 2003; Pew Foundation, 2008; Schorr & Marchand, 2007). Second, the field has recognized the simultaneous needs of moving all children (i.e., irrespective of background and age) to permanent family situations while also being cognizant of the need to nurture the child development of children who remain involved in the child welfare service system beyond a 3-month protective services intervention (Berrick et al., 1998; Kerman, Maluccio, & Freundlich, 2009). Third, racial and ethnic disproportionality in the provision of services and achievement of permanency outcomes are increasingly acknowledged problems. (Chibnall et al., 2003; Derezotes, Poertner, & Testa, 2005; Hines, Lemon, Wyatt, & Merdinger, 2004; U.S. Government Accountability Office, 2007). A discussion of these and other policy issues follows.

Key Child Welfare Policy and Legislation

A number of public policies influence child welfare programs and affect the families receiving child welfare services. Listed below are some of the key federal policies that are related to child welfare. These policies include adoption, child protection, income support, education, early intervention, family support, and foster care. (For more information see Appendix A in Pecora et al., 2009.) Medical care, which is also important for child welfare, is discussed more thoroughly in Chapter 6 of this volume.

- *Child Abuse Prevention and Treatment Act of 1974 (P.L. 93–247:* Provides some financial assistance for demonstration programs for the prevention, identification, and treatment of child abuse and neglect; mandates that states must provide for the reporting of known or suspected instances of child abuse and neglect (Stein, 1984).
- *Juvenile Justice and Delinquency Prevention Act of 1974 (P.L. 93–415):* Provides funds to reduce the unnecessary or inappropriate detention of juveniles and to encourage state program initiatives in the prevention and treatment of juvenile delinquency and other status offenses (see http://www.ojjdp.ncjrs .gov/about/ojjjjact.txt).

- *Title XIX of the Social Security Act:* provides health care to income-eligible persons and families. One of the sections of this act established the Early and Periodic Screening, Diagnosis, and Treatment program, which provides cost-effective health care to pregnant women and young children (see http://www.ssa.gov/OP_Home/ssact/title19/1900.htm).
- *The Education for All Handicapped Children Act of 1975 (P.L. 94–142):* This law supports education and social services for handicapped children. The act requires states to (a) offer programs for the full education of handicapped children between the ages of 3 and 18, (b) develop strategies for locating such children, (c) use intelligence testing that does not discriminate against the child racially or culturally, (d) develop an individualized education plan (IEP) for each child, and (e) offer learning opportunities in the *least restrictive educational environment* possible, with an emphasis on mainstreaming—integrating handicapped children into regular classrooms (see http://www .projectidealonline.org/publicPolicy.php).
- *The Individuals with Disabilities Education Act (IDEA):* The Individuals with Disabilities Education Act (IDEA) began as the Education for All Handicapped Children Act of 1975 (P.L. 94–142) and gave all children with disabilities the right to a free and appropriate public education. This watershed civil rights law resulted from sustained advocacy by parents of children with disabilities. Special education has been shaped by the six core principles that formed the nucleus of the Education for All Handicapped Children Act: (1) zero reject, meaning schools could not opt to exclude any children with disabilities from instruction; (2) nondiscriminatory evaluation, by which every child receives an individualized, culturally and linguistically appropriate evaluation before being placed in special education; (3) IEP, a plan delineating current performance, progress on past objectives, goals, and services for the school year, and evaluation of outcomes; (4) least restrictive environment, which is in settings with nondisabled children; (5) due process, which codifies the legal steps to ensure a school's fairness and accountability in meeting the child's needs and how parents can obtain relief via a hearing or by second opinions; and (6) parental participation, whereby parents have the right to access their child's education records and participate in IEP planning (Kirk, Gallagher, & Anastasiow, 1993, pp. 51–52).
- Another part of IDEA that is important for children served by child welfare agencies is early intervention, which has as its purpose the provision of prevention and treatment services to improve cognitive, social, and emotional development of the youngest children (under the age of 3). Children receiving early intervention services either are considered at risk for delayed development or have been identified as having a developmental disability (Ramey & Ramey, 1998).
- *The Indian Child Welfare Act of 1978 (P.L. 95–608):* Strengthens the standards governing the removal of Native American children from their families. Provides for a variety of requirements and mechanisms for tribal government overseeing and services for children (see http://www.nicwa.org/ law/; Plantz, Hubbell, Barrett, & Dobrec, 1989).

- *The Adoption Assistance and Child Welfare Act of 1980 (P.L. 96–272):* This is one of the key laws for child welfare reform because it used funding incentives and procedural requirements to implement a wide range of placement prevention and permanency planning (see http://www.ssa.gov/OP_Home/comp2/F096-272.html; Pine, 1986).
- *Independent Living Initiative (P.L. 99–272):* Provides funding for services to prepare adolescents in foster care for living in the community on an independent basis (Mech, 1988).
- *Personal Responsibility and Work Opportunity Reconciliation Act (PRWORA):* Funds the Temporary Assistance to Needy Families (TANF), the largest income transfer program for poor families. This is part of the nation's welfare system—administered by the states and funded jointly by state and federal governments. Low-income families of children with disabilities can also receive income transfers through TANF, which is the limited welfare program enacted in 1996 by PRWORA. TANF replaced Aid to Families with Dependent Children (AFDC), which limits program participation (with some exceptions) to 60 months. TANF allows states to exempt up to 20% of their welfare caseload from work requirements, but states have the discretion to establish more strict work participation rules (see http://www.cbpp.org/cms/?fa=view&id=936).
- *Foster Care Independence Act of 1999 (P.L. 106–169):* Authorized the Education Training Voucher (ETV) program. Congress provided federal funding of $42 million for the first time in FY 2003 and increased funding to $45 million for FY 2004. In both years, the president requested $60 million in his budget (see http://www.acf.hhs.gov/programs/cb/laws_policies/cblaws/public_law/p1106_169/p1106_169.htm).
- The voucher program is a component of the Chafee Independent Living Program, which helps older youth leaving foster care to get the higher education, vocational training, and other education supports they need to move to self-sufficiency. Up to $5,000 per year is available to a young person for the cost of attending college or vocational school. ETV funds are distributed to the states using the same formula as the Chafee Independent Living Program under the Foster Care Independence Act. If a state does not apply for funds for the ETV program, the funds are reallocated to other states based on their relative need. Although states are generally doing a good job of distributing these funds, more foster youth could take advantage of the vouchers if their availability were more widely known. An additional $60 million is needed for ETVs for youth leaving foster care at age 18 and those adopted from foster care at age 16 or older (Child Welfare League of America, 2004).
- *Keeping Children and Families Safe Act (PL 108–36):* Reauthorizes the Child Abuse Prevention and Treatment Act. Authorizes funds for grants to state child welfare agencies, competitive grants for research and demonstration programs, and grants to states for the establishment of community-based programs and activities designed to strengthen and support families, all of which support services to prevent and treat child abuse and neglect. The act

amends the Adoption Reform Act of 1978 (Adoption Opportunities), focusing on the placement of older foster children in adoptive homes with an emphasis on child-specific recruitment strategies and efforts to improve interjurisdictional adoptions. This act also includes amendments to the Abandoned Infants Assistance Act, making aid a priority to infants who are infected with the HIV virus, have a life-threatening disease, or have been exposed perinatally to a dangerous drug. The act also includes an amendment to the Family Violence Prevention and Services Act, extending from FY 2004 through FY 2008 authorization of appropriations for specified family violence prevention programs (see www.naesv.org/Resources/FVPSA.pdf).

- *The Adoption Incentive Program (P.L. 108–145):* The Adoption Incentive Program was first enacted as part of the Adoption and Safe Families Act in 1997 to promote permanence for children. In 2003, Congress passed the Adoption Promotion Act of 2003 (P.L. 108–145) to reauthorize the program with modifications. The Adoption Incentive Program is designed to encourage states to finalize adoptions of children from foster care, with additional incentives for the adoption of foster children with special needs. States receive incentive payments for adoptions that exceed an established baseline. The Adoption Promotion Act revises the incentive formula in current law, creating four categories of payment (see http://www.childwelfare.gov/systemwide/laws_policies/federal/index.cfm?event=federalLegislation.viewLegis&id=85).

- *Runaway, Homeless, and Missing Children Protection Act (Title III of the 3 Juvenile Justice and Delinquency Prevention Act of 1974), 4 as Amended by the 5 Runaway, Homeless, and Missing Children Protection Act (P.L. 108–96):* Authorizes funds for the establishment and operation of centers to provide shelter, protection from sexual and other abuse, counseling, and related services to runaway and homeless youth under 18 years of age. The act authorized local groups to open "maternity group homes" for homeless pregnant teens or for those that have been abused. These homes are required to educate runaway youth about parenting skills, child development, family budgeting, health and nutrition, and related skills to promote long-term independence and the health and well-being of youth in their care (see http://www.acf.hhs.gov/programs/fysb/content/aboutfysb/RHYComp.pdf; and http://www.acf.hhs.gov/programs/fbci/progs/fbci_rhyouth.html).

The most recent major child welfare related law to be enacted and funded by Congress is the Fostering Connections to Success and Increasing Adoptions Act (H.R. 6893/P.L. 110–351) of 2008. This law helps children and youth in foster care by ensuring permanent placements for them through kinship and adoption and improving educational and health care outcomes. It will also extend federal support for youth to age 21. The act offers for the first time substantial support to American Indian children residing in child protective custody. Key provisions are listed below:

- Offers federal support to children who leave foster care to live permanently with relative guardians through a federal subsidized guardianship program.
- Help relatives connect the children with the services and supports they need by using kinship navigator programs.
- Includes separate licensing standards to address non-safety licensing requirements that create barriers to children living with relatives in foster care.
- Provides additional support to older youth and increase their opportunities for success by:
  - Continuing federal support for children in foster care after age 18—The law allows states, at their option, to provide care and support to youth in foster care until the age of 19, 20, or 21.
  - Transition support: The act requires child welfare agencies to help youth make this transition to adulthood by requiring, during the 90-day period immediately before a youth exits from care at 18, 19, 20, or 21, the development of a personalized transition plan that identifies options for housing, health insurance, education, local opportunities for mentoring, continuing support services, workforce supports, and employment services.
  - Grants tribes direct access to Title IV-E: The law ensures that Indian tribes have direct access to IV-E funded programs.
  - Improves education outcomes for children who live in out-of-home care by improving educational stability by requiring states to ensure that placement of the child in foster care takes into account the appropriateness of the current educational setting and the proximity to the school in which the child is enrolled at the time of placement.
  - Promotes coordinated health care for children in out-of-home care by requiring that states develop a plan for the oversight and coordination of health, mental health, and dental services for children in foster care.
- Expands and improves adoption assistance programs:
  - Improves the child welfare workforce: The law allows states to be reimbursed for training provided to an expanded group of individuals and organizations including kinship caregivers, court personnel, court-appointed special advocates, and nonagency workers providing child welfare services.

Current Policy Challenges

Child welfare faces a number of policy challenges, some of which are underscored by the mixed success the United States is having in meeting the basic needs of children; ensuring children's safety, health, relationships, and opportunities; and supporting families as the foundation for positive child development. These challenges include the following 15 issues.

1. Early intervention services are underfunded and lack federal leadership. Early intervention services have long been recognized as helping families avoid involvement with the child welfare system. Best practices for early intervention programs involve provision of a range of family-centered services that focus on meeting the needs of the child within the context of the family as well as the larger environment. For example, early intervention might include referring parents to job assistance or adult education and providing parents with assistance in obtaining housing and health care. Child-centered early intervention programs have been linked with improved child development across multiple domains (Karoly, Kilburn, Caulkins, & Cannon, 2000; Kilburn & Karoly, 2008). It is quite possible that the design, development, and delivery of improved early intervention services could reduce the incidence of child maltreatment.

However, implementing early intervention programs will require a more unified leadership with a cohesive plan for family support at both the federal and state levels. Communities interested in early intervention will need to invest public resources in evidence-based programs that support parents and strengthen families. Furthermore, those interested in child welfare must work toward increasing the supply of affordable child care and increasing the awareness among policymakers of the importance of *family economic security.* This need is emphasized by the large proportion of children entering child welfare as a result of parental neglect. As previously mentioned, more effective mental health and substance abuse interventions for parents could also reduce youth entry into foster care.

A risk, resilience, and protective factor perspective undergirds the philosophy supporting early intervention. Early intervention should aim to disrupt risk processes, promote protective mechanisms, and stimulate resilience. Ideally, early intervention services promote well-being and optimal development by providing comprehensive community-based support services to help improve child developmental outcomes. Two examples of such interventions are Point of Engagement (Marts, Lee, McCroy, & McCroskey, 2008) and the Prevention Intervention Development Initiative in Los Angeles (McCroskey et al., 2009). Unfortunately, these types of services are underfunded, and states lack the flexibility to reallocate federal funds designated for placement services to fund family support programs.

2. Family support services are not backed by coherent funding strategies. Family support programs, which include parent hotlines, crisis nursery services, environmental adaptations, personal assistance, and mental health and crisis interventions are often "lifelines." These services allow families to care for their children at home rather than placing a child in out-of-home care, which is expensive and generally publicly financed (Bruns & Burchard, 2000; Schorr & Marchand, 2007). The goals of family support services include enabling families to raise children at home by reducing stress and by strengthening and enhancing caregiving capacities (Pew Foundation, 2008; Walton, Sandau-Beckler, & Mannes, 2001). Family caregivers' acceptance and use of formal support services play a significant role in reducing the burdens and stress associated with caring for a child and in helping families obtain services for unmet needs. Across the United States, family support services are usually jointly financed by the federal and state governments, often using Medicaid resources, and are typically administered by state or county governments. Not surprisingly, given the differences among the states in the provision of social services, there is variability across states in the funding levels for family support and in the types of services available (Parish, Pomeranz, & Braddock, 2003). Consequently, these services are often not only underfunded but also among the first to be cut during periods of economic downturns.

3. Changes to key child welfare funding mechanisms require careful consideration. A number of proposals that would allow states to use federal foster care funds not only to support children in out-of-home care but also to support child abuse prevention and postadoption services have been presented to Congress. For example, several proposals would change the system for funding key child welfare programs, including foster care entitlement under Title IV-E of the Social Security Act. One such proposal is described in the accompanying text box.

These and other proposals can be seen as efforts to address the family support issue. However, the downside to these proposals is that the overall budget for children's services would decrease if all the areas under proposed legislation are considered. Based on what occurs with the federal block grant process for Medicaid and the Supplemental Nutrition Assistance Program (SNAP, formerly the food stamp program), families would no longer have an entitlement. Therefore, educational efforts are needed to inform the public and policymakers of the importance of policies that preserve the open-ended entitlement for key child welfare programs. In addition, child and family advocates need to raise awareness among policymakers and the public that program funds should be tied to performance. Results should be rewarded, and savings due to lowered rates of foster care should be reinvested to improve the quality of child welfare services (Annie E. Casey Foundation, 2009; Casey Family Programs, 2010a).

4. Policies and funding to treat mental health and substance abuse problems must be coordinated with child welfare services. Fragmented funding streams and policies for mental health, substance abuse, developmental disabilities, and child welfare services unduly complicate the treatment of parents and children with co-morbid conditions (Kessler & Magee, 1993). A significant percentage of the families with children who have been placed in out-of-home care also have substance abuse problems (Barth, Gibbons, & Guo, 2006; Besinger, Garland, Litrownik, & Landsverk, 1999). To serve the dual needs of these families, many agency administrators are diverted from other activities while trying to "braid" or cobble together sources of funding to cover the costs of drug treatment and other programs. Such efforts highlight the need for increased program coordination at the federal and state levels to maximize the effectiveness of existing resources (Johnson, Knitzer, & Kaufmann, 2003). This type of increased coordination requires a system of care approach. (For a discussion of systems of care in mental health, see Chapter 5 in this volume.)

Overhaul of Foster Care Eyed
by Cheryl Wetzstein

The nation's foster care system would undergo sweeping changes, akin to welfare reform, under a bill recently introduced by House Republicans. "The way the federal government pays for foster care is perverse," said House Majority Leader Tom DeLay, Texas Republican and co-sponsor of the Child Safety, Adoption, and Family Enhancement Act. "We are spending billions of dollars to pay for the room and board of children in temporary foster care, but doing little else to actually improve these children's lives," he said.

The bill, introduced by Rep. Wally Herger, California Republican and chairman of the House Ways and Means subcommittee on human resources, is "like welfare reform for child welfare," said one congressional aide. As in the 1996 welfare reform, the bill would combine major child-welfare funding streams into a capped grant to states. The grant would grow $200 million a year,

(Continued)

(Continued)

and when per-child adoption-bonus payments are added in, child-welfare funding is estimated to increase from $7.7 billion in 2005 to nearly $11 billion in 2014.

Congress also would remove outdated child-welfare rules, giving states more flexibility in how to spend their funds. However, states would have to ensure "better outcomes" for children, such as stronger efforts to prevent children from entering state care and improved management of children's cases when they are in care.

"This bill is designed to fundamentally change the child-welfare system to focus on outcomes rather than process," said Mr. Herger, who has been holding hearings for months on child-welfare issues.

House Democrats have not endorsed the bill, saying their Child Protective Services Improvement Act, introduced in 2003, is better. The Herger bill correctly provides more resources, but caps the grant—which "threatens the safe haven needed when children must be removed from their homes," said Rep. Benjamin L. Cardin, Maryland Democrat. Foster care is the "safety net of last resort for our most vulnerable children, and I cannot see the wisdom in cutting a hole in that net," said Mr. Cardin, who said the Herger bill erred in not requiring states to pay relatives who become legal guardians of foster children or resolving work force problems in child welfare.

Separately this week, leaders in child welfare and law enforcement said they are working together to respond more effectively when foster children run away, are abducted from care, or otherwise become "lost in the system."

The number of "missing" foster children is unknown, said Shay Bilchik, president and chief executive of the Child Welfare League of America, which, in collaboration with the National Center for Missing and Exploited Children, has released its first in-depth report on "Children Missing from Care."

The problem is likely to grow, however, because the number of teens and preteens in foster care steadily has risen. About 40 percent of children in foster care are 13 or older, compared with 25 percent in 1997, and older foster children are more likely to run away, said Bryan Samuels, director of the Illinois Department of Children and Family Services.

5. Differential approaches to child protective services intake need additional testing. New intake approaches are attempting to divert low-risk families (i.e., those with a low risk for a subsequent maltreatment referral) to supportive programs other than child protective services. Although promising, these approaches need further testing and evaluation to inform policymakers' decisions about the roles of law enforcement; medical, legal, and social services personnel; and voluntary agencies. If new intake procedures accurately distinguish low- from high-risk families, such procedures would complement family support interventions that have been heavily researched and found cost-effective. For example, practice, administrative, policy, and other system reform strategies exist that can improve conditions for maltreated children and accelerate permanency planning. Using these strategies safely reduces the number of children in foster care. Especially in times of fiscal constraints, programs are needed that will result in a reduction in foster care rates so that placement-cost savings can be reinvested in higher quality services for the children for whom out-of-home care is the best, most appropriate option. Shown in Table 3.4, the following placement reduction interventions have evidence of cost-effectiveness:

- Chicago Child Parent Centers
- Home Visiting: *Nurse–Family Partnership* for Low-Income Families
- Intensive Family Preservation and Reunification Services (Homebuilders® model)
- *Parent–Child Interaction Therapy*
- *TripleP—Positive Parenting Program*

6. Kinship care funding, licensing, and practice policies need to be aligned. More than 6.7 million children—about 1 in every 12 U.S. children—are living in households headed by grandparents or other relatives. The number of children raised in relative-headed households has increased significantly. U.S. Census data show that 2.4 million grandparents are taking primary responsibility for the basic needs of their grandchildren. Kinship caregivers often lack the information and range of supports they need to fulfill their parenting role. In an effort to remedy this situation, a group of advocates from child welfare, aging and research organizations prepared a set of revised kinship care fact sheets (Children's Defense Fund, 2008). These sheets provide state-specific data and information directing grandparents or other kinship caregivers to support services that can help make their jobs easier. The new Fostering Connections

Table 3.4   Prevention Program Costs and Benefits

Program	Total Benefit-to-Cost Ratio (dollars in benefits for every $1 of program cost per participant)	Total Benefits Minus Costs (per participant)
Programs That Directly Reduce Foster Care		
Intensive Family Preservation and Reunification Service Programs (Homebuilders® model) [a,c]	$2.54	$4,775
Parent–Child Interaction Therapy (Oklahoma) [a]	$5.93	$4,962
TripleP–Positive Parenting Program [d]	$4.09 (1 year of benefit)	Not applicable
Other Prevention Programs		
Chicago Child Parent Centers [a]	$4.82	$31,036
Nurse Family Partnership for Low-Income Families [a,b]	$3.02	$18,054

a. 2008 estimates from Washington State Institute for Public Policy (2008).

b. The Nurse–Family Partnership and home-visiting meta-analysis data are from Lee, Aos, and Miller (2008). The program cost data are net present value, 2007 dollars compared to the cost of alternative. The program benefit data are net present value, 2007 dollars. The RAND Corporation has independently estimated that the return for each dollar invested in Nurse–Family Partnership was $5.70 for the higher risk population served and $2.88 for the entire population served (in 2003 dollars). Their estimate does not include cost savings attributable to reductions in subsequent pregnancies or preterm births. Actual cost savings are likely to be larger given the significant expenses associated with these conditions (see Karoly, Kilburn, & Cannon, 2005).

c. WSIPP presented a single benefit–cost analysis for Homebuilders®-style Intensive Family Preservation Service Programs here. In a meta-analytic table, they presented effect size estimates in three ways: (1) for IFPS programs focused on reunification of children already placed out of home, (2) for programs focused on preventing children from being removed from home, and (3) for all IFPS programs. The benefit–cost estimates were nearly identical for the reunification and prevention programs, so the estimates were combined (Lee et al., 2008).

d. See also the Triple-P websites available at http://www.triplep.net/ and http://www.paxis.org/triplep/PPP_flash.aspx.

legislation (P.L. 110–351) authorizes federal support for *kinship navigators* to advise these parents. However, more work needs to be done to help resolve the policy inconsistencies in licensing and support of these families.

7. Tribal access to federal child welfare services funding should be increased and existing infrastructure should be improved. Consistent with their cultures, Native American tribes have exercised jurisdiction over their children, but most tribes have seriously underdeveloped services. Tribal entities need to build a variety of service infrastructures such as management information systems and quality improvement programs. The new Fostering Connections legislation enables American tribes to access Federal Title IV-E funds directly.

8. Agency policies should promote better assessment and support of gay, lesbian, bisexual, and transgendered youth in out-of-home care. Child welfare service delivery systems have not encouraged staff members and foster parents to protect and nurture gay, lesbian, bisexual, and transgendered youth. Such youth are vulnerable to victimization, depression, suicide, and placement disruption because of their sexual orientation. Special efforts are needed both to assess the needs of these youths and to devise supportive services for them (Mallon, 1999; Wornoff & Mallon, 2006).

9. Cross-systems collaboration should be strengthened. The risk and protective factors related to child maltreatment bear remarkable resemblance to risk and protective factors for other social and health problems. This suggests that a more integrated and coordinated approach to family support and children's services could be designed to address common risk factors. Income assistance, education, mental health, intimate partner violence, law enforcement, juvenile justice, and child welfare agencies need to work more toward a common purpose and minimize operating in isolation from each other. Cross-systems collaboration—sometimes called a system of care—is needed to strengthen provision of services to families with concurrent occurrences of child maltreatment, depression, drug abuse, and partner violence.

10. Transition policies and support for emancipating youth must be overhauled. Too many graduates of the foster care system are undertrained and underemployed. Many alumni are part of a large group of marginalized youth who age out of the system without adequate skills for independent living and without a support system. Graduates of foster care vary widely in their level of preparation for emancipation from foster care in terms of education and income (Courtney et al., 2007; Goerge et al., 2002).

Programmatically, child welfare systems should promote investment in culturally relevant services, support, and opportunities to ensure that every youth in foster care makes a safe, successful transition to adulthood. Preparation for independent living must be redesigned to start at age 10 years, rather than the current age of 17 years. A comprehensive transition plan should be developed for every child. This type of comprehensive plan should include planning for supportive relationships, community connections, education, life skills assessment and development, identity formation, housing, employment, physical health, and mental health (Casey Family Programs, 2001; Massinga & Pecora, 2003; Wald & Martinez, 2003). Employment training and work experience should be expanded for many youth while they are in care. Policies and incentives should ensure that no young person leaves foster care without housing, access to health care, employment skills, and permanent connections to at least one adult.

11. All youth in high school should receive the tutoring and employment experiences that build work-related skills. Youth preparing to emancipate must have greater access to experiential life skills and classroom-based training. However, systems change is essential to accomplish this goal. Among others, the MacArthur Foundation transition scholars have documented the failure of major American institutions to keep pace with societal changes that require new ways of working (Carnegie Council on Adolescent Development, 1989; First Focus, 2008).

12. Policies should provide fiscal incentives to improve high-school graduation rates and to support postsecondary education and training for children and youth in foster care. Recent changes in the federal Higher Education Act, reauthorized in 2008 as the Higher Education Opportunity Act (HEOA; P.L. 110–315), provide more consideration of the special needs of children and youth in foster care. Further policy innovations are needed to strengthen elementary and secondary education programs, including special education initiatives. In addition, federal and state policies must maintain the financial viability and array of services within the Medicaid and State Children's Health Insurance Program (SCHIP) programs for youth in foster care and ensure that no young person leaves foster care without access to appropriate health care.

13. Policies should increase the likelihood that youths will achieve and maintain permanency in a reasonable period through foster care, reunification, relative placement, guardianship, or adoption. In many states, a substantial number of children have a case goal of *alternative planned living arrangement* (APLA), such as emancipation from foster care at age 18 or exit before age 18 via independent living. APLA is not a legal form of permanence, and it does not provide children with a long-term supportive relationship with an adult. Reforms that are needed include crafting policies to ensure that kinship care families have access to adequate resources that will allow them to raise healthy children in stable home environments (Casey Family Programs, 2010b). Adoption policy must more thoroughly address how to better respond to the legal concerns expressed in the Multi-Ethnic Placement Act and Inter-Ethnic Adoption Provisions Act.

14. Policymakers need to recognize the seriousness of and make changes to reduce racial and ethnic disproportionality. Although the disproportionate numbers of children of color in the child welfare system, and the disparities in the outcomes of those children, are slowly being recognized as major ethical, policy, and program issues, much needs to be done to fully address these issues. First, we need to promote the investment of public resources into gathering critical data about African American, Native American, Asian American, and Hispanic children who are involved in the child welfare system. This information ranges from the level of access to services of birth parents for children of color in the child welfare system to data concerning use of substance abuse and mental health services both before entering and during their contact with the system (Hill, 2007; Hines et al., 2004). Second, using this information, officials must enhance national awareness of the disproportionate number of children of color in the foster care system and pinpoint the reasons for this disproportionality. Finally, communities should launch efforts to reduce disparities. The goal of these efforts should be to remove race and ethnicity as a predictor of outcome in child welfare services. Table 3.5 provides an example of a Point of Engagement strategy used in Los Angeles to reduce racial and ethnic disparities in child welfare.

15. Performance-based contracting should be fully implemented. Attempts to implement state and county policies to promote performance-based contracting have been hampered by a lack of knowledge of

Table 3.5   Point of Engagement and Up-Front Assessment Services in Los Angeles

The process works as follows:

- An upfront assessment is recommended when an emergency response worker suspects a problem connected with mental health, substance abuse or domestic violence and needs additional expertise about the degree of involvement.
- An assessment is not made if a safety issue indicates immediate removal or if the hotline allegation is unfounded.
- The assessment is voluntary. If the parent agrees to the assessment, a trained clinician from a community-service organization goes to the home no later than 48 hours after the referral.
- The assessment is an expanded bio/psycho/social analysis that looks at seven major areas of functioning: physical health, mental health, substance use, educational and occupational functioning, social relationships, domestic violence/domestic relationships and criminal activity. The assessor uses a computer-based, online tool called a Behavioral Severity Assessment Program (BSAP) and interviews caregivers separately. The assessment is comprehensive, looking at strengths as well as needs, and often taking two hours to complete. SHEILDS' supervision and program manager Trevor Daniels explained: "You have to get a full understanding about the dynamics of a family's world. You have to understand people's functional level, and whether there's a risk to the kids because of their parents' problems."
- The assessors do not make recommendations about child placement. Removal—or not—is the responsibility of the Department of Child and Family Services (DCFS). Rather the assessor talks to the family and to DCFS about the results of the assessment and makes recommendations to DCFS for services.
- DCFS makes the decision about removal and services. Because the agency conducting the assessments is a community provider with expertise in domestic violence, mental health and substance abuse and because it has information on what the caregivers really need, it can start services right away.
- Ideally a Team Decision Meeting takes place soon after the assessment, and the community agency participates with family members, DCFS, and others in determining a plan of action.

SOURCE: Casey Family Programs. (2009). *Stories of practice change: What flexible funding means to the children and families of Los Angeles County.* Seattle, WA: Casey Family Programs, pp. 7–8. Reprinted with permission.

baseline conditions, concrete target goals, and infrastructure funding gaps. Clear performance criteria, cohort-based and longitudinal data analyses, and quality improvement systems must be in place to enable agencies to improve performance-based contracting and the implementation of evidence-based practice models (Mordock, 2002; Pecora, Selig, Zirps, & Davis, 1996; Wulczyn et al., 2009).

Using Knowledge of Risk, Protection, and Resilience to Achieve Service Integration

We have described the major policies that influence the well-being of children and families involved with the child welfare system. The challenges of fragmented funding and the lack of service integration were noted as well as many policy developments that illustrate how risk-reduction strategies could improve child welfare services. To disrupt the risk mechanisms that lead to child maltreatment and that complicate recovery from victimization, child welfare agencies need adequate funding, as well as new and more effective ways to link funding to effective programs.

It is worth noting that a number of authors have commented on the lack of alignment among child welfare policy, performance incentives, and current best practices (e.g., Wulczyn et al., 2009). Critics argue that the child welfare system needs to be overhauled to better address risk factors leading to child abuse and neglect (Adams & Nelson, 1995; Edna McConnell Clark Foundation, 2004; Lindsey, 2004; Thomas, 1994; Whittaker & Maluccio, 2002). In addition, the emerging literature on protective processes, which buffer children from risk and promote recovery from victimization, holds potential to influence policy and practice.

To underscore the complexity of the challenges incumbent in reform, a case study is presented in the accompanying box. The case describes a family in which multiple forms of child neglect are present. This family situation illustrates how child neglect can have serious consequences for child development. The complexity of this family situation is evident; it is the too frequent situation in which genuine love for children is interwoven with mental health problems, partner violence, poverty, and deficits in parenting skills. In this scenario, the concepts of risk, resiliency, and protective factors have utility for guiding case decision making and the choice of interventions.

A Case Example

Children Who Are Not Headliners

Introduction

This case example involves multiple forms of child neglect. An intergenerational cycle may be at work here: a "passing on of infantilism, mother to daughter, through processes of deprivation leading to detachment (the deprivation-detachment hypotheses), failure to provide stimulation, and the child's identification with an inadequate role model. Hence the cycle of neglect might be said to derive from a cycle of infantilism" (Polansky, Chalmers, Buttenweiser, & Williams, 1981, p. 43). Although it must be emphasized that generalizing these families is not wise because of their diversity, some of the research data depict a group of neglectful caregivers who are generally (a) less able to love; (b) less capable of working productively; (c) less open about feelings; (d) more prone to living planlessly and impulsively; (e) susceptible to psychological symptoms and to phases of passive inactivity and numb fatalism; (f) more likely to live in a situation of family conflict, to be less organized and more chaotic; (g) less verbally expressive; and (h) less positive and more negative in affect (Gaudin, Polansky, Kilpatrick, & Shilton, 1996; Polansky et al., 1981; Polansky, Gaudin, & Kilpatrick, 1992). Although many families involved with substance abuse never come to the attention of child welfare agencies, when they do they very often are identified as having problems related to child neglect (U.S. Department of Health and Human Services, 1999).

In a sense, the parenting/nurturing instinct has been weakened or distorted in its aim, or overwhelmed by the parent's struggle in personal survival. This stunting or crippling of parenting or nurturing is not often an emergent response to current stress but is predictable from the social history of the parent and the lack of nurturance in his or her childhood (Polansky et al., 1981, pp. 147–157). Some of those risk factors (and family strengths and resources) are illustrated by the following case example.

The family consists of Mona Stay, twenty-three, and her common-law husband Frank Brown, aged twenty-six. There are three children: Frank Stay, three and a half, Sylvia Stay, eighteen months, and Wilma, seven months. The Stay-Browns have been together over five years. Although they quarrel and separate periodically, they seem very mutually dependent and likely to remain a couple.

Their original referral was from a nurse who had become aware of the eldest child's condition. He was difficult to discipline, was eating dirt and paint chips, and seemed hyperactive. Although over two, he was not speaking. His father reacted to him with impatience. He was often slapped, and hardly ever spoken to with fondness. The caseworker got Mona to cooperate in taking young Frank in for a test for lead poisoning, and for a full developmental evaluation. This child had had several bouts with impetigo, had been bitten through the eyelid by a stray dog, and had a series of ear infections resulting in a slight hearing loss. Although physically normal, he appeared already nearly a year delayed.

Often this child was found outside the house alone when the caseworker came to see the family. On one occasion he was seen hanging from a broken fire escape on the second floor. The worker was unable to rouse his mother, or to enter the house until she got help from the nearby landlord, after which she ran upstairs and rescued the child. Only then did the sleeping Mona awaken!

With much effort having been expended on his behalf, this child had been attending a therapeutic nursery. His speech is already improved after four or five months, and his hyperactivity has calmed. He comes through as a lovable little boy.

Sylvia is surprisingly pale . . . and indeed, suffers from severe anemia. This child has had recurrent eye infections, and had a bout with spinal meningitis at age three months which, fortunately, seems to have left no residual effects. Much effort has gone into working with Mona concerning Sylvia's need for proper diet and iron supplement. After a year of contact this is still a problem.

The baby was born after the family had become known to the agency. Despite the agency's urging, Mona refused to go for prenatal care until she was in her second trimester, but she did maintain a fairly good diet, helped by small "loans" from the agency when her money for food ran out. When Wilma was born, she had to remain for a time at the hospital for treatment of jaundice. After she went home, she was left to lie most of the time in her bassinet, receiving very little attention from either parent. At four months of age, Wilma weighed only five pounds and was tentatively diagnosed as exhibiting "failure to thrive" by the hospital. Thereafter the mother avoided going to the clinic, and the caseworker spent much effort concerning the feeding and sheer survival of Wilma. The baby is now slowly gaining weight but is still limp and inactive.

(Continued)

(Continued)

In addition to an active caseworker, a homemaker was assigned to this family for months. Much more was involved than trying to help Mona learn to organize her day: she had almost no motivation to get started. Rather than learning how to manage, she tried to manipulate the homemaker into doing her housework for her. However, with time and patience, Mona has been persuaded to go with the caseworker on shopping trips, is learning how to buy groceries to best advantage, and from time to time manages to get the laundry into and out of the laundromat. So far as her plans for herself, Mona has talked of seeking training as a beauty operator, but has never followed through on this or on other positive plans.

The family's sole support is public assistance. Frank Brown, the father, was on drugs earlier in their relationship, but managed to get off them. Now, however, he drinks heavily, and although he manages to work, he never contributes to the household.

Mona, apparently, was herself a neglected child, and was removed from her parents in infancy. Placed with an adoptive family, there was constant friction during her growing up, and she ran away from home several times. During her teens, she was placed in an institution for incorrigible girls. Later she spent a period in a mental hospital during which she was withdrawn from heroin addiction. It is a commentary on her life that she regards this period in the adolescent ward as one of her happiest ever. Her adoptive mother is now dead, and her father wants nothing more to do with her, so she was more or less living on the streets when she met with Frank and set up their present establishment.

Frank and Mona, despite his obvious exploitativeness, seem to love each other and their children, and to want to keep the family together. They are able to relate to those who try to help them, so at least one is not operating constantly against hostile resistance. Mona is an intelligent woman and now shows adequate ability to handle the children. She can be an excellent cook—when there is food. Yet this remains a disorganized household. Bills are never paid, clothes are thrown around, the children never sleep on clean sheets, trash is piled around the house so that flies and maggots abound. Mona still leaves the youngsters quite alone for brief periods. There is no heat in the house, and the family will soon have to move, with neither any idea where to go nor funds for rent deposits and the like. Mona, at least, is currently wearing an IUD.

The Stay-Brown menage was not invented, although of course we have altered names and some facts to protect all concerned. These are real people, and they are clearly involved in child neglect. The failures center on poor feeding, uncleanliness, extremely bad housing, filthy circumstances which make the children prone to infections, lack of medical care, inadequate supervision and protections from danger, lack of intellectual stimulation, inattentiveness to the children bordering on rejection—one could go on. The fine staff trying to help Mona improve her child care finally gave up and closed her case after about fifteen months of effort. The care was improving slowly, if at all, and there were recurrent instances of regression.

Frank proved superficially amenable to suggestions when he could be seen, but in fact evaded any real responsibility for the household. The time, money, and—more importantly—motivation for hard work with such families are chronically in short supply. So the decision was made to try to help someone else who might be more treatable.

Meanwhile these children are with their parents. Since they have not literally been abandoned, it is uncertain whether a local judge would decide the home is so bad that the children must be removed. If a catastrophe were to occur, if one were to read that these three children had burned to death in a fire, one would be saddened but not greatly surprised. If one of the three were to die of an infectious disease or an undiagnosed appendicitis, one would not be surprised either. For the present, however, they are among the group child-protection workers know well, but that the public does not, because they do not make headlines—or at least not yet.

SOURCE: Polansky, Chalmers, Buttenweiser, & Williams, *Damaged Parents: An Anatomy of Child Neglect,* pp. 5–7. Copyright © 1981. Reprinted with permission of the University of Chicago Press.

Summary

In this chapter, we have reviewed policies and legislation in American child welfare, and discussed a number of critical issues and potential reforms. The utility of a risk and resilience perspective was explored. From the concepts of protection and resilience, models of service that consider child and family development in the context of community and culture may be useful in future child welfare initiatives. Historically, private child welfare programs played a major role in protecting and nourishing maltreated children who were placed in state custodial care. Policy experts would be wise to consider this framework as debates continue about ways to improve child welfare services and increase funding.

On balance, our review suggests that child welfare needs to adopt a broader framework to protect children from maltreatment. The growing knowledge base regarding risk and resilience, combined with the growing number of studies showing that child maltreatment can be prevented, present a clear challenge to design "upstream" prevention-focused services while concurrently improving services for maltreated children. Meeting this challenge will demand a measure of leadership and accountability that is visionary.

QUESTIONS FOR DISCUSSION

1. What are the implications of the literature on risk and protective factors for the design of policies and programs for family support, foster care, and permanency planning?

2. What policy changes would you recommend to better integrate service delivery and to provide an evidence-based system of child welfare services for families with children at risk of child maltreatment?

3. In what ways might the increasing federal and state emphasis on measurable outcomes promote service delivery approaches that are culturally appropriate and oriented to child well-being?

Notes

1. There were 3 million reports involving the welfare of about 5 million children in 2001 and 1.8 million in 2002. For the most recent federal child maltreatment statistics, see U.S. DHHS (2009a, pp. iii and 3). In 1990, there were an estimated 611,924 victims, based on projections using data from 35 states. See U.S. DHHS (1999, pp. 4–2); for the 2002 statistics, see http://www.acf.hhs.gov/programs/cb/publications/cm02/summary.htm.

2. These data are from the federal Adoption and Foster Care Analysis and Reporting System (AFCARS), which derived these estimates using data from 45 states and other jurisdictions (e.g., Washington, D.C., and Puerto Rico; U.S. DHHS, 2009b). For total children served in 2008, see U.S. DHHS (2009c). Note that AFCARS data are periodically updated; therefore, the data cited in this chapter may not match the data on the current website.

3. The concept of *epigenetic change*—alterations in gene expression that are due to environmental or other reasons not related to DNA—is an important idea

in child development. There is ample evidence that subtle changes in the early environment influence adulthood disease appearance; this early environment is not restricted to the fetal period but is expanded to encompass the plastic phase of early child development. Moreover, evidence supports that our genetic background, which is the result of our evolution, is an important contributor to susceptibility to perinatal imprinting. However, rapid adjustment and optimization, which are necessary at times for survival, require a type of plasticity that the genome sequence alone cannot achieve. Without changing the genomic backbone, epigenetic modulation, in reaction to a given environment, results in functional adaptation of the genomic response. Thus, evolutionarily acquired genomic susceptibilities and environmentally induced epigenomic modulations occurring early in life impact on later development of human diseases (Tremblay & Harnet, 2008).

4. Family structure reflects the number of parents in the household and their relationship to the child; living arrangement reflects their marital or cohabitation status. Considering both factors, the NIS-4 classified children into six categories: living with two married biological parents, living with other married parents (e.g., stepparent, adoptive parent), living with two unmarried parents, living with one parent who had an unmarried partner in the household, living with one parent who had no partner in the household, and living with no parent.

5. The NIS-4 could identify a grandparent as a child's caregiver under three conditions: when the grandparent was the child's primary caregiver, when the primary caregiver did not have a spouse or partner and the grandparent was the secondary caregiver, and when the grandparent was a caregiver and maltreated the child.

6. To contend with missing data on individual items, the NIS-4 analyses combined three indicators into a general measure of socioeconomic status: household income, household participation in any poverty program, and parents' education. Low socioeconomic status households were those in the bottom tier on any indicator: household income below $15,000 a year, parents' highest education level less than high school, or any member of the household a participant in a poverty program, such as TANF, food stamps, public housing, energy assistance, or subsidized school meals.

7. It is possible that the lower rates at these younger ages reflect some undercoverage of these age groups. That is, prior to attaining school age, children are less observable to community professionals.

8. This section draws from policy briefs and position statements from the following sources:

- Children's Defense Fund and the Center for the Study of Law and Social Policy. (2008). *Fostering Connections to Success and Increasing Adoptions Act* (HR6893) Summary. Washington, DC: Author.
- Kids Count: A Project of the Annie E. Casey Foundation: www.kidscount.org.

- Summaries prepared by the Public Policy team of Casey Family Programs with the consultation of Children's Defense Fund, Child Welfare League of America, American Public Human Services Association, and the Alliance for Children

References

Adams, P., & Nelson, K. (1995). *Reinventing human services: Community and family-centered practice.* Hawthorne, NY: Aldine de Gruyter.

Ainsworth, M. D. S. (1989). Attachments beyond infancy. *American Psychologist, 44,* 709–716. doi:10.1037/0003-066X.44.4.709

American Humane Association, Children's Division; American Bar Association, Center on Children and the Law; Annie E. Casey Foundation; The Casey Family Program; Casey Family Services; and Institute for Human Services Management. (1998). *Assessing outcomes in child welfare services: Principles, concepts, and a framework of core indicators.* Englewood, CO: The Casey Outcomes and Decision-Making Project. Retrieved from http://www.aecf.org/upload/publicationfiles/assessing%20framework.pdf

American Psychological Association Task Force on Resilience and Strength in Black Children and Adolescents. (2008). *Resilience in African American children and adolescents: A Vision for optimal development.* Washington, DC: Author. Retrieved from http://www.apa.org/pi/families/resources/resiliencerpt.pdf

Annie E. Casey Foundation. (2009). *Rebuild the nation's child welfare system* (Issue brief). Baltimore: Author. Retrieved from http://www.aecf.org/~/media/PublicationFiles/Child_Welfare_issuebrief2.pdf

Avery, R. (1998). *Public agency adoption in New York State: Phase I report. Foster care histories of children freed for adoption in New York State: 1980–1993.* Ithaca, NY: Cornell University Press.

Barnett, D., Manly, J. T., & Cicchetti, D. (1993). Defining child maltreatment: The interface between policy and research. In D. Cicchetti & S. Toth (Eds.), *Child abuse, child development and social policy* (pp. 7–74). Norwood, NJ: Ablex.

Barth, R. P., Gibbons, C., & Guo, S. (2006). Substance abuse treatment and the recurrence of maltreatment among caregivers with children living at home: A propensity score analysis. *Journal of Substance Abuse Treatment, 30,* 93–104. doi:10.1016/j.jsat.2005.10.008

Berrick, J. D., Needell, B., Barth, R. B., & Johnson-Reid, M. (1998). *The tender years: Toward developmentally sensitive child welfare services for very young children.* New York: Oxford University Press.

Besinger, B. A., Garland, A. F., Litrownik, A. J., & Landsverk, J. A. (1999). Caregiver substance abuse among maltreated children placed in out-of-home care. *Child Welfare, 78*(2), 221–239.

Briere, J. (1992). *Child abuse trauma theory and treatment of the lasting effects.* Newbury Park, CA: Sage.

Bronfenbrenner, U. (1979). *The ecology of human development.* Cambridge, MA: Harvard University Press.

Bronfenbrenner, U. (1986). Ecology of the family as a context to human development: Research perspectives. *Developmental Psychology, 22,* 723–742. doi:10.1037/ 0012–1649.22.6.723

Bronfenbrenner, U. (2004). *Making human beings human: Bioecological perspectives on human development.* Thousand Oaks, CA: Sage.

Bronfenbrenner, U., & Morris, P. A. (1998). The ecology of developmental processes. In W. Damon (Ed.), *Handbook of child psychology* (5th ed., pp. 993–1028). New York: John Wiley.

Brooks-Gunn, J., & Duncan, G. J. (1997). The effects of poverty on children. *Future of Children, 7,* 55–71. doi:10.2307/1602387

Brooks-Gunn, J., Klebanov, P. K, & Liaw, F. (1995). The learning, physical, and emotional environment of the home in the context of poverty: The Infant Health and Development program. *Children and Youth Services Review, 17,* 251–276. doi:10.1016/0190–7409(95)00011-Z

Bruns, E. J., & Burchard, J. D. (2000). Impact of respite care services for families with children experiencing emotional and behavioral problems. *Children's Services: Social Policy, Research, and Practice, 3,* 39–61. doi:10.1207/S15326918CS0301_3

Caplan, G. (1974). *Support systems and community mental health: Lectures on concept development.* New York: Behavioral Publications.

Carey, J. (2009, March 9). The spirit level: Why more equal societies almost always do better by Richard Wilkinson and Kate Pickett [Book review]. *London Sunday Times.* Retrieved from http://entertainment.timesonline.co.uk/tol/ arts_and_entertainment/books/non-fiction/article5859108.ece

Carnegie Council on Adolescent Development. (1989). *Turning points: Preparing youth for the 21st century.* Washington, DC: Author.

Casey Family Programs. (2001). *It's my life—A framework for youth transitioning from foster care to successful adulthood.* Seattle, WA: Author. Retrieved from http://www .casey.org/Resources/Publications/pdf/ItsMyLife_Framework.pdf

Casey Family Programs. (2003a). *Family, community, culture: Roots of permanency— A conceptual framework on permanency from Casey Family Programs.* Seattle, WA: Author.

Casey Family Programs. (2010a). *Public policy agenda: A comprehensive finance reform package framework.* Seattle, WA: Author.

Casey Family Programs. (2010b). *No time to lose: An ecological practice model for adolescent and young adult permanency* (Preliminary title). Seattle, WA: Author.

Catalano, R. F., & Hawkins, J. D. (1996). The social developmental model: A theory of antisocial behavior. In J. D. Hawkins (Ed.), *Delinquency and crime: Current theories* (pp. 149–197). New York: Cambridge University Press.

Chamberlain, P. (2003). *Treating chronic juvenile offenders: Advances made through the Oregon multidimensional treatment foster care model.* Washington, DC: American Psychological Association. doi:10.1037/10596–000

Chibnall, S., Dutch, N., Jones-Harden, B. Brown, A., Gourgine, R., Smith, J., Boone, A., & Snyder, S. (2003). *Children of color in the child welfare system: Perspectives from the child welfare community.* Washington, DC: U.S. Department of Health and Human Services. Retrieved from http://www.childwelfare.gov/pubs/otherpubs/children/

Child Welfare Information Gateway, Children's Bureau, FRIENDS National Resource Center For Community-Based Child Abuse Prevention. (2010). *Strengthening families and communities: 2010 resource guide.* Washington, DC: Author. Retrieved from http://www.childwelfare.gov/pubs/res_guide_2010/

Child Welfare League of America. (2004). *Making children a national priority: A framework for community action.* Washington, DC: Author.

Children's Defense Fund. (2008). *State factsheets for grandparents or other relatives raising children.* Retrieved from http://www.childrensdefense.org/child-research-data-publications/data/state-data-repository/grandparents-other-relatives-raising-children-state-factsheets.html

Cicchetti, D., & Lynch, M. (1993). Toward an ecological/transactional model of community violence and child maltreatment: Consequences for children's development. *Psychiatry, 56,* 96–118.

Cohen, J. A., Mannarino, A. P., Zhitova, A. C., & Capone, M. E. (2003). Treating child abuse-related posttraumatic stress and comorbid substance abuse in adolescents. *Child Abuse & Neglect, 27,* 1345–1365. doi:10.1016/j.chiabu.2003.08.001

Coll, C. G., & Magnuson, K. (2000). Cultural differences as sources of developmental vulnerabilities and resources. In J. P. Shonkoff & S. J. Meisels (Eds.), *Handbook of early childhood intervention* (2nd ed., pp. 94–114). Cambridge, UK: Cambridge University Press.

Courtney, M.E., Dworsky, A., Cusick, G.R., Keller, T., Havlicek, J. , Perez, A., Terao, S., & Bost, N. (2007). *Midwest evaluation of adult functioning of former foster youth: Outcomes at age 21.* Chicago: University of Chicago, Chapin Hall Center for Children.

Crary, D. (2010, February 2). *U.S. study shows drop in child abuse* (Associated Press). Retrieved from http://www.thefreelibrary.com/APNewsBreak%3a+US+study+shows+drop+in+child+abuse-a01612134912

Dalla, R. L., Defrain, J., Johnson, J., & Abbott, D. A. (2009). *Strengths and challenges of new immigrant families: Implications for research, education, policy, and service.* Lanham, MD: Lexington Books.

De Anda, D. (2003). *Social work with multicultural youth.* New York: Haworth Press.

DePanfilis, D. (1996). Social isolation of neglectful families: A review of social support assessment and intervention. *Child Maltreatment, 1*(1), 37–52. doi:10.1177/1077559596001001005

Derezotes, D., Poertner, J., & Testa, M. (Eds.). (2005). *Race matters in child welfare: The overrepresentation of African American children in the system.* Washington, DC: Child Welfare League of America Press

Downs, A. C., & Pecora, P. J. (2004). *Application of Erikson's psychosocial theory to the effects of child abuse and ameliorative foster care* (Working Paper No. 2). Seattle, WA: Casey Family Programs.

Edna McConnell Clark Foundation. (2004). *Theory of change behind the program for children.* New York: Author. Retrieved from http://www.emcf.org/programs/children/indepth/theory.htm

Erikson, E. H. (1985). *The life cycle completed.* New York: Norton.

Finkelhor, D, & Jones, L. (2006). Why have child maltreatment and child victimization declined? *Journal of Social Issues, 62*(4), pp. 685–716.

First Focus. (2008). *Big ideas for children: Investing in our nation's future.* Washington, DC: Author.

Fraser, M. W. (Ed.). (2004). *Risk and resilience in childhood: An ecological perspective* (2nd ed.). Washington, DC: NASW Press.

Garbarino, J. (1992). *Children and families in the social environment.* New York: Aldine de Gruyter.

Garbarino, J., & Ganzel, B. (2000). The human ecology of early risk. In J. P. Shonkoff & S. J. Meisels (Eds.), *Handbook of early childhood intervention* (2nd ed., pp. 76–93). Cambridge, UK: Cambridge University Press.

Garmezy, N. (1983). Stressors of childhood. In N. Garmezy & M. Rutter (Eds.), *Stress, coping and development in children* (pp. 43–84). New York: McGraw-Hill.

Garmezy, N. (1985). Stress resistant children: The search for protective factors. In J. E. Stevenson (Ed.), *Recent research in developmental psychopathology* (pp. 76–93). Oxford, UK: Pergamon Press.

Gaudin, J. M., Polanksy, N. A., Kilpatrick, A. C., & Shilton, P. (1996). Family functioning in neglectful families. *Child Abuse & Neglect, 20,* 363–377. doi:10.1016/0145-2134(96)00005-1

Goerge, R., Bilaver, L., Lee, B. L., Needell, B., Brookhart, A., & Jackman, W. (2002). *Employment outcomes for youth aging out of foster care. Final report.* Chicago: University of Chicago, Chapin Hall Center for Children. Retrieved from http://aspe.hhs.gov/hsp/fostercare-agingout02/

Hanson, R. F., Smith, D. W., Saunders, B. E., Swenson, C. C., & Conrad, L. (1995). Measurement in child abuse research: A survey of researchers. *The APSAC Advisor, 8,* 7–10.

Haskins, R., Wulczyn, F., & Webb, M.B. (Eds.). (2007). *Child protection: Using research to improve policy and practice.* Washington, DC: Brookings Press.

Hill, R. B. (2007). *Analysis of racial/ethnic disproportionality and disparity at the national, state and county levels.* Washington, DC: The Casey-CSSP Alliance for Racial Equity and the Center for the Study of Social Policy.

Hines, A. M., Lemon, K., Wyatt, P., & Merdinger, J. (2004). Factors related to the disproportionate involvement of children of color in the child welfare system: A review and emerging themes. *Children and Youth Services Review, 26,* 507–527. doi:10.1016/j.childyouth.2004.01.007

Hodges, V. (1994). Assessing for strengths and protective factors in child abuse and neglect: Risk assessment with families of color. In P. J. Pecora, & D. J. English (Eds.), *Multi-cultural guidelines for assessing family strengths and risk factors in child protective services* (pp. II–1–11). Seattle: University of Washington School of Social Work, and Washington State Department of Social Services.

Johnson, K., Knitzer, J., & Kaufmann, R. (2003). *Making dollars follow sense: Financing early childhood mental health services to promote healthy social and emotional development in young children.* New York: Columbia University, National Center on Children in Poverty.

Karoly, L. M., Kilburn, R. M., & Cannon, J. S. (2005). *Early childhood interventions: Proven results, future promise* (RAND Doc. No. MG-341-PNC). Santa Monica, CA: RAND Corporation. Retrieved from http://www.rand.org/pubs/monographs/MG341

Karoly, L. M., Kilburn, R. M., Caulkins, J. P., & Cannon, J. S. (2000). *Assessing costs and benefits of early childhood intervention programs: Overview and application.* Santa Monica, CA: RAND Corporation.

Kendall-Tackett, K. (2003). *Treating the lifetime health effects of childhood victimization.* Kingston, NJ: Civic Research Institute.

Kerman, B., Maluccio, A. N., & Freundlich, M. (2009). *Achieving permanence for older children and youth in foster care.* New York: Columbia University Press.

Kessler, R. C., & Magee, W. J. (1993). Childhood adversities and adult depression: Basic patterns of association in a US national survey. *Psychological Medicine, 23,* 679–690. doi:10.1017/S0033291700025460

Kilburn, M. R., & Karoly, L. A. (2008). *The economics of early childhood policy: What the dismal science has to say about investing in children* (RAND Doc. No. OP-227-CFP). Santa Monica, CA: RAND Corporation.

Kirk, S., Gallagher, J., & Anastasiow, N. (1993). *Educating exceptional children* (7th ed.). Boston: Houghton Mifflin.

Lee, S., Aos, S., & Miller, M. (2008). *Evidence-based programs to prevent children from entering and remaining in the child welfare system: Interim report* (WSIPP Doc. No. 08–05–3902). Olympia: Washington State Institute for Public Policy. Retrieved from Washington http://www.wsipp.wa.gov/pub

Lindsey, D. (2004). *The welfare of children* (2nd ed.). New York: Oxford University Press.

Maier, H. W. (1978). *Three theories of child development* (3rd ed.). New York: Harper & Row.

Mallon, G. P. (1999). *Let's get this straight: A gay- and lesbian-affirming approach to child welfare.* New York: Columbia University Press.

Maluccio, A. N., Pine, B. A., & Tracy, E. M. (2002). *Social work practice with families and children.* New York: Columbia University Press.

Mann, A. (2003). Relationships matter: Impact of parental, peer factors on teen, young adult substance abuse. *NIDA Notes, 18*(2), 11–13. doi:10.1151/v18i2RMIPPFTYASA

Marts, E. J., Lee, R., McCroy, R., & McCroskey, J. (2008). Point of engagement: Reducing disproportionality and improving child and family outcomes. *Child Welfare, 87*(2), 335–358.

Massinga, R., & Pecora, P. J. (2003). Providing better opportunities for older children in the child welfare system. *Future of Children, 14*, 151–173. Retrieved from http://www.futureofchildren.org/futureofchildren/publications/docs/14_01_08.pdf

McCroskey, J., Christie, T., Lorthridge, J., Chambers, R., Pecora, P. J., Azzam, T. , Fleischer, D., Rosenthal, E., Weisbart, A., Custodio, C., Franke, T., Nunn, P., Carter, S., Yoo, J., Bowie, P., & Wold, C. (2009). *Prevention Initiative Demonstration Project (PIDP): Year one evaluation summary report.* Los Angeles: Casey Family Programs. Retrieved from http://www.casey.org/Resources/Publications/pdf/pidp_fr.pdf

McDonald, J., Salyers, N., & Shaver, M. (2004). *The foster care straitjacket: Innovation, federal financing & accountability in state foster care reform.* Urbana-Champaign: University of Illinois at Urbana-Champaign, Fostering Results Project. Retrieved from http://www.pewtrusts.org/our_work_report_detail.aspx?id=17842

McIntosh, N. (1991). Identification and investigation of properties of social support. *Journal of Organizational Behavior Management, 12*, 201–217. doi:10.1002/job.4030120304

Mech, E. V. (Ed.). (1988). Independent-living services for at-risk adolescents. *Child Welfare, 67*, 483–634.

Mordock, J. B. (2002). *Managing for outcomes: A basic guide to the evaluation of best practices in the human services.* Washington, DC: Child Welfare League of America Press.

Morgan, L. J., Spears, L. S., & Kaplan, C. (2003). *A framework for community action: Making children a national priority.* Washington, DC: Child Welfare League of America Press.

National Coalition for Child Protection Reform. (2008). *The trouble with child and family services reviews: The federal government's failed attempt to measure child welfare system performance.* Alexandria, VA: Author. Retrieved from http://www.nccpr.org/reports/cfsr.doc

O'Connell, M. E., Boat, T., & Warner, K. E. (Eds.). (2009). *Preventing mental, emotional and behavioral disorders among young people: Progress and possibilities.* Washington, DC: National Academies Press. Retrieved from http://www.nap.edu/catalog.php?record_id=12480

Osofsky, J. D., & Thompson, D. (2000). Adaptive and maladaptive parenting: Perspectives on risk and protective factors. In J. P. Shonkoff & S. J. Meisels (Eds.), *Handbook of early childhood intervention* (2nd ed., pp. 54–75). Cambridge, UK: Cambridge University Press.

Parish, S. L., Pomeranz, A. E., & Braddock, D. (2003). Family support in the United States: Financing trends and emerging initiatives. *Mental Retardation, 41,* 174–187. doi:10.1352/0047–6765(2003)41<174:FSITUS>2.0.CO;2

Pecora, P. J., Kessler, R. C., Williams, J., Downs, A. C., English, D.J., & White, J., & O'Brien, K. (2010). *What works in family foster care? Key components of success from the Northwest foster care alumni study.* New York and Oxford: Oxford University Press.

Pecora, P. J., Selig, W., Zirps, F., & Davis, S. (Eds.). (1996). *Quality improvement and program evaluation in child welfare agencies: Managing into the next century.* Washington, DC: Child Welfare League of America Press.

Pecora, P. J., Whittaker, J. K., Maluccio, A. N., Barth, R. P., & Depanfilis, D. (with R. Plotnick). (2009). *The child welfare challenge: Policy, practice, and research* (3rd ed.). Piscataway, NJ: Aldine-Transaction.

Pecora, P. J., Williams, J., Kessler, R. J., Downs, A.C., O'Brien, K., Hiripi, E., & Morello, S. (2003). *Assessing the effects of foster care: Early results from the Casey National Alumni Study.* Seattle, WA: Casey Family Programs. Retrieved from http://www.inpathways.net/casey_alumni_studies_report.pdf

Pew Foundation. (2008). *Time for reform: Investing in prevention: Keeping children safe at home.* Philadelphia: Author. Retrieved from http://kidsarewaiting.org/tools/reports/files/0011.pdf

Pine, B. A. (1986). Child welfare reform and the political process. *Social Service Review, 60,* 339–359. doi:10.1086/644381

Plantz, M. C., Hubbell, R., Barrett, B. J., & Dobrec, A. (1989). Indian Child Welfare Act: A status report. *Children Today, 18,* 24–29.

Polansky, N. A., Chalmers, M. A., Buttenweiser, E., & Williams, D. P. (1981). *Damaged parents: An anatomy of child neglect.* Chicago: University of Chicago Press.

Polansky, N. A., Gaudin, J. M., Jr., & Kilpatrick, A. C. (1992). Family radicals. *Children and Youth Services Review, 14,* 19–26. doi:10.1016/0190–7409(92)90010-S

Rae-Grant, N., Thomas, B. H., Offord, D. R., & Boyle, M. H. (1989). Risk, protective factors, and the prevalence of behavioral and emotional disorders in children and adolescents. *Journal of American Academy Child and Adolescent Psychiatry, 28,* 262–268. doi:10.1097/00004583–198903000–00019

Ramey, C. T., & Ramey, S. L. (1998). Early intervention and early experience. *American Psychologist, 53,* 109–120. doi:10.1037/0003–066X.53.2.109

Ridge, T. (2009). *Living with poverty: A review of the literature on children's and families' experiences of poverty* (Research Report No. 594). Colegate, Norwich: United Kingdom Department for Work and Pensions. Retrieved from http://research.dwp.gov.uk/asd/asd5/rports2009–2010/rrep594.pdf

Rutter, M. (1979). Protective factors in children's responses to stress and disadvantage. In M. W. Kent & J. E. Rolf (Eds.), *Primary prevention of psychopathology: Vol. 3. Social competence in children* (pp. 49–74). Hanover, NH: University Press of New England.

Rutter, M. (1981). Stress, coping and development: Some issues and some questions. *Journal of Child Psychology & Psychiatry, 22,* 323–356. doi:10.1111/j.1469 7610.1981.tb00560.x

Rutter, M. (1985). Resilience in the face of adversity: Protective factors and resistance to psychiatric disorder. *British Journal of Psychiatry, 147,* 598–611. doi:10.1192/bjp.147.6.598

Rutter, M. (1987). Psychosocial resilience and protective mechanisms. *American Journal of Orthopsychiatry, 57,* 316–331.

Rutter, M. (1989). Intergenerational continuities and discontinuities in serious parenting difficulties. In D. Cicchetti & V. Carlson (Eds.), *Child maltreatment: Theory and research on the causes and consequences of child abuse and neglect* (pp. 317–348). Cambridge, UK: Cambridge University Press.

Rutter, M. (1990). Psychosocial resilience and protective mechanisms. In J. Rolf (Ed.), *Risk and protective factors in the development of psychopathology* (pp. 42–73). New York: Cambridge University Press.

Ryan, J., & Testa, M. (2004). *Child maltreatment and juvenile delinquency: Investigating the role of placement and placement instability.* Champaign-Urbana: University of Illinois at Urbana-Champaign, School of Social Work, Children and Family Research Center.

Schorr, E., & Marchand, V. (2007). *Pathway to the prevention of child abuse and neglect.* Washington, DC: Project on Effective Interventions, Pathways Mapping Initiative Retrieved from http://www.cssp.org/uploadFiles/PCANPDFFI NAL11–14–07.pdf

Sedlak, A. J., Mettenburg, J., Basena, M., Petta, I., McPherson, K., Greene, A., & Li, S. (2010). *Fourth National Incidence Study of Child Abuse and Neglect (NIS-4): Report to Congress.* Washington, DC: U.S. Department of Health and Human Services, Administration for Children and Families. Retrieved from http://www.acf.hhs.gov/programs/opre/abuse_neglect/natl_incid/nis4_ report_congress_full_pdf_jan2010.pdf

Shonkoff, J., & Phillips, D. (Eds.). (2000). *From neurons to neighborhoods: The science of early childhood development.* Washington, DC: National Academies Press. Retrieved from http://books.nap.edu/openbook.php?record_id=9824&page=R1

Stahmer, A. C., Leslie, L. K., Hurlburt, M. S., Barth, R., Webb, M. B., Landsverk, J., & Zhang, J. (2005). Developmental and behavioral needs as predictors of service use for young children in child welfare. *Pediatrics, 116,* 891–900. doi:10.1542/peds.2004–2135

Stein, T. (1984). The Child Abuse Prevention and Treatment Act. *Social Service Review, 58,* 302–314. doi:10.1086/644194

Testa, M. F., & Poertner, J. (2010). *Fostering accountability: Using evidence to guide and improve child welfare policy.* New York: Oxford University Press.

Thomas, G. (1994). Travels in the trench between child welfare theory and practice: A case study of failed promises and prospects for renewal. *Child and Youth Services Review, 17,* 1–31. doi:10.1300/J024V17N01_01

Tremblay, J., & Harnet, P. (2008). Impact of genetic and epigenetic factors from early life to later disease. *Metabolism, 57*(Suppl.), S27-S31.

U.S. Census Bureau. (2009a). *As baby boomers age, fewer families have children under 18 at home* [Press release]. Retrieved from http://www.census.gov/Press-Release/www/releases/archives/families_households/013378.html

U.S. Census Bureau. (2009b). *Income, poverty, and health insurance coverage in the United States: 2008* (Report P60–236). Retrieved from http://www.census.gov/prod/2009pubs/p60–236.pdf .

U.S. Census Bureau. (2010). *State single year of age and sex population estimates: April 1, 2000 to July 1, 2007 resident.* Retrieved from http://www.census.gov/popest/datasets.html

U.S. Department of Health and Human Services, Administration on Children, Youth and Families. (1999). *Child maltreatment 1997: Reports from the states to the National Child Abuse and Neglect Data Systems.* Washington, DC: Government Printing Office. Retrieved from http://www.acf.hhs.gov/programs/cb/pubs/ncands97/index.htm

U.S. Department of Health and Human Services, Administration on Children, Youth and Families, Children's Bureau. (2003a). *Safety, permanency and well-being: Child welfare outcomes 1998, 1999, & 2000.* Washington, DC: Government Printing Office.

U.S. Department of Health and Human Services, Administration for Children, Youth, and Families, Children's Bureau. (2003b). *AQ1 Emerging practices in the prevention of child abuse and neglect.* Washington, DC: Author.

U.S. Department of Health and Human Services, Administration on Children, Youth and Families. (2010). *Child maltreatment 2008.* Washington, DC: Government Printing Office. Retrieved from http://www.acf.hhs.gov/programs/cb/pubs/cm08/index.htm

U.S. Department of Health and Human Services, Administration for Children and Families, Children's Bureau. (2009a). *The AFCARS report:* Preliminary FY 2008 Estimates as of October 2009 (16). Washington DC: Author. Retrieved from http://www.acf.hhs.gov/programs/cb/stats_research/afcars/tar/report16.htm

U.S. Department of Health and Human Services, Administration for Children and Families, Children's Bureau. (2009b). *Trends in foster care and adoption—FY 2002-FY 2008.* Washington DC: Author. Retrieved from http://www.acf.hhs.gov/programs/cb/stats_research/afcars/trends.htm

U.S. General Accounting Office. (2004). *Child and family services reviews: Better use of data and improved guidance could enhance HHS's oversight of state performance* (GAO-04–333). Washington, DC: Government Printing Office. Retrieved from http://www.gao.gov/cgi-bin/getrpt?GAO-04–333

U.S. Government Accountability Office. (2007). *African American children in foster care: Additional HHS assistance needed to help states reduce the proportion in care* (GAO 07–816; Report to the Chairman, Committee on Ways and Means, House of Representatives). Washington, DC: Author. Retrieved from http://www.gao.gov/new.items/d07816.pdf

Wald, M., & Martinez, T. (2003). *Connected by 25: Improving the life chances of the country's most vulnerable 14–24 year olds* (Working Paper). Menlo Park, CA: William and Flora Hewlett Foundation. Retrieved from http://betterfutures.fcny.org/betterfutures/connected_by_25.pdf

Walton, E., Sandau-Beckler, P., & Mannes, M. (Eds.). (2001). *Balancing family-centered services and child well-being: Exploring issues in policy, practice, and research.* New York: Columbia University Press.

Wang, C-T., & Holton, J. (2008). *Total estimated cost of child abuse and neglect in the United States.* Chicago: Prevent Child Abuse America.

Webb, M. B., Dowd, K., Jones-Harden, B., Landsverk, J., & Testa, M. (Eds.). (2010). *Child welfare and child well-being: New perspectives from the National Survey of Child and Adolescent Well-Being.* New York: Oxford University Press.

Weinfield, N. S., Ogawa, J. R., & Sroufe, L. A. (1997). Early attachment as a pathway to adolescent peer competence. *Journal of Research on Adolescence, 7,* 241–265.

Werner, E. E. (1989). High-risk children in young adulthood: A longitudinal study from birth to 32 years. *American Journal of Orthopsychiatry, 59,* 72–81.

Whittaker, J. K., & Maluccio, A. N. (2002). Rethinking "child welfare": A reflective essay. *Social Service Review, 76,* 107–134. doi:10.1086/324610

Wilkinson, R., & Pickett, K. (2009). *The spirit level: Why more equal societies almost always do better.* New York: Penguin.

Wilson, M. (1984). Mothers' and grandmothers' perceptions of parental behavior in three-generational Black families. *Child Development, 55,* 1333–1339. doi:10.2307/1130003

Wornoff, R., & Mallon, G.P. (Eds.). (2006). *Lesbian, gay, bisexual, and transgender issues in child welfare.* Washington, DC: Child Welfare League of America Press.

Wulczyn, F., Barth, R.P., Yuan, Y.Y., Jones-Harden, B., & Landsverk, J. (2005). *Beyond common sense: Child welfare, child well-being, and the evidence for policy reform.* Somerset, NJ: Transaction Aldine.

Wulczyn, F. H., Hislop, K. B., & Chen, L. (2007). *Foster care dynamics: 2003–2005: A report from the multistate foster care data archive.* Chicago: Chapin Hall at the University of Chicago.

Wulczyn, F. H., Orlebeke, B., & Haight , J. (2009). *Finding the return on investment: A framework for monitoring local child welfare agencies.* Chicago: Chapin Hall at the University of Chicago. Retrieved from http://www.chapinhall.org/sites/default/files/Finding_Return_On_Investment_07_20_09.pdf

Additional Reading

Chibnall, S., Dutch, N., Jones-Harden, B., Brown, A., Gourgine, R., Smith, J., Boone, A., & Snyder, S. (2003). *Children of color in the child welfare system: Perspectives from the child welfare community.* Washington, DC: U.S. Department of Health and Human Services Administration for Children and Families Children's Bureau, Administration for Children and Families. Retrieved from http://www.childwelfare.gov/pubs/otherpubs/children/

Child Welfare League of America. (2003). *Making children a national priority: A framework for community action.* Washington, DC: Author. Retrieved from http://www.cwla.org/membersonly/cig021009b.pdf

Shonkoff, J. P., & Meisels, S. J. (Eds.). (2000). *Handbook of early childhood intervention* (2nd ed.). New York: Cambridge University Press.

Wulczyn, F., Barth, R. P., Yuan, Y. Y., Jones Harden, B., & Landsverk, J. (2005). *Beyond common sense: Evidence for child welfare policy reform.* New York: Transaction De Gruyter.

Wulczyn, F. H., Orlebeke, B., & Mitchell-Herzfeld, S. (2005). *Improving public child welfare agency performance in the context of the federal child and family services reviews.* Chicago: Chapin Hall at the University of Chicago. Retrieved from http://www.chapinhall.org/research/report/improving-public-child-welfare-agency-performance-context-federal-child-and-family-s

Web-Based Resources

American Psychological Association, Task Force on Resilience and Strength in Black Children and Adolescents. (2008). *Resilience in African American children and adolescents: A vision for optimal development.* Retrieved from http://www.apa.org/pi/families/resources/resiliencerpt.pdf

Child Trends for key statistical summaries, child and family trend data and issue summaries, http://www.childtrends.org

U.S. Children's Bureau for state outcomes and foster care statistics, http://www.acf.hhs.gov/programs/cb/publications

Resilience and strength in Black children and adolescents, http://psychcentral.com/news/2008/08/21/resiliency-among-black-youth/279

4

Education Policy for Children, Youth, and Families

Andy J. Frey

Hill M. Walker

Armon R. Perry

Public education in the United States occurs in the context of a complex and often contentious system composed of diverse interest groups. Several competing viewpoints about the primary purpose of education are at the heart of debates on education policy. These competing interests include preparing students for the workforce, teaching basic academic skills, developing social and cognitive skills, and preparing youth to be future citizens who participate productively in society (Sadovnik, Cookson, & Semel, 2001). Given the broad scope of this set of interacting purposes, it is not surprising that their presence creates enormous policy and program challenges. The purpose of this chapter is to identify and describe significant education policies of the past century in the context of a risk, protection, and resilience framework. Herein, we discuss the prevalence and trends for school dropout and failure; identify and describe the primary risk and protective factors associated with school adjustment and achievement problems; summarize the past and present education policies; and consider and discuss ways in which principles of risk, protection, and resilience might be used to develop or enhance education policy.

Trends in School Failure and Academic Achievement

Public education is often referred to as the great equalizer. This label suggests that access to education plays a prominent role in the acquisition of economic and social benefits associated with gainful employment. Unfortunately, evidence from years of research indicates that access to quality public education is far from equal. In 2006, nearly 3.7 million children dropped out of school before earning a high school diploma, a number that represents 9.3% of the nation's youth (U.S. Census Bureau, 2008). Historically, marginalized groups have faced severe challenges and discrimination in their attempts to take advantage of educational opportunities. Despite progress on many fronts, recent reports have indicated that the American education system is still struggling in its effort to reach all students effectively. Although it is widely known that a lack of educational attainment has a deleterious impact on future economic status, many children begin school without the necessary readiness skills and embrace a pattern of failure that leads to dropout and poor prospects for employment.

Studies have shown that student-specific factors are associated with dropout and academic failure (Patterson, Reid, & Dishion, 1992). These student-specific risk factors include low academic achievement, student misbehavior, suspensions and expulsions, negative narrative comments in school records, frequent referrals for in- and out-of-school problems (Arcia, 2006; Finn, Fish, & Scott, 2008), number of elementary schools attended, and early involvement in the juvenile justice system (Sweeten, 2006). In addition to these individual risk factors, larger environmental influences also affect school failure and dropout rates. The notion of school engagement is central to the influence of environmental factors. Students perform better and achieve at higher levels when they feel a sense of attachment to school, which is characterized by bonding or connection that occurs through a process of school engagement (Hawkins, Catalano, Kosterman, Abbott, & Hill, 1999). Conversely, students who are unable to establish a connection to school and thus cannot fully engage in the schooling process are at increased risk for dropout (Kemp, 2006). Lack of engagement may occur among students whose families move frequently (South, Haynie, & Bose, 2007) and those who have negative interactions with school personnel or who are minimally involved in extracurricular activities (Kemp, 2006).

For other students, particularly for youth of color, school structure and culture is often quite different from the structure and culture of their homes. This disparity often alienates students and contributes to disengagement and subsequent dropout (Patterson, Hale, & Stessman, 2007). Youth of color are at greatest risk for school adjustment problems during the elementary grades, and they are more likely than others to become school dropouts (Patterson et al., 2007; Ripple, 1994; Substance Abuse and Mental Health Services Administration, 2008). This pattern also contributes to higher dropout rates in urban areas that are heavily populated by racial and ethnic minorities (Patterson et al.). As shown in Table 4.1, males and females have similar dropout rates, and overall dropout rates have declined for all racial and ethnic groups since 2000; however, in 2000 and 2007, both African American and Hispanic students had higher rates of school dropout than their White counterparts. In a recent study, Carpenter and Ramirez (2007) examined reasons for school dropout and found that being retained in a grade, or held back, predicted school dropout for all races, whereas family composition and time spent on homework were factors related to school dropout only for White and Hispanic students. Among African American students, the number of suspensions and level of parental involvement in school predicted dropout (Carpenter & Ramirez). Most important, these findings suggest that many racial and ethnic differences in academic achievement and dropout rates might stem from key differences in risk status at family, school, and neighborhood levels.

Risk and Protective Factors for School Adjustment and Achievement Problems

The term *risk factor* is defined by Fraser and Terzian (2005) as "any event, condition, or experience that increases the probability that a problem will be formed, maintained, or exacerbated" (p. 5). Risk factors for school-related problems may be either specific or general in nature. Within the context of education, nonspecific risk factors such as poverty are not directly related to

Table 4.1   Status Dropout Rates of 16 to 24 Year Olds, 2000 and 2007

	2000	2007
	%	%
Gender		
Male	12.0	9.8
Female	9.9	7.7
Race/ethnicity		
White	6.9	5.3
African American	13.1	8.4
Hispanic	27.8	21.4
Total	10.9	8.7

SOURCE: Cataldi, Laird, and Kewal-Ramani (2009).

NOTE: Status dropouts include the percentage of individuals in a given age range who are not in school and have not earned a high school diploma or equivalency credential.

school adjustment and achievement problems. Nevertheless, such factors have the potential to create maladaptive emotional and behavioral contexts and outcomes, which in turn, can have an adverse affect on academic performance (Greenberg, Domitrovich, & Bumbarger, 1999). Nonspecific risk factors may set into motion what Fraser and colleagues have called a chain of risk (Fraser, Kirby, & Smokowski, 2004), which can culminate in negative outcomes such as academic failure.

Other risk factors directly affect the likelihood of school adjustment and academic failure. For example, factors such as low commitment to school contribute to truancy, poor grades, and poor overall academic performance (Carnahan, 1994). As shown in Table 4.2, risk factors occur at the individual level or in the context of families, schools, or neighborhoods.

Protective factors are characteristics or traits that buffer exposure to risk. In situations of high risk, protective factors, such as attachment to teachers or other adults at school, have the potential to reduce risk and decrease the likelihood of school-related problems. In the absence of risk, protective factors have a neutral effect. The concept of promotion is closely related to protection. *Promotive factors* are defined as resources that exert positive influences on behavior, irrespective of the presence or absence of risk (Sameroff & Gutman, 2004). Examples of promotive factors include high intelligence or strong social skills, which can promote positive behavioral outcomes regardless of risk exposure. Table 4.3 summarizes protective and promotive factors that affect academic performance.

Table 4.2   Risk Factors for Academic Failure by Level of Influence

Level of Influence	Risk Factors
Individual	Learning related social skills (listening, participating in groups, staying on task, organizational skills) Substance use Pregnancy Social behavior Limited intelligence Presence of a disability Minority status Special education status Inability to read by the fourth grade
Family	Residential mobility Early exposure to familial antisocial behavior Parent–child conflict Lack of connectedness with peers, family, school, and community
School	Large school size Limited school resources High staff turnover Inconsistent classroom management practices Percentage of low socioeconomic status students Negative school and classroom climate School violence Overcrowding High student to teacher ratios Insufficient curricular and course relevance Weak, inconsistent adult leadership Poor building design Overreliance on physical security measures
Neighborhood	Poverty Low percentage of affluent neighbors

Table 4.3   Promotive and Protective Factors for Academic Failure by Level of Influence

Level of Influence	Promotive Factors	Protective Factors
Individual	Cognitive skills (e.g., intelligence, the ability to work collaboratively with others, and the capacity to focus in the face of distraction) High socioemotional functioning Ability to adapt to changes in school or work schedule Effective and efficient communication skills Ability to use humor to de-escalate negative situations Social skills Understanding and accepting capabilities and limitations Maintaining a positive outlook Involvement in extracurricular activities	
School	Positive and safe environment Setting high academic and social expectations Positive relationships with teachers School bonding Positive and open school climate Positive ratings for overall educational performance	School climate Classroom management strategies that reduce classroom disruption and increase learning School bonding Consistent and firm rules for students
Peer		Acceptance by pro-social peers Involvement in positive peer groups

Education Policy: Past and Present

Our review of education policy in the United States begins with the recognition that American educational practices are profoundly influenced by political ideology, which is most frequently viewed in terms of a conservative or liberal stance. Historically, a conservative view of education has promoted the idea that individual students have the capacity to earn—or fail to earn—their place among the academic elite. Policy approaches based on conservative views tend to emphasize knowledge-centered education, traditional forms of learning and curricula, respect for authority and discipline, and the adoption of rigorous academic standards. In contrast, educational approaches based on liberal perspectives tend to support curricula that are responsive to the individual as well as to social and environmental contexts (Apollonia & Abrami, 1997). Educational policies and programs in the past 100 years are reviewed and summarized in Table 4.4; the impact of policies that have been subjected to evaluation is also discussed.

Early Public Policy

From its inception, public education was thought of as a social vehicle for minimizing the importance of class and wealth and for determining who might excel economically. Social policy in the late 19th and early 20th centuries was based on the liberal ideas of Horace Mann and John Dewey. In the mid-19th century, Mann proclaimed that education, more than any other process, was the great equalizer of people from various walks of life (Cremin, 1957). Similarly, Dewey's (1916) philosophy of education held the role of education as the "leveler" of the socially advantaged and disadvantaged. Education policy also stemmed from the conservative notion that mass education was necessary to ensure that the citizenry could obey the law, vote, pay taxes, serve on juries, and participate in the armed forces (Derezinski, 2004). The Massachusetts Compulsory School Attendance Act of 1852 required public school attendance for all able-bodied children of a certain age unless a child's parent could establish that the child was obtaining equivalent instruction outside the public schools. By 1918, 48 states had adopted similar attendance policies (Derezinski). This change resulted in programs based on the idea that all children must attend school and graduate; these assertions were nonexistent before compulsory attendance laws. At this point, segregated education was determined to be constitutional, as evidenced by the separate-but-equal clause in *Plessey v. Ferguson* (1896), which supported separate transportation systems for African American and White people; the ruling was later applied to children in the context of public school integration.

Education Policy From 1930 to 1970

In the post-World War I era, education policy was dominated by debates about the academic and social goals of education and by

(Text continued on page 126)

Table 4.4 Major American Education Policies, Court Cases, and Public Reports, 1852–2010

Policy, Court Case, or Public Report	Date	Summary	Influence on Education
Compulsory School Attendance Act	1852	Required public school attendance for all able-bodied children of a certain age, unless the parent of the child could establish that the child was obtaining equivalent instruction outside of the public schools.	Resulted in programs designed to have all children attend school and graduate. Existing programs would need to change to accommodate a very different student population that had not previously attended school.
Plessey v. Ferguson	1896	Commonly referred to as "separate but equal," this decision supported separate transportation systems for Blacks and Whites.	Validated the belief that separate schools for Blacks and Whites was a constitutionally sound practice.
Brown v. Board of Education	1954	The U.S. Supreme Court ruled that laws assigning students to schools based on race were unconstitutional. The court ruled unanimously that such laws violated the Fourteenth Amendment's guarantee that the rights of all Americans deserved equal protection. The rationale for the verdict was that being separated from White students could result in feelings of inferiority in students of color and compromise their futures.	Desegregation gained momentum and competed for attention in the national spotlight and attempted to force school districts to desegregate.

Policy, Court Case, or Public Report	Date	Summary	Influence on Education
Numerous Public Reports	Late 1960s and early 1970s	Highlighted the structural inequalities in the educational system (particularly for African American children and those from disadvantaged backgrounds) and the relationship between socioeconomic status and unequal educational outcomes.	Justified busing students between schools and between school districts, suggesting that reassigning poor students to schools with middle-class students would improve poor students' academic achievement.
Head Start Act	1965	Head Start was designed to address a wealth of factors that affect poor children and their families, with the ultimate goal of increasing early school readiness by providing health, educational, nutritional, family support, social, and other services for 3- and 4-year-old children from low-income households.	The first primary prevention program of its kind, designed to prepare disadvantaged children on a universal level for kindergarten.
Elementary and Secondary Education Act (ESEA)	1965	The ESEA of 1965 provided funds for schools that had high percentages of disadvantaged students (Title I). Goals were to promote safe and drug-free learning environments (Title IV), help linguistically diverse children (Title VII), and promote the inclusion and participation of women in	Title I and Title IV have had the greatest impact on high-risk youth. Title I has been the largest source of federal funding for poor children in schools, serving 10 million children in more than 50,000 schools.

Table 4.4 (Continued)

Policy, Court Case, or Public Report	Date	Summary	Influence on Education
		all aspects of education (Title IX). These funds were used to support whole school reform, compensatory education, and remediation for the country's most disadvantaged children and to provide free and reduced-cost lunches for children in need.	
Milliken v. Bradley	1974	The courts declared that if segregation was the result of an individual's choice, school districts could not be forced to remedy the situation.	Released a district from desegregation orders after it demonstrated it had done everything possible to desegregate schools. This ruling set a precedent for similar rulings that resulted in an end to racially balanced schools in many American cities.
Education of All Handicapped Children Act, PL-94–142	1975	Provided screening and identification for children with a wide range of disabilities and required schools to provide a variety of services for children based on an individualized education plan developed by a multidisciplinary team.	Altered the education of those with disabilities for many years to come.
A Nation at Risk	1983	Cited high rates of adult illiteracy and low	Federal, state, and local policy switched

Policy, Court Case, or Public Report	Date	Summary	Influence on Education
		achievement test scores as indicators of declining literacy and educational standards. The report recommended that educational policies strive to improve education for all students and develop more rigorous and measurable standards to assess academic performance. It highlighted the failure of education to ameliorate social problems and blamed these policies for producing mass mediocrity in education that resulted in the decline of authority and standards in schools.	to the improvement of curriculum, school-based management, the tightening of standards, the importance of discipline, and the establishment of academic goals and assessment.
Individuals with Disabilities Act (PL 94-142 Reauthorized)	1990	Recommended that behavior intervention plans based on a functional behavior assessment should be developed for children suspected of having severe emotional disturbance. Behavior intervention plans were mandated for children with disabilities who had been suspended for 10 days or more before a change of placement could be initiated.	Marked the beginning of a trend in educational policy to promote positive, proactive strategies for children with challenging behavior.
America 2000	1992	President George H. Bush called for voluntary testing in Grades 4, 8, and 12 and proposed six goals for education, called America 2000	Began what would become a major movement toward education policy aligned with the conservative ideology.

(Continued)

Table 4.4 (Continued)

Policy, Court Case, or Public Report	Date	Summary	Influence on Education
Goals 2000	1994	President Bill Clinton proposed this initiative, which would have set into law the six national education goals proposed by President George H. Bush.	Continued the trend toward standards and accountability testing.
Gun-Free Schools Act	1994	This act provided funds only for schools that adopted zero-tolerance policies for guns and drugs on school grounds.	Resulted in the expansion of zero-tolerance policies for less severe student infractions. Led to promising prevention and intervention services such as teacher involvement/ training; the restructuring of schools to increase student engagement, attendance, performance, and family involvement; and the establishment of clear behavior expectations in schools
No Child Left Behind	2000	NCLB is the most recent reauthorization of the ESEA. It is designed to create a stronger, more accountable education system; seeks to change the culture of education; and purports to use evidence-based strategies found to be effective through rigorous research.	Initiated focus on evidence-based strategies in regular education and provided a much stronger emphasis on accountability testing than previous policies.

Policy, Court Case, or Public Report	Date	Summary	Influence on Education
		NCLB holds students accountable to high educational outcomes and standards. NCLB requires each state to set clear and high standards and to put an assessment system in place to measure student progress toward those standards.	
Individuals with Disabilities Education Improvement Act (PL 94-142 Reauthorized)	2004	Mandated the use of interventions known to be effective and placed a premium on primary prevention by substantially altering the screening and identification procedures for children with disabilities.	Continued the trend to promote positive, proactive interventions and to adopt interventions supported by the scientific literature.
Parents Involved in Community Schools v. Seattle School District No. 1 (2007)	2007	The U.S. Supreme Court struck down voluntary student assignment plans in Louisville, Kentucky, and Seattle, Washington, thereby continuing and extending the trend toward resegregation in the public schools.	Extended the trend toward resegregation in public schools and illustrated the deep divisions between the liberal and conservative factions of the newly configured Supreme Court. The ruling applied pressure on school districts that rely on race-conscious criteria to assign students to schools to revisit their plan so it fits within the context of this precedent.

discussions about whether all children should receive the same quality education. Although the focus on curriculum and teaching methods remained, a values-based debate ensued that was associated with the issues of equity and excellence. By 1930, the direction of education policy shifted toward equality in education. During the 1930s, the National Association for the Advancement of Colored People initiated a campaign to overthrow the *Plessey v. Ferguson* (1896) decision, with school desegregation as a major goal. As the achievement gap between advantaged and disadvantaged students became increasingly clear, efforts at desegregation in public education gained momentum and competed for policy attention in the national spotlight.

The achievement gap between White and African American students as well as the achievement gap between economically advantaged and disadvantaged children became the most important educational issues of the century in the 1940s. The debate that ensued served as a catalyst for efforts to close the achievement gap and to maximize educational opportunities for people of color. The integration movement scored a significant victory in 1954, when the U.S. Supreme Court ruling in *Brown v. Board of Education of Topeka* (1954) established that laws assigning students to schools based on race were unconstitutional. The Supreme Court ruled unanimously that such laws violated the 14th Amendment's guarantee that the rights of all Americans deserved equal protection. The rationale for the verdict was that separating African American students from White students could result in feelings of inferiority in students of color and serve to compromise the quality of their education. It took nearly two decades for all states to comply with the court's order to desegregate schools, and many of the initial advancements achieved by integration have since given way.

During this same period, conservatives attacked progressive directions in education, suggesting the American education system was sacrificing intellectual goals for social ends. The discussion between the progressives, who saw the educational arena as the most legitimate vehicle for leveling the playing field, and the critics, who demanded more academic rigor in education, became known as "The Great Debate" (Ravitch, 1983). The debate was fueled by the Soviet launching of the space satellite Sputnik, which seemed to warn that the United States might no longer lead the world in scientific research and development. From the mid-1950s to the mid-1960s, the pursuit of excellence, standards-based education, curriculum reform, assessment, and

accountability gained momentum. However, standards-based education would not take center stage in education policy until the 1980s.

The 1960s witnessed great divisiveness in education policy as illustrated
by the tension evident in the eventual move toward a more liberal reform
orientation. This change mirrored larger societal issues, predominantly the
emphasis on equity issues raised by the Civil Rights Movement. In the
1960s and early 1970s, several influential books highlighted the structural
inequalities in the educational system, particularly for African American
children and children from disadvantaged backgrounds (Clark, 1965; Kohl,
1967; Kozol, 1967; Rosenfeld, 1971). These books, along with a report by
Coleman (1966) titled *Equality of Educational Opportunity,* highlighted the
relationship between socioeconomic status and disparity in educational
outcomes. The Coleman report suggested that the composition of the
student body within schools was highly correlated with student
achievement (Sadovnik et al., 2001). The implications of the report were
shocking, primarily because Coleman set out to demonstrate that the
achievement gap between African American and White students could be
attributed to the organizational structure of American schools. The
Coleman report justified busing students between schools and between
school districts, suggesting that reassigning poor students to schools with
middle-class students would equalize educational opportunities. The
report was challenged by many researchers, who questioned the premise,
method, and findings.

Other progressive policies also emerged in the 1960s. In 1965, the Head
Start Act funded an innovative preschool program for disadvantaged
children. Head Start was designed to address a wealth of factors that
affected poor children and their families, and specifically school
readiness. The goal of the program was to increase early school readiness
by providing health, educational, nutritional, family support, social, and
other services to preschool children from low-income households. The
Head Start program was the first federally supported primary prevention
program of its kind.

Congress also passed the Elementary and Secondary Education Act
(ESEA) in 1965. Similar to the Head Start Act, the ESEA was passed on the
assumption that inequities in educational opportunities were largely
responsible for the achievement gap between advantaged and disadvantaged children. ESEA provided funds for schools that had high percentages of disadvantaged students to promote safe and drug-free learning
environments (Title IV). The act also supported linguistically diverse

children (Title VII) and promoted the inclusion and participation of women in all aspects of education (Title IX). These funds were used for whole school reform, compensatory education, remediation for the country's most disadvantaged children, and free and reduced-price lunches for children in need. ESEA has been revised and reauthorized every 5 years since 1965. Provisions of the act are currently responsible for funding bilingual education, drug education, and school lunch and breakfast programs (Nelson, Palonsky, & McCarthy, 2004).

Title I and Title IV of ESEA have had the greatest impact on vulnerable and high-risk youth. Title I has been the largest source of federal funding for poor children in schools for 40 years (Cook, 2005), serving more than 27 million students in more than 58,000 schools (National Center for Education Statistics, 2008). Title IV provides early screening; remedial academic support; and prevention programming that addresses issues of violence, substance abuse, sexual abuse, and teenage pregnancy. In addition, Title IV funds support transition programs for youth coming to public schools from residential and juvenile justice settings.

Education Policy From 1970 to 2000

The 1970s brought new attempts to integrate schools through complex busing plans and magnet schools designed to attract White students to neighborhood schools that they would not ordinarily attend (Cecelski, 1994). However, desegregation became increasingly difficult to maintain as a host of court cases gradually began to undo the *Brown* mandate. In the 1974 case of *Milliken v. Bradley*, the U.S. Supreme Court declared that if segregation was the result of an individual's choice, school districts could not be forced to remedy the situation. Put simply, once a district had done all it could to desegregate its schools, the district was released from further desegregation orders. Similar rulings led to renewed efforts to achieve a racial balance in schools in many American cities (Nelson et al., 2004).

In 1975, Congress passed the Education of All Handicapped Children Act (EHA; P.L.-94–142), which altered educational patterns for students with disabilities. EHA provided screening and identification for children with a wide range of disabilities and required schools to offer a variety of services for children based on an individualized education plan developed by a multidisciplinary team. The EHA contained four components: (a) screening and identification of children with disabilities,

(b) intervention services for children with disabilities, (c) inclusion of students with nondisabled students to the greatest extent possible, and (d) discipline provisions for students with disabilities.

In the late 1970s, many proponents of conservative policy pointed to the government's inability to solve social problems in the schools. Some spoke critically of the way in which EHA interfered with individual freedoms (Nelson et al., 2004). Many experts argued that progressive reforms had not only failed to narrow the achievement gap between advantaged and disadvantaged children but also had increased problems in the schools related to discipline and other behavioral issues. This belief was fueled by *A Nation at Risk* (Anyon, 1997), a report issued by the National Commission on Excellence (1983). The report was issued in 1983 under Terrel Bell, President Ronald Reagan's secretary of education; it discussed an ongoing problem of declining literacy and education standards, leading to high rates of adult illiteracy and low achievement test scores. The report recommended that educational policies should strive to improve education for all students and to develop more rigorous and measurable standards to assess academic performance (Nelson et al.). *A Nation at Risk* paved the way for educational reform efforts focused on excellence for all students, rather than concentrating on subgroups of children such as disabled or high-risk youth. The report highlighted the failure of education to ameliorate social problems and blamed past policies for producing mass mediocrity in education, which resulted in the decline of authority and standards in schools.

Subsequently, the focus of most federal, state, and local policy switched to the improvement of curriculum, school-based management, tightening of standards and discipline, and the establishment of academic goals and assessments. School-based management emphasized a structural shift away from bureaucratic boards of education to local forms of control. New policies were developed to engage parents, teachers, and administrators in decision-making processes. Teacher empowerment, a concept closely related to school-based management, was emphasized as a way to give teachers more decision-making power within schools. In addition, school choice options, such as vouchers, charter schools, and magnet schools, were created to provide parents with alternatives to the traditional public school offerings.

A 1990 reauthorization of EHA, the Individuals with Disabilities in Education Act (IDEA), was the first in a series of policy efforts aimed to ensure that children with disabilities were exposed to positive and

proactive interventions. Specifically, IDEA recommended certain measures for any student who might have a severe emotional disturbance.
The first step was for qualified professionals to conduct a functional
behavioral assessment of the student and then construct a behavior
intervention plan based on that assessment. In addition, a new or
revised behavior plan was mandated after a child with a disability had
been suspended for more than 10 days or before a change of placement
to a more restrictive setting (i.e., alternative classroom or school). IDEA
was also noteworthy for mandating the inclusion of parents in the planning
process for their child.

Partially because the discipline provisions in IDEA made expelling a
student with a severe emotional disturbance nearly impossible, the
Gun-Free Schools Act of 1994 was passed, which provided funds only to
those schools that adopted zero-tolerance policies for guns and drugs on
school grounds. Public and political concern over discipline-related
policies also heightened in the mid-1990s with the outbreak of mass
shootings in schools (Jenson & Howard, 1999). This heightened awareness of the safety risk in the school environment resulted in the expansion of zero-tolerance policies for less severe infractions. Alternative
schools and increased school security strategies were also implemented
to address school safety issues. However, a substantial body of evidence
suggests that exclusionary discipline measures such as office referrals,
suspension and expulsion, additional security, and other punitive alternatives exacerbate the very problems they are intended to address
(Skiba, 2002). Furthermore, the evidence supports that children of color,
particularly African Americans, are disproportionately represented
among the students receiving such discipline, which is also evidence of
institutional biases inherent in the use of exclusionary discipline (Skiba,
Michael, Nardo, & Peterson, 2000). The overreliance on punishment and
exclusionary practices in the presence of convincing evidence to suggest
the practices are ineffective has resulted in the development of policies
during the past decade that mandate the use of evidence-based, or
empirically supported practices.

Finally, Head Start, which has served as a laboratory for a variety of
prevention, early intervention, and program evaluation research since its
inception in 1965, was expanded in 1995 (Love, Tarullo, Raikes, &
Chazen-Cohen, 2006). Specifically, Early Head Start was launched to
expand Head Start services to pregnant women and to children during

the birth-to-3-year period, thereby providing earlier opportunities for preventive interventions. Federal appropriations for Head Start tripled during the 1990s, both to increase the number of children served and to improve the quality of programs, but funding has remained level since the early 2000s. In fiscal year 2006, the Head Start and Early Head Start programs served 909,201 children in more than 50,000 classrooms located in more than 18,800 centers funded through 1,600 grantees (Administration for Children and Families, 2007). With an overall federal budget of $6.7 billion, the average annual cost per child is currently calculated as $7,209 (Administration for Children and Families).

Current Education Policy, 2000 to 2010

The momentum of educational reforms in the 1990s culminated in the passage of the 2002 No Child Left Behind Act (NCLB). NCLB has been described as the most sweeping federal reform in education since ESEA was passed in 1965 (Nelson et al., 2004). Technically, NCLB was the most recent reauthorization of ESEA. However, NCLB added many new initiatives. For example, NCLB was designed to create a stronger, more accountable education system, to change the culture of education, and to use evidence-based strategies that have been determined effective through rigorous research. Rather than providing specific resources for at-risk youth, NCLB proposed assisting children and youth by holding them accountable to high educational outcomes and standards. NCLB required each state to set clear and high standards and to put an assessment system in place to measure student progress toward those standards (Paige, 2002). Specifically, NCLB required states to test all students annually in Grades 3 through 8 in reading and math. Scores reported by states must be disaggregated by poverty, race, ethnicity, disability, and English language proficiency so that potential achievement gaps can be identified. Schools that fail to make adequate yearly progress toward identifiable goals are identified for improvement and are subject to corrective action (Paige). NCLB mandates that teachers use strategies that have been shown to be effective. In addition to its emphasis on early reading programs, NCLB is noteworthy for its attention to the critical role that parents play in children's educational experiences. NCLB has dramatically affected educational practices, which now place a premium on students meeting standards of learning and assessment and on school-based management, teacher empowerment, and school choice (e.g., vouchers, magnet schools, charter schools, and privatization options).

The Individuals with Disabilities Education Improvement Act of 2004 (IDEIA), a reauthorization of IDEA (P.L. 94–142), continued the trend of promoting the adoption of effective interventions and placed a premium on primary prevention by altering substantially the screening and identification procedures for children with disabilities. Specifically, IDEIA permits school districts to use a process that determines if the child responds to scientific, research-based intervention as a part of the evaluation procedures used to assess functional capacity. This modified method can replace assessment using the discrepancy between ability and achievement to identify students with learning difficulties. This approach, referred to as Response to Intervention, has been applied to academic and behavioral supports in special and routine education. Batsche et al. (2005) defined Response to Intervention as the practice of (a) providing effective instruction and interventions based on students' needs and (b) regularly monitoring students' progress to guide decisions about changes in instruction or goals. The model suggests that more intensive interventions should be considered for individual students based on their response (or lack thereof) to less intensive, high-quality interventions.

In 2007, the U.S. Supreme Court struck down voluntary student assignment plans in Louisville, Kentucky, and Seattle, Washington, thereby continuing and extending the trend toward resegregation in public schools. In the 2007 case, *Parents Involved in Community Schools v. Seattle School District No. 1*, the petitioners contended that assigning students to schools solely to achieve racial balance in the schools was a violation of individuals' rights guaranteed under the 14th Amendment (e.g., Equal Protection Clause), as well as the Civil Rights Act of 1964. The Louisville and Seattle districts argued unsuccessfully that educational and social benefits such as socialization and good citizenship are derived from an educationally diverse learning environment and that because racial diversity was their primary interest, promoting that interest using race-conscious criteria alone was necessary and justified. Although the justices were sharply divided in a 5–4 vote, the Court's opinion allows districts to use race-conscious measures so long as such measures do not use race to treat individual students differently "solely on the basis of a systematic individual typing by race" (*Parents Involved in Community Schools v. Seattle School District No. 1*, 2007, p. 7). Even though the decision appears likely to result in increased educational resegregation, it does not overtly forbid school districts seeking diversity to pursue that goal by using race-conscious means.

Summary of Federal Policy

Public education in the United States has gone through a number of reform movements in the past century. From the end of World War I until the mid-1940s, education policy focused on equity and attempted to narrow or eliminate the achievement gap between advantaged and disadvantaged youth. From the 1950s to the 1970s, issues of equity dominated federal education policy. However, policies favoring equity in education were not without criticism during these years; many critics of equity policies believed intellectual and academic goals were being sacrificed for social ends. These attacks created fertile ground for alternative strategies to spring forth, such as the adoption of standards, curriculum reform, and accountability systems. Since the mid-1970s, most education policies and programs have been more closely aligned with conservative ideology, which focuses on improving education for all students rather than helping at risk children or youth with school adjustment or academic achievement problems.

Principles of Risk, Protection, and Resilience in Education Policy

Evidence exists to both support and criticize the effectiveness of the policies and programs discussed in the prior section. Next, we briefly evaluate the extent to which historic and current educational policies and programs have been based on principles of risk and resilience; we begin with those that are clearly within this framework.

Several policies illustrate the relationship between risk, protection, and educational approaches to change and reform. For example, Head Start, EHA/IDEA/IDEIA, and NCLB emphasize principles that are consistent with the models of risk and resilience discussed earlier in this chapter. Head Start targets youth who are at highest risk for academic failure because of low socioeconomic status. The program attempts to bolster school readiness skills, and this approach is consistent with evidence suggesting that the preschool years represent a critical developmental phase for prevention and early intervention services (Reid, 1993). Although IDEIA permits intervention with children before they enter school and targets children at risk of developing disabilities and school failure, most IDEIA funding is intended for children who are already identified as having a disability. In addition, NCLB attempts to raise awareness of the achievement gap and encourages school districts to address the gap by requiring states to report standard test scores disaggregated by poverty, race/ethnicity, disability, and English language proficiency. The recent NCLB emphasis on standards-based education sets high academic expectations for all students, and such expectations are an identified protective factor against school failure and drop out (Furlong & Morrison, 2000).

The emphasis on evidence-based prevention efforts highlighted in IDEIA is compatible with risk and protective factors. This emphasis should result in improvements to the learning environment, such as school connectedness, school climate, teacher expectations, family involvement, and community services to support students and families. Many of these improved environmental conditions have been high-lighted previously as key protective influences for children (Haberman, 2000; Hawkins et al., 1999).

Other policies appear to ignore principles of risk and resilience, at best, and undermine or contradict such principles at worst. Specifically, standards such as those promoted in NCLB have the potential to be counterproductive to children and youth who are not able to compete academically. Some experts have argued that standards-based policies may actually be contrary to principles of risk and resilience because those policies may lower teachers' expectations of students and subsequently have a negative impact on achievement (Nelson et al., 2004). In addition, zero-tolerance policies, particularly those that apply to minor infractions, have been shown to increase risk of poor outcomes among high-risk children, in general, and youth of color specifically (Skiba & Peterson, 1999).

In sum, the application of risk and protective factors to the design of educational policy is inconsistent. Some policies (e.g., the Compulsory School Attendance Act, the Head Start Act, EHA, and IDEIA), court cases (e.g., *Brown v. Board of Education*), and programs (e.g., Head Start and special education) support the constructs of risk and resilience. Other policies (e.g., NCLB and Gun-Free Schools Act) and court cases (e.g., *Plessey v. Ferguson* and *Milliken v. Bradley*) ignore or may even reject the constructs of risk and resilience. New and sustained efforts are needed to implement a risk and resilience framework in education policy.

Using Principles of Risk, Protection, and Resilience to Achieve Integrated Education Policy

Principles of risk, protection, and resilience can be applied to education policy in two fundamental ways. One option requires policymakers to focus efforts on youth who are most likely to experience school adjustment and achievement problems. Such a strategy tends to concentrate program and policy efforts on youth from disadvantaged backgrounds because socioeconomic status is a key risk factor for educational failure (Brooks-Gunn & Duncan, 1997). A second approach uses knowledge of risk, protection, and resilience to design promotive educational policies and programs that are beneficial for all children regardless of risk exposure. We begin our discussion with policy recommendations for programs that promote healthy outcomes for all children and youth.

Promotive Interventions and Strategies

We recommend educational policies and programs that promote social competence, develop caring relationships, and create high expectations for all students. Policies that promote participation in positive academic and social groups, enhance school bonding or connectedness, and create positive and safe learning environments should receive priority in national policy and program debates. Simply adopting effective promotion interventions and strategies is not sufficient to produce sustainable change. Specific promotion strategies include the following:

- Establishing positive behavioral and rigorous academic expectations for all students
- Making environmental arrangements and providing active supervision
- Applying consequences to encourage desired behavior and discourage undesirable behavior
- Developing school and community linkages
- Developing school and home linkages (Frey, Lingo, & Nelson, 2010)

Other programs designed to positively affect school culture, such as conflict resolution, peer mediation, and antibullying strategies, illustrate the growing emphasis on changing peer and institutional culture and are likely to have protective value. Recent research has demonstrated that many strategies and programs work for a short time, but then effects quickly fade; thus, there is a need to know more about the specific conditions and settings in which intervention effects can be sustained over time (Duncan, 2009). A report by the Center for Mental Health in Schools (2002) indicated that school-based reform efforts have been unsuccessful because projects and services designed to remove barriers to learning are usually viewed as supplementary services. This viewpoint has left policy experts interested in removing barriers largely absent from the decision-making table. The result may be seen in the fragmentation of services, marginalization of professionals, and overall inadequacies in policy reform. Service providers, including school social workers, school psychologists, speech language specialists, school nurses, and school counselors, must be trained to support the primary mission of schools. Furthermore, policies must be designed to enhance standards while promoting reasonable professional-to-student ratios for all schools and students.

A critically important element in effecting positive change in schools is the process of *enculturation,* or "the manner in which a school embeds a systems change process into its own unique culture, assumes 'ownership' of the process, and has the process become a part of business as usual at the school" (Sailor, Wolf, Choi, & Roger, 2009, p. 664). Policies and programs must also foster service cohesion by addressing the need for multiple interventions within schools in an integrated fashion. Walker and colleagues (1996) suggested that prevention efforts have generally lacked coordination and integration because no comprehensive strategic plan for coordinating and linking behavioral supports existed at the school or district level. Evidence from efficacious school-based practices also supports the need to attend to interactions among key individual and environmental factors. Over the past several decades, our knowledge of "what works" in school-based prevention programs has increased dramatically. For example, it is now clear that interventions are far more effective if they are integrated and coordinated with other interventions along a continuum of support representing primary, secondary, and tertiary levels of intervention (Dunlap, Sailor, Horner, & Sugai, 2009). Within this continuum, the promise of primary prevention is increasingly emphasized because it not only is efficient and effective but also increases the likelihood that the needs of students with elevated risk status will be targeted for intervention. We believe that targeted educational policies and programs should focus on schools that have high percentages of students living in poverty, and identification of and intervention with high-risk students should occur as early as possible. Examples of targeted policies and programs are reviewed next.

Targeted Interventions and Strategies

Redistribution of Tax Dollars to Support Schools in Low-Income Neighborhoods

The most obvious recommendation for using principles of risk and protection in targeted educational policy may involve school financing. Nearly 50% of school funding comes from local property taxes (Nelson et al., 2004). Therefore, adequately funding schools in low-income neighborhoods is an ongoing and persistent challenge to policy officials and school administrators. To address this problem, a larger percentage of school financing may need to come from state and federal taxes rather than from local tax bases. Equalizing the funding base between advantaged and disadvantaged communities is not likely to produce equal educational outcomes, given variations in individual, family, neighborhood, and community risk factors across schools and communities. Furthermore, providing more money to disadvantaged schools would require people in wealthy districts to partially fund poor districts, which is a practice that runs counter to the beliefs of many Americans. However, such a strategy may well be necessary to create positive change and promote effective policies based on principles of risk and protection.

Early Identification and Intervention at the Point of School Entry

Between 9.5% and 14.2% of children up to 5 years old experience social or emotional problems that adversely affect their functioning and development (e.g., school readiness skills), with children living in poverty more likely to experience these problems (Brauner & Stephens, 2006; Duncan, Brooks-Gunn, & Klebanov, 1994). Whether in preschool or early elementary school, the importance of early screening for risk factors that lead to poor educational outcomes cannot be overstated. Given the proper tools, it requires minimal effort for educators to predict—with great accuracy—which children will require extensive academic or behavioral supports. Systemwide screening, particularly for emotional and behavioral indicators leading to school failure, may be a cost-effective strategy to improve educational outcomes. Many experts argue that enhancing school readiness skills should be the primary focus of policy reforms (Nelson et al., 2004). We concur and recommend increased funding for intervention programs that target school readiness skills.

As noted, several federal programs, such as those promoted through Title IV and Title V funds, provide nonspecific funding to address a wide range of educational issues. Title I is consistent with the risk and protection framework because the primary criteria to access these funds are linked to students' socioeconomic status. However, there is no mandate requiring that interventions created with these funds address known risk and protective factors. In addition, there are no mandates requiring the funds, or a portion of the funds, to be used for evidence-based practices. Policymakers should address these gaps in funding mandates to ensure that funds are used for effective early intervention programs that have sustained effects. For example, early intervention programs that focus on family-risk factors are particularly promising; Duncan and Brooks-Gunn (2000) report that interventions targeting parenting practices can mediate up to half of the impact of poverty on child development.

The presence of high-quality primary prevention programs is increasingly being recognized as a prerequisite for intensive interventions (Greenberg, 2004; Scott, Anderson, Mancil, & Alter, 2009). In sum, a series of policy and system reforms is necessary to improve the condition of the country's schools. Principles of risk, protection, and resilience promotion offer a framework for thinking more systematically about a continuum of education policy defined by levels of service. Moreover, integration of policy and programs across other systems of care should be a part of such a continuum.

Targeted and Intensive Strategies to Integrate Education Policy

It is both exciting and challenging to envision integrating educational policies and programs across service domains such as child welfare, substance abuse, mental health, juvenile justice, developmental disabilities, and health. In many respects, the compartmentalized approach used to channel federal and state funding as well as the isolated educational training of professionals in each problem area runs counter to the vision of cohesive integrated services. Given the number of children involved in the educational system, the number of hours children spend in school, and the numbers of families and communities that can be linked by mobilized schools, we believe that the education system is an ideal context in which to identify children in need of services across many domains.

A Case for Integrated Service Delivery

Jeremy is a 14-year-old male who was physically and sexually abused as a young child. His mother was incarcerated when he was 6 years old, and her parental rights were terminated when Jeremy was 8 years old. He experienced six out-of-home placements before age 10, when he was finally placed in a stable foster care home with loving and supportive parents.

Jeremy has struggled socially and emotionally in school since kindergarten, but he was not identified for special education services under the severe emotionally disturbed (SED) category until his current foster parents advocated for an evaluation at age 11 years. He has done well in some settings, but he was suspended 13 times last year during his first year of middle school. Jeremy has been convicted twice for misdemeanor charges and is currently on probation.

He receives a variety of support services from a learning specialist and a school social worker at his middle school, a counselor at the local mental health agency, and a child protection caseworker. Jeremy reports to a probation officer regularly and sees a psychiatrist yearly for medication monitoring. These individuals have never met together, and many of the services provided to Jeremy are duplicated across settings.

Cross-system funding for education, health, and social services may be one means to achieve integrated policy. Cross-system funds could be used to

- provide early screening to identify children most at risk;
- promote school readiness skills for high-risk youth;
- deliver comprehensive services and case management to children who display signs of adjustment problems before the second grade;

- provide seamless access to and provision of educational, health, and social services through support service providers and family resource or youth service centers; and
- implement primary prevention programs at key developmental stages.

An integrated approach to service delivery would be very beneficial to youth such as Jeremy and his foster parents in several ways. First, if the services provided by his teacher, learning specialist, school social worker, counselor, caseworker, probation officer, and psychiatrist were monitored and coordinated, each provider would know what other services Jeremy was receiving and how he was functioning in other aspects of his life. Such an approach could reduce redundancy in service provision and likely would be more cost-effective. An integrated service delivery system would facilitate communication between professionals and allow each provider easy access to the information the other providers possess. Furthermore, an integrated approach would also produce one set of goals, one treatment plan, and one system to evaluate progress. In addition, an integrated strategy would likely make it easier for his foster parents to attend the requisite meetings associated with each service. Last, it is exciting to imagine the range and quality of services that could be put in place if the requisite departments of education, juvenile justice, and child welfare shared costs, problem ownership, and approaches for all the services directed toward complex cases such as Jeremy's. Most important, if an integrated approach had been in place to offer assessment and service delivery early in Jeremy's life, it is possible his early antisocial behavior and school failure would have raised warning flags that might have altered Jeremy's path to later destructive outcomes.

Summary

Education policy in the past century has vacillated among liberal, progressive, and conservative ideologies, which has led to inconsistent and constantly changing practices in schools. According to Anyon (1997), education policy continues to revolve "around the tensions between equity and excellence, between the social and intellectual functions of schooling, and over differing responses to the questions, 'Education in whose interests?' 'Education for whom?'" (p. 87). Policy directed at the nation's schools has lacked a guiding set of consistent principles. Principles of risk, protection, and resilience offer promise as a systematic method of designing and enhancing education policy and programs. Policymakers at all levels would do well to incorporate these principles into the nation's struggling educational system.

QUESTIONS FOR DISCUSSION

1. What are some of the major risk factors for school failure? Which of these risk factors should receive the most attention in educational policy and why?

2. What educational policies and programs over the past 100 years have best served the concept of risk and resilience? Why?

3. What factors inhibit the integration of policies and programs across problem domains?

4. What are some possible solutions to the barriers to the integration of policies and programs across problem domains?

References

Administration for Children and Families. (2007). *Head Start fact sheet.* Washington, DC: U.S. Department of Health and Human Services. Retrieved from http://www.acf.hhs.gov/programs/hsb/research/factsheets.htm

Anyon, J. (1997). *Ghetto schooling: A political economy of urban reform.* New York: Teachers College Press.

Apollonia, S., & Abrami, P. C. (1997). Student ratings: The validity of use. *American Psychologist, 52,* 1199–1208.

Arcia, E. (2006). Achievement and enrollment status of suspended students: Outcomes in a large, multicultural school district. *Education & Urban Society, 38,* 359–369.

Batsche, G. M., Elliott, J., Graden, J. L., Grimes, J., Kovaleski, J. F., & Prasse, D. (2005). *Response to intervention: Policy considerations and implementation.* Alexandria, VA: National Association of State Directors of Special Education.

Brauner, C. B., & Stephens, B. C (2006). Estimating the prevalence of early childhood serious emotional/behavioral disorder: Challenges and recommendations. *Public Health Reports, 121,* 303–310.

Brooks-Gunn, J., & Duncan, G. J. (1997). The effects of poverty on children. *Future of Children, 7,* 55–71.

Brown v. Board of Education of Topeka, 347 U.S. 483 (1954).

Carnahan, S. (1994). Preventing school failure and dropout. In R. J. Simeonsson (Ed.), *Risk, resilience, and prevention: Promoting the well-being of all children* (pp. 103–124). Baltimore: Paul H. Brooks.

Carpenter, D. M., & Ramirez, A. (2007). More than one gap: Dropout rate gaps between and among Black, Hispanic, and White students. *Journal of Advanced Academics, 19,* 32–64.

Cataldi, E. F., Laird, J., & Kewal-Ramani, A. (2009). *High school dropout and completion rates in the United States: 2007* (NCES 2009–064). Washington, DC: U.S. Department of Education, National Center for Education Statistics.

Cecelski, D. (1994). *Along freedom road.* Chapel Hill: University of North Carolina Press.

Center for Mental Health in Schools. (2002). *An introductory packet: About mental health in schools* (ERIC Document No. 463509).Los Angeles: University of California at Los Angeles. Retrieved from http://www.eric.ed.gov/ERICDocs/data/ericdocs2sql/content_storage_01/0000019b/80/19/f2/3a.pdf

Clark, K. (1965). *Dark ghetto: Dilemmas of social power.* New York: Harper & Row.

Coleman, J. S. (1966). *Equality of educational opportunity* (No. OE-38001). Washington, DC: National Center for Education Statistics.

Cook, G. (2005). Title I at 40. *American School Board Journal, 192,* 24–26.

Cremin, L. A. (1957). *The republic and the school: Horace Mann on the education of free men.* New York: Teachers College Press.

Derezinski, T. (2004). School attendance. In P. Allen-Meares (Ed.), *Social work services in schools* (4th ed., pp. 95–118). Boston: Allyn & Bacon.

Dewey, J. (1916). *Democracy and education.* New York: Macmillan.

Duncan, A. (2009, June 8). Plenary address. Paper presented at the Annual Institute of Education Sciences conference, Washington, DC.

Duncan, G. J., & Brooks-Gunn, J. (2000). Family poverty, welfare reform, and child development. *Child Development, 71,* 188–161. doi:10.1111/1467–8624.00133

Duncan, G. J., Brooks-Gunn, J., & Klebanov, P. K. (1994). Economic deprivation and early childhood development. *Child Development, 65,* 296–318. doi:10.2307/1131385

Dunlap, G., Sailor, W., Horner, H. F., & Sugai, G. (2009). Overview and history of positive behavior support. In W. Sailor, G. Dunlap, G. Sugai, & H. F. Horner (Eds.), *Handbook of positive behavior support: issues in clinical child psychology* (pp. 3–16). New York: Springer. doi:10.1007/978–0-387–09632–2_1

Finn, J. D., Fish, R. M., & Scott, L. A. (2008). Educational sequelae of high school misbehavior. *Journal of Educational Research, 101,* 259–274. doi:10.3200/JOER.101.5.259–274

Fraser, M. W., Kirby, L. D., & Smokowski, P. R. (2004). Risk and resilience in childhood. In M. W. Fraser (Ed.), *Risk and resiliency in childhood: An ecological perspective* (2nd ed, pp. 13–66). Washington, DC: NASW Press.

Fraser, M. W., & Terzian, M. A. (2005). Risk and resilience in child development: Practice principles and strategies. In G. P. Mallon & P. M. Hess (Eds.), *Handbook of children, youth, and family services: Practices, policies, and programs* (pp. 55–71). New York: Columbia University Press.

Frey, A. J., Lingo, A., & Nelson, C. M. (2010). Implementing positive behavior support in elementary schools. In M. R. Shinn & H. M. Walker (Eds.), *Interventions for achievement and behavior problems in a three-tier model including RTI* (pp. 397-434). Bethesda, MD: National Association of School Psychologists.

Furlong, M., & Morrison, G. (2000). The school in school violence. *Journal of Emotional & Behavioral Disorders, 8,* 71–82. doi:10.1177/106342660000800203

Greenberg, M. T. (2004).Current and future challenges in school-based prevention: The researcher perspective. *Prevention Science, 5,* 5–13. doi:10.1023/B:PREV .0000013976.84939.55

Greenberg, M. T., Domitrovich, C., & Bumbarger, B. (1999). *Preventing mental disorders in school-age children: A review of the effectiveness of prevention programs.* University Park: Pennsylvania State University, Prevention Research Center for the Promotion of Human Development.

Haberman, M. (2000). Urban schools: Day camps or custodial centers? *Phi Delta Kappan, 82*(3), 203–208.

Hawkins, J. D., Catalano, R. F., Kosterman, R., Abbott, R. D., & Hill, K. G. (1999). Preventing adolescent health-risk behaviors by strengthening protection during childhood. *Archives of Pediatrics & Adolescent Medicine, 153,* 226–234.

Jenson, J. M., & Howard, M. O. (1999). *Youth violence: Current research and recent practice innovations.* Washington, DC: NASW Press.

Kemp, S. (2006). Dropout policies and trends for students with and without disabilities. *Adolescence, 41,* 235–250.

Kohl, H. (1967). *36 children.* New York: New American Library.

Kozol, J. (1967). *Death at an early age: The deconstruction of the hearts and minds of Negro children in the Boston public schools.* Boston: Houghton Mifflin.

Love, J. M., Tarullo, L. B., Raikes, H., & Chazen-Cohen, R. (2006). Head Start: What do we know about its effectiveness? What do we need to know? In K. McCartney & D. Phillips (Eds.), *Blackwell handbook on early childhood development* (pp. 550–575). Malden, MA: Blackwell. doi:10.1002/9780470757703.ch27

Milliken v. Bradley, 418 U.S. 717 (1974).

National Center for Education Statistics. (2008). *Public elementary and secondary school universe survey.* Washington, DC: U.S. Department of Education.

National Commission on Excellence. (1983). *A nation at risk. The imperative for educational reform.* Washington, DC: Author. Retrieved from http://www2.ed.gov/ pubs/NatAtRisk/index.html

Nelson, J. L., Palonsky, S. B., & McCarthy, M. R. (2004). *Critical issues in education: Dialogues and dialectics* (5th ed.). Boston: McGraw-Hill.

Paige, R. (2002). An overview of America's education agenda. *Phi Delta Kappan, 83*(9), 708–713.

Parents Involved in Community Schools v. Seattle School District No. 1, 127 U.S. 2738 (2007).

Patterson, J. A., Hale, D., & Stessman, M. (2007). Cultural contradictions and school leaving: A case study of an urban high school. *High School Journal, 91,* 1–15. doi:10.1353/hsj.2008.0001

Patterson, G. R., Reid, J., & Dishion, T. J. (1992). *Antisocial boys*. Eugene, OR: Castalia Press.

Plessey v. Ferguson, 163 U.S. 537 (1896).

Ravitch, D. (1983). *The troubled crusade: An American education, 1945–1980*. New York: Basic Books.

Reid, J. B. (1993). Prevention of conduct disorder before and after school entry: Relating interventions to developmental findings. *Development and Psychopathology, 5*, 243–262. doi:10.1017/S0954579400004375

Ripple, R. P. (1994). Intergenerational education: Breaking the downward achievement spiral of teen mothers. *Clearing House, 67*, 143–147.

Rosenfeld, G. (1971). *"Shut those thick lips!" A study of slum school failure*. New York: Holt, Rinehart, & Winston.

Sadovnik, A. R., Cookson, P. W., & Semel, S. F. (2001). *Exploring education: Introduction to the foundations to education*. Needham Heights, MA: Allyn & Bacon.

Sailor, W., Wolf, N., Choi, H., & Roger, B., (2009). Sustaining positive behavior support in a context of comprehensive school reform. In W. Sailor, G. Dunlap, G. Sugai, & R. Horner (Eds.), *Handbook of positive behavior support: Issues in clinical child psychology* (pp. 633–670). New York: Springer. doi:10.1007/978-0-387-09632-2_26

Sameroff, A. J., & Gutman, L. M. (2004). Contributions of risk research to the design of successful interventions. In P. Allen-Meares & M. W. Fraser (Eds.), *Intervention with children and adolescents: An interdisciplinary perspective* (pp. 9–26). Boston: Allyn & Bacon.

Scott, T. M., Anderson, C. M., Mancil, R., & Alter, P. (2009). Function-based supports for individual students in school settings. In W. Sailor, G. Dunlap, G. Sugai & H. F. Horner (Eds.), *Handbook of positive behavior support: Issues in clinical child psychology* (pp. 421–441). New York: Springer. doi:10.1007/978-0-387-09632-2_18

Skiba, R. (2002). Special education and school discipline: A precarious balance. *Behavioral Disorders, 27*, 81–97.

Skiba, R., Michael, R. S., Nardo, A.C., & Peterson, R. (2000). *The color of discipline: sources of racial and gender disproportionality in school punishment*. Retrieved December 13, 2009, from http://www.indiana.edu/~safeschl/cod.pdf

Skiba, R., & Peterson, R. (1999). The dark side of zero tolerance: Can punishment lead to safe schools? (ERIC Document No.ED 456 546). *Phi Delta Kappan, 80*, 381–382.

South, S. J., Haynie, D.L., & Bose, S. (2007). Student mobility and school drop out. *Social Science Research, 36*, 68–94. doi:10.1016/j.ssresearch.2005.10.001

Substance Abuse and Mental Health Services Administration. (2008). *National household survey on drug abuse: Main findings*. Washington, DC: U.S. Department of Health and Human Services.

Sweeten, G. (2006). Who will graduate? Disruption of high school education by arrest and court involvement. *Justice Quarterly, 23,* 462–480.

U.S. Census Bureau. (2008). *Current population survey (CPS).* Washington, DC: Author.

Walker, H., Horner, R. H., Sugai, G., Bullis, M., Sprague, J. R., Bricker, D., & Kaufman, M. J. (1996). Integrated approaches to preventing antisocial behavior patterns among school-age children and youth. *Journal of Emotional & Behavioral Disorders, 4,* 193–256. doi:10.1177/106342669600400401

Additional Reading

Fraser, M. W., Kirby, L. D., & Smokowski, P. R. (2004). Risk and resilience in childhood. In M. W. Fraser (Ed.), *Risk and resiliency in childhood: An ecological perspective* (2nd ed., pp. 13–66.). Washington, DC: NASW Press.

Nelson, J. L., Palonsky, S. B., & McCarthy, M. R. (2004). *Critical issues in education: Dialogues and dialectics* (5th ed.). Boston: McGraw-Hill.

Sadovnik, A. R., Cookson, P. W., & Semel, S. F. (2001). *Exploring education: Introduction to the foundations to education.* Needham Heights, MA: Allyn & Bacon.

Sailor, W., Dunlap, G., Sugai, G, & Horner, R. (2009). *Handbook of positive behavior support.* New York: Springer. doi:10.1007/978-0-387-09632-2

Sprague, J. R., & Walker, H. (2000). Early identification and intervention for youth with antisocial and violent behavior. *Exceptional Children, 66,* 367–379.

Walker, H., & Shinn, M. K. (2010). *Interventions for achievement and behavior problems: Preventive and remedial approaches* (Vol. 3). Bethesda, MD: National Association of School Psychologists.

Web-Based Resources

Education Policy Institute, http://www.educationalpolicy.org/

Education Policy and Leadership Center, http://www.eplc.org/about_description.html

Center on Education Policy, http://www.cep-dc.org/

Education Commission of the States, http://www.ecs.org/

5

Child Mental Health Policy

Promise Without Fulfillment?

Mary E. Fraser

Children and their families are our nation's most valuable and perhaps most endangered resource. Today's children and families face unprecedented challenges, including exposure to persistent poverty, alcohol and other drugs, and violence. It is no wonder that one of every five children and adolescents in the United States has a diagnosable emotional or behavioral disorder that can lead to school failure, alcohol or other drug use, violent conduct, or suicide (Burns et al., 1995; Costello, Mustillo, Erkanli, Keeler, & Angold, 2003). The increasing prevalence of emotional and behavioral disorders is becoming a major public health concern in this country.

According to the Surgeon General's (1999) report on mental health, at least 1 in 10 young people, or as many as 6 million youth, meet the criteria for serious emotional disturbances (SED). Children and adolescents with SED are so ill that their symptoms often disrupt their social, academic, and emotional functioning. Many are in out-of-home placements or are at risk for such placement. Although many youth with SED have multiple social and health problems that lead to referral or involvement in the mental health, special education, child welfare, and juvenile justice systems (Brendenberg, Freidman, & Silver, 1990), only 59% of children with mental health needs receive any type of formal mental health care (Commonwealth Fund, 2006)

The 7-year National Adolescent and Child Treatment Study identified a number of risk factors that are common among youth with SED. Researchers leading the investigation found that youth with SED had poorer social skills, lower academic achievement, less financial independence, and more limited interpersonal relationships than youth without SED (Greenbaum et al., 1996). In addition, the study showed that youth with SED were more involved in substance abuse and illegal activity than youth with no SED symptoms.

The Greenbaum et al. (1996) findings were consistent with those from the National Longitudinal Transitional Study of special education students with SED. In this investigation, Davis and Vander Stoep (1997) found that young people with SED—compared to either youth with other disabilities or the general population—were more likely to drop out of school, to be arrested, and to have less competitive employment. Indeed, as compared with a 6% arrest rate for all students, 20% of students with SED are arrested at least once before they leave school, and that number jumps to nearly 50% within 5 years of leaving school (U.S. Department of Education, 1994).

Without comprehensive policies and interventions that diminish risk and strengthen protection for youth with SED, the adult outcomes for these at-risk youth can be expected to be poor. This forecast is supported by a body of literature on risk factors associated with emotional and behavioral problems in childhood as well as a growing body of evidence on protective factors that mitigate the effects of these problems. Because children with SED are found in all public child-serving agencies, public policies that promote cross-agency, integrated approaches to providing effective risk and protection interventions are needed.

This chapter reviews the literature on risk and protective factors related to emotional and behavioral disorders in children and adolescents and summarizes the complex evolution of child mental health policy in the United States. Two case examples of state policies that were designed to improve and integrate services for youth with SED are described. Finally, suggestions are made for future policies that combine the risk and resilience perspective with integrated service structures.

Prevalence of Child Mental Health Disorders

A defining feature of the mental health field is the use of a system of classification that relies on diagnostic categories linked to service strategies, both psychosocial and pharmacological. One of the primary classification sources used in the United States is the *Diagnostic and Statistical Manual of Mental Disorders* (*DSM*), published by the American Psychiatric Association (2000). This manual is currently in its fourth edition (*DSM-IV-TR*), and a fifth edition is under review and scheduled for publication in May 2013. Table 5.1 displays the most common *DSM-IV-TR* diagnoses found in youth ages 9 to 17 years old. The first column shows national prevalence rates for each diagnosis, and the second column shows the diagnostic prevalence rates for each disorder within the subgroup of youth who have SED.

Table 5.1   Diagnostic Prevalence Rates for Children 9 to 17 Years Olds

Diagnosis	U.S. Population[a]	SED Population[ab]
Anxiety Phobias, separation anxiety disorder, generalized anxiety disorder, obsessive-compulsive disorder, posttraumatic stress disorder	8–10%	41%
Depression Major depressive disorder, dysthymia	6%	19%
Disruptive disorders Conduct disorder Oppositional defiant disorder	4–10%	67%
Attention deficit hyperactivity disorder (ADHD)	5%	12%
Childhood schizophrenia	0.3%	-
Eating disorders Bulimia nervosa Anorexia nervosa	1–3% 0.5–1%	

a. Friedman, Katz-Levey, Manderschied, and Sondheimer (1996).

b. Greenbaum et al. (1996).

Anxiety is the most common mental health problem found in childhood and adolescence (Costello et al., 1996). Anxiety manifests in a variety of forms, including phobias, separation anxiety disorders, generalized anxiety disorders, and obsessive-compulsive disorders. *Phobias* are unreasonable fears. One of the most common phobias among children and adolescents is social anxiety disorder, which is characterized by an unremitting fear of embarrassment in social and performance situations that sometimes leads to full-blown panic attacks. Children and adolescents with this disorder tend to avoid social situations and try to avoid going to school.

Separation anxiety disorder occurs in about 4% of children and young adolescents and is characterized by irrational fears that parents will be killed or taken away, which may lead to clinging behavior, difficulty falling asleep at night, and inability to participate in school and social events away from home. The disorder can last for many years and can be a precursor to panic disorder and agoraphobia experienced as an adult.

Generalized anxiety disorder is characterized by excessive and persistent worry. Children and adolescents with this anxiety disorder tend to be perfectionists and insecure.

Obsessive-compulsive disorder is characterized by recurrent, time-consuming, obsessive, or compulsive behaviors that cause distress or impairment. The obsessions may be intrusive images, thoughts, or impulses. Compulsive behaviors, such as hand washing and other cleaning rituals, are considered to be attempts to displace obsessive thoughts. Prevalence estimates range from less than 1% in children to as high as 2% in adolescents (Surgeon General, 1999).

Posttraumatic stress disorder (PTSD) is a prolonged, pathologic anxiety that occurs in both adults and adolescents following a severe trauma. The onset of PTSD in adolescence is common and may impair the acquisition of life skills needed for independent, self-sufficient living. PTSD is common among youth who have been victims of physical or sexual abuse and who have witnessed violence in their homes or neighborhoods.

Depression in children and adolescents usually presents in two different forms. A diagnosis of *major depressive disorder* requires either a depressed, irritable mood or a diminished interest or pleasure in activities. Accompanying symptoms must include some combination of significant weight change, either gain or loss; sleep disturbance; loss of energy or feelings of extreme fatigue; psychomotor agitation or retardation; feelings of worthlessness or inappropriate guilt; diminished ability to think or concentrate; and recurrent thoughts of death. These symptoms must be present for at least 2 weeks and produce significant functional impairment. Diagnostic criteria for *dysthymia* also require a depressed or irritable mood that has continued for a period longer than 1 year and requires many of the same accompanying symptoms as major depression. Although the description of dysthymia appears similar to that of major depressive disorder, the symptoms of major depressive disorder are more debilitating than those of dysthymia. However, dysthymia tends to be chronic, more persistent, and longer lasting than major depressive disorder.

A disruptive disorder, *conduct disorder,* is based on a repetitive and persistent pattern of behavior in which the basic rights of others or the major age-appropriate social norms or rules are violated. Characteristic behaviors of conduct disorder include aggression toward persons or animals, destruction of property, deceitfulness, or theft. Girls with a conduct disorder are prone to early sexual activity and homelessness. About 40% of youth with a conduct disorder develop an antisocial personality disorder and become involved in the criminal justice system. Those with an early onset of conduct disorder have a worse prognosis and are at higher risk for adult antisocial disorder. Conduct disorder frequently co-occurs with attention deficit and hyperactivity disorder.

Oppositional defiant disorder (ODD) is typically characterized by problem behaviors such as persistent arguing, habitual fighting, and frequent loss of temper. Children and adolescents with this disorder frequently test limits, deliberately refuse to comply with adult requests, and intentionally annoy others. These behaviors lead to difficulties with family members, peers, and teachers. ODD is sometimes a precursor of conduct disorder.

As implied by the name, *attention deficit and hyperactivity disorder* (ADHD) is made up of two distinct sets of symptoms. Although these two problems often co-occur, one set of symptoms can be present without the other. Children with attention deficit disorder have difficulty paying attention and are easily distracted. These children are often disorganized, and they have difficulty following through with tasks. The symptoms of hyperactivity include the compulsion to move that may be expressed as fidgeting, squirming, or wriggling around when seated or getting up and moving around the room. Children with ADHD often perform poorly at school and have difficulties with peer relationships. Hyperactive behavior is often associated with the development of conduct and oppositional defiant disorders.

Eating disorders, such as anorexia nervosa and bulimia nervosa, are potentially life-threatening conditions, with 10% of cases ending in death (Steiner & Lock, 1998). The prevalence of eating disorders is a particular concern because these disorders are among the most common chronic illnesses of adolescent girls, following obesity and asthma (Lucas, Beard, O'Fallon, & Kurland, 1991; Stice & Agras, 1998). Anorexia nervosa is characterized by a distorted body image that triggers an intense fear of gaining weight. The symptoms of bulimia nervosa include recurrent episodes of binge eating and purging.

Although rare, *childhood schizophrenia* is a serious illness. Children with schizophrenia may experience auditory and visual hallucinations and feel detached from the real world. It is sometimes difficult to distinguish between childhood schizophrenia and autism. Onset of adult schizophrenia usually occurs between puberty and young adulthood. Children with an earlier onset of schizophrenia generally experience symptoms that are longer lasting and more severe (American Psychiatric Association, 2000).

In this chapter, the terms *serious emotional and behavioral disorders* and *SED* are used interchangeably. Although not diagnostically specific, either term may include any or several of the diagnostic categories listed earlier. However, readers should note that simply having a diagnosis of one of these disorders does not mean that a child is seriously emotionally disturbed or impaired. Moreover, it is important to recognize that the different diagnostic categories relate to different risks and intervention strategies. For example, children with eating disorders differ markedly from those with conduct disorders. Thus, child mental health policies must address a wide range of behaviors and conditions that are differentially categorized by diagnostic labels and terms such as SED.

A Risk, Protection, and Resilience Perspective on Mental Health Disorders

Allen-Meares and Fraser (2004) outlined a set of empirically supported principles to describe the concepts of risk, protection, and resilience. These principles inform our discussion of mental health disorders and child mental health policy. Allen-Meares and Fraser argued that (a) identifiable risk and protective factors exist for social and mental health problems in childhood; (b) cumulative risk is generally more predictive of developmental outcomes than any single risk factor; (c) some risk factors are more responsive than others to change strategies; (d) reduction of risk can produce improved outcomes; and (e) more salutary outcomes occur when risk factors are reduced and protective factors are increased. In addition, Allen-Meares and Fraser noted important differences between protective and promotive factors. Protective factors reduce, suppress, and buffer risk but are neutral (i.e., have no effect) in the absence of risk. In contrast, promotive factors, which are the opposite of risk factors, operate actively to promote positive developmental outcomes for all youths. Universal prevention strategies focus on promotive factors, whereas targeted interventions strengthen protective factors to reduce known risks. We apply these definitions to the discussion that follows.

Most serious childhood emotional disorders are considered to be biosocial in nature. Although children endure countless negative life experiences, most children are naturally resilient. That is, when faced with adversity, children tend to make self-righting adaptations. However, such adaptations do not happen in isolation. Resilience results from the nexus of individual effort and environmental conditions that facilitate adaptations. Most people share the viewpoint that mental health problems emerge in children and adolescents when there is a biological vulnerability combined with exposure to adverse environmental factors (Surgeon General, 1999). The principles of risk and resilience can be used to better understand not only which biological and environmental factors might predict serious emotional and behavioral disorders in children and adolescents but also which children should be targeted for prevention and early intervention efforts. A touch point for this chapter, these principles can also be used to determine which protective factors should be bolstered to promote resilience.

Risk Factors

Biological risk. Shown in Table 5.2, biological risk factors can occur at either the individual or family level. Common examples of biological risk factors include genetics, chemical imbalances, and damage to the central nervous system through trauma or prenatal exposure to alcohol and drugs. Researchers have established clear genetic links to some conditions, including ADHD, mood and anxiety disorders, and childhood schizophrenia (Goodman & Stevenson, 1989; Jellinek & Synder, 1998; Maziade & Raymond, 1995; Rutter, Silberg, O'Conner, & Simonoff, 1999). Although the genetic mechanism of many disorders remains unclear, having a parent, sibling, or even a grandparent with a mental health problem increases a person's odds for developing a mental disorder.

Gender is correlated with diagnosis of certain emotional and behavioral disorders in children. For instance, girls are at greater risk than boys for internalizing mental health problems such as depression, anxiety, and suicide (Spirito et al., 1993). By age 15 years, girls are twice as likely to be depressed as boys (Nolen-Hoeksema & Girgus, 1994). Girls are also more likely than boys to be diagnosed with an eating disorder (Rogers, Resnick, Mitchel, & Blum, 1997), whereas boys are more likely than girls to be diagnosed with a conduct disorder and ADHD (Piquero & Chung, 2001; Robins, 1991; Ross & Ross, 1982).

Once a child is diagnosed with one disorder, the risk of having additional mental problems and co-morbid disorders is increased. Children and youth with a history of psychiatric disorder have been found to be three times more likely to have a subsequent diagnosis of psychiatric disorder. It is not unusual to see a progression from one diagnosis to another, such as from a diagnosis of depression to a diagnosis of anxiety and from a diagnosis of anxiety back to a diagnosis of depression. Similarly, a common diagnosis pattern might start with ADHD and move to ODD, or start with a diagnosis of anxiety and conduct disorder and expand to include a diagnosis of substance abuse. Sequential diagnosis may be more common among girls (Costello et al., 2003).

Evidence supports that a child's difficult early temperament is related to emotional and behavioral problems later in life. Agitated and tearful infants have been found to show symptoms of anxiety by the age of 4 years (Kagan, Snidman, & Arcus, 1998). Connections between difficult infant temperaments and conduct disorder have also been observed (Olds et al., 1998).

Environmental Risk

A child's social environment is an equal—or possibly more important—determinant of later mental health problems than constitutionally based factors (Sameroff & Gutman, 2004). Bronfenbrenner's (1979) ecological model of child and adolescent development stressed the importance of contextual factors, including families, communities, and social institutions. Youth at high risk for serious emotional disorders are more likely to be raised in environments that heighten the effects of biological vulnerability (Resnick & Burt, 1996). Some of the more common environmental risks that exacerbate vulnerability include poverty, dysfunctional family, exposure to violence, and parental psychopathology or criminality.

Poverty is often associated with mental health problems in children and adolescents. Children with SED have been found to be overrepresented in low-income families (Mark & Buck, 2006). Werner and Smith (1992) found that low parental income was the single greatest predictor of emotional disturbances in youth under 18 years of age. Although African American and Latino youth have also been found to be overrepresented in SED samples (Mark & Buck), the factor of race/ethnicity, once thought to be a strong predictor of certain emotional and behavioral problems, loses its strength when adjusted for income (Neal, Lilly, & Zakis, 1993; Peeples & Loeber, 1994; Robins, 1991; Siegel, Aneshensel, Taub, Cantwell, & Driscoll, 1998). Moreover, early childhood poverty has been shown to have an association with depression, antisocial behavior, adolescent anxiety, and adolescent hyperactivity (McLeod & Shanahan, 1996; Pagani, Boulerice, Tremblay, & Vitaro, 1997).

Poverty is also associated with increased violence and substance abuse (Rutter, 1985; Spearly & Lauderdale, 1983). The Children's Defense Fund (1995) has estimated that each year between 3 million and 10 million children are witnesses to domestic violence. Witnessing violent acts can have long-term deleterious effects on children (Jenkins & Bell, 1997).

Exposure to substantial incidents of violence can impair a child's capacity for emotional regulation (Gerrity & Folcarelli, 2008). In turn, a child's problems with controlling his or her anger and modulating mood can seriously complicate the child's ability to perform in school and to develop healthy peer relations (Fairbank, Putnam, & Harris, 2007). Child abuse and neglect can negatively affect both neurological and psychosocial development, including the formation of personal morals and values, the capacity for relationships, the development of respect for social institutions and mores, and the ability to comply with rules of social conduct (Putnam, 2006). Although the risk process is not well understood, the experience of physical and sexual abuse increases a child's risk for major depressive and anxiety disorders (Dykman et al., 1997; Flisher et al., 1997; Silverman, Reinherz, & Giaconia, 1996), conduct disorders (Livingston,

Table 5.2   Risk Factors for Child and Adolescent Mental Health Disorders

Individual Level	Familial Level	Extrafamilial Level
Genetic vulnerability to a mental health disorder	Low socioeconomic status	Frequent violence
Victim of physical or sexual abuse	Multiple moves	High stress
Poor self-esteem	Parental substance abuse	Rejection by peers
Difficult temperament	Parental mental illness	Social isolation
Chronic childhood illness or developmental delay	Poor maternal bonding and attachment	
Race/ethnicity	Poor parenting skills	
Previous diagnosis of a mental health disorder	Four or more siblings in the home	
Gender Girls: depression, anxiety, eating disorders Boys: conduct disorder	Parental criminality	

Lawson, & Jones, 1993), ADHD (Wolfe, Sas, & Wekerle, 1994), and eating disorders (Douzinas, Fornari, Goodman, Sitnick, & Packman, 1994).

Trauma exposure is widespread. For example, a longitudinal study of children living in a primarily rural area in North Carolina found that by age 16 years, more than 67% of the children reported exposure to at least one traumatic event (Copeland, Keeler, Angold, & Costello, 2007). Those events included child maltreatment or domestic violence, a major medical trauma, traffic injury, traumatic loss of a significant other, or sexual assault (Copeland et al., 2007). Although the role trauma exposure plays in the development of various disorders is not clear, experiencing trauma appears to affect emotional regulation and the processing of social information.

Similarly, poor social and economic conditions have been correlated with family pathology, child abuse, and poor parental supervision. However, the causal pathway is uncertain. It may be that poverty itself does not cause poor mental health outcomes in children and adolescents. Instead, living in poverty may produce poor child mental health outcomes because the parental experience of financial strain and economic loss diminishes some parents' capacity to provide involved and supportive parenting (Linver, Fuligni, Hernandez, & Brooks-Gunn, 2004; Oyserman, 2004).

Dysfunctional parenting—rejection, neglect, maltreatment, and inability to provide appropriate structure and supervision—is associated with increased risk of emotional and behavioral disorders in children and adolescents (Johnson, Cohen, Kasen, Smailes, & Brook, 2001; Resnick & Burt, 1996). In one review, Loeber and Stouthamer-Loeber (1996) noted that poor parental supervision and lack of parental involvement were among the strongest correlates of conduct disorder in children. Other research has linked harsh, abusive, and inconsistent discipline patterns to serious conduct problems in children (Lahey et al., 1995; Robins, 1991; Shaw, Gillion, Ingoldsby, & Nagin, 2003). In stressed or large families, parental attention can be in short supply and may be unduly focused on negative behaviors. Because such behaviors garner much-desired parental attention, the negative and aggressive behaviors are reinforced, which may lead to patterns of antisocial behaviors (Surgeon General, 1999).

In addition, a number of studies have linked poor family management and emotional climate to depression in children. As compared with families raising children who are not depressed, families of children with depression tend to be less emotionally expressive, more hostile, more critical, and less accepting. Families with depressed children also have family structures that are less cohesive, more disorganized, and more conflictual in nature than families without depressed children (Gilbert, 2004).

Parents who are depressed themselves find it hard to provide consistent discipline, supervision, and emotionally positive interactions with their children (Zahn-Waxler, Iannotti, Cummings, & Denham, 1990). Children and adolescents of parents with depression have been found to be at increased risk for anxiety disorders, conduct disorders, and alcohol dependence (Wickramaratne & Weissman, 1998). Not surprisingly, parental mental illness itself is associated with poor parenting ability (Oyserman, Mowbray, Allen-Meares, & Firminger, 2000).

Negative life events have also been associated with poor emotional and behavioral outcomes in children and adolescents (Gerrity & Folcarelli, 2008; Goodyer, 1990; Kessler, 1997; Tiet et al., 2001). Examples of negative life events include multiple moves; loss of a parent through death, divorce, or out-of-home placement; physical assault; exposure to violent acts; and injury.

In a 1999 review of the mental health research literature, the U.S. Surgeon General noted that exposure to emotional abuse and physical violence disrupted the normal development of children and adolescents and had profound effects on mental, physical, and emotional health. The review found that children's exposure to abuse and violence were associated with characteristics such as insecure attachment; impaired social functioning with peers; and psychiatric disorders such as PTSD, ADHD, conduct disorder, and depression (Surgeon General, 1999). When compared with peers who did not experience adverse events in childhood, people who experienced four or more categories of child-hood adverse events (e.g., having witnessed violence, having a parent who abused alcohol or drugs, or having lived in poverty) had a 4- to 12-fold increased risk for alcoholism, drug abuse, depression, and suicide attempts (Felitti et al., 1998).

Certain groups of disorders are more closely associated with negative life events than are others. In addition, the effect of negative life events also appears to differ by gender. For example, depression is associated with loss and grief, particularly in girls (Breier et al., 1988; Goodyer, 2001; Moore, Rohde, Seeley, & Lewinsohn, 1999). The earlier a child experiences the loss of a parent or caretaker, the more severe the outcome. Being a victim of a crime, a violent act, or an assault is strongly associated with PTSD and conduct disorder in both girls and boys (Famularo, Kinscherff, & Fenton, 1992); however, the association between being a victim of crime, violence, or assault and the occurrence of ODD is particularly strong among girls (Tiet et al., 2001). Among boys, a parent being arrested and jailed is strongly associated with conduct disorder and dysthymia, whereas the effect of parental arrest for girls is more often seen in cases of conduct disorder and overanxious disorder.

In sum, a number of risk factors are associated with emotional and behavioral disorders in children and adolescents. These risk factors can be grouped at the individual, familial, and extrafamilial levels. The level of individual risk appears to be related to the number of risk factors a child has in various domains (Fergusson, Horwood, & Lynsky, 1994; Rutter, 1979). Moreover, cumulative risk appears to be more important than any single risk factor (Sameroff & Gutman, 2004).

Indeed, it is estimated that nearly half of children entering kindergarten have at least one risk factor (Zill & West, 2001). Similarly, the Adverse Childhood Experiences Study, which was conducted in a primary-care setting, found that more than 50% of respondents had experienced at least one type of adverse experience in childhood, and 25% reported more than two types (Felitti et al., 1998). Moreover, increased exposure to adverse experiences in childhood is related to a greater likelihood of developing a variety of behavioral, health, and mental health problems, including smoking, multiple sexual partners, heart disease, cancer, lung disease, liver disease, sexually transmitted diseases, substance abuse, depression, and suicide attempts (Lu, Mueser, Rosenberg, & Jankowski, 2008). Table 5.2 summarizes risk factors for mental health disorders at the individual, familial, and extrafamilial levels.

Protective Factors

Protective factors reduce risk. Indeed, the impact of risk factors on children's outcomes can be moderated by protective factors. Furthermore, just as a greater number of risk factors are associated with increased risk, resilience can be a function of the number of protective and promotive factors present in a child or adolescent's life (Sameroff, Bartko, Baldwin, Baldwin, & Seifer, 1999). Garmezy (1993) identified three broad sets of variables that have potential to operate as protective factors. These variables include (a) child characteristics, such as easy temperament, cognitive skills, and social skills; (b) family characteristics, such families that are marked by warmth, cohesion, and structure; and (c) the social characteristic of having a support system available. Shown in Table 5.3, social-adaptive behavior is an important protective factor that is related to most emotional and behavioral disorders.

According to the NACT longitudinal study of youth with SED, risk can be mitigated with adaptive social behavior, such as interpersonal relationship skills or coping skills (Armstrong, Dedrick, & Greenbaum, 2003). Good communication skills have also been found to be protective against hospital readmissions among children with SED (Greenbaum et al., 1996).

Life history reports of adolescents treated for mental health problems indicate that young people who had positive life outcomes tended to have

Table 5.3   Protective Factors Against Child and Adolescent Mental Health Disorders

Individual Level	Familial Level	Extrafamilial Level
Good social skills	Parental monitoring	Presence of nurturing/caring adults
Academic achievement	Good communication and cohesion	Opportunities and support for achievement
Easy-going temperament; good problem-solving skills		

had more stable living situations, better family relationships, and more positive relationships with peers. In addition, children who seemed to prevail over adversities were more goal-oriented and experienced more successes and fewer stresses (McConaughy & Wadsworth, 2000). Findings from studies sponsored by the World Health Organization have suggested that adversities such as the long-term disability associated with childhood schizophrenia can be minimized through supportive relationships with family or community members (Hopper & Wanderling, 2000). Thus, just as poor parenting practices are risk factors for many antisocial behaviors (Loeber, Farrington, Stouthamer-Loeber, & Van Kammen, 1998), warm, supportive family relationships and parental monitoring appear to function as protective factors for both boys and girls (Fraser, 2004; Green, 1995; Santilli & Beilenson, 1992). Table 5.3 shows protective factors for mental health disorders summarized at the individual, familial, and extrafamilial levels.

History of Child Mental Health Policy in the United States

Whereas risk and protection are relatively new concepts, the concept of childhood mental illness has a history dating to the late 19th century. The first discussion in a textbook of psychological problems in children was Maudsley's chapter on "The Insanity of Early Life" in 1867 (Hergenhahn,

2001; Parry-Jones, 1989). However, the prevailing thought was that people could not "go mad" until they had reached adulthood. Children and adolescents who exhibited serious emotional or behavioral symptoms were hospitalized or imprisoned alongside adults. A public system devoted solely to child mental health did not emerge for another 100 years.

Precursors of Mental Health Policy

The earliest public mental health efforts on behalf of children were a result of changes that came about at the turn of the 20th century in approaches to handling "wayward" youth. Public policy in juvenile justice was changing from an approach that focused on punitive measures to an approach that sought corrective measures. The nation's first juvenile court was established in Chicago in 1899. In 1909, several members of the Hull House Association board became impressed with the new juvenile courts and created the Juvenile Psychopathic Institute to study the problems of juvenile offenders. The institute's first director, William Healy, M.D., was a pioneer in the field and applied emerging psychiatric theory related to children and adolescents to individualize treatment of juvenile offenders. Growing from Healy's influence, juvenile court clinics developed across the country, providing the first publicly funded community mental health services to troubled youth. Even though mental health theory and practice provided a foundation for much of the evolving juvenile justice and child welfare policies, no formal child mental health policy had yet been developed (Jones, 1999).

During the 1920s, juvenile court clinics began serving more than just children with antisocial problems, and they became attached to a variety of new structures such as charities, universities, and teaching hospitals. Referred to as child guidance clinics, their major areas of concentration became school and home problems. Child guidance clinics primarily served children and adolescents with internalizing problems, and the clinicians used Freudian and Ericksonian developmental theories in addressing those problems.

The federal government first became involved in child mental health policy in the 1930s through the advocacy of the federal Children's Bureau, which supported the development of a child mental health field and advocated for the expansion of child guidance clinics. Child guidance clinics became the major source of mental health care for children and youth until the 1970s.

World War II brought an unexpected focus to the mental health needs of children. Because of the huge military draft, life histories were available for hundreds of thousands of young soldiers from varied backgrounds and socioeconomic levels. By the end of the war, it was apparent that soldiers who had behavior problems as children were much more likely to be prematurely discharged, disciplined, wounded, or killed (Schowalter, 2003). The country learned that mental illness is blind to both color and income and that the outcomes of mental health problems are costly to both individuals and society.

Community Mental Health Centers

In 1963, President John F. Kennedy signed the Mental Retardation Facilities and Community Mental Health Center Act, which changed the face of mental health care nationally. Focused primarily on adults with mental illness, the law established funding for community mental health centers. These centers were designed to provide mental health services in community rather than in hospital settings. Similar to the child guidance movement that had preceded it, the Community Mental Health Center Act provided mental health services to only a small percentage of children with SED. The act did not mandate that affordable mental health services be provided to all children in need (Lourie & Hernandez, 2003), and little, if any attention was afforded to prevention or early intervention.

However, advocacy efforts on behalf of children and youth with emotional problems continued to grow, which eventually led Congress to establish the Joint Commission on Mental Health of Children. In its 1969 report, the commission found that millions of children and youth were not receiving the mental health services they needed. Moreover, many of those receiving care were served in inappropriately restrictive settings such as state psychiatric hospitals. In 1975, Congress acted to require community mental health centers to serve children and adolescents.

Despite the congressional mandate to provide mental health services to children and adolescents, community mental health centers were slow to respond. A report issued by the President's Commission on Mental Health (1978) strongly criticized community mental health centers for their failure to address the needs of children and youth with serious emotional and behavioral problems. President Jimmy Carter's Mental Health Commission also noted that few communities were providing either the number or the continuum of services needed. Therefore, the commission recommended that a community-based network of integrated services be developed to meet the needs of seriously emotionally disturbed children and adolescents.

Although similar recommendations had been voiced throughout the 1970s, it was not until the 1982 publication of Jane Knitzer's widely read book, *Unclaimed Children,* that Congress mobilized to take action. Knitzer boldly stated that of 3 million children and adolescents with SED in the United States, 2 million did not receive the services they needed. Furthermore, Knitzer reported that at least 40% of hospital placements for children were in inappropriately restrictive settings, including facilities for people with mental retardation and adult psychiatric hospital wards. She observed that most states had no specific policies for children with SED and noted that millions of "unclaimed" children were adrift in the public health, mental health, education, juvenile justice, and child welfare systems, and these children were not receiving appropriate mental health services (Knitzer, 1982).

Systems of Care

Knitzer (1982) documented a lack of services; poor coordination among service agencies; overuse of residential and institutional care; and failure of the federal, state, and local governments to respond to the crisis. In suggesting ways to improve these conditions, she coined the term *system of care* to describe a new approach to mental health. In 1984, Congress appropriated funds to the National Institute of Mental Health (NIMH) to establish a national agenda to deal with the problems outlined by Knitzer. In response, NIMH created the Child and Adolescent Service System Program (CASSP).

Following the example of the innovative Community Support Program for adults with serious and persistent mental illness, CASSP focused on the needs of children with SED by providing financial incentives to states to develop systems of care to serve these children. The CASSP initiative was the first federal mental health program to clearly identify youth with SED as its target population. CASSP created a movement and momentum for change. It became the vehicle for the development and articulation of federal and state child mental health policy.

The CASSP program was based on the following four assumptions:

1. Children and adolescents with serious emotional disorders are found in all of the nation's public health, mental health, education, juvenile justice, and child welfare systems.

2. Most children and adolescents with serious problems are served in more than one of these agencies at the same time.

3. Regardless of the agencies with which children are affiliated, the mental health needs of children have been overlooked and have not been addressed appropriately.

4. Few states have planning mechanisms to identify children and adolescents who are served across multiple systems.

The policy imperative in the CASSP initiative was to develop a multi-agency approach to the delivery of mental health services.

In a widely circulated monograph, Stroul and Friedman (1986) defined Knitzer's concept of a system of care (SOC) as "a comprehensive spectrum of mental health and other necessary services, which are organized into a coordinated network to meet the multiple and changing needs of children and adolescents with severe emotional disturbances and their families" (p. iv). These authors stated that an SOC should be a community-based, child-centered, family-focused, and culturally competent approach to integrating services. The multiple needs of each child and family should be met by providing a full range of services, including mental health, substance abuse, health, social, educational, and vocational services, with case management providing the mechanism to guide the family toward the appropriate mix and timing of services. Figure 5.1 illustrates a model SOC for mental health service delivery.

The ideal SOC includes enough flexibility to allow services to be tailored to the specific needs of the child and family involved, regardless of which agency has overall responsibility for the child or which system provided the services. For example, a child or adolescent with an SED might have psychological needs that require intervention by a mental health center, special education needs filled by the school system, and residential needs for a structured living environment provided by a social services agency.

Stroul and Friedman's (1986) outline of an SOC was used as the blueprint by the CASSP program for organizing child mental health services across the country. To receive federal funding, states were expected to create a protocol for interagency cooperation that would effectively coordinate all child-serving agencies and services. Coordination and cooperative development were to start at the state level and then be replicated at the local level. States were urged to develop strategies and methods for pooling financial resources among agencies so that all needed

Figure 5.1   A System of Care Framework for Children and Adolescents

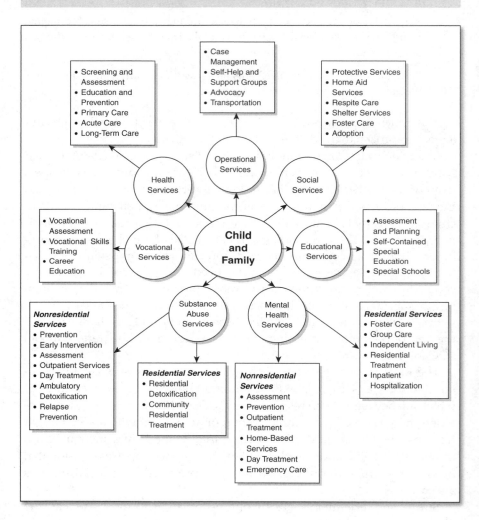

services could be provided, regardless of the child's service eligibility or insurance coverage. By the fall of 1990, all 50 states and the District of Columbia had received CASSP grants. By 1995, all states had at least one state-level, full-time, child mental health specialist working to develop a statewide system of care (Davis, Yelton, Katz-Leavy, & Lourie, 1995).

Systems of Care and Mental Health Policy

The policy of creating SOCs to serve the mental health needs of the nation's youth was formally endorsed in 1992 when Congress passed the Children's and Community Mental Health Services Improvement Act. (See Table 5.4 on page 171 for a listing of federal mental health policy initiatives.) This act created a program called the Comprehensive Community Mental Health Services for Children and Their Families. Administered by the Center for Mental Health Services in the Substance Abuse and Mental Health Administration (SAMHSA), this program provided grants to states to expand the SOC concept. To date, this program is the largest federal initiative supporting the development of children's mental health services.

By the close of the 20th century, at least half of the states had enacted laws requiring some sort of SOC (Davis, Yelton, & Katz-Leavy, 1995). The Children's and Community Mental Health Services Improvement Act provided nearly $460 million in federal funding to 67 local SOCs that served more than 40,000 children across the country (Center for Mental Health Services, 1999). Now, many years after their initial authorization, SOCs continue to be the primary policy approach to governing public mental health systems. Congress continues to provide annual funding through a competitive grant structure to states wishing to enhance their SOCs. The major principles underlying this approach remain intact.

Service Integration Within a System of Care

A growing body of literature has described the overall characteristics of children with SED and their families (Epstein, Cullinan, Quinn, & Cumblad, 1995; Quinn & Epstein, 1998; Wagner, Kutash, Duchnowski, Epstein, & Sumi, 2005). Most of these studies report that children with SED have a number of common risk factors, including inadequate social skills, poor academic performance, family violence, alcohol and drug use, and mental illness. Despite these commonalities, there is no single system of mental health care for these youth. In fact, more youth with SED are found in other service systems than are treated within the child mental health system. For example, up to 80% of all children entering the juvenile justice system have mental health disorders (President's New Freedom Commission on Mental Health, 2003), and researchers have estimated that 20% of incarcerated youth have SED, which is double the rate of SED found in the general population (Mears & Aron, 2003). Nearly 20% of children with SED are involved in the child welfare system; a staggering 70% of youth with SED receive mental health services from local school systems (Burns et al., 1995).

It is clear that children in these separate systems need appropriate mental health care that is tailored to meet their individual needs. Over the past 20 years, mental health leaders, policymakers, and service providers have been struggling with how to best integrate mental health services into these systems. The most common state-level integration approaches involve coordinating mental health, child welfare, and juvenile justice services using one of the following three structures:

1. Separate agencies are maintained as individual departments. In this model, coordination of services is accomplished through formal interagency planning structures.

2. A part or all of the three agencies (mental health, child welfare, and juvenile justice) are housed within a single umbrella department such as a department of human services. Each division maintains its own staff, policy development process, and budget. Coordination is facilitated because each agency reports to a single department director, and departmental rules and procedures that might inhibit service integration can be changed without legislative intervention.

3. The three agencies are combined into a single departmental agency, with a single agency budget and policy-making body.

A quick review of these three options might lead a person to conclude that combining all child services into a single agency would be the most advantageous option. However, such an arrangement has costs as well as benefits. Single, integrated agencies tend to be quite large, making management time-consuming, cumbersome, and often inefficient. Turf issues remain problematic. In addition, many child advocates object to the fact that the allocation of funds across different child populations would occur within a single budget process that might not be open to the public for review and comment.

States have found that restructuring alone does not overcome turf issues, policy conflicts, leadership challenges, and inadequate or disproportionate funding. Arguably the most important elements of successful service integration are agreeing on a common target population and blending funding streams so that an appropriate set of individually tailored services can be provided. Which agency provides the actual services may not be as important as having an arrangement in place so that services are provided to children who need them, regardless of the child's custody status or the family's financial ability to pay for services.

Systems of Care Implementation Evaluations

On the clinical level, integrated SOCs appear to produce positive developmental outcomes for children and adolescents involved in them. The Comprehensive Community Mental Health Services for Children and Their Families program is evaluated annually by SAMHSA. Findings from these evaluations have been detailed in "short reports," provided on the SAMHSA website (SAMHSA, 2009). These evaluations have used parent and teacher reports of youth behavior as well as youth self-reports from model SOCs. The findings have indicated that youth served in these SOCs demonstrate positive benefits as compared with their pre-enrollment behavior, including fewer emotional and behavioral problems, improved school performance, and less likelihood of engaging in harmful behaviors.

Despite the positive outcomes of model SOCs, and notwithstanding the large level of federal and private foundation support allocated to states, SOCs have proven difficult to implement. The model requires many systems-level alterations, including developing links among child-serving agencies, creating a continuum of community-based services, blending funding streams, developing interagency policy, and organizing treatment teams to coordinate care.

The Center for Mental Health Services conducted reviews of SOC implementation in 1995 and 2002. Researchers from both reviews found substantial changes had occurred in each funded site. Indeed, changes in policies and procedures had been made that facilitated cross-agency training, programming, and co-location of services. The researchers also found changes that enhanced interagency communication and collaboration. Even so, no site had implemented all the aspects required of a comprehensive SOC model. (Stroul, 2006; Vinson, Brannan, Baughman, Wilce, & Gawron, 2001).

A number of interagency coordination issues emerged as significant barriers in the SOC approach. Sometimes called "turf problems," these issues revolved around poor interagency collaboration, which was attributable to factors such as a lack of trust, a sense of competition, a fear of sharing resources, and a lack of understanding regarding the partner agencies' mandates and capacities. In addition to these turf problems, the greatest barrier to full-scale change was likely the sheer amount of time required to develop meaningful collaborations (Behar, 2003).

At the state level, many states have also struggled to sustain and expand their SOC approach after the federal funding period (Stroul & Manteuffel, 2007). Few states are able to support child mental health services with state dollars that are not also attached to federal Medicaid funds. The Medicaid program was created in 1965 as a health care financing program; it is governed by federal rules and jointly managed by federal and state authorities. Medicaid pays for about 50% of all mental health services provided to poor children and adolescents (Kenny, Oliver, & Poppe, 2002). Thus, policies flowing from federal and state Medicaid offices are as influential on state child mental health delivery systems as the federal policy initiatives that come through NIMH or the Center for Mental Health Services.

Unfortunately, state spending limits for Medicaid and expansion initiatives for mental health services are frequently in conflict. Although federal Medicaid policies have become more flexible over the past years, most state policies on Medicaid spending have become increasingly restrictive. Because Medicaid spending has been the highest growth factor in most states' budgets, state-level Medicaid policies are frequently focused on cost containment, especially in times of economic downturn or recession. In turn, the state mental health departments try to stretch their limited funds by matching state appropriations to federal Medicaid funds. In addition, the Medicaid program has inherent limitations and barriers related to supporting SOC structures.

The Fort Bragg Study

During the early 1990s, the Department of Defense and NIMH funded a major research study to test the impact of developing comprehensive and coordinated continuums of care for youth with SED at Fort Bragg, North Carolina. The demonstration program sought to fill the service gap between outpatient therapy and inpatient hospitalization by providing non-clinic-based services such as in-home crisis stabilization, afterschool group treatment, therapeutic foster care, and crisis management.

The Fort Bragg study demonstrated substantial system improvements, including increased service capacity, enhanced collaboration among service agencies, and reduced use of hospitals and residential treatment facilities. However, the demonstration program did not produce significant clinical outcomes with regard to alleviation of symptoms, increased functioning, or reduction of impairments (Bickman et al., 1995). The findings of the Fort Bragg project were in line with the evaluation results of the Robert Wood Johnson Foundation Mental Health Services Program for Youth program, which examined the development of SOCs in eight communities over a 10-year period (Cross & Saxe, 1997; Johnsen, Morrissey, & Calloway, 1996).

These disappointing findings caused ongoing debate in the child mental health field. Some researchers have advocated for a change in policy emphasis from system development to service effectiveness (Salzer & Bickman, 1997), whereas others continued to support large systems reforms (Hernandez & Hodges, 2003). Recent policy discourse has suggested requiring simultaneous system reform and the delivery of evidence-based interventions (Burns, 2001; Rosenblatt & Woodbridge, 2003). Although the risk and resilience framework for targeting interventions is not yet widely used within the mental health field, many policy leaders and advocates are focusing attention on identifying and using evidence-based practices that will provide cost-effective client-level improvements.

Evidence-Based Care and Mental Health Policy

In 1998, the American Psychological Association (APA) convened a special task force to systematically evaluate the evidence base (i.e., the available evidence from empirical research using rigorous scientific methods) for treating individual disorders in children and adolescents (Chambless & Ollendick, 2001). In its report, the APA Task Force determined two levels of criteria against which to evaluate the evidence base of particular interventions. The first, more rigorous criterion was "well established," and the other, less rigorous, was "probably efficacious." The major distinction between the two criteria is the strength of the supporting evidence. A *well-established treatment* is one that has been shown to be superior to either a placebo or another treatment, whereas a *probably efficacious treatment* needs to be shown only as superior to the outcomes of either a waiting list condition or a no-treatment control group. Evidence of the effectiveness of well-established treatments must be supported by at least two separate research teams. Using these criteria, Lonigan, Elbert, and Johnson (1998) conducted a review of psychosocial interventions for children and adolescents and found that most did not meet the first level of empirical support. In the years since the Lonigan et al. review, several more well-established treatments have been shown to be effective for children and adolescents with diagnoses of anxiety, ADHD, autism, bipolar disorder, conduct disorder/ODD, phobia, or depression. These treatments include behavioral parent training and classroom behavior modification for ADHD and parent training, functional family therapy, and multisystemic therapy for conduct disorder and ODD. In addition, graduated exposure, participant modeling, and reinforced practice were found to be well-established interventions for children and adolescents with phobias.

A number of other treatments, including those based on cognitive-behavioral therapy, have been identified. Cognitive-behavioral techniques have been shown to be effective with ADHD; depression; anxiety disorders, including PTSD; conduct disorders; and phobias. In addition, several skills-training interventions appear to be effective for children with major depression and conduct disorders. Other promising interventions include (a) school-based contingency management for children with ADHD and conduct disorders (Brestan & Eyberg, 1998; Pelham, Wheeler, & Chronis, 1998); (b) classroom-based social skills training for conduct problems, which is delivered in combination with parent training and systematic communication with teachers (Fraser, Day, Galinsky, Hodges, & Smokowski, 2004; Reid, Eddy, Fetrow, & Stoolmiller, 1999); and classroom-based social skills training for elementary school-aged children with depression (Gillam, Reivick, Joaycox, & Seligman, 1995).

Many of the interventions commonly used in the child mental health system either have not been tested in controlled research investigations or have not met the scientific rigor necessary for inclusion in the APA Task Force Report. Examples of this lack of scientific rigor include studies assessing the effects of partial hospitalization, day treatment, case management, and home-based services (Surgeon General, 1999).

Unfortunately, no single resource exists for the increasingly long list of evidence-based interventions. SAMHSA developed the National Registry of Evidenced-Based Programs and Practices (available at http://nrepp .samhs.gov). Several professional and advocacy organizations have also created listings of evidence-based services for children and youth. Several of these resources are listed at the end of this chapter.

Given all of the policy rhetoric, it is surprising that no national legislation has yet been drafted to support evidence-based practices. However, many states are beginning to enact legislative language that requires the use of empirically supported interventions in child mental health SOCs. In this context, state mental health statutes often include the requirement to create interagency SOCs, within which evidence-based services are provided to children with SED and their families.

Table 5.4   Major Federal Mental Health Policy Initiatives

Policy	Date	Impact
Mental Retardation Facilities and Community Mental Health Center Construction Act (P.L. 88-164)	1963	Established funding to build and staff community mental health centers
Community Mental Health Center Act Amendments of 1965 (P.L. 91-211)	1965	Grants provided to support the development of mental health services in low-income areas. Included a new program of grants to support further development of children's services. Extended grant eligibility to centers serving those with alcohol and substance abuse problems.
Social Security Amendments of 1965	1965	Provided funding for medically necessary services to low-income families, pregnant women, and persons who are aged, blind, and disabled. Coverage of most mental health services was optional to states.
Education of All Handicapped Children Act (P. L. 94–162)	1974	Required that schools provide mental health services to children with serious emotional disturbances (SED) as part of their Individual Education Plan (IEP)
Community Mental Health Center Act Amendment (P.L. 94-63)	1975	Required community mental health centers to provide mental health services to children and adolescents
Mental Health Systems Act (P.L. 96-398),	1980	Based on recommendations of President's Commission on Mental Health and designed to improve services for people with severe, persistent mental disorders

(Continued)

Table 5.4 (Continued)

Policy	Date	Impact
Omnibus Budget Reconciliation Act (OBRA; P.L. 97-35)	1981	Repealed the Mental Health Systems Act and consolidated social services funding into a single block grant that allows each state to determine spending of its funds. Act required that 10% of mental health block grant funds be spent on children and adolescents. Federal role becomes providing technical assistance to improve state and local providers of mental health services.
Alcohol, Drug, and Mental Health Administration (ADAMHA) Appropriations Act	1984	Directed the National Institute of Mental Health (NIMH) to provide incentive grants to states to develop state and local-level child mental health structures to coordinate care to children with SED and their families. NIMH created the Child and Adolescent Service System Program (CASSP)
Children's and Community Mental Health Services Improvement Act	1992	Created the Comprehensive Community Mental Health Services for Children and Their Families Program within the Center for Mental Health Services, which provided funding to states to develop systems of care for children with SED
Surgeon General's Reports	2000	Called for increased research on and use of evidence-based mental health practices
President's New Freedom Commission Report on Mental Health and the Federal Action Agenda	2003–2005	Called for a transformation of the mental health system, recommending a public health approach that emphasizes mental health promotion, early identification, and treatment

Risk, Protection, and Resilience Framework and Mental Health Policy

The risk, protection, and resilience perspective provides a promising new framework in which to develop new mental health policies as it offers a valuable cross-problem, multidisciplinary approach for individually tailored interventions within an integrated SOC. Although it is not yet used widely within the mental health field, there are several good examples of its potential benefit. The Ventura County System of Care and the *Willie M. Program* will be described here as case examples. The *Willie M. Program*, which grew out of a class action lawsuit, provides a good example of using the risk and resilience framework to individualize care. The Ventura County System of Care was enacted by state statute and required its county agencies to work together. Ventura County's success in providing integrated services to SED youth led to statewide legislation supporting SOCs and has opened the door for multi-agency prevention and early intervention approaches targeted at children and youth at risk for mental health problems.

Program and Case Example

The Willie M. Program

The *Willie M. Program* grew out of a class action lawsuit (*Willie M. et al. v. James B. Hunt, Jr. et al.*, 1980) filed against the State of North Carolina on behalf of children with serious emotional disorders (SED) and aggressive behavior who were institutionalized because of inadequate community-based care. Seeing the negotiations to settle the lawsuit as an opportunity to improve the service structure, administrators in the North Carolina Division of Mental Health, Developmental Disabilities, and Substance Abuse Services (MH/DD/SAS) created a comprehensive continuum of community-based care for high-risk and hard-to-manage children and adolescents with SED.

To be represented and served under the class action suit, youths had to meet criteria as a class member: be younger than 18 years old; have a serious emotional, mental, or neurological disorder; have a history of violent or chronically aggressive behavior; have been placed in public custody, such as institutions,

(Continued)

(Continued)

or be at risk of such placement; or have been denied access to needed treatment or educational services. Although many youths met the criteria, four youths were ultimately named as plaintiffs in the litigation. Willie M., the first of four plaintiffs, was an 11-year-old boy diagnosed as emotionally disturbed with unsocialized aggression.

The North Carolina Department of Human Services avoided a trial by agreeing to the court's complaints and demands. Each member of the class was guaranteed individualized treatment in the least restrictive setting possible. The treatment was to be based on the child's needs rather than the availability of service providers to provide a service or set of services. If needed services did not exist, such services were to be created.

Leaders within the Division of MH/DD/SAS welcomed the challenge and advocated for the development of local systems of care (SOCs) within which they could create and provide services to class members. The *Willie M. Program* became among the first model SOCs in the country, serving as many as 1,500 severely aggressive youth with SED a year; two thirds of them lived in specialized foster care or group homes. The SOC required cooperative arrangements among the multiple agencies serving these youth. Court officers monitored the interagency relationships, making sure that public education, child welfare, and juvenile justice personnel worked in concert with the Division of MH/DD/SAS on behalf of these children. Comprehensive case management, also called *wraparound case management,* was the primary tool used to tailor services to the individual needs of members of the class action lawsuit. Each class member was required to have an individual habilitation plan. Beginning in 1995, the individual habilitation plan was based on an assessment process that reviewed both risk and protective factors.

An Assessment and Outcomes Instrument (AOI) was created to assess and to measure the progress of children in the *Willie M. Program.* The instrument used a risk and protective factor perspective and measured both fixed characteristics (i.e., factors that could not be changed through intervention, such as the loss of a parent) and dynamic characteristics (i.e., factors that were malleable in treatment, such as school performance). Risk factors included family-level characteristics (e.g., living in poverty; parental loss; parental mental health and substance abuse problems, parental criminality, and large family size) and individual-level characteristics (e.g., fetal substance exposure, neurologic or developmental disorders, poor mother-infant attachment, difficult or shy early temperament, witness to violent acts, and history of physical and sexual abuse, school failure, and delinquent behavior). Of the possible 30 risk factors assessed by the AOI, each of the *Willie M.* class members had experienced an average of 13 risk factors—a number that far exceeds most definitions of a high-risk youth (e.g., Rutter, 1979). Consistent with the literature on risk and conduct disorders, most *Willie M.* class members with poor behavioral outcomes had histories of negative parent–child interactions and poor academic performance. Better behavioral outcomes were predicted by protective factors such as having good skills in areas such as problem solving, interpersonal relationships, and reading; having social support networks available, including involvement with family members and prosocial peers; and having a parent who was consistently employed (Vance, Bowen, Fernandez, & Thompson, 2002).

Each member's individual rehabilitation plan specified interventions that were likely to result in positive behavioral changes. Because most risk factors associated with *Willie M.* class members were fixed historical experiences and family features that were not amenable to change, few options were available that would reduce the impact of those risk factors on current behaviors. However, evaluations of the *Willie M. Program* found that strengthening protective factors was directly associated with improved behavioral outcomes (Bowen & Flora, 2002; Vance et al., 2002). Depending on individual needs, protective factors such as reading skills, relationships with adults, social skills, positive beliefs and attitudes, and involvement in community activities were strengthened through a variety of targeted interventions. In addition, parental and caretaker positive discipline skills were strengthened. The protective factors that were found to be strongly associated with behavioral improvement included increased levels of home and school social skills. Interventions targeting these factors included teaching skills in anger management, empathy development, and making and keeping friends (Bowen & Flora, 2002). Because of these positive behavioral changes, youth served in the *Willie M. Program* attended school more often and had fewer arrests. Class member and family satisfaction with services was high. As an individualized SOC was successfully developed, the *Willie M.* class action lawsuit was resolved in 2000.

The *Willie M. Program* in North Carolina was both successful and expensive. The court demanded the provision of needed services, regardless of cost. Many state legislators resented this open-checkbook approach. As costs went up for class members' services, appropriations to other parts of the mental health system declined or were not increased accordingly. Once the class action lawsuit was resolved and its mandates removed, funding for the *Willie M. Program* was reduced and realigned within the Division of MH/DD/SAS.

Ventura County System of Care

In 1985, the California State Legislature passed a landmark bill (AB 3920) authorizing a demonstration program to integrate mental health services across a core group of service systems, including child welfare, public education, and juvenile justice. The legislation provided for creation of a comprehensive, coordinated system of care (SOC) and facilitated interagency cooperation by integrating numerous federal and state statutes that addressed public mental health services for children and by amending various statutes and regulations. Ventura County was selected as one of three demonstration sites under Assembly Bill 3920. As part of the demonstration program, all child-serving agencies in Ventura County were required to engage in interagency planning and to develop interagency protocols and agreements that emphasized providing services to children in their homes or in the least-restrictive setting.

The Ventura County System of Care had five interdependent components as outlined in the enabling legislation: (a) a clearly defined target population, (b) a systemwide goal to preserve family unity and locally based treatment, (c) a commitment to developing collaborative programs of services and standards tailored to individual needs of children and their families, (d) a continuum of service options and settings that cross agency boundaries, and (e) a mechanism for system evaluation.

Client outcomes for the Ventura County System of Care reflected a cross-agency perspective. The overarching goal was for children with serious emotional disturbances to remain or to be reunified with their families, to attend and progress in public schools, and—as appropriate—to desist from problem behavior such as delinquency and drug use. A cross-agency target population experiencing serious emotional disturbance (SED) was identified, including populations within each agency that had been mandated for services. The target population included emotionally or behaviorally disordered youth, such as (a) court dependents whose histories included neglect, physical or sexual abuse, multiple foster home placements, residential treatment, and psychiatric hospitalization; (b) court wards for whom the public sector had legal responsibility because of delinquent behavior and who were at risk of out-of-home placement; (c) special education pupils who required mental health services to benefit from their Individual Education Plans; and (d) children who were not part of a formal agency other than mental health and who were at risk of out-of-home placement to state hospitals or residential treatment.

Mental health treatment was integrated into the service systems of the other major child-serving public agencies. The county mental health department was given responsibility for serving the mental health needs of the targeted children involved in the public school, child welfare, and juvenile justice systems. Mental health staff located their services in places where targeted children lived and went to school, a step that required reorganization of the Department of Mental Health. Most of the mental health staff was deployed to agency and school settings to provide or supervise mental health services in those settings. Depending on the needs of the agency, mental health staff provided consultation, assessments, case management, counseling, day treatment, special day classes, in-home care, family therapy, enriched foster-home care services, or crisis intervention.

The state legislation that created the demonstration project also facilitated the blending of categorical funds so that each agency domain was enabled to determine the array of mental health services it needed. Specific roles and relationships between agencies were delineated in interagency agreements and facilitated by a number of interagency coordinating mechanisms. An interagency juvenile justice council became the policy-making body of the county system. This policy-making body was created to serve as a vehicle for identifying problems, developing interagency solutions, and working through agency conflicts. The council's permanent members included the county counselor, public defender, district attorney, sheriff, chief administrative officer of the juvenile court, director of probation, a member of the board of supervisors, the superintendent of schools, the director of the Department of Child Welfare, and the director of the Department of Mental Health. Still in operation today, the council reviews all agency budgets and looks for ways to mingle and coordinate funding streams.

The Ventura County demonstration project met the system-level performance outcomes required by the statute. By integrating mental health services into each system, more children were served—especially children from ethnic minority backgrounds—and fewer youth required placement in restrictive and costly state hospitals or residential treatment centers. The project netted a substantial savings to the state. The demonstration program was expanded to more counties in 1989. In 1992, the California State Legislature enacted the Children's Mental Health Services Act, which expanded the SOC model to all counties. In 2001, the legislature enacted a law requiring an agency-integrated SOC statewide (Stortz, 2003).

(Continued)

(Continued)

California can be a beacon for other states. Its formal adoption of SOC principles and policies in statute has provided fiscal incentives for many local county collaborations. The state's shift to the rehabilitative option for federal Medicaid billing has allowed clinical staff to work outside of their offices and support field-based, in-home, and wraparound service delivery models. A state match to the federal EPSDT (Early and Periodic Screening, Detection, and Treatment) program has provided an important fiscal engine to expand and sustain services and supports to children and youth 0 to 21 years old. Most recently, the California Mental Health Services Act (Proposition 63), enacted in 2007, has provided additional and ongoing state funds to further transform the mental health system in California with increased funding for mental health promotion, prevention, and early intervention services to children and adolescents statewide (Hodges, Ferreira, Israel, & Mazza, 2007).

Criticisms of Child Mental Health Policies

Child mental health policies in the United States have been widely criticized over the past 50 years. The mental health services and programs resulting from these policies have been described as fragmented, spotty, nontargeted, and generally ineffective (Joint Commission on the Mental Health of Children, 1969; Knitzer, 1982; Lourie & Hernandez, 2003; President's Commission on Mental Health, 1978). In response to this criticism, Congress supported the creation of SOCs to coordinate and enhance mental health care to youth with SED. Private funding sources, such as the Robert Wood Johnson and Annie E. Casey foundations, also contributed millions of dollars to develop model SOCs across the country. Unfortunately, the evaluations of many of these model programs have produced only mixed results.

Although supportive of the SOC concept, child mental health advocacy groups such as the Federation of Families for Children's Mental Health and the Child and Adolescent Network (a branch of the National Alliance for the Mentally Ill) remain frustrated by and critical of the slow process of implementation. These advocacy groups have not seen policy rhetoric translated into significant changes at the child or family level.

These criticisms were echoed in both the Surgeon General's (2000) *National Action Agenda* and the report of the President's New Freedom Commission on Mental Health (2003). The Surgeon General (2000) stated that despite the existence of mental health programs in many communities, the nation lacked a basic infrastructure for adequate mental health care, and that "unmet need for services remains as high today as it was 20 years ago" (p. 13).

Two years after the Surgeon General's report, President Bush signed Executive Order 13263 establishing the President's New Freedom Commission on Mental Health. The executive order charged the commission with the responsibility of conducting a comprehensive study of the problems and gaps in the nation's mental health service system. In his cover letter to the President's New Freedom Commission on Mental Health (2003) final report, Michael Hogan, chair of the Commission, wrote,

> Today's mental health care system is a patchwork relic—the result of disjointed reforms and policies. Instead of ready access to quality care, the system presents barriers that all too often add to the burden of mental illnesses for individuals, their families, and our communities. (p. 1)

Transformation of the Mental Health System

As a way to address these gaps and fundamentally transform how mental health care is delivered in America, the New Freedom Commission on Mental Health's report recommended a public health model of mental health care that would support mental health promotion and early intervention efforts, as well as direct treatment services. SAMSHA followed up on the commission's report by creating a Federal Mental Health Action Agenda and inviting key federal agencies to help propose a set of action steps to address the commission's vision and to move its agenda forward (SAMSHA, 2005). The key federal agencies contributing to this agenda of action steps included the departments of Education, Housing and Urban Development, Justice, Labor, and Veterans' Affairs, all the divisions within the Department of Health and Human Services, and the Social Security Administration.

In 2009, Kathryn Power, director of the Center for Mental Health Services, reported that the federal government was committed to the transformation of the mental health system. It appears that "transformation of the mental health system" is fast becoming the 21st century's de facto policy on child mental health. However, it remains unclear how this policy will evolve.

Summary

In 2008, the National Center for Children in Poverty published a study as a 25-year follow-up to Jane Knitzer's heralded report, *Unclaimed Children: The Failure of Public Responsibility to Children in Need of Mental Health Services*. In the intervening years, although there has been an explosion of knowledge about the biological and social determinants of children's mental health issues, new understanding about how children and their problems develop, and new ways of providing preventive and treatment services, the report found that state policies and the SOCs in place for most troubled children and youth appear all too similar to those criticized 25 years earlier (Cooper et al., 2008).

This is not to say that there has been no change. The vast majority of states were found to have taken tangible steps to improve their mental health delivery systems for children. However, a closer analysis revealed that those changes, while promising, are often limited in scope and depth. Although nearly all 50 states report that they have incorporated SOC values and principles into their delivery systems, only 18 states have taken steps to sustain these efforts through legislation and regulation, practice standards, and strategic planning. Too few resources were expended for states to develop a workable, comprehensive policy framework for addressing the needs of children and youth with serious mental health conditions. Even fewer resources have been committed by states to implement service systems and approaches grounded in the public health framework of mental health prevention, promotion, and early intervention (Cooper et al., 2008).

Much can be learned, however, from the Ventura County System of Care and the Willie M. Program case examples provided in this chapter. In addition, lessons about the effectiveness of mental health policies and programs can be derived from many other state and local efforts on behalf of children and adolescents with mental health problems. Based these examples and evidence provided in this chapter, at least four core strategies for policy reform in child mental health should be considered:

1. Structures should be developed to integrate mental health services into key child-serving agencies, such as public education, child welfare, and juvenile justice.

2. Systematic assessment should identify malleable risk and protective factors.

3. Evidence-based interventions should be selected and provided to reduce risk and strengthen protective factors.

4. Services should be developmentally and culturally appropriate and sequenced sufficiently early in childhood to disrupt negative developmental trajectories.

We know that most mental health disorders occur at the same rate in young children as they do in older children and adolescents (Kenny, Oliver, & Poppe, 2002). It is unfortunate that these disorders are not usually diagnosed and treated until youth are older. State legislatures spend millions of dollars annually treating older youth with serious emotional and behavioral disorders. Too often, these funds are expended in the juvenile justice and child welfare systems, which begs the question, "Are these efforts too little, too late?" Increasingly, many experts think this is the case.

In many communities, mental health services are now being integrated into public schools through programs such as school-based health clinics. These clinics improve access to primary health care and provide a less stigmatized entry into mental health services for many youth (Wu, Katic, Liu, Fan, & Fuller, 2010). School-based health clinics provide preventive and early intervention screenings for many health conditions that inhibit learning. Regular screenings for emotional and behavioral problems can also be incorporated into clinic services.

For these reasons, schools may be the best public setting in which to identify troubled children and to link them with appropriate services. More than 52 million youth attend U.S. public schools (President's New Freedom Commission on Mental Health, 2003). The integration of mental health and public school policies has the potential to save public money and private heartache by positioning resources to detect and treat mental health problems before they become florid disorders.

The good news is that some federal policymakers are taking notice and have proposed legislation that emphasizes mental health promotion and risk prevention in school settings. For instance, in 2007 Senators Christoper J. Dodd, Pete Domenici, and Edward M. Kennedy proposed legislation that would fund local education agencies to expand school mental health efforts through community–family–school partnerships. Two other recent Senate bills reflect growing federal support for school-based mental health services: House of Representatives Bill 3003, the School-Based Health Clinic Establishment Act of 2009; and Senate Bill 1034, the Healthy Schools Act of 2009. Although these measures did not pass into law, prevention-, promotion-, and treatment-oriented school-based mental health initiatives continued to gain resonance with policymakers, culminating in the inclusion of school-based health centers (SBHCs) in President Obama's health care reform bill (the Patient Protection and Affordable Care Act, 2010).

Becoming a federally authorized program is a historic victory for SBHCs, as it recognizes them as part of the federally supported health care system. This historic health reform legislation allows eligible SBHCs to receive funds supporting management and operation of programs, salaries for health care professionals and other personnel, purchase or lease of equipment, construction projects, and training. However, the SBHC authorization will be a hollow victory unless it is followed by appropriations. Until funds are appropriated, only limited federal support exists for SBHC operations, leaving little hope for the expansion that has been called for by many, including U.S. Department of Health and Human Services' Secretary, Kathleen Sebelius (2010): "We are thrilled that part of the [health reform] legislation calls for an expanded footprint of school-based health clinics. . . . I can't think of a better way to deliver primary and preventive care to not only students, but their families, than through school-based clinics."

We now know a great deal about risk and protective factors for childhood mental health disorders. Arguably the most important is that identifying, diagnosing, and treating high-risk children early may interrupt developmental trajectories that lead to poor outcomes in adolescence and adulthood. Improving our abilities to prevent or minimize these poor outcomes should become the goal to which mental health, child welfare, public education, and juvenile justice policymakers and leaders direct their concerted efforts.

1. What child mental health policies and practices have inhibited the integration of mental health services into other child-serving systems such as juvenile justice and child welfare?

2. Are there reasons to keep child-serving agencies organizationally separate at the state level? Local level?

3. Given what we know about risk factors for a variety of emotional and behavioral disorders, how can we combine mental health and public education resources to support prevention and early intervention strategies?

References

Allen-Meares, P., & Fraser, M. W. (2004). *Intervention with children and adolescents: An interdisciplinary perspective.* Boston: Allyn & Bacon.

American Psychiatric Association. (2000). *Diagnostic and statistical manual of mental disorders* (4th ed., Text revision). Washington, DC: Author.

Armstrong, K. H., Dedrick, R. F., & Greenbaum, P. E. (2003). Factors associated with community adjustment in young adults with serious emotional disturbance: A longitudinal analysis. *Journal of Emotional and Behavioral Disorders, 1,* 66–76. doi:10.1177/106342660301100201

Behar, L. B. (2003). Mental health management environments: Children's mental health services—The challenge of changing policy and practice. In W. R. Reid & S. B. Silver (Eds.), *Handbook of mental health administration and management* (pp. 149–162). New York: Brunner-Routledge.

Bickman, L., Guthrie, P. R., Foster, E. M., Lamber, E. W., Summerfelt, W. T., Breda, C. S., & Heflinger, C. A. (1995). *Evaluating managed mental health services: The Fort Bragg experiment.* New York: Plenum.

Bowen, N. K., & Flora, D. B. (2002). When is it appropriate to focus on protection in interventions for adolescents? *American Journal of Orthopsychiatry, 72,* 526–538. doi:10.1037/0002–9432.72.4.526

Breier, A., Kelsoe, J. R., Kirwin, P. D., Bellar, S. A., Wolkowitz, O. M., & Pickar, D. (1988). Early parental loss and development of adult psychopathology. *Archives of General Psychiatry, 45,* 987–993.

Brendenberg, N., Freidman, R., & Silver, S. (1990). The epidemiology of childhood psychiatric disorders: Prevalence findings from recent studies. *Journal of the American Academy of Child and Adolescent Psychiatry, 29,* 76–83.

Brestan, E. V., & Eyberg, S. M. (1998). Effective psychosocial treatments of conduct-disordered children and adolescents: 29 years, 82 studies, and 5,272 kids. *Journal of Child Clinical Psychology, 27,* 180–189. doi:10.1207/s15374424jccp2702_5

Bronfenbrenner, U. (1979). *The ecology of human development: Experiments by nature and design.* Cambridge, MA: Harvard University Press.

Burns, B. J. (2001). Commentary on the special issue on the National Evaluation of the Comprehensive Community Mental Health Services for Children and Their Families Program. *Journal of Emotional and Behavioral Disorders, 9*, 71–76. doi:10.1177/106342660100900108

Burns, B. J., Costello, E. J., Angold, A., Tweed, D., Stangl, D., Farmer, E. M., & Erkanli, A. (1995). Children's mental health service use across service sectors. *Health Affairs, 14*, 147–159. doi:10.1377/hlthaff.14.3.147

Center for Mental Health Services. (1999). *Annual report to Congress on the evaluation of the Comprehensive Community Mental Health Services for Children and Their Families Program.* Atlanta, GA: ORC Macro.

Chambless, D. L., & Ollendick, T. H. (2001). Empirically supported psychological interventions: Controversies and evidence. *Annual Review of Psychology, 52*, 685–716.

Children's Defense Fund. (1995). *The state of America's children yearbook: 1995.* Washington, DC: Author.

Commonwealth Fund, Commission on a High Performance Health System. (2006). *Why not the best? Results from a National Scorecard on U.S. Health System Performance.* Retrieved from http://www.commonwealthfund.org/Content/Publications/Fund-Reports/2006/Sep/Why-Not-the-Best-Results-from-a-National-Scorecard-on-U-S-Health-System-Performance.aspx

Cooper, J. L., Aratani, Y., Knitzer, J., Douglas-Hall A, Masi, R., Banghard, P., & Dababnah, S. (2008). *Unclaimed children revisited: The status of children's mental health policy in the United States.* New York: The National Center for Children in Poverty.

Copeland, W. E., Keeler, G., Angold, A., & Costello, E. J. (2007). Traumatic events and posttraumatic stress in childhood. *Archives of General Psychiatry, 64*, 577–584. doi:10.1001/archpsyc.64.5.577

Costello, E. J., Mustillo, S, Erkanli, A, Keeler, G. & Angold, A. (2003). Prevalence and Development of Psychiatric Disorders in Childhood and Adolescence. *Archives of General Psychiatry, 60*, 837–844. doi:10.1001/archpsyc.60.8.837

Cross, T. P., & Saxe, L. (1997). Many hands make mental health systems a reality: Lessons from the mental health services program for youth. In C. T. Nixon & D. A. Northrup (Eds.), *Children's mental health services: Research, policy, and evaluation* (pp. 45–72). Thousand Oaks, CA: Sage.

Davis, M., & Vander Stoep, A. (1997). The transition to adulthood for youth who have serious emotional disturbance: Developmental transition and young adult outcomes. *Journal of Mental Health Administration, 24*, 400–427.

Davis, M., Yelton, S., & Katz-Leavy, J. (1995). *State child and adolescent mental health: Administration, policies, and laws.* Tampa: University of South Florida, Florida Mental Health Institute.

Davis, M., Yelton, S., Katz-Leavy, J., & Lourie, I. (1995). Unclaimed children revisited. *Journal of Mental Health Administration, 22*, 142–166.

Douzinas, N., Fornari, V., Goodman, B., Sitnick, T., & Packman, L. (1994). Eating disorders and abuse. *Child Psychiatric Clinics of North America, 3,* 777–796.

Dykman, R. A., McPherson, B., Ackerman, P. T., Newton, J. E., Mooney, D. M., Wherry, J., & Chaffin, M. (1997). Internalizing and externalizing characteristics of sexually and/or physically abused children. *Integrative Physiological & Behavioral Science, 32,* 62–74. doi:10.1007/BF02688614

Epstein, M. H., Cullinan, D., Quinn, K. P., & Cumblad, C. (1995). Personal, family, and service use characteristics of young people served by an interagency community-based system of care. *Journal of Emotional and Behavioral Disorders, 3,* 55–64. doi:10.1177/106342669500300107

Fairbank, J. A., Putnam, F. W., & Harris, W. W. (2007). The prevalence and impact of child traumatic stress. In M. J. Friedman, T. M Keane, & P. A. Resick (Eds.), *A handbook of PTSD: Science and practice* (pp. 229–251). New York: Guilford Press.

Famularo, R., Kinscherff, R., & Fenton, T. (1992). Psychiatric diagnoses of maltreated children: Preliminary findings. *Journal of American Academy of Child and Adolescent Psychiatry, 31,* 863–867.

Felitti, V. J., Anda, R. F., Nordenberg, D., Williamson, D. F., Spitz, A. M., Edwards, V., .Koss, M. & Marks, J. S. (1998). Relationship of childhood abuse and household dysfunction to many of the leading causes of death in adults: The Adverse Childhood Experiences (ACE) Study. *American Journal of Preventive Medicine, 14,* 245–258. doi:10.1016/S0749–3797(98)00017–8

Fergusson, D. M., Horwood, L. J., & Lynsky, M. T. (1994). The childhoods of multiple problem adolescents: A 15-year longitudinal study. *Journal of Child Psychology and Psychiatry, 35,* 1123–1140. doi:10.1111/j.1469–7610.1994.tb01813.x

Flisher, A. J., Kramer, R. A., Hoven, C. W., Greenwald, S., Alegria, M., Bird, H. R., Canino, G., Connell, R., & Moore, R. E. (1997). Psychosocial characteristics of physically abused children and adolescents. *Journal of the American Academy of Child and Adolescent Psychiatry, 36,* 123–131. doi:10.1097/00004583–199701000–00026

Fraser, M. W. (Ed.). (2004). *Risk and resilience in childhood: An ecological perspective* (2nd ed.). Washington, DC: NASW Press.

Fraser, M. W., Day, S. H., Galinsky, M. J., Hodges, V. G., & Smokowski, P. R. (2004). Conduct problems and peer rejection in childhood: A randomized trial of the Making Choices and Strong Families programs. *Research on Social Work Practice, 14,* 313–324. doi:10.1177/1049731503257884

Friedman, R. M., Katz-Levey, J. W., Manderschied, R. W., & Sondheimer, D. L. (1996). Prevalence of serious emotional disturbance in children and adolescents. In R. W. Manderscheid & M. A. Sonnenschein (Eds.), *Mental health, United States, 1996* (pp. 71–88) (DHHS Publication No. SMA96–3098). Washington, DC: Government Printing Office.

Garmezy, N. (1993). Children in poverty: Resilience despite risk. *Psychiatry, 56*, 127–136.

Gerrity, E., & Folcarelli, C. (2008). *Child traumatic stress: What every policymaker should know.* Durham, NC: National Center for Child Trauma Stress.

Gilbert, C. (2004). Childhood depression: A risk factor perspective. In M. W. Fraser (Ed.), *Risk and resilience in childhood: An ecological perspective* (2nd ed., pp. 315–346). Washington, DC: NASW Press.

Gillam, F., Reivick, K., Joaycox, L, & Seligman, M.E.P. (1995). Prevention of depressive symptoms in school children: Two-year follow-up. *Psychological Science, 6*, 343–351. doi:10.1111/j.1467–9280.1995.tb00524.x

Goodman, R., & Stevenson, J. (1989). A twin study of hyperactivity. II. The etiological role of genes, family relationships and perinatal adversity. *Journal of Child Psychology and Psychiatry, 30*, 691–709. doi:10.1111/j.1469–7610.1989.tb00782.x

Goodyer, I. (1990). *Life experiences, development, and childhood psychiatry.* New York: John Wiley.

Goodyer, I. (2001). Life events: Their nature and effects. In I. M. Goodyer (Ed.), *The depressed child and adolescent* (2nd ed., pp. 204–232). New York: Cambridge University Press.

Green, W. (1995). Family, peer, and self factors as predictors of male and female adolescent substance abuse at 9th and 12th grade. *Dissertation Abstracts International: Section B: Sciences and Engineering, 55*, 2771.

Greenbaum, P. E., Dedrick, R. F., Friedman, R., Kutash, K., Brown, E., Lardieri, S., & Pugh, A. (1996). National adolescent and child treatment study (NACTS): Outcomes for individuals with serious emotional and behavioral disturbance. *Journal of Emotional and Behavioral Disorders, 4*, 130–146. doi:10.1177/106342669600400301

Hergenhahn, B. R. (2001). *An introduction to the history of psychology* (4th ed.). Belmont, CA: Wadsworth.

Hernandez, M., & Hodges, S. (2003). Building upon the theory of change for systems of care. *Journal of Emotional and Behavioral Disorders, 11*, 19–26. doi:10.1177/106342660301100104

Hodges, S., Ferreira, K., Israel, N., & Mazza, J. (2007). *Strategies for system of care development: Locally identified factors for system implementation* (Supplement to issue brief 2, Lessons from successful systems: Critical factors in system of care implementation). Tampa: University of South Florida, Louis de la Parte Florida Mental Health Institute, Research and Training Center for Children's Mental Health.

Hopper, K., & Wanderling, J. (2000). Revisiting the developed versus developing country distinction in course and outcome in schizophrenia: Results from IsoS, the WHO collaborative followup project. International study of schizophrenia. *Schizophrenia Bulletin, 26*, 835–846.

Jellinek, M., & Synder, J. (1998). Depression and suicide in children and adolescents. *Pediatrics in Review, 19,* 255–265.

Jenkins, E., & Bell, C. (1997). Exposure and response to community violence among children and adolescents. In J. Osofsky (Ed.), *Children in a violent society* (pp. 9–31). New York: Guilford Press.

Johnsen, M. C., Morrissey, J. P., & Calloway, M. O. (1996). Structure and change in child mental health service delivery networks. *Journal of Community Psychology, 24,* 275–289. qqdoi:10.1002/(SICI)1520–6629(199607)24:3<275::AID-JCOP7>3.0.CO;2-W

Johnson, J. G., Cohen, P., Kasen, S., Smailes, E., & Brook, J. S. (2001). Association of maladaptive parental behavior with psychiatric disorder among parents and their offspring. *Archives of General Psychiatry, 58,* 453–460. doi:10.1001/archpsyc.58.5.453

Joint Commission on the Mental Health of Children. (1969). *Crisis in child mental health: Challenges for the 1970s.* New York: Harper & Row.

Jones, K (1999). *Taming the troublesome child: American families, child guidance, and the limits of psychiatric authority.* Cambridge, MA: Harvard University Press.

Kagan, J., Snidman, N., & Arcus, D. (1998). Childhood derivatives of high and low reactivity in infancy. *Child Development, 69,* 1483–1493.

Kenny, H., Oliver, L., & Poppe, J. (2002). *Mental health services for children: An overview.* Washington, DC: National Conference of State Legislatures.

Kessler, R. C. (1997). The effects of stressful life events on depression. *Annual Review of Psychology, 48,* 191–214. doi:10.1146/annurev.psych.48.1.191

Knitzer, J. (1982). *Unclaimed children.* Washington, DC: Children's Defense Fund.

Lahey, B. B., Loeber, R., Hart, E. L., Frick, P. J., Applegate, B., Zhang, Q., Green, S. M., & Russo, M. F. (1995). Four-year longitudinal study of conduct disorder in boys: Patterns and predictors of persistence. *Journal of Abnormal Psychology, 104,* 83–93. doi:10.1037/0021–843X.104.1.83

Linver, M., Fuligni, A., Hernandez, M., & Brooks-Gunn, J. (2004). Poverty and child development: Promising interventions. In P. Allen-Meares & M. W. Fraser (Eds.), *Intervention with children and adolescents: An interdisciplinary perspective* (pp. 106–129). Boston: Allyn & Bacon.

Livingston, R., Lawson, L., & Jones, J. G. (1993). Predictors of self-reported psychopathology in children abused repeatedly by a parent. *Journal of the American Academy of Child and Adolescent Psychiatry, 32,* 948–953. doi:10.1097/00004583-199309000-00009

Loeber, R., Farrington, D. P., Stouthamer-Loeber, M., & Van Kammen, W. B. (1998). Multiple risk factors for multi-problem boys: Co-occurrence of delinquency, substance use, attention deficit, conduct problems, physical aggression, covert behavior, depressed mood, and shy/withdrawn behavior. In R. Jessor (Ed.), *New perspectives on adolescent risk behavior* (pp. 90–149). Cambridge, UK: Cambridge University Press.

Loeber, R., & Stouthamer-Loeber, M. (1996). The development of offending. *Criminal Justice and Behaviour, 23,* 12–24. doi:10.1177/0093854896023001003

Lonigan, C. J., Elbert, J. C., & Johnson, S. B. (1998). Empirically supported psychosocial interventions for children: An overview. *Journal of Clinical Child Psychology, 27,* 138–145. doi:10.1207/s15374424jccp2702_1

Lourie, I. S., & Hernandez, M. (2003). A historical perspective on national child mental health policy. *Journal of Emotional and Behavioral Disorders, 2,* 5–9. doi:10.1177/106342660301100102

Lu, W., Mueser, K. T., Rosenberg, S. D., & Jankowski, M. K. (2008). Correlates of adverse childhood experiences among adults with severe mood disorders. *Psychiatric Services, 59,* 1018–1026. doi:10.1176/appi.ps.59.9.1018

Lucas, A. R., Beard, C. M., O'Fallon, W. M., & Kurland, L. T. (1991). 50-year trends in the incidence of anorexia nervosa in Rochester, MN: A population-based study. *American Journal of Psychiatry, 148,* 917–922.

Mark, T. L., & Buck, J. A. (2006). Characteristic of U.S. youth with Serious Mental disturbances: Data from the National Health Interview Study. *Psychiatric Services, 57,* 1573–1578. doi:10.1176/appi.ps.57.11.1573

Maziade, M., & Raymond, V. (1995). The new genetics of schizophrenia. In C. L. Shriqui & H. A. Nasrallah (Eds.), *Contemporary issues in the treatment of schizophrenia* (pp. 61–79). Washington, DC: American Psychiatric Press.

McConaughy, S. H., & Wadsworth, M. E. (2000). Life history reports of young adults previously referred for mental health services. *Journal of Emotional and Behavioral Disorders, 8,* 202–215. doi:10.1177/106342660000800401

McLeod, J. D., & Shanahan, M. J. (1996). Poverty, parenting and children's mental health. *American Sociological Review, 58,* 351–366. doi:10.2307/2095905

Mears, D. P., & Aron, L. Y. (2003). *Addressing the needs of youth with disabilities in the juvenile justice system: The current state of knowledge* (The Urban Institute). Retrieved from http://www. urban. org/UploadedPDF/410885_youth_with_disabilities.pdf

Moore, S. M., Rohde, P. L., Seeley, J. R., & Lewinsohn, P. M. (1999). Life events and depression in adolescence: Relationship loss as a prospective risk factor for first onset of major depressive disorder. *Journal of Abnormal Psychology, 108,* 606–614. doi:10.1037/0021–843X.108.4.606

Neal, A. M., Lilly, R. S., & Zakis, S. (1993). What are African American children afraid of? *Journal of Anxiety Disorders, 7,* 129–139. doi:10.1016/0887–6185(93)90011–9

Nolen-Hoeksema, S., & Girgus, J. S. (1994). The emergence of gender differences in depression during adolescence. *Psychological Bulletin, 115,* 424–443. doi:10.1037/0033–2909.115.3.424

Olds, D., Henderson, C. R., Jr., Cole, R., Eckenrode, J., Kitzman, H., Luckey, D., Pettitt, L., Sidora, K., Morris, P., & Powers, J. (1998). Long-term effects of nurse home visitation on children's criminal and antisocial behavior. *Journal of the American Medical Association, 280,* 1238–1244. doi:10.1001/jama.280.14.1238

Oyserman, D. (2004). Depression during the school-aged years. In P. Allen-Meares & M. W. Fraser (Eds.), *Intervention with children and adolescents: An interdisciplinary perspective* (pp. 264–281). Boston: Allyn & Bacon.

Oyserman, D., Mowbray, C. T., Allen-Meares, P. A., & Firminger, K. B. (2000). Parenting among mothers with a serious mental illness. *American Journal of Orthopsychiatry, 70,* 296–315. doi:10.1037/h0087733

Pagani, L., Boulerice, B., Tremblay, R. E., & Vitaro, F. (1997). Behavioral development in children of divorce and remarriage. *Journal of Child Psychology and Psychiatry, 38,* 769–781. doi:10.1111/j.1469–7610.1997.tb01595.x

Parry-Jones, W. L. (1989). Annotation: The history of child and adolescent psychiatry: Its present day relevance. *Journal of Child Psychology and Psychiatry, 30,* 3–11. doi:10.1111/j.1469–7610.1989.tb00766.x

Peeples, F., & Loeber, R. (1994). Do individual factors and neighborhood context explain ethnic differences in juvenile delinquency? *Journal of Quantitative Criminology, 10,* 141–158. doi:10.1007/BF02221156

Pelham, W. E., Jr., Wheeler, T., & Chronis, A. (1998). Empirically supported psychosocial treatments for attention deficit hyperactivity disorder. *Journal of Clinical Child Psychology, 27,* 190–205. doi:10.1207/s15374424jccp2702_6

Piquero, A. R., & Chung, H. L. (2001). On the relationships between gender, early onset, and the seriousness of offending. *Journal of Criminal Justice, 29,* 189–206. doi:10.1016/S0047–2352(01)00084–8

Power, A. K. (2009). Focus on transformation: A public health model of mental health for the 21st century. *Psychiatric Services, 60,* 580–584. doi:10.1176/appi.ps.60.5.580

President's Commission on Mental Health. (1978). *Report of the sub-task panel on infants, children and adolescents.* Washington, DC: Government Printing Office.

President's New Freedom Commission on Mental Health. (2003). *Achieving the promise: Transforming mental health care in America* (Final report, DHHS Pub. No. SMA-03–3832). Rockville, MD: U.S. Department of Health and Human Services.

Putnam, F. W. (2006). The impact of trauma on child development. *Juvenile and Family Court Journal, 57*(1), 1–11. doi:10.1111/j.1755–6988.2006.tb00110.x

Quinn, K. P., & Epstein, M. H. (1998). Characteristics of children, youth, and families serviced by local interagency systems of care. In M. H. Epstein, K. Kutash, & A. Duchowski (Eds.), *Outcomes for children and youth with emotional and behavioral disorders and their families: Programs and evaluation best practices* (pp. 81–114). Austin, TX: PRO-ED.

Reid, J. B., Eddy, M. J., Fetrow, R. A., & Stoolmiller, M. (1999). Description and immediate impacts of preventive intervention for conduct problems. *American Journal of Community Psychology, 27,* 483–517. doi:10.1023/A:1022181111368

Resnick, G., & Burt, M. R. (1996). Youth at risk: Definitions and implications for service delivery. *American Journal of Orthopsychiatry, 66,* 172–188. doi:10.1037/h0080169

Robins, L. N. (1991). Conduct disorder. *Journal of Child Psychology and Psychiatry and Allied Disciplines, 32,* 193–212. doi:10.1111/j.1469–7610.1991.tb00008.x

Rogers, L., Resnick, M. D., Mitchel, J. E., & Blum, R. W. (1997). The relationship between socioeconomic status and eating disorders in a community sample of adolescent girls. *International Journal of Eating Disorders, 22,* 15–23. doi:10.1002/(SICI)1098–108X(199707)22:1<15::AID-EAT2>3.0.CO;2–5

Rosenblatt, A., & Woodbridge, M. W. (2003). Deconstructing research on systems of care for youth with EBD: Frameworks for policy research. *Journal of Emotional and Behavior Disorders, 11,* 27–37. doi:10.1177/106342660301100105

Ross, D. M., & Ross, S. A. (1982). *Hyperactivity: Current issues, research, and theory.* New York: John Wiley.

Rutter, M. (1979). Protective factors in children's responses to stress and disadvantage. In M. W. Kent & J. E. Rolf (Eds.), *Primary prevention of psychopathology: Vol. 3. Social competence in children* (pp. 49–74) Hanover, NH: University Press of New England.

Rutter, M. (1985). Resilience in the face of adversity: Protective factors and resistance to psychiatric disorders. *British Journal of Psychiatry, 147,* 598–611. doi:10.1192/bjp.147.6.598

Rutter, M., Silberg, J., O'Conner, T., & Simonoff, E. (1999). Genetics and child psychiatry: I. Advances in quantitative and molecular genetics. *Journal of Child Psychology and Psychiatry and Allied Disciplines, 40,* 3–18. doi:10.1111/1469–7610.00422

Salzer, M., & Bickman, L. (1997). Delivering effective children's services in the community: Reconsidering the benefits of system interventions. *Applied & Preventive Psychology, 6,* 1–13. doi:10.1016/S0962–1849(05)80062–9

Sameroff, A. J., Bartko, W. T., Baldwin, A., Baldwin, C., & Seifer, R. (1999). Family and social influences on the development of child competence. In M. Lewis & C. Feiring (Eds.), *Families, risk, and competence* (pp. 167–185). Mahwah, NJ: Lawrence Erlbaum.

Sameroff, A. J., & Gutman, L. M. (2004). Contributions of risk research to the design of successful interventions. In P. Allen-Meares & M. W. Fraser (Eds.), *Intervention with children and adolescents: An interdisciplinary perspective* (pp. 9–26). Boston: Allyn & Bacon.

Santilli, J. S., & Beilenson, P. (1992). Risk factors for adolescent sexual behavior, fertility and sexually transmitted diseases. *Journal of School Health, 62,* 271–279. doi:10.1111/j.1746–1561.1992.tb01243.x

Schowalter, J. E. (2003, September 1). A history of child and adolescent psychiatry in the United States. *Psychiatric Times, 20*(9). Retrieved from http://www.psychiatrictimes.com/display/article/10168/48051?pageNumber=1

Sebelius K. (2010, April 7). Opening plenary remarks. Presented at Coalition for Community Schools National Forum, Philadelphia.

Shaw, D. S., Gillion, M., Ingoldsby, E. M., & Nagin, D. (2003). Trajectories learning to school-age conduct problems. *Developmental Psychology, 39,* 189–200. doi:10.1037/0012–1649.39.2.189

Siegel, J. M., Aneshensel, C. S., Taub, B., Cantwell, D. P., & Driscoll, A. K. (1998). Adolescent depressed mood in a multiethnic sample. *Journal of Youth and Adolescence, 27,* 413–427. doi:10.1023/A:1022873601030

Silverman, A. B., Reinherz, H. Z., & Giaconia, R. M. (1996). The long-term sequelae of child and adolescent abuse: A longitudinal community study. *Child Abuse and Neglect, 20,* 709–723. doi:10.1016/0145–2134(96)00059–2

Spearly, J., & Lauderdale, M. (1983). Community characteristics and ethnicity in the prediction of child maltreatment rates. *Child Abuse and Neglect, 7,* 91–105. doi:10.1016/0145–2134(83)90036–4

Spirito, A., Bond. A., Kurkjian, J., Devost, L., Bosworth, T., & Brown, L. K. (1993). Gender differences among adolescent suicide attempters. *Crisis, 14,* 178–184.

Steiner, H., & Lock, L. (1998). Anorexia nervosa and bulimia nervosa in children and adolescents: A review of the past 10 years. *Journal of the American Academy of Child and Adolescent Psychiatry, 37,* 352–359.

Stice, E., & Agras. W. S. (1998). Predicting onset and cessation of bulimic behaviors during adolescence: A longitudinal grouping analysis. *Behavior Therapy, 29,* 257–276. doi:10.1016/S0005–7894(98)80006–3

Stortz, M. (2003). *The tale of two settings: Institutional and community-based mental health services in California since realignment in 1991.* Oakland: California Protection and Advocacy. Retrieved from http://www.disabilityrightsca.org/pubs/540301.pdf

Stroul B. A. (2006). *The sustainability of systems of care: Lessons learned. A report on the special study on the sustainability of systems of care.* Atlanta, GA: ORC Macro.

Stroul, B. A., & Friedman, R. M. (1986). *A system of care for severely emotionally disturbed children and youth.* Washington, DC: Georgetown University Center for Child and Human Development.

Stroul, B. A., & Manteuffel, B.A. (2007). The sustainability of systems of care for children's mental health: Lessons learned. *Journal of Behavioral Health Services and Research, 34,* 237–259. doi: 10.1007/s11414–007–9065–3

Substance Abuse and Mental Health Services Administration. (2005). *Transforming mental health care in America: The federal action agenda: First steps.* Rockville, MD: Author.

Substance Abuse and Mental Health Services Administration. (2009). *Working together to help youth thrive in schools and communities.* Retrieved January 11, 2010 from http://www.samhsa.gov/children/docs/shortreport.pdf

Surgeon General. (1999). *Mental health: A report from the Surgeon General.* Washington, DC: Department of Health and Human Services.

Surgeon General. (2000). *Report of the surgeon general's conference on children's mental health: A national action agenda.* Washington, DC: Department of Health and Human Services.

Tiet, Q. Q., Bird, H. R., Hoven, C. W., Moore, R., Wu, P., Wicks, J., Jensen P., Goodman S., & Cohen, P. (2001). Relationship between specific adverse life events and psychiatric disorders. *Journal of Abnormal Child Psychology, 29,* 153–164. doi:10.1023/A:1005288130494

U.S. Department of Education, Office of Special Education Programs. (1994). *National agenda for achieving better results for children and youth with serious emotional disturbances* (ERIC Document No. ED376690). Washington, DC: Author.

Vance, J. E., Bowen, N. K., Fernandez, G., & Thompson, S. (2002). Risk and protective factors as predictors of outcome in adolescents with psychiatric disorder and aggression. *Journal of the American Academy of Child & Adolescent Psychiatry, 41,* 36–43. doi:10.1097/00004583–200201000–00009

Vinson, N. B., Brannan, A. M., Baughman, L. N., Wilce, M., & Gawron, T. (2001). The system-of-care model: Implementation in twenty-seven communities. *Journal of Emotional and Behavioral Disorders, 9,* 30–42. doi:10.1177/106342660100900104

Wagner, M., Kutash, K., Duchnowski, A. J., Epstein, M. H., & Sumi, W. C. (2005). The children and youth we serve: A national picture of the characteristics of students with emotional disturbances receiving special education. *Journal of Emotional and Behavioral Disorders, 13,* 79–96. doi:10.1177/10634266050130020201

Werner, E. E., & Smith, R. S. (1992). *Overcoming the odds: High risk children from birth to adulthood.* Ithaca, NY: Cornell University Press.

Wickramaratne, P. J., & Weissman, M. M. (1998). Onset of psychopathology in offspring by developmental phase and parental depression. *Journal of the American Academy of Child and Adolescent Psychiatry, 37,* 933–942. doi:10.1097/00004583–199809000–00013

Willie, M. v. James B. Hunt, Jr., et al., Civil No. C-C-79-294-M (W.D. N.C. 1980).

Wolfe, D. A., Sas, L., & Wekerle, C. (1994). Factors associated with the development of posttraumatic stress disorder among child victims of sexual abuse. *Child Abuse and Neglect, 18,* 37–50. doi:10.1016/0145–2134(94)90094–9

Wu, P., Katic, B. J., Liu, X, Fan, B., & Fuller, C. J. (2010). Mental health service use among suicidal adolescents: Findings from a U.S. national community survey. *Psychiatric Services, 61,* 17–24. doi:10.1176/appi.ps.61.1.17

Zahn-Waxler, C., Iannotti, R., Cummings, E. M., & Denham, S. (1990). Antecedents of problem behaviors in children of depressed mothers. *Development and Psychopathology, 2,* 271–291. doi:10.1017/S0954579400000778

Zill, N., & West, J. (2001). *Entering kindergarten: A portrait of American children when they begin school: Findings from The Condition of Education 2000* (NCES 2001–035). Washington, DC: Department of Education, Government Printing Office. Retrieved from

Additional Reading

Allen-Meares, P., & Fraser, M. W. (2004). *Intervention with children and adolescents: An interdisciplinary perspective.* Boston: Allyn & Bacon.

American Psychiatric Association. (2000). *Diagnostic and statistical manual of mental disorders* (4th ed.). Washington, DC: Author.

Center for Mental Health Services. (1999). *Annual report to Congress on the evaluation of the Comprehensive Community Mental Health Services for Children and Their Families Program.* Atlanta, GA: ORC Macro. Retrieved from http://mentalhealth .samhsa.gov/publications/allpubs/CB-E199/default.asp

Costello, E. J., Angold, A., Burns, B. J., Stangl, D. K., Tweed, D. L., Erkanli, A., & Worthman, C. M. (1996). The Great Smoky Mountains Study of youth: Goals, design, methods, and the prevalence of *DSM-III-R* disorders. *Archives of General Psychiatry, 53,* 1129–1136. PMID: 8956679

Gerrity, E., & Folcarelli, C. (2008). *Child traumatic stress: What every policymaker should know.* Durham, NC: National Center for Child Trauma Stress. Retrieved from http://www.nctsnet.org/nctsn_assets/pdfs/PolicyGuide_CTS2008.pdf

Mark, T. L., & Buck, J. A. (2006). Characteristics of U.S. youth with serious mental disturbances: Data from the National Health Interview Study. *Psychiatric Services, 57,* 1573–1578.

National Alliance for the Mentally Ill. (2001). *Families on the brink: The impact of ignoring children with serious mental illness.* Arlington, VA: Author.

President's New Freedom Commission on Mental Health. (2003). *Achieving the promise: Transforming mental health care in America.* Rockville, MD: U.S. Department of Health and Human Services. Retrieved from http://www.mentalhealth commission.gov/reports/FinalReport/toc.html

Stroul, B., & Friedman, R. (1986). *A system of care for severely emotionally disturbed children and youth* (ERIC Document No. 330167). Washington, DC: CASSP Technical Assistance Center, Georgetown University. Retrieved from http://www.eric.ed.gov/ERICDocs/data/ericdocs2sql/content_storage_ 01/0000019b/80/22/d8/2b.pdf

Substance Abuse and Mental Health Services Administration. (2005). *Transforming mental health care in America: The federal action agenda: First steps.* Rockville, MD: Author.

Surgeon General. (1999). *Mental health: A report from the Surgeon General.* Washington, DC: Department of Health and Human Services. Retrieved from http://mental health.samhsa.gov/cmhs/surgeongeneral/surgeongeneralrpt.asp

Surgeon General. (2000). *Report of the surgeon general's conference on children's mental health: A national action agenda.* Washington, DC: Office of the Surgeon General. Retrieved from http://www.surgeongeneral.gov/topics/cmh/ childreport.html

Web-Based Resources (General)

Bazelon Center for Mental Health and Law, http://www.bazelon.org/
Federation of Families for Children's Mental Health, http:/www.ffcmh.org
National Alliance for the Mentally Ill, http://www.nami.org/Hometemplate.cfm
National Institute of Mental Health, http://www.nimh.nih.gov/
Mental Health America, http://www.nmha.org/
Substance Abuse and Mental Health Services Administration, http://www.mental
    health.samhsa.gov/

Web-Based Resources (Evidence-Based Practices)

Association for Cognitive and Behavioral Therapies & Society of Clinical Child and
    Adolescent Psychology. (n.d.). *Evidence-based mental health treatment for children and
    adolescents.* Retrieved from http://www.effectivechildtherapy.com/
National Child Traumatic Stress Network. (2010). *Empirically supported treatments
    and promising practices.* Retrieved from http://www.nctsnet.org/nccts/nav.do?
    pid=ctr_top_trmnt_prom
Substance Abuse and Mental Health Services Administration. (2007). *A guide to
    evidence-based practices on the web.* Retrieved from www.samhsa.gov/
    ebpWebGuide/index.asp
Substance Abuse and Mental Health Services Administration. (2010). *National registry
    of evidence-based practices: NREPP.* Retrieved from www.nrepp.samhsa.gov/

6

Health Policy for Children and Youth

Kathleen A. Rounds

Guadalupe V. Huitron

Thomas C. Ormsby

Purpose and Overview of Health Policies for Children and Youth

The primary purpose of health policies aimed at children and youth is to provide access to preventive and medical care. Access is defined as the ability to obtain needed care: Lack of access is an indication of unmet health care needs of children and youth (Shi & Singh, 2001). Access to health care encompasses a number of dimensions, including

- Availability—Does the service exist?
- Cultural acceptability—Is there a fit between the cultural belief systems and languages of the client and the provider?
- Convenience—Does the client have transportation to the service, and can the client access the service at a convenient time?
- Affordability—Can the client pay for the service, or does the client have private or public insurance to cover the cost? (Anderson, 1995; Donabedian, 1973)

The U.S. health care environment is distinguished from health care systems in other industrialized nations by three critical features. First, the United States is the only country in the Western world that does not have universal health care coverage for its children and adolescents (Stein, 1997). Second, the U.S. health care delivery system is a heavily privatized delivery system financed by public dollars. Federal, state, and local dollars constitute about 45% of all health care expenditures (Centers for Disease Control and Prevention [CDC], 2009b). The current system is an amalgam of private and government sources that operates in a market-oriented, commodity-driven economy in which many of the key players are motivated by profit margins (Halfon & Hochstein, 1997; Shi & Singh, 2001). Third, in large part, U.S. health care is poorly coordinated, a fragmented system (Shortell, Gillies, Anderson, Erickson, & Mitchell, 2000).

Halfon and Hochstein (1997) posed two major policy questions regarding the delivery of health care for children and youth. The first question is referred to as the "insurance question." It focuses on expanding access to health insurance for children and youth in addition to the elimination of nonfinancial barriers to access (e.g., outreach and transportation). Halfon and Hochstein labeled the second question the "systems question." It asks how health care services might be organized and integrated with other systems to meet the needs of children and youth more effectively.

Federal health care policies affect all children, youth, and their families. However, these policies have a more dramatic affect on low-income households, which are disproportionately African American, Latino, or other racial/ethnic minorities. According to the Kaiser Commission on Medicaid and the Uninsured, "The gaps in our nation's health coverage system fall at the doorstep of low-income families" (Williams et al., 2004, p. 2). These families are more likely to have children with health problems, and they are less likely to have health insurance (Starfield, 1997).

Because of special vulnerabilities, some federal health care policies specifically target infants, very young children, or adolescents. For example, eligibility for public health insurance programs (e.g., Medicaid) has been expanded to provide access to greater numbers of infants and young children, who otherwise would likely have unmet health needs. This policy change was based on the recognition that a child's early years are important not only for preventive care (i.e., well-baby checkups and immunizations) but also for screenings to detect developmental and health problems.

Adolescents are another developmentally vulnerable group because they have a high likelihood of engaging in high-risk behaviors (e.g., unprotected sex, substance use, smoking) that have long-term health consequences. During early adolescence, most youths develop health behaviors that persist into adulthood (Greydanus, Patel, & Greydanus, 2003).

Federal health policy also targets children who meet the definition of "children with special health care needs." However, uncertainty over which children made up this population prompted the Maternal and Child Health Bureau [MCHB] of the U.S. Department of Health and Human Services [DHHS] to form a work group expressly to establish a clear definition. This definition has been adopted by the DHHS as well as the American Academy of Pediatrics: "Children who have, or are at increased risk for, chronic physical, developmental, behavioral, or emotional conditions and who also require health and related services of a type or amount beyond that required by children generally" (McPherson et al., 1998, p. 138). Based on this definition, children with special health care needs compose 13.9% of U.S. children ages 0 to 17. The prevalence of special health care needs has been estimated at one of every five U.S. households with children (Data Resource Center for Child and Adolescent Health, n.d.); however, this number does not include children in the at-risk category that is encompassed in the definition used by the MCHB (Bethell, Read, Blumberg, & Newacheck, 2008).

In this chapter, we review the prevalence of four health problems experienced by children and youth: low birth weight, asthma, overweight and obesity, and sexually transmitted infections. We identify the risk and protective factors associated with these health problems. We summarize the historical development of child health policy and examine ways in which child health policy has been based on risk and protective factors. Using a case example, we discuss strategies for integrating health care with other service systems that serve children and youth.

Risk and Protective Factors for Health Problems in Childhood and Adolescence

Infants, children, and adolescents in the United States experience a range of health problems, with the most frequent being low birth weight, asthma, overweight or obesity, and sexually transmitted infections. In this chapter, we focus on the prevalence of these health problems; health disparities associated with race, ethnicity, and socioeconomic status; and risk factors across multiple system levels. (See Table 6.1 for prevalence data on low birth weight, asthma, overweight, and obesity.) This section concludes with a discussion of protective factors related to access to health care services.

Low Birth Weight

Infants with low birth weight (LBW) are defined as those weighing less than 2,500 grams (about 5.5 pounds). The incidence of LBW is increasing in the U.S. population and has become a serious public health concern because it can lead to adverse health outcomes throughout life. Between 1990 and 2007, the prevalence of LBW increased by 17% in the United States (CDC, 2009b). In 2007, infants with LBW represented 8.2% of U.S. live births, which was the highest percentage in more than 30 years (CDC, 2009e). Moreover, 1.5% of live births in the same year were *very low birth weight* (VLBW) infants, who weighed less than 1,500 grams, or about 3.3 pounds (CDC, 2009e). LBW and VLBW infants are at increased risk for a host of health and developmental problems, including neonatal mortality, neurodevelopmental disorders (Jaffee & Perloff, 2003), respiratory distress syndrome, cardiac problems (March of Dimes Foundation, 2008), and delayed cognitive functioning (Reuner, Hassenpflug, Pietz, & Philippi, 2009). Compared with infants of normal birth weight, LBW infants face a greater than fivefold increase in risk of death during their first year, and VLBW infants incur a 100-fold increase risk of death in their first year (CDC, 2009b).

Racial and ethnic disparities in the incidence of LBW and VLBW infants present a serious public health issue in the United States. The rate of LBW live births among non-Hispanic African American mothers in 2007 (13.8%) was about 2 times the rate reported for either non-Hispanic White mothers (7.2%) or Hispanic mothers (6.9%; CDC, 2009e). In addition, non-Hispanic African American mothers were nearly 2 times more likely to have a VLBW live birth than Hispanic mothers (3.2% and 1.2%, respectively; CDC, 2009e). Jaffee and Perloff (2003) suggested that one factor contributing to the racial/ethnic disparities in the prevalence of LBW might be the inequality of living conditions. Indeed, a recent study examining four sources of stress thought

Table 6.1   Estimated Prevalence of Health Conditions Among Children and Adolescents in the United States

	U.S. Population (all races)	African American (not Hispanic or Latino)	Latino or Hispanic	White (not Hispanic or Latino)
Low Birth Weight				
2007: Percent of Live Births < 2,500 grams	8.2	13.8	6.9	7.2
2007: Percent of Live Births < 1,500 grams	1.5	3.2	1.2	1.2
Overweight				
2003–2006: Percent Overweight[a] Children 6–11 years				
Boys	11.7	14.4	21 (Mexican American only)	8.7
Girls	11.1	19.7	14 (Mexican American only)	9.1
Adolescents 12–19 years				
Boys	13.9	15.3	15.9 (Mexican American only)	13.1
Girls	11.1	19.6	14.1 (Mexican American only)	9.1
2008: Asthma < age 18				
Percent ever told had asthma	14	21	11	13
Percent had asthma attack in past 12 months (data presented for children < age 15)	4.3	8.6	5	4.6

a. Overweight is defined as Body Mass Index (BMI) at or above the sex- and age-specific 95th percentile BMI cutoff points from the 2000 Centers for Disease Control growth charts.

to contribute to LBW among African American mothers found that neighborhood disorganization had the most robust effect (Holland, Kitzman, & Veazie, 2009).

A variety of factors, including genetics, lifestyle, and environmental conditions, can substantially affect birth weight. Maternal characteristics that are risk factors for LBW include smoking or drug use during pregnancy, limited or late prenatal care, and the number of previous pregnancies (Jaffee & Perloff, 2003). In the decades since Simpson's 1957 report on the prenatal effects of maternal smoking, smoking during pregnancy has been well established as a major risk factor for LBW. In addition, maternal smoking has been recognized as the most significant risk factor for LBW in developed countries (Kramer, 1987). These findings are supported by 2007 data that show 12% of U.S. mothers who smoked during pregnancy had a LBW newborn as compared with 7.7% of nonsmoking mothers (CDC, 2009b). Researchers investigating the effects of maternal smoking on birth outcomes found that infants born to mothers who smoked weighed an average of 170 to 260 grams less (about 0.4 to 0.6 pounds) than infants of nonsmoking mothers (Aagaard-Tillery, Porter, Lane, Varner, & Lacoursiere, 2008).

Early childbearing (i.e., maternal age 15 years or younger) has been noted as a significant risk factor for VLBW. A study of U.S. singleton first births between 1995 and 2006 showed VLBW infants were born to very young mothers (15 years or younger) at nearly double the rate among mothers between 20 and 24 years old (21.7/1,000 live births and 10.4/1,000 live births, respectively; Chen et al., 2007). Furthermore, this study showed that VLBW rates declined for older adolescent mothers as compared with the youngest adolescent mothers (14.9/1,000 live births for mothers 16 to 17 years old, and 12.3/1,000 live births among mothers 18 to 19 years old; Chen et al., 2007). Additional findings from the Chen and colleagues' study revealed that mothers 15 years or younger had higher rates of inadequate prenatal care, which is a risk factor for LBW. Although early childbearing occurs across the socioeconomic spectrum, researchers investigating maternal age trends have argued that the incidence of early childbearing is disproportionately high among ethnic minority and impoverished young women (Chen, Wen, Fleming, Yang, & Walker, 2008). Chen and colleagues noted that the poverty faced by many young women also contributes to their delayed entry into prenatal care, to their inadequate weight gain during pregnancy, and to their increased incidence of perinatal medical complications. The nutritional demands of normal physiological development during adolescence may be one factor contributing to the increased prevalence of LBW among adolescent mothers because these demands create a maternal-fetal competition for nutrients (Chen et al., 2008). This competition may be exacerbated in low-income households, which often cannot afford food and in communities where nutritional foods may be less available or cost prohibitive.

In recent years, the United States has experienced a significant increase in the rate of multiple births, which—in part—is the result of increased use of fertility drugs and procedures. Between 1980 and 2002, the United States experienced a 6.5% increase in the rate of twin births. Similarly, between 1980 and 1998, the rate of higher order multiple births increased from 37 births to 193.5 births per 100,000 live births (Alexander, Slay Wingate, Salihu, & Kirby, 2005). These increases in multiple births, particularly twin births, have had a significant impact on raising the incidence rate of LBW, preterm delivery, and prenatal mortality in the United States (Boulet et al., 2008).

Childhood Asthma

Asthma, a long-term lung disease that is characterized by recurrent periods of inflammation in the airways, shortness of breath, coughing, and wheezing, is the most common chronic illness and the most prevalent cause of disability among children in the United States (Williams, Sternthal, & Wright, 2009; Wu, Smith, Bokhour, Hohman, & Lieu, 2008). Indeed, the prevalence of childhood asthma has more than doubled since 1980 (Akinbami, 2006). Data for 2008 show that 10 million U.S. children and adolescents younger than 18 years old had been diagnosed with asthma at some point in their lives, which represented 14% of the U.S. population younger than 18 years (CDC, 2009g). Furthermore, records for 2009 indicated that 5.4% of all U.S. children younger than 15 years old experienced an asthma attack in the previous 12 months (CDC, 2009a). Asthma is the third leading cause of hospitalization among children younger than 15 years, and each year asthma accounts for 12.8 million missed school days (CDC, 2009c).

The prevalence of asthma varies by race and ethnicity. Non-Hispanic African American children (21%) are more likely than either non-Hispanic White children (13%) or Hispanic children (11%) to have been diagnosed with asthma (CDC, 2009g). In a population-based study of 6,004 children in Los Angeles County, the prevalence of childhood asthma among African

American children was 15.8% as compared with 7.3% among Whites and 3.9% among Hispanics (Simon, Zeng, Wold, Haddock, & Fielding, 2003). Similar disparities exist in health outcomes and receipt of health care related to childhood asthma. Compared with White children, African American children are 4 times more likely to be hospitalized because of their asthma and 5 times more likely to die from asthma (Wu et al., 2008).

Although the exact causes of asthma remain unknown, an array of risk factors increases children's risk of developing asthma; many of these risk factors are related to a household's low socioeconomic status. Poverty status and family income have been found to be associated with both previous asthma diagnosis and incidence of asthma attacks (Williams et al., 2009). Children living below the federal poverty level were more likely to have been diagnosed with asthma (16.9%) than those living between 100% and 200% of federal poverty guidelines (15.1%) and those living at or above 200% of the federal poverty level (11.7%; CDC, 2009j). In 2004, 7.2% of children in families receiving public assistance through Temporary Assistance for Needy Families (TANF) had asthma as compared with 5.4% of children in non-TANF families (Child Trends Databank, 2009). Children receiving Medicaid were much more likely to have been diagnosed with asthma (17.4%) at some point in their lives than children with private insurance or no insurance (11.8 % and 8.1%, respectively; CDC, 2009j). In part, the lower prevalence of lifetime asthma diagnosis among uninsured children may be attributable to limited access to health care, which results in a decreased likelihood of a formal diagnosis of asthma. The effect of household economic status on prevalence of childhood asthma is further supported by data showing that children living in single-parent households headed by a female were markedly more likely to have been diagnosed with asthma (17.6%) than children living with two parents (11.7%), which typically report higher income levels than single-mother-headed households (CDC, 2009j).

Research has established that certain environmental conditions appear to be associated with the development of childhood asthma, and the presence of indoor and outdoor environmental pollutants may exacerbate existing asthma (Woodruff et al., 2004). For example, environmental tobacco smoke (i.e., secondhand smoke), most commonly from parental smoking in the household, is a risk factor for increased likelihood of developing childhood asthma as well as exacerbating existing asthma (Baena-Cagnani, Gomez, Baena-Cagnani, & Canonica, 2009; Gerald et al., 2009). In addition, other environmental elements, such as dust mite and cockroach allergens, have been linked to asthma-related health problems among inner-city children (Wang et al., 2009). One study found that exposure to cockroaches at some point in childhood significantly increased the risk for developing childhood asthma, and exposure to cockroach allergens during infancy was associated with a twofold increase in risk for developing asthma (Salam, Li, Langholz, & Gilliland, 2004). Current research has also suggested that poverty at the individual, household, and community level is directly associated with both increased risk of developing asthma and increased risk of experiencing greater severity of asthma "attacks" or acute episodes (Williams et al., 2009).

Various other factors also affect children's risk of asthma. Research findings have suggested that prenatal exposure to tobacco smoke increases the risk that the child will subsequently develop childhood asthma (Baena-Cagnani et al., 2009; Jaakola & Gissler, 2004). Another recent study suggested an association between LBW and childhood asthma (Ahmad et al., 2009). Factors as seemingly unrelated as early day-care attendance and a history of recurrent ear infections have been shown to be associated with increased risk for childhood asthma (Ahmad et al.; Caudri et al., 2009). A recent study of 102,300 children from birth to 17 years indicated that overweight and obese children were nearly 1.3 times more likely to be diagnosed with new-onset asthma and that overweight and obese boys in all age groups were more frequently diagnosed with new-onset asthma (Ahmad et al.).

Overweight and Obesity Among Children and Adolescents

Overweight and obesity are terms used to describe ranges of body weight that are "greater than what is considered healthy for a given height" (CDC, 2009f, para. 1). The problem of overweight has become epidemic among the U.S. population and is the most common health problem facing the country's children (Ogden, Carroll, & Flegal, 2008). The CDC defines weight status using measures of body mass index (BMI), which is a ratio of weight to height. For children, the CDC defines *overweight* as "a BMI at or above the 85th percentile and lower than the 95th percentile" whereas *obesity* is defined as "a BMI at or above the 95th percentile for children of the same age and sex" (CDC, 2009f, para. 2). The BMI percentiles are based on CDC Growth Charts for children

(CDC, 2009f). Overall, boys 6 to 11 years old have been found more likely to be overweight than girls (18% versus 15.8%, respectively; Ogden et al., 2008). Significant disparities in the prevalence of overweight exist between racial and ethnic groups. From 2003 to 2006, the prevalence rate of overweight among Mexican American boys aged 6 to 11 years was 27.5% as compared with 18.6% among non-Hispanic African American boys, and 15.5% among non-Hispanic White boys (Ogden et al., 2008). Among U.S. girls aged 6 to 11 years, the prevalence of overweight was highest among non-Hispanic African American girls (24.0%) as compared with both Mexican American and non-Hispanic White girls (19.7% and 14.4%, respectively; Ogden et al., 2008). Overweight and obesity among younger children have been found to be a significant risk factor for subsequent obesity in adolescence and adulthood as well as the development of diabetes, hypertension, hyperlipidemia, asthma, and sleep apnea (Sharma et al., 2009).

Marked racial and ethnic differences in childhood overweight prevalence are also seen among U.S. adolescents 12 to 19 years old (CDC, 2009f). Based on data from 2003 to 2006, for U.S. adolescent males 12 to 19 years old, 22.1% of Latino adolescents of Mexican descent (i.e., Mexican Americans) were overweight, which was a significantly higher percentage than either their African American or White counterparts (18.5% and 17.3%, respectively; CDC, 2009f). Among U.S. female adolescents 12 to 19 years old, African American females (27.7%) were more likely to be overweight than either Mexican Americans (19.9%) or Whites (14.5%; CDC, 2009f). Between 1998 and 2006, overweight prevalence increased the most among African American females (14.5%) and Mexican American females (10.7%; CDC, 2009f). Even so, since 1999, there has been no significant overall change in the overweight prevalence among U.S. children and adolescents (Ogden et al., 2008).

Studies across disciplines have demonstrated that childhood obesity is caused by the interplay of several factors (Gable & Lutz, 2000). Findings from a study by Stettler, Zemel, Kumanyika, and Stallings (2002) revealed that a pattern of rapid weight gain in the first 3 months of life was associated with overweight status at 7 years. Findings from another research study showed an association between clinically significant behavior problems in normal-weight children and an increased risk of becoming overweight within the subsequent 2-year period (Lumeng, Gannon, Cabral, Frank, & Zuckerman, 2003). Behaviors such as excessive television viewing have been identified as a significant risk factor for childhood overweight

(Zimmerman & Bell, 2009). Proctor (2003) found that children who viewed television 3 hours or more each day had greater body fat and a greater BMI than children who viewed television less than 1.75 hours each day. One randomized controlled school-based intervention to reduce television, videotape, and video game use among elementary school students produced statistically significant decreases in participants' BMI scores as compared with controls (Robinson, 1999). Powell and Bao (2009) posited that food intake and eating habits depend on food availability in the home and that food availability and quality depends largely on food prices and the availability of restaurants and food outlets in the household's neighborhood. Powel and Bao concluded that a 10% price increase for fruits and vegetables available at neighborhood food outlets was positively associated with an increase in child BMI of 0.7%.

Sexually Transmitted Infections Among Adolescents

Sexually transmitted infections (STIs) are a significant health problem facing adolescents in the United States. Compared to older adults, adolescents and young adults are at increased risk for acquiring STIs (CDC, 2009i). Although those between the ages of 15 and 24 years represent only 25% of the sexually experienced population in the United States, this age group accounts for almost half of the estimated 19 million new STI cases each year (CDC, 2009h).

Unprotected sexual intercourse can lead not only to STIs but also to unwanted pregnancy; therefore, teen pregnancy rates are considered an indicator of rates of high-risk sexual behavior. Despite a steady decline in the teen pregnancy rate in the United States between 1995 and 2005, the United States experienced a 3% increase in teen pregnancy rates in 2006 (Alan Guttmacher Institute [AGI], 2010). Although it is too soon to determine whether this increase is simply a short-term fluctuation or the beginning of a long-term increase, preliminary data for 2007 indicate a further increase in teen pregnancy rates (AGI, 2010). The connection between unintended teen pregnancies and STI risk is crucial because risky sexual behaviors that may result in pregnancy also place teens at high risk for STIs.

It is difficult to estimate national STI rates because states have different reporting requirements. Currently, chlamydia, gonorrhea, syphilis, HIV, hepatitis C, and hepatitis B are the only STIs reported by every state to the CDC (CDC, 1997). The accurate collection of incidence and prevalence data is profoundly inhibited by the wide variation in the quality of surveillance data at local and state levels as well as the lack of standard-ized state reporting mechanisms for many common STIs, including geni-tal herpes (herpes simplex viruses type 1 and type 2 and human papillomavirus. Disparities in reporting between public and private health care providers further challenge accurate STI data collection, resulting in the potential underestimation of STIs diagnosed in the private health sector (Rounds, 2004). In addition, many STIs can be asymptomatic and remain undetected, which further contributes to the underestimation of STI rates among adolescents (Rounds, 2004). Lack of access to health care—a significant issue among many adolescents—may also add to the underestimation of STI rates.

Table 6.2   Common Risk Factors for Risky Adolescent Sexual Behaviors

System Level		
Individual Characteristics	**Family Conditions**	**Environmental Conditions**
• Inadequate communication skills • Substance abuse • Depression • Sense of invulnerability • Negative attitudes, beliefs, and intentions about safer sex practices • Inadequate perception of risk • Lack of knowledge about sexuality and safer sex practices • Having been sexually abused • Early puberty • Early initiation of sexual activity • Incomplete cognitive development • Intention to initiate intercourse • Inability to use condoms properly	• Poor parental supervision • Family sexual abuse • Older siblings who are sexually active • Chaotic family life • Family norms that accept early initiation of sexual intercourse and multiple partners • Poor parent–adolescent relationship and communication	• Limited sexuality education (e.g., abstinence-only) • Lack of easy/free condom availability in community • Peer pressure • Community norms that accept early initiation of sexual intercourse and multiple partners • Media that sexualize women and promote risky sexual practices • Lack of emphasis on prevention • Environments or activities where alcohol and drugs are used • High-risk environment

Chlamydia and gonorrhea are the most prevalent among the STIs that states are required to report to the CDC, and each can cause serious health consequences if undetected or left untreated, particularly in young women (CDC, 2009j). In 2008, nearly 71% of all reported chlamydia infections (that included age data) were among young people 15 to 24 years old (CDC, 2009i). Among women in 2008, the highest age-specific reported prevalence rate of chlamydia was in young women 15 to 19 years old, with 3,275.8 cases per 100,000 females; this rate was significantly higher than the rate of chlamydia among males in the same age group (CDC, 2009i). According to CDC (2009i) data collected in prenatal clinics, the 2008 median state-specific chlamydia rate among young women 15 to 24 years old was 7.4%. Compared with many other STIs, syphilis and Hepatitis B are relatively rare among U.S. adolescents and young adults. Prevalence rates of syphilis for 2008 are based on estimates of reported cases and indicate about 4.2 reported cases per 100,000 persons 15 to 19 years old and 11.4 reported cases per 100,000 persons 20 to 24 years old (CDC, 2009i). In 2008, there were 0.9 reported cases of Hepatitis B per 100,000 among those 13 to 24 years old (CDC, 2009i).

Nearly 61% of gonorrhea infections reported in 2008 were among those 15 to 24 years old (CDC, 2009i). In 2008, the incidence was highest among women between the ages of 15 and 24 years and among men between 20 and 24 years old (CDC, 2009i). For young women (15 to 19 years old) in 2008, there were 636.8 cases of gonorrhea per 100,000, representing a slight increase from 2004 (CDC, 2009i). Among young males (15 to 19 years old) in 2008, the gonorrhea prevalence rate was significantly lower at 278.3 cases per 100,000 (CDC, 2009i).

As previously noted, states are not required to report cases of herpes simplex virus and human papillomavirus to the CDC (CDC, 1997). Both of these viral infections can be asymptomatic and, therefore, are frequently transmitted to others by those unaware of their infection. There is little precise information about the prevalence or incidence of either STI among adolescents in the United States, although both are widely prevalent among young people. However, the prevalence of these STIs is an important public health concern because prior exposure to STIs has been linked to predisposition for contracting the HIV virus (Hook et al., 1992).

The overall U.S. STI rates do not reflect the disproportionate impact of STIs on certain high-risk adolescent populations such as youth involved with the juvenile justice system. Youth in the juvenile justice system have elevated rates of engaging in sexual risky behavior and have higher rates of STIs than their peers. These rates may be attributable to three factors: youth involved in the juvenile justice system report onset of sexual activity at younger ages and with more partners than their peers; youth involved in the juvenile justice system are disproportionately African American, and African Americans are disproportionately affected by STIs; and youth involved in the juvenile justice system have higher rates of psychiatric disorders, which are associated with engaging in high-risk sexual behaviors, than the general population (Elkington et al., 2008). The prevalence rates of chlamydia and gonorrhea in juvenile detention settings are consistently higher than in any other subpopulation group (CDC, 2009i). In 2008, the median chlamydia prevalence rate among adolescent females entering juvenile correction facilities was 14.5% as compared with 8.5% of women entering adult corrections facilities (CDC, 2009i). Among young men entering juvenile correctional facilities in 2008, the median prevalence of chlamydia was 6.4% (CDC, 2009i). The median site-specific gonorrhea rate among adolescent females entering 63 juvenile correctional facilities in 2008 was 4.6%, compared with 1.1% among males entering 110 facilities (CDC, 2009i). One study of adolescents in two juvenile detention facilities found that 22.2% of females had chlamydia as compared with 8.7% of males (Kelly, Bair, Baillargeon, & German, 2000).

Youths' sexual risk behaviors and violent behaviors are assessed through the national Youth Risk Behavior Survey (YRBS), which collects self-report data from a representative sample of public and private school students in 9th through 12th grades. Results from the 2006 YRBS showed the prevalence of chlamydia among adolescent females was 4.6% versus 2.3% among same-age males (CDC, 2009h). Chlamydia has also been found to be highly prevalent among economically disadvantaged young women (16 to 24 years) based on longitudinal data collected through the National Job Training Program, which is a federally funded program that requires universal screening for STIs (CDC, 2009i). In each year since 1990, an average of 20,000 young women entering the National Job Training Program have been screened for chlamydia; in 2003, the overall chlamydia prevalence rate among the sample was 9.9%, whereas the 2007 overall rate was 13.7% (Satterwhite, Tian, Braxton, & Weinstock, 2010). More than 1.2 million cases of chlamydia were reported to the CDC during 2008, which was the greatest number of cases ever reported for any STI (CDC, 2009j).

Human immunodeficiency virus (HIV), the virus that over time leads to acquired immunodeficiency syndrome (AIDS), disproportionately affects adolescents in the United States. Researchers estimate that in 2006, about 34% of all new HIV infections in the United States occurred among young people between 13 to 29 years old, the majority of which acquired the virus through sexual transmission (Hall, 2008). Within this age group, women, men who have sex with men, and African Americans are particularly affected by HIV/AIDS (CDC, 2009d). In 2007, young women 13 to 19 years old accounted for 31% of all new cases of HIV whereas women 20 to 24 years old accounted for 23% of new HIV cases (CDC, 2009d). From 2004 to 2007, the majority of new HIV/AIDS cases among male adolescents and young adults 13 to 24 years old were attributed to male-to-male sexual contact (CDC, 2009d). In addition, there is a racial disparity in the HIV/AIDS epidemic in the United States, with African American adolescents disproportionately affected. In localities with confidential HIV reporting, African American adolescents 13 to 19 years old accounted for only 17% of the total population but 72% of new diagnoses of HIV/AIDS (CDC, 2009d). The link between HIV and other STIs is important because the presence of an STI places an individual at greater risk for contracting HIV when exposed to the virus through sexual contact (CDC, 2009i).

As compared with older adults, many biological, developmental, and social factors place sexually active adolescents at higher risk for contracting STIs. Table 6.2 presents a summary of risk factors associated with adolescents' risky sexual behaviors. Adolescents are more likely than are older adults to have unprotected sex and multiple sex partners (either concurrent or sequential), which increases the risk of exposure to an STI-infected partner (Monasterio, Hwang, & Shafer, 2007). According to the 2007 YRBS, only half of all sexually active adolescents 15 to 19 years old reported using a condom during their last sexual intercourse (CDC, 2009h). One in four sexually active high-school seniors reported having used alcohol or other drugs before their last sexual intercourse, and 3 in 10 females reported having had two or more lifetime sex partners (CDC, 2009h). As compared with young men, the higher rates of STIs among young women appear to be based both in behavior and physiology. Behaviorally, young women have a greater likelihood of choosing older, experienced, sexual partners, which increases their potential exposure to STIs (Manlove, Terry-Humen, & Ikramullah, 2006). The higher rates of STIs among young women are also accounted for, in part, by anatomy, which makes females physiologically more susceptible to many STIs than males (Manlove et al., 2006)

Multiple studies have found that adolescent females who self-report a history of childhood and adolescent sexual abuse are more likely to have had consensual intercourse at a younger age, to have not used birth control, to have had multiple sex partners, and to have used alcohol or drugs during their most recent sexual experience (Senn, Carey, & Vanable, 2008). Findings from Raj, Silverman, and Amaro (2000) revealed that both adolescent males and females who reported a history of sexual abuse also reported engaging in risky sexual behaviors. Morrison-Beedy, Carey, Feng, and Tu (2008) found that adolescent females with a history of psychological distress were at increased risk for multiple adverse sexual and reproductive health outcomes. Lee, O'Riordan, and Lazebnik (2009) posited that depressed individuals may engage in risky sexual behaviors as a way of coping with depressive symptoms. In a study of African American adolescent females, a history of depressive symptoms was associated with a greater number of lifetime sexual partners, history of STIs, and previous or current pregnancy (Lee et al., 2009) Adolescents may face numerous barriers to accessing high-quality STI prevention and treatment services. Lack of insurance or alternative payment source, lack of youth-friendly services, lack of transportation, and confidentiality concerns can all inhibit adolescents from accessing quality services that address sexual health needs (Monasterio et al., 2007).

Access to Care as a Protective Factor

Although research has clearly identified biological, developmental, lifestyle, and environmental risk factors associated with health problems, research on protective factors has been more limited. In the case of children and youth at risk for poor health outcomes, access to health care is a protective factor. A host of factors that facilitate access to health care may also be seen as providing a protective effect. Health insurance and health care delivery models that make health care accessible (e.g., community-based care, school-based care, convenient hours, support services, perceived confidentiality among adolescents, and culturally competent services) have a major impact on whether services are accessible and used. Access to health care (i.e., an acceptable provider is available, the individual can get to the provider, and the individual has health insurance to pay for medical care) serves as a protective factor when a child needs medical care (Fraser & Terzian, 2005). That is, access to medical treatment may reduce or buffer the effect of the health condition. For example, ongoing medical treatment for asthma reduces the likelihood that a child will experience an acute episode requiring treatment in the emergency room. Access to health care can also serve as a protective factor by interrupting a chain of risk (Fraser & Terzian, 2005). For instance, early medical treatment for chlamydia, combined with counseling and education on safe sexual practices, may reduce the likelihood that an adolescent girl will develop long-term reproductive-health problems. As a protective factor, access to care can also prevent or block the onset of a risk factor (Fraser & Terzian). One example is the case of a mother whose access to ongoing preventive health services may prevent her young child from becoming at risk for obesity.

Access to health services, or the lack thereof, is closely related to the discussion of poverty-related risk factors identified for each of the previously discussed childhood and adolescent health problems. According to U.S. national data, older adolescents, racial/ethnic minorities, sexually active youth, and uninsured youth are more likely to have neglected health care—a significant risk factor for a wide array of health problems (CDC, 2009b). In 2007, 6.8% of children in the United States had no usual source of health care (CDC, 2009b). In addition, children under 100% of the federal poverty level were 3 times more likely to have an unmet health care need than those from households with income at 200% or more above the poverty threshold.

Availability of health insurance as one component of access to care is a critical protective factor to increase the likelihood that children and adolescents will receive health care. It is estimated that 10% of children in the United States had no form of health insurance in 2008 (U.S. Census Bureau, 2009a). Adolescents without health insurance, either public or private, are more likely to lack a usual health care provider, to have unmet health needs, and to miss at least annual contact with a health care provider (CDC, 2009b).

Although the absence of insurance coverage is a major factor related to access to health care, health insurance alone may not be enough to ensure that children and adolescents receive needed health care services, particularly among those who are low income (DeVoe et al., 2007). As previously noted, having a usual source of care may reduce many barriers to accessing health care services, although it does not ensure that such services will be used or received when needed (Szilagyi, Schuster, & Cheng, 2009). Many nonfinancial factors also appear to affect health care accessibility and utilization. These factors include delivery system structure, provider availability, preventive care education, enabling services (e.g., transportation and translation), child care, and appointment reminders (Newacheck, Hung, Park, Brindis, & Irwin, 2003).

Risk, Resilience, and Protection in Health Policy for Children and Youth

In this section, we present a brief overview of the development of child health policy from the beginning of the 20th century to the present. We also examine the effectiveness of health policies in meeting the health care needs of children and youth. We conclude by discussing the extent to which policy has been based on risk and protective factors.

Historical Development of Child Health Policy

Child health policy has developed in a piecemeal way, with policy initiatives often having been episodic responses to the failure of the private marketplace (Barr, Lee, & Benjamin, 2003). Although the federal government was involved to some extent in responding to children's health and mental health needs through the establishment of the Children's Bureau in 1912 and then later through the establishment of the Maternal and Child Health service system, it did not become heavily involved in financing health care for children and youth until the establishment of the Medicaid program in 1965. Table 6.3 provides a chronological listing of major policy initiatives and their primary purposes.

At the turn of the 20th century, living conditions were so poor for many American families that the average state infant mortality rate was 150/1,000. In some industrial cities, it was as high as 180/1,000 (Margolis, Cole, & Kotch, 1997). In response to this high infant mortality rate, social workers joined forces with public health workers and advocates from the fields of education, medicine, and labor to lobby for passage of legislation to establish the Children's Bureau in 1912 (Margolis et al., 1997). The Children's Bureau was initially created with a mandate to study the problem of infant mortality and address the problem by disseminating information on promising interventions to the states. Based on the success of the Children's Bureau, Congress passed the Sheppard-Towner Maternity and Infancy Act in 1921, creating the first national maternal and child health program that provided grants-in-aid to states. The Sheppard-Towner Act represented the first federal effort to establish a maternal and child health infrastructure within the states, and it laid the groundwork for future collaboration between state and federal governments to

Table 6.3   Chronology of Key Child Health Policy Legislation 1900 to Present

Year	Legislation	Purpose
1912	Children's Bureau established	Studied and began to address the high rates of infant mortality
1921	Sheppard-Towner Maternity and Infancy Act	Established the first national Maternal and Child Health program, provided grants-in-aid to states to develop local and state maternal and child health infrastructures
1935	Social Security Act, including Title V Maternal and Child Health Program	Title V—Created a coordinated Maternal and Child Health service system based on a federal–state partnership
1965	Title XIX amended the Social Security Act to establish the Medicaid program	Provided health insurance to children and families in poverty
1981	Omnibus Budget Reconciliation Act of 1981 (OBRA '81) Maternal and Child Health Services Block Grant Amendments to Title V	Shifted program planning, control, and accountability for Maternal and Child Health programs from federal to state and local governments
1989	Omnibus Budget Reconciliation Act (OBRA '89)	Established stricter reporting requirements for Title V and supported development of systems of care for Children with Special Health Care Needs (CSHCN); expanded the Early and Periodic, Screening, Diagnosis, and Treatment (EPSDT) program; mandated Medicaid coverage of children younger than 6 years with family income up to 133% of federal poverty level (FPL)
1996	Personal Responsibility Work and Opportunity Reconciliation Act (PRWORA)	Delinked Medicaid eligibility and public assistance
1997	Title XXI (SSA), State Child Health Insurance Program (SCHIP) established	Expanded the health insurance safety net to cover more low-income children who were not eligible for Medicaid and whose families could not afford private insurance

(Continued)

Table 6.3 (Continued)

Year	Legislation	Purpose
2003	Jobs and Growth Tax Relief Reconciliation Act	Raised all state Medicaid matching rates by 2.95 percentage points for the period of April 2003 through June 2004 as a temporary federal fiscal relief for the states due to the downturn of the economy, provided that the state maintains its Medicaid eligibility levels
2006	Deficit Reduction Act of 2005 (DRA)	Allowed states to impose cost-sharing for most services on children eligible for Medicaid on an "optional" basis (generally those with family incomes above 100% of the FPL); required all children and parents who apply for Medicaid and who claim to be U.S. citizens to document their citizenship and identity, Medicare beneficiaries and most individuals with disabilities are exempt from this requirement; allowed states to offer disabled children under 19 with family incomes below 300% of FPL to purchase Medicaid coverage by paying income-related premiums
2009	Children's Health Insurance Program Reauthorization Act (CHIRPA)	Expanded Child Health Insurance Program (CHIP) to an additional 4 million children; gave states the option to eliminate a 5-year waiting period for legal immigrant children and pregnant women to be eligible for Medicaid and CHIP; rescinded the August 17 Directive, which had restricted states' ability to cover children in families with income above 250% of the FPL
2009	American Recovery and Reinvestment Act (ARRA)	Provided enhanced Medicaid matching funds to states from October 1, 2008, through December 31, 2010, to help states maintain Medicaid eligibility levels and enrollment
2010	Patient Protection and Affordable Care Act and Health Care and Education Reconciliation Act	Expands health insurance coverage to 32 million people by 2019; prevents states from reducing income eligibility threshold for SCHIP and maintains current income eligibility for children's Medicaid until 2019; regulates insurance companies to prevent insurers from dropping individuals when they become sick and denying coverage for pre-existing conditions

address maternal and child health (Kessel, Jaros, & Harker, 2003; Margolis et al., 1997). During the 8 years the act was in effect, the number of permanent maternal and child health centers and state child hygiene and welfare programs increased.

The Sheppard-Towner Act was not renewed in 1929, and the Great Depression had a major impact on the ability of states to provide maternal and child health services. These events contributed to an increase in infant mortality across the nation. In response to rising infant mortality rates and the widespread poverty among women and children, Title V of the Social Security Act was passed in 1935. Title V had three parts that were administered under the Children's Bureau: (1) Maternal and Child Health Services (MCH) enabled states to expand services that had been provided by the Sheppard-Towner Act; (2) Services for Crippled Children's Program enabled states to locate and provide medical and other services for children who had "crippling conditions"; and (3) Child Welfare Services enabled states to provide services to homeless, dependent, and neglected children (Kessel et al., 2003). Title V funding through the Services for Crippled Children's Program was the only source of federal funding for children with special health care needs (the majority of whom needed orthopedic treatment as a result of the polio epidemic) until 1965, when the Medicaid program was established.

Title V has been amended numerous times over the past decades. The Omnibus Budget Reconciliation Act of 1981, P.L. 97–35, consolidated seven Title V categorical programs into a block grant program. The Omnibus Budget Reconciliation Act of 1989 (OBRA '89), P.L. 101–239, introduced stricter requirements for state planning and reporting regarding use of Title V funds. OBRA '89 gave authority to the Maternal and Child Health Bureau to help develop systems of care for children with special health care needs and their families, and expanded the mission of related programs to promote the development of community-based systems of services (McPherson et al., 1998). State health departments administer the Title V MCH Services Block Grant Program (Maternal and Child Health Bureau, n.d.). The federal government requires states to conduct a statewide needs assessment every 5 years and to submit a plan for meeting those needs. Title V block grant funds are used primarily for service system development to reduce infant mortality and the incidence of disabilities and to provide and ensure access to health care for women of reproductive age, access to preventive and primary care services for children, and access to family-centered, community-based, coordinated care for children with special health care needs.

The Medicaid program was enacted in 1965 as a joint state and federally funded health insurance program for women who were on public assistance and their children and other persons who were elderly, blind, or disabled. Each state administers its own Medicaid program according to federal guidelines. The federal government provides matching funds for some of the state Medicaid costs (on average about 57% of costs are matched). In 1967, the Early and Periodic Screening, Diagnosis, and Treatment Program (EPSDT) was created as a unique prevention component of the Medicaid program to ensure that children receiving Medicaid would receive preventive health services in addition to acute and chronic medical care (Sardell & Johnson, 1998). The EPSDT program requires states to offer age-appropriate screenings and immunizations, follow-up diagnostic services, and medical treatment. Because many states never fully implemented their EPSDT program and to increase the number of children receiving preventive care, Congress included provisions in the Omnibus Budget Reconciliation Act (OBRA '89) that expanded the EPSDT program. The expanded provisions required states to conduct aggressive outreach and case-finding efforts as well as to provide enabling services such as case management, transportation, and translation services (Rosenbach & Gavin, 1998).

During the 1980s and 1990s, the rates of children and youth covered by private health insurance substantially declined. This decline was the result of several factors, including the loss of manufacturing jobs, which often offered employees and their families affordable health insurance, and the concomitant rise in lower paying service jobs, which often did not offer employees health insurance. The proportion of workers who were hired to fill contract or part-time positions, which typically do not carry health insurance benefits for the worker or his or her family, also increased. In addition, during this period, the cost of health insurance for employers rose significantly, and many employers changed policies to cover only the employee and not the family (Moniz & Gorin, 2003).

To deal with the loss of private health insurance coverage and the resulting increase in uninsured children and youth, Congress passed a series of Medicaid expansions beginning in the mid-1980s. For example, the Omnibus Budget Reconciliation Act of 1989 (OBRA '89) required states to cover pregnant women and children up to the age of 6 years with family incomes that were up to 133% of federal poverty guidelines. The early expansions focused solely on infants and young children. Later, the

Omnibus Budget Reconciliation Act of 1990 (OBRA '90) mandated coverage of adolescents up to 16 years of age with family incomes of as much as 100% of the federal poverty guidelines (Newacheck, Brindis, Cart, Marchi, & Irwin, 1999).

These Medicaid expansions began the "delinking" of Medicaid and public assistance status. This delinking process was finally completed in 1996 with the passage of the Personal Responsibility Work and Opportunity Reconciliation Act (PRWORA; Moniz & Gorin, 2003). PRWORA separated the determination of eligibility for Medicaid from receipt of public assistance, which was called Temporary Assistance for Needy Families (TANF). Currently, the federal government requires states to provide Medicaid coverage for children up to age 5 years in families with incomes of as much as 133% of the poverty guidelines and to cover children from the ages of 6 to 19 years old in families with incomes at or below the federal poverty level.

The Balanced Budget Act of 1997 created the State Children's Health Insurance Program (SCHIP) to address the large number of uninsured children of low-income working families who were not eligible for Medicaid because their family income exceeded the eligibility criteria. Unlike Medicaid, SCHIP is not an entitlement program. Under federal legislation, states have been given tremendous flexibility to use SCHIP allocations to create separate SCHIP programs, expand their Medicaid programs, or develop a combination of both. States are also allowed to determine SCHIP eligibility; among the states, eligibility ranges from less than 200% to 400% of the federal poverty guidelines. State dollars are matched by federal dollars. States with lower per capita income receive a higher federal match rate. States are also allowed to require monthly premiums or co-payments for participation in their SCHIP programs. In 2009, premiums were required by 35 states, with some premiums as high as $100 or more per month (Henry J. Kaiser Family Foundation, 2009b).

The success of SCHIP has been highly variable and largely dependent on each state conducting aggressive and effective outreach, enrollment, and renewal efforts. Although Medicaid and SCHIP provide health insurance coverage for many low-income children, nearly 7.3 million children are uninsured, and it is estimated that a significant number of these are eligible for Medicaid or SCHIP (U.S. Census Bureau, 2009b). Because of barriers to enrollment and renewal, many eligible children are currently not enrolled. In addition, because of constraints on state budgets, outreach efforts have been reduced in many states, and some states have enacted measures to restrict coverage in their SCHIP programs (Henry J. Kaiser Family Foundation, 2009a). According to some reports, if Medicaid and SCHIP were to be implemented in a way that included aggressive outreach to all eligible children, coverage for immigrant children, and a modest expansion to include more low-income families, these programs could provide coverage to all children in the United States with family income less than 200% of federal poverty guidelines (Baron, Kleinmann, & Sylvester, 2003).

Landmark health care reform legislation, The Patient Protection and Affordable Care Act and the Health Care and Education Reconciliation Act of 2010, was signed into law by President Barack Obama in March 2010. Key provisions of the act include barring insurance companies from dropping individuals from coverage when they become ill, developing a new program to provide health insurance to uninsured adults with pre-existing conditions, and allowing young adults to remain on their parents' insurance until they reach 26 years of age. In addition, the law prevents states from reducing the income eligibility threshold for SCHIP and requires them to maintain children's Medicaid eligibility until 2019. Beginning in 2014, individuals will be required to have minimal health insurance coverage or pay a penalty; federal subsidies or tax credits will be used to help offset costs for low- and middle-income people who must purchase individual plans. At the time of this writing, the Department of Health and Human Services had not released specific details regarding how the various provisions would be implemented.

The Degree to Which Policy Has Been Based on Risk and Protective Factors

As stated earlier in this chapter, for many children and youth, access to care serves as a protective factor in the face of health risk. Federal health policy has primarily attempted to address risk factors associated with poor health outcomes by increasing access to preventive and medical care services. It has been addressed in two ways: (1) through the creation of public health insurance programs for low-income children (first through Medicaid and then through SCHIP) and (2) through supporting infrastructure development to ensure that services are delivered in a coordinated and accessible manner (primarily through Title V of the Social Security Act).

Protective Role of Health Insurance

Numerous studies have demonstrated the key role that health insurance plays in increasing access to health care for children and youth (Newacheck et al., 1999; Newacheck, Pearl, Hughes, & Halfon, 1998). Beginning in the 1980s, with the expansion of eligibility for Medicaid, and extending through the implementation of the SCHIP program, the federal insurance safety net has covered an increasing percentage of low-income children. A study of the New York state SCHIP program demonstrated that enrollment in SCHIP reduced preexisting racial/ethnic disparities in unmet need and access to and continuity of care among 2,290 children (Shone, Dick, Klein, Zwanziger, & Szilagyi, 2005). Kempe and associates (2005) in a study of Colorado's SCHIP program found that one year after enrollment, families ($N = 480$) reported improved access to care, a decrease in unmet medical needs, an increase in routine care visits, and a higher perception of quality care. Experts argue that the most effective way to ensure that children have health insurance coverage and receive needed care is to approach insurance coverage at the family level as opposed to the individual level. DeVoe, Tillotson, and Wallace (2008) found that, compared with insured children who had at least one insured parent, children with uninsured parents were more likely to have never received preventive counseling services, to have insurance coverage gaps, and to have unmet health care needs.

Concept of a "Medical Home"

Although public insurance programs such as Medicaid and SCHIP have provided an important health insurance safety net for children and youth, insurance coverage alone is not sufficient for ensuring access to health services (Newacheck et al., 2003). Coordinated systems of care also need to be in place to respond to the health care needs of children and youth. Federal policymakers have addressed systems issues primarily through programs funded by Title V of the Social Security Act. For example, one of the hallmarks of coordinated care is to ensure that children have continuous access to routine health care and that medical services are integrated with other child and youth services. The

American Academy of Pediatrics and other advocacy groups have worked closely with the MCHB to implement the "medical home" concept for all children, especially children with special health care needs (American Academy of Pediatrics, 2010). Although the term *medical home* was originally defined as a physical location, it has evolved to define a partnership with families to ensure that children and youth are receiving care that is "accessible, family centered, coordinated, comprehensive, continuous, compassionate, and culturally effective" (Sia, Tonniges, Osterhus, & Taba, 2004, p. 1473). Examining data from the National Survey of Children with Special Health Care Needs, investigators found that when children have a medical home, they experience significantly less delay in seeking care and have fewer unmet health care needs and fewer unmet needs for family support services (Strickland et al., 2004). One of the child health objectives in *Healthy People 2010* is to "increase the proportion of children with special health care needs who have access to a medical home" (U.S. DHHS, n.d.). The Head Start program and the Maternal and Child Health Bureau Services V Block Grant program require that states report on how and to what extent they are achieving this objective.

Another systems-change approach to increasing access to health care for children and youth is to deliver health care in settings where the majority of children spend a large portion of their day. This approach is reflected in policy initiatives to support the development and ongoing operation of school-based and school-linked health centers. Delivering integrated services through school-based health centers will be discussed in the next section on service integration.

The Case of "Abstinence Only" Versus More Comprehensive Programs

One area of controversy regarding how well federal health policy has been informed by risk and protective factors is that of adolescent sexual health. Comprehensive sexual health education can serve as a protective factor by providing youth with the knowledge and skills necessary to make healthy decisions about sexual behavior. In fiscal year 2008, the federal government allocated $176 million for abstinence-only education. At this time, there was no federal program that supported comprehensive sex education to teach young people about both abstinence and contraception (Boonstra, 2009). Federal law required that abstinence-only sexuality education teach that sexual activity outside of marriage is wrong and harmful for everyone, irrespective of age (Boonstra). This mandate kept educators from providing information on contraceptive methods, with the exception of emphasizing their ineffectiveness (Boonstra). Perhaps most disturbing is that after years of evaluation of abstinence-only programs, no credible evidence has shown that such restrictive education delays adolescent sexual activity (Boonstra). However, empirical evidence does suggest that abstinence-only models may reduce contraceptive use among sexually active young people, thereby increasing their risk for STIs and unplanned pregnancies (Boonstra; Rosenbaum, 2009). Furthermore, research has demonstrated that the most effective sexuality education programs are comprehensive in nature, incorporating both abstinence promotion and discussion of safer sex options (Kohler, Manhart, & Lafferty, 2008). In 2009, the Obama administration introduced a new initiative that replaced the Community Based Abstinence Program. This initiative, called the Teen Pregnancy Prevention Initiative, focuses on replicating programs that have proven effectiveness and allocates funds to develop and test innovative models and new strategies for preventing teen pregnancy (National Campaign to Prevent Teen and Unplanned Pregnancy, 2010).

Using Knowledge of Risk, Protection, and Resilience to Achieve Service Integration in Health Policy

Meeting the needs of children and youth, especially those involved in multiple service systems, requires policies that promote integration and collaboration among service systems. In this section, we use a case study of an adolescent with multiple problems to illustrate how integrated service systems can best meet the needs of children and youth. We use the school-based health center model as an example of how services can be integrated to respond to the multiple challenges of children and youth. School-based health centers serve as an important safety net for primary care—more than two thirds of students who have access to such centers are ethnic minorities, and a substantial proportion of schools are in low-income communities (National Assembly on School-Based Health Care [NASBHC], 2007). These centers have been successful at integrating health and mental health care with educational services because services are delivered in the school setting where the majority of children and youth spend a large portion of their day. For adolescents in particular, who are more likely to use health care services on a "spontaneous basis" (Pastore & Techow, 2004, p. 195), school-based health centers offer location, convenience, confidentiality, and trust—all factors associated with the utilization of health and mental health services by adolescents (Brandis et al., 2003).

Background and Current Status of School-Based Health Centers

During the 1970s, several communities established school-based health clinics to serve low-income children. The Robert Wood Johnson Foundation joined these efforts in 1978 by underwriting a 5-year School Health Services Program that put nurse practitioners in elementary schools serving 150,000 students in Colorado, New York, North Dakota, and Utah. In response to a national concern over the deteriorating health status of children and adolescents, the foundation launched the Community Care Funding Partners Program in 1981. Five of the eight cities in this program located community health centers in secondary schools. Based on the success of this program, the foundation in 1986 launched the School-Based Adolescent Health Care Program, which was designed to evaluate whether school-based health centers could be sustained by communities and could effectively deliver comprehensive medical and mental health services to teens. The foundation used strict criteria to fund 24 centers in 14 cities. The criteria emphasized the need for community advisory committees and coalition building among corporations, foundations, schools, and health and welfare agencies (Brodeur, 2000).

Early Findings

A 1993 evaluation of the School-Based Adolescent Health Care Program found that although the program had little effect on decreasing high-risk behavior, the centers had increased access to care for students (especially low-income students) who had previously not received care. More than half of the students who were enrolled in the participating schools were receiving care from the centers. Another critical issue revealed in the evaluation was that the centers had not been sufficiently successful in obtaining reimbursement from third-party insurers, including Medicaid.

Through the early 1990s, local health departments, private foundations, and the MCHB funded school-based health centers. Because of limited funding to support the development of centers, the Robert Wood Johnson Foundation initiated "Making the Grade: State and Local Partnerships to Establish School-Based Health Centers." The goal of this initiative was to reorganize state and local funding policies to support comprehensive health care for children and adolescents as well as to improve administrative procedures enabling school-based health centers to receive reimbursements through Medicaid (Brodeur, 2000).

Recent Findings

Recent data on school-based health centers indicate that the centers are no longer in a demonstration phase, with nearly 70% of U.S. centers now in place for 5 years or more (NASBHC). The record demonstrates that school-based centers are an effective means through which young people can access health and mental health services. The summary of the results from the national survey, *School Based Health Centers National Census School Year 2004–2005* (NASBHC), identified 1,709 school-based health programs. This number includes school-based, mobile, and linked programs. Hospitals, local health departments, and community health centers represent 68% of sponsors. About 65% of the centers provide mental health services. Since the last NASBHC census conducted during the 2001–2002 school year, 152 new centers have opened. Once primarily located in urban areas, school-based health centers have expanded to suburban and rural schools (NASBHC). Today, nearly 30% of all centers are located in rural communities (NASBHC).

Providing Concurrent Health and Mental Health Care Through School-Based Clinics

According to the NASBHC report, nearly all school-based health centers offer the following services: comprehensive health assessments (96%), minor acute illness care (97%), psychological development assessments (71%), dental screenings/diagnostic (42%), and immunizations (90%). About 81% of programs have a licensed mental health provider, 12% report having a drug and alcohol counselor on site, and 10% report having a psychiatrist. Services offered include crisis intervention, assessment and diagnosis, long-term therapy, and tobacco use counseling. In the secondary-school centers, 42% provide gynecological exams and 62% provide diagnosis and treatment of STIs (NASBHC, 2007). Other studies have shown that school-based health centers are an important secondary access point for teens, especially with regard to behavioral health care services. In a 3-year study conducted in the greater Cincinnati area, Guo, Wade, and Keller (2008) found that young adolescents who were enrolled in a school with a school-based health center were more likely to access mental health services. There was a statistically significant increase in mental health services utilization in urban (5.6%) and rural (5.9%) schools with school-based health centers, whereas the slight increase in utilization in urban (2.6%) and rural (.2%) schools without a center was not statistically significant. In an evaluation of a school-based health center serving two schools in New York City, Pastore and Techow (2004) concluded that "on-site mental health services and their immediate availability for crisis intervention allow teenagers to engage in individual, family, and group treatment before problems become so severe that they interfere with their education" (p. 194).

The following case study illustrates how a school-based health center serves as a protective factor by providing access to care to a youth with several risk factors for poor health and mental health outcomes. Because of their location in school settings and the collaborative philosophy and interdisciplinary approach to providing services, school-based health centers are well positioned to integrate services for children and youth.

Case Study

James, a 14-year-old African American male, lives with his 31-year-old single mother and 8-year-old sister in a public housing project on the outskirts of town. James's mother works in a local fast-food restaurant and has no health insurance. As a freshman in high school, James is experiencing a great deal of anxiety about fitting in with his classmates, often feels sad, is not sleeping well, and is falling behind in his course work because of his lack of motivation and problems concentrating. Like many of his friends, James is experimenting with alcohol, marijuana, and other drugs and has recently become sexually active. He had unprotected vaginal sex at a party the previous week, and for the past 2 days, he has been experiencing a fire-like burning during urination. James is worried that he might have gonorrhea, but he has no idea of where to go for help. He is very uncomfortable and does not want to go to school, yet he feels that there is no way he can let his mom find out about his condition.

James is fortunate in that he attends a school with a school-based health center that offers comprehensive services. On the urging of his best friend, who has had several good experiences at the center, James drops by the center for a visit during lunch. Because his mother signed an enrollment form for the health center when James entered high school, he is able to receive confidential services without the center contacting her. A nurse practitioner sees him initially for assessment and medical treatment of his STI. The social worker also conducts an initial psychosocial assessment and schedules a time to meet with James the next day. She plans to follow-up with his concerns about school and his feelings of sadness and to learn more about his recent drug and alcohol use and sexual behavior. James has given the social worker permission to access his school records and talk with his teachers and school counselor. The social worker will be able to contact other staff at the health center for assistance in evaluating James and providing him with needed services. A psychiatrist provides consultation services to the school-based health center staff. The psychiatrist also conducts psychiatric evaluations and prescribes and monitors psychiatric medications. In addition, the health center staff provides counseling and conducts groups on a number of health and mental health topics, such as substance abuse, sexual health, and coping with relationships. The health center has recently begun participating in an innovative SCHIP outreach initiative to increase the enrollment of eligible youth. The social worker thinks that James probably meets the eligibility criteria and, with James's permission, she will contact his mother to assist her in enrolling both of her children. James' enrollment in the SCHIP program will allow the center to be reimbursed for services and will help the social worker access additional health and mental health services for James if he needs them.

Case Study Questions for Discussion

- What would most likely happen to James if a school-based health center did not exist in his school?
- How would he find out how to get care?
- Where would he receive care and when?
- Who would pay for his care?
- How comprehensive would his care likely be?
- What is the likelihood that James would be assessed and treated for any other conditions or problems than his presenting symptoms (i.e., burning on urination)?

Summary

In this chapter, we have reviewed risk factors for several major health problems (LBW, asthma, overweight and obesity, and STIs) experienced by children and youth. Although there are risk factors that are unique to each of these health problems, two major risk factors are common across health problems: poverty and living in socially and physically unhealthy environments (Fraser, 2004; Moniz & Gorin, 2003). Access to care, which includes both access to health insurance and availability of coordinated systems of care, plays a major role in decreasing the risk for poor health outcomes and protecting children and youth from developing health problems.

U.S. health care policy has increased children's access to health services through the creation of public health insurance programs (e.g., Medicaid and SCHIP). Through Title V of the Social Security Act and other initiatives, the federal government has supported the development of a more coordinated and comprehensive service system. The concepts of the medical home and school-based health centers are examples of efforts at coordination and integration. School-based health centers are a promising example of integration of health, mental health, and educational services provided in a location that is accessible to children and youth enrolled in schools. However, attempts to fully integrate services for children and youth across major service systems (health, mental health, education, child welfare, and juvenile justice) are still in their infancy and much remains to be accomplished. Furthermore, federal policy has had very limited success in reducing the number of children living in poverty or near poverty or ensuring that children and youth live in healthy environments. To truly make a significant difference in the health of children and youth, federal policy cannot be constrained to the mere creation of coordinated systems of care, although this would be a substantial achievement. National policy must also address the poverty and social inequities associated with poor health and well-being.

QUESTIONS FOR DISCUSSION

1. How do socioeconomic inequalities and physical and social environments contribute to health outcomes of children and youth? Given the existence of these inequalities, what effect will the recent passage of health care reform legislation, which expands insurance coverage to the uninsured and thereby increases access to medical care, have on the existing racial health disparities among children and youth?

2. Given the success of school-based health clinics in integrating service systems for children and youth, why has their establishment not been more widespread?

3. What other service delivery models are you aware of that integrate service systems, including health care for children and youth? What policies need to be in place for these service delivery models to be created?

References

Aagaard-Tillery, K. M., Porter, T. F., Lane, R. H., Varner, M. W., & Lacoursiere, D. Y. (2008). In utero tobacco exposure is associated with modified effects of maternal factors on fetal growth. *American Journal of Obstetrics and Gynecology, 198*(1), 66.e1–66.e6. doi:10.1016/j.ajog.2007.06.078

Ahmad, N., Biswas, S., Bae, S., Meador, K. E., Huang, R., & Singh, K. P. (2009). Association between obesity and asthma in US children and adolescents. *The Journal of Asthma, 46*(7), 642–646. doi:10.1080/02770900802503123

Akinbami, L., (2006). *The state of childhood asthma, United States, 1980–2005* (Advance Data Series No. 381, Centers for Disease Control and Prevention). Retrieved from http://www.cdc.gov/nchs/data/ad/ad381.pdf

Alan Guttmacher Institute. (2010). *U.S. teenage pregnancies, births and abortions: National and state trends and trends by race and ethnicity.* Retrieved from http://www.guttmacher.org/pubs/USTPtrends.pdf

Alexander, G. R., Slay Wingate, M., Salihu, H., & Kirby, R. S. (2005). Fetal and neonatal mortality risks of multiple births. *Obstetrics and Gynecology Clinics of North America, 32,* 1–16. doi:10.1016/j.ogc.2004.10.005

American Academy of Pediatrics. (2010). *National Center for Medical Home Implementation: What is a medical home?* Retrieved from http://www.medical homeinfo.org/index.html

Anderson, R. M. (1995). Revisiting the behavioral model and access to medical care: Does it matter? *Journal of Health and Social Behavior, 36,* 1–10.

Baena-Cagnani, C. E., Gomez, R. M., Baena-Cagnani, R., & Canonica, G. W. (2009). Impact of environmental tobacco smoke and active tobacco smoking on the development and outcomes of asthma and rhinitis. *Current Opinion in Allergy and Clinical Immunology, 9,* 136–140. doi:10.1097/ACI.0b013e3283294038

Baron, J., Kleinmann, J. H., & Sylvester, K. (2003). Health insurance for children: Issues and ideas. *Future of Children, 13,* 1–32.

Barr, D. A., Lee, P. R., & Benjamin, A. E. (2003). Health care and health care policy in a changing world. In H. M. Wallace, G. Green, & K. Jaros (Eds.), *Health and welfare for families in the 21st century* (2nd ed., pp. 262–42). Boston: Jones & Bartlett.

Bethell, C. D., Read, D., Blumber, S. J., & Newacheck, P. (2008). What is the prevalence of children with special health care needs: Towards an understanding of variations in findings and methods across three national surveys. *MCH Journal, 12,* 1–14. doi:10.1007/s10995-007-0220-5.

Boonstra, H. D. (2009). Advocates call for a new approach after the era of "abstinence-only" sex education. *Guttmacher Policy Review, 12*(1), 6–11. Retrieved from http://www.guttmacher.org/pubs/gpr/12/1/gpr120106.html

Boulet, S. L., Schieve, L. A., Nannini, A., Ferre, C., Devine, O., Cohen, B., . . . Macaluso, M. (2008). Perinatal outcomes of twin births conceived using assisted reproduction technology: A population-based study. *Human Reproduction, 23*(8), 1941–1948. doi:10.1093/humrep/den169

Brandis, C. D., Klein, J., Schlitt, J., Santelli, J., Juszcak, L., & Nystrom, R. (2003). School-based health centers: Accessibility and accountability. *Journal of Adolescent Health, 32S,* 98–107.

Brodeur, P. (2000). School-based health clinics. In S. L. Isaacs & J. R. Knickman (Eds.), *To improve health and health care: The Robert Wood Johnson Foundation anthology* (pp. 121–149). San Francisco: Jossey-Bass.

Caudri, D., Wijga, A., Scholtens, S., Kerkhof, M., Gerritsen, J., Ruskamp, J. M., . . . de Jongste, J. C. (2009). Early daycare is associated with an increase in airway symptoms in early childhood but is no protection against asthma or atopy at 8 years. *American Journal of Respiratory and Critical Care Medicine, 180,* 491–498. doi:10.1164/rccm.200903–03270C

Centers for Disease Control and Prevention. (1997). Case definitions for infectious conditions under public health surveillance. *Morbidity and Mortality Weekly Report, 44*(No. RR-10), 1–5.

Centers for Disease Control and Prevention. (2009a). *Early release of selected estimates based on data from the January–June 2009 National Health Interview Survey: Asthma episodes and current asthma.* Retrieved from http://www.cdc.gov/nchs/data/nhis/earlyrelease/200912_15.pdf

Centers for Disease Control and Prevention. (2009b). *Health, United States, 2009.* Retrieved from http://www.cdc.gov/nchs/data/hus/hus09.pdf

Centers for Disease Control and Prevention. (2009c). *Healthy schools healthy youth: Asthma.* Retrieved from http://www.cdc.gov/HealthyYouth/asthma/index.htm

Centers for Disease Control and Prevention. (2009d). *HIV/AIDS surveillance in adolescents and young adults (through 2007).* Retrieved from http://www.cdc.gov/hiv/topics/surveillance/resources/slides/adolescents/index.htm

Centers for Disease Control and Prevention. (2009e). *National vital statistics reports births: Preliminary data for 2007.* Retrieved from http://www.cdc.gov/nchs/data/nvsr/nvsr57/nvsr57_12.pdf

Centers for Disease Control and Prevention. (2009f). *Overweight and obesity.* Retrieved from http://www.cdc.gov/obesity/childhood/defining.html

Centers for Disease Control and Prevention. (2009g). *Provisional—Summary health statistics for U.S. children: National interview survey, 2008.* Retrieved from http://www.cdc.gov/nchs/data/series/sr_10/sr10_244.pdf

Centers for Disease Control and Prevention. (2009h). Sexual and reproductive health of persons aged 10–24—United States, 2002–2007. *Morbidity and Mortality Weekly Report, 58*(No. SS-6), 1–60.

Centers for Disease Control and Prevention. (2009i). *Sexually transmitted diseases surveillance, 2008.* Retrieved from http://www.cdc.gov/std/stats08/surv 2008-Complete.pdf

Centers for Disease Control and Prevention. (2009j). *Summary health statistics for U.S. children: National Health Interview Survey, 2007.* Retrieved from http://www .cdc.gov/nchs/data/series/sr_10/sr10_239.pdf

Chen, X., Wen, S. W., Fleming, N., Demissie, K., Rhoads, G. G., & Walker, M. (2007). Teenage pregnancy and adverse birth outcomes: A large population based retrospective cohort study. *International Journal of Epidemiology, 36,* 368–373. doi:10.1093/ije/dy1284

Chen, X. K., Wen, S. W., Fleming, N., Yang, Q., & Walker, M. C. (2008). Increased risks of neonatal and postneonatal mortality associated with teenage pregnancy had different explanations. *Journal of Clinical Epidemiology, 61,* 688–694. doi:10.1016/j.jclinepi.2007.08.009

Child Trends Databank. (2009). *Asthma.* Retrieved from http://www.childtrends databank.org/indicators/43Asthma.cfm

Data Resource Center for Child and Adolescent Health. (n.d.). *Focus areas: Who are children with special health care needs?* Retrieved from http://www.childhealth data.org/content/Default.aspx

DeVoe, J. E., Baez, A., Angier, H., Krois, L., Edlund, C., & Carney, P. A. (2007). Insurance + access not equal to health care: Typology of barriers to health care access for low-income families. *Annals of Family Medicine, 5,* 511–518. doi:10.1370/afm.748

DeVoe, J. E., Tillotson, C., & Wallace, L. S. (2008). Uninsured children and adolescents with insured parents. *Journal of the American Medical Association, 300,* 1904–1913. doi:10.1001/jama.2008.516

Donabedian, A. (1973). *Aspects of medical care administration.* Cambridge, MA: Harvard University Press.

Elkington, K. S., Teplin, L. A., Mericle, A. A., Welty, L. J., Romero, E. G., & Abram, K. M. (2008). HIV/sexually transmitted infection risk behaviors in delinquent youth with psychiatric disorders: A longitudinal study. *Journal of the American Academy of Child and Adolescent Psychiatry, 47,* 901–911. doi: 10.1097/ CHI.0b013e318179962b

Fraser, M. W. (2004). The ecology of childhood: A multisystems perspective. In M. W. Fraser (Ed.), *Risk and resilience in childhood: An ecological perspective* (2nd ed., pp. 1–12). Washington, DC: NASW Press.

Fraser, M. W., & Terzian, M. A. (2005). Risk and resilience in child development: Practice, principles, and strategies. In G. P. Mallon & P. McCartt Hess (Eds.), *Child welfare for the 21st century: A handbook of practices, policies, and programs.* New York: Columbia University Press.

Gable, S., & Lutz, S. (2000). Household, parent, and child contributions to childhood obesity. *Family Relations, 49,* 293–300. doi:10.1111/j.1741–3729.2000 .00293.x

Gerald, L. B., Gerald, J. K., Gibson, L., Patel, K., Zhang, S., & McClure, L. A. (2009). Changes in environmental tobacco smoke exposure and asthma morbidity among urban school children. *Chest, 135,* 911–916. doi:10.1378/chest.08–1869

Greydanus, D. E., Patel, D. R., & Greydanus, E. K. (2003). Adolescent health. In H. M. Wallace, G. Green, & K. Jaros (Eds.), *Health and welfare for families in the 21st century* (2nd ed.). Boston, MA: Jones & Bartlett.

Guo, J. J., Wade, T. J., & Keller, K. N. (2008). Impact of school-based health centers on students with mental health problems. *Public Health Reports, 123*(6), 768–780.

Halfon, N., & Hochstein, M. (1997). Developing a system of care for all: What the needs of vulnerable children tell us. In R. E. K. Stein & P. Brooks (Eds.), *Health care for children: What's right, what's wrong, what's next* (pp. 303–338). New York: United Hospital Fund.

Hall, H. I. (2008). Estimation of HIV incidence in the United States. *Journal of the American Medical Association, 300,* 520–529. doi:10.1001/jama.300.5.520

Henry J. Kaiser Family Foundation. (2009a). *Enrolling uninsured low-income children in Medicaid and SCHIP.* Retrieved from http://www.kff.org/medicaid/upload/2177_06.pdf

Henry J. Kaiser Family Foundation. (2009b). *The uninsured: A primer, key facts about Americans without health insurance.* Retrieved from http://www.kff.org/uninsured/upload/7451–05.pdf

Holland, M. L., Kitzman, H., & Veazie, P. (2009). The effects of stress on birth weight in low-income, unmarried Black women. *Women's Health Issues, 19,* 390–397.

Hook, E. W., III, Cannon, R. O., Nahmias, A. J., Lee F. F., Campbell, C. H., Jr., Glasser, D., & Quinn, T. C. (1992). Herpes simplex virus infection as a risk factor for human immunodeficiency virus infection in heterosexuals. *Journal of Infectious Diseases, 165,* 251–255.

Jaakola, J. K., & Gissler, M. (2004). Maternal smoking in pregnancy, fetal development, and childhood asthma. *American Journal of Public Health, 94,* 136–140.

Jaffee, K. D., & Perloff, J. D. (2003). An ecological analysis of racial differences in low birth weight: Implications for maternal and child health social work. *Health and Social Work, 28,* 9–22.

Kelly, P. J., Bair, R. M., Baillargeon, J., & German, V. (2000). Risk behaviors and the prevalence of *Chlamydia* in a juvenile detention facility. *Clinical Pediatrics, 39,* 521–528.

Kempe, A., Beaty, B. L., Crane, L. A., Stokstad, J., Barrow, J., Belman, S., & Steiner, J. F. (2005). Changes in access, utilization, and quality of care after enrollment into a state child health insurance plan. *Pediatrics, 115,* 364–371. doi:10.1542/peds.2004–0475

Kessel, W., Jaros, K., & Harker, P. T. (2003). The Social Security Act and maternal and child health services: Securing a bright future. In H. M. Wallace, G. Green, & K. Jaros (Eds.), *Health and welfare for families in the 21st century* (2nd ed., pp. 164–170). Boston, MA: Jones & Bartlett.

Kohler, P. K., Manhart, L. E., & Lafferty, W. E. (2008). Abstinence-only and comprehensive sex education and the initiation of sexual activity and teen pregnancy. *Journal of Adolescent Health, 42,* 344–351. doi:10.1016/j.jadohealth.2007.08.026

Kramer, M. S. (1987). Intrauterine growth and gestational duration determinants. *Pediatrics, 80,* 502–511.

Lee, S. H., O'Riordan, M. A., & Lazebnik, R. (2009). Relationships among depressive symptoms, sexually transmitted infections, and pregnancy in African-American adolescent girls. *Journal of Pediatric and Adolescent Gynecology, 22,* 19–23. doi:10.1016/j.jpag.2007.12.003

Lumeng, J. C., Gannon, K., Cabral, H. J., Frank, D. A., & Zuckerman, B. (2003). Association between clinically meaningful behavior problems and overweight in children. *Pediatrics, 112,* 1138–1145.

Manlove, J., Terry-Humen, E., & Ikramullah, E. (2006). Young teenagers and older sexual partners: Correlates and consequences for males and females. *Perspectives on Sexual and Reproductive Health, 38,* 197–207. doi:10.1363/psrh.38.197.06

March of Dimes Foundation. (2008). *Low birth weight.* Retrieved from http://www.marchofdimes.com/professionals/14332_1153.asp

Margolis, L. H., Cole, G. P., & Kotch, J. B. (1997). Historical foundations of maternal and child health. In J. B. Kotch (Ed.), *Maternal and child health: Programs, problems, and policy in public health* (pp. 19–43). Gaithersburg, MD: Aspen.

Maternal and Child Health Bureau. (n.d.). *Programs: Title V block grant to states.* Retrieved from http://mchb.hrsa.gov/programs/

McPherson, M., Arango, P., Fox, H., Lauver, C., McManus, M., Newacheck, P. W., . . . Strickland, B. (1998). A new definition of children with special health care needs. *Pediatrics, 102,* 137–140. doi:10.1542/peds.102.1.137

Moniz, C., & Gorin, S. (2003). *Health and health care policy: A social work perspective.* Boston: Allyn & Bacon.

Monasterio, E., Hwang, L. Y., & Shafer, M. A. (2007). Adolescent sexual health. *Current Problems in Pediatric and Adolescent Health Care, 37,* 302–325. doi:10.1016/j.cppeds.2007.07.006

Morrison-Beedy, D., Carey, M. P., Feng, C., & Tu, X. M. (2008). Predicting sexual risk behaviors among adolescent and young women using a prospective diary method. *Research in Nursing & Health, 31,* 329–340. doi:10.1002/nur.20263

National Assembly on School-Based Health Care. (2007). *School-based health centers national census school year 2004–2005.* Retrieved from http://ww2.nasbhc.org/RoadMap/Public/EQ_2005census.pdf

National Campaign to Prevent Teen and Unplanned Pregnancy. (2010). *Latest developments from the Obama administration and Capitol Hill.* Retrieved from http://www.thenationalcampaign.org/federalfunding/latest.aspx

Newacheck, P. W., Brindis, C. D., Cart, C. U., Marchi, K., & Irwin, C. E., Jr. (1999). Adolescent health insurance coverage: Recent changes and access to care. *Pediatrics, 104,* 195–202. doi:10.1542/peds.104.2.195

Newacheck, P. W., Hung, Y. Y., Park, M. J., Brindis, C. D., & Irwin, C. E., Jr. (2003). Disparities in adolescent health and health care: Does socioeconomic status matter? *Health Services Research, 38,* 1235–1252. doi:10.1111/1475–6773.00174

Newacheck, P. W., Pearl, M., Hughes, D. C., & Halfon, N. (1998). The role of Medicaid in ensuring children's access to care. *Journal of the American Medical Association, 280,* 1789–1793. Doi:10.1001/jama.280.20.1789.

Ogden, C. L., Carroll, M. D., & Flegal, K. M. (2008). High body mass index for age among US children and adolescents, 2003–2006. *Journal of the American Medical Association, 299,* 2401. doi:10.1001/jama.299.20.2401

Pastore, D., & Techow, B. (2004). Adolescent school-based health care: A description of two sites in their 20th year of service. *Mount Sinai Journal of Medicine, 71,* 191–196.

Powell, L. M., & Bao, Y. (2009). Food prices, access to food outlets and child weight. *Economics and Human Biology, 7*(1), 64–72. doi:10.1016/j.ehb.2009.01.004

Proctor, M. H. (2003). Television viewing and change in body fat from preschool to early adolescence: The Framingham children's study. *International Journal of Obesity, 27,* 827–33. doi:10.1038/sj.ij0.0802294

Raj, A., Silverman, J. G., & Amaro, H. (2000). The relationship between sexual abuse and sexual risk among high school students: Findings from the 1997 Massachusetts Youth Risk Behavior Survey. *Maternal and Child Health Journal, 4,* 125–134. doi:10.1023/A:1009526422148

Rauh, V. A., Andrews, H. F., & Garfinkel, R. S. (2001). The contribution of maternal age to racial disparities in birthweight: A multilevel perspective. *American Journal of Public Health, 91,* 1815–1824. doi:10.2105/AJPH.91.11.1815

Reuner, G., Hassenpflug, A., Pietz, J., & Philippi, H. (2009). Long-term development of low-risk low birth weight preterm born infants: Neurodevelopmental aspects from childhood to late adolescence. *Early Human Development, 85,* 409–413. doi:10.1016/j.earlhumdev.2009.01.007

Robinson, T. N. (1999). Reducing children's television viewing to prevent obesity. *Journal of the American Medical Association, 282,* 1561–1567. doi:10.1001/jama.282.16.1561

Rosenbach, M. L., & Gavin, N. I. (1998). Early and periodic screening, diagnosis, and treatment and managed care. *Annual Review of Public Health, 19,* 507–525. doi:10.1146/annurev.publhealth.19.1.507

Rosenbaum, J. E. (2009). Patient teenagers? A comparison of the sexual behavior of virginity pledgers and matched nonpledgers. *Pediatrics, 123*(1), e110-e120. doi:10.1542/peds.2008–0407

Rounds, K. A. (2004). Preventing sexually transmitted infections among adolescents. In M. W. Fraser (Ed.), *Risk and resilience in childhood: An ecological perspective* (2nd ed., pp. 251–280). Washington, DC: NASW Press.

Salam, M. T., Li, Y. F., Langholz, B., & Gilliland, F. D. (2004). Early-life environmental risk factors for asthma: Findings from the children's health study. *Environmental Health Perspectives, 112,* 760–765.

Sardell, A., & Johnson, K. (1998). The politics of EPSDT policy in the 1990s: Policy entrepreneurs, political streams, and children's health benefits. *The Milbank Quarterly, 76,* 175–205. doi:10.1111/1468–0009.00086

Satterwhite, C. L., Tian, L. H., Braxton, J., & Weinstock, H. (2010). Chlamydia prevalence among women and men entering the National Job Training Program: United States, 2003–2007. *Sexually Transmitted Diseases, 37,* 63–67. doi:10.1097/OLQ.0b013e3181bc097a

Senn, T. E., Carey, M. P., & Vanable, P. A. (2008). Childhood and adolescent sexual abuse and subsequent sexual risk behavior: Evidence from controlled studies, methodological critique, and suggestions for research. *Clinical Psychology Review, 28,* 711–735. doi:10.1016/j.cpr.2007.10.002

Sharma, A. J., Grummer-Strawn, L. M., Dalenius, K., Galuska, D., Anandappa, M., Borland, E., . . . Smith, R. (2009). Obesity prevalence among low-income, preschool-aged children—United States, 1998–2008. *MMWR.Morbidity and Mortality Weekly Report, 58*(28), 769.Retrieved from http://www.cdc.gov/mmwr/preview/mmwrhtml/mm5828a1.htm

Shi, L., & Singh, D. (2001). *Delivering health care in America: A systems approach* (2nd ed.). Gaithersburg, MD: Aspen.

Shone, L. P., Dick, A. W., Klein, J. D., Zwanziger, J., & Szilagyi, P. G. (2005). Reduction in racial and ethnic disparities after enrollment in the State Children's Health Insurance Program. *Pediatrics, 115,* e697–705. doi:10.1542/peds.2004–1726

Shortell, S. M., Gillies, R. R., Anderson, D. A., Erickson, K. M., & Mitchell, J. B. (2000). *Remaking health care in America: The evolution of organized delivery systems* (2nd ed.). San Francisco: Jossey-Bass.

Sia, C., Tonniges, T. F., Osterhus, E., & Taba, S. (2004). History of the medical home concept. *Pediatrics, 113,* 1473–1478.

Simon, P. A., Zeng, Z., Wold, C. M., Haddock, W., & Fielding, J. E. (2003). Prevalence of childhood asthma and associated morbidity in Los Angeles County: Impacts of race/ethnicity and income. *Journal of Asthma, 40,* 535–543. doi:10.1081/JAS-120018788

Simpson, W. J. (1957). A preliminary report on cigarette smoking and the incidence of prematurity. *American Journal of Obstetrics and Gynecology, 73,* 808–815.

Starfield, B. (1997). Social, economic, and medical care determinants of children's health. In R.E.K. Stein & P. Brooks (Eds.), *Health care for children: What's right, what's wrong, what's next?* (pp. 39–52). New York: United Hospital Fund.

Stein, R. E. K. (1997). Changing the lens: Why focus on children's health? In R. E. K. Stein & P. Brooks (Eds.), *Health care for children: What's right, what's wrong, what's next?* (pp. 1–12). New York: United Hospital Fund.

Stettler, N., Zemel, B. S., Kumanyika, S., & Stallings, V. A. (2002). Infant weight gain and childhood overweight status in a multicenter, cohort study. *Pediatrics, 109,* 194–199. doi:10.1542/peds.109.2.194

Strickland, B., McPherson, M., Weissman, G., van Dyck, P., Huang, Z. J., & Newacheck, P. (2004). Access to the medical home: Results of the National Survey of Children With Special Health Care Needs. *Pediatrics, 113*, 1485–1492.

Szilagyi, P. G., Schuster, M. A., & Cheng, T. L. (2009). The scientific evidence for child health insurance. *Academic Pediatrics, 9*(1), 4–6. doi:10.1016/j.acap.2008.12.002

U.S. Census Bureau. (2009a). *Health insurance coverage: 2008: Highlights.* Retrieved from http://www.census.gov/hhes/www/hlthins/hlthin08/hflth08asc.html

U.S. Census Bureau. (2009b). *Income, poverty, and health insurance coverage in the United States: 2008.* Retrieved from http://www.census.gov/prod/2009pubs/p60–236.pdf

Wang, J., Visness, C. M., Calatroni, A., Gergen, P. J., Mitchell, H. E., & Sampson, H. A. (2009). Effect of environmental allergen sensitization on asthma morbidity in inner-city asthmatic children. *Clinical and Experimental Allergy: Journal of the British Society for Allergy and Clinical Immunology, 39*, 1381–1389. doi:10.1111/j.1365–2222.2009.03225.x

Williams, C., AZA Consulting, Rosen, J., Hudman, J., O'Malley, M., & The Kaiser Commission on Medicaid and the Uninsured. (2004). *Challenges and tradeoffs in low-income family budgets: Implications for health coverage.* Menlo Park, CA: The Henry J. Kaiser Family Foundation.

Williams, D. R., Sternthal, M., & Wright, R. J. (2009). Social determinants: Taking the social context of asthma seriously. *Pediatrics, 123*, S174–84. doi:10.1542/peds.2008–2233H

Woodruff, T. J., Axelrad, D. A., Kyle, A. D., Nweke, O., Miller, G. G., & Hurley, B. J. (2004). Trends in environmentally related childhood illnesses. *Pediatrics, 113*, 1133–1140.

Wu, A. C., Smith, L., Bokhour, B., Hohman, K. H., & Lieu, T. A. (2008). Racial/Ethnic variation in parent perceptions of asthma. *Ambulatory Pediatrics, 8*(2), 89–97. doi:10.1016/j.ambp.2007.10.007

Zimmerman, F. J., & Bell, J. F. (2009). Associations of television content type and obesity in children. *American Journal of Public Health, 200*, 334–340. doi:10.2105/AJPH.2008.155119

Additional Reading

Baron, J., Kleinmann, J. H., & Sylvester, K. (2003). Health insurance for children: Issues and ideas. *Future of Children, 13*, 1–32.

Cecil-Karb, R., & Grogan-Kaylor, A. (2009). Childhood body mass index in community context: Neighborhood safety, television viewing, and growth trajectories of BMI. *Health & Social Work, 34*(3), 169–177.

Rounds, K. A. (2004). Preventing sexually transmitted infections among adolescents. In M. W. Fraser (Ed.), *Risk and resilience in childhood: An ecological perspective* (2nd ed., pp. 251–280). Washington, DC: NASW Press.

Sparks, P. J. (2009). Do biological, sociodemographic, and behavioral characteristics explain racial/ethnic disparities in preterm births? *Social Science & Medicine, 68,* 1667–1675. doi: 10.1016/j.socscimed.2009.02.026

Strolin-Goltzman, J. (2010). The relationship between school-based health centers and the learning environment. *Journal of School Health, 80,* 153–159. doi: 10.1111/j.1746–1561.2009.00480.x

Web-Based Resources

Center for Health and Health Care in Schools, http://www.healthinschools.org

Centers for Disease Control and Prevention, http://www.cdc.gov/

Child Trends DataBank, http://www.childtrendsdatabank.org

Families USA, http://www.familiesusa.org

The Future of Children, http://www.futureofchildren.org

Kaiser Commission on Medicaid and the Uninsured, The Henry J. Kaiser Family Foundation, http://www.kff.org/about/kcmu.cfm

March of Dimes, http://www.modimes.org/

Maternal and Child Health Bureau, http://mchb.hrsa.gov/

Maternal and Child Health Information Resource Center, Maternal and Child Health Bureau, http://www.mchb.hrsa.gov/mchirc/

The National Assembly on School Based Health Care, http://www.nasbhc.org/

The Robert Wood Johnson Foundation, http://www.rwjf.org

7

Policies and Programs for Children and Youth With Disabilities

Susan L. Parish

Alison W. Saville

Jamie G. Swaine

Children with disabilities (i.e., conditions producing functional limitations in mobility, self-care, communication, or learning) make up about 12.3% of the U.S. population between the ages of 5 to 17 years old (Hogan, Msall, Rogers, & Avery, 1997). In addition, many more children younger than 5 years old have impairments of this level of severity. Although the increasing prevalence of childhood disability is well documented (Newacheck, Stein, Bauman, & Hung, 2003), the reasons for this increase are not well understood. One view holds that medical and technological advances have enabled more children with disabilities to survive, and that increased public awareness has led to a greater identification of impairments. The prevalence of disability is higher among African Americans than Whites. Studies attribute racial disparities in disability prevalence to the increased likelihood of African American children living in poverty (e.g., Newacheck et al., 2003); however, these findings must be substantiated with further research. The prevalence of disability also varies by gender and disability condition. For example, autism is more common among males (Yeargin-Allsopp et al., 2003), whereas Rett Syndrome is found almost exclusively among females.

Most programs for children with disabilities determine eligibility based on a child's diagnosis or disability category, which may vary over the life course. In addition, how a policy or program defines disability can significantly affect the number of children who are deemed eligible to receive services. In the absence of a uniform definition of disability, children who are eligible for one program based on their diagnosis may not be eligible for another program, even if its mission is to serve children with the same disabilities (Beers, Kemeny, Sherritt, & Palfrey, 2003). Differential eligibility is more noticeable in state-run programs such as maternal and child health services because these services are administered under Title V of the Social Security Act, which gives each state the latitude to determine its own program structures and processes (Beers et al., 2003).

Terminology. When a child does not reach expected benchmarks or developmental milestones such as turning over, crawling, walking, or talking, this is referred to as a *developmental delay*. Developmental delays are noted frequently in young children before a specific condition is formally diagnosed. They may be a temporary or a lifelong condition. *Developmental disabilities* are lifelong impairments that manifest during childhood and result in substantial functional limitations, including intellectual disabilities (i.e., mental retardation), autism, cerebral palsy, Down syndrome, and other related disorders. Young adults with one or more than one of these disorders who are transitioning out of high school are often described as having a developmental disability, which is used as a general diagnostic category.

Increasing Prevalence of Disability

Medical and technological advances during the latter half of the 20th century substantially improved prenatal and perinatal care and brought about dramatic changes in the survival rates of children born with impairments. For example, between 1984 and 1998, there was a four-fold reduction in perinatal mortality in high-risk pregnancies (Creasy & Resnik, 1999). These advances have translated into increased numbers of children with disabilities living into adolescence and adulthood and explain, at least in part, the increasing prevalence of disability among children.

Children with developmental disabilities often need a lifetime of assistance, including a developmentally appropriate sequence of special services and individualized supports (Developmental Disabilities Assistance and Bill of Rights Act of 2000). Conditions such as autism, sickle cell anemia, cystic fibrosis, or cerebral palsy result in elevated needs for both primary medical care and specialized therapeutic care. To maximize their cognitive, emotional, academic, and physical development, these children's special needs may include rehabilitation therapies, environmental adaptations, assistive devices, personal assistance, and mental health, home health, or respite care (Perrin, 2002). Ongoing therapies, specialized interventions, and ancillary and supportive services play a pivotal role in allowing children to maximize their capacity for independence and fully participate in daily activities and community life. Furthermore, ancillary and supportive services such as respite care and other family support services enable parents to care for their children at home rather than seek expensive out-of-home care, which is usually publicly financed (Abelson, 1999; Bruns & Burchard, 2000; Curran, Sharples, White, & Knapp, 2001).

A wide array of policies governs the services received by children with disabilities and their families. Some policies are designed for children with disabilities (e.g., special education, disability income transfers), and others are designed for a broader population of children (e.g., provision of health-related services to children eligible for Medicaid). Policies directed at families often provide supports intended to reduce out-of-home placements and mitigate the physical, emotional, and financial burdens associated with caring for children with disabilities.

Although the overarching goal of these policies is to enhance development and adaptation, the service system for children with disabilities can best be characterized as fragmented. Numerous organizations control the delivery of services (e.g., local school districts, state disability offices, state or county social service agencies), and revenues typically come from two or more levels of government (i.e., federal, state, and local). Poor coordination and collaboration across agencies complicate the challenges families face in seeking assistance, and the barriers often seem insurmountable.

In the subsequent sections of this chapter, we review risk and protective factors related to childhood disability and outline the major social policies that have been directed toward children with disabilities and their families. The ways in which concepts of risk and protection operate within these policies are examined. Finally, recommendations of strategies to promote greater service integration are presented. However, before plunging into these tasks, we briefly describe the theoretical models that guide our analysis.

Three Theoretical Frameworks

Three theoretical frameworks underpin this chapter: the ecological model, models of risk and protective factors, and the social or minority model of disability. The ecological model espoused by Bronfenbrenner (1979, 1986) posited that individual development occurs and can be understood only within a larger family and social-environmental context. In this model, an understanding the interplay of factors at the level of the individual, the family, and the environment is necessary to understand what appear to be individual behavior and individual outcomes. Child developmental outcomes arise from the complex interplay of these interwoven elements.

Conceptually, risk and protective factors are those elements that influence the chances of adverse outcomes and optimal development, respectively (Fraser, Kirby, & Smokowski, 2004). We build our analysis from the elaboration of the risk and resilience framework presented by Fraser and his colleagues (2004) and the introductory chapter of this volume. The ecological perspective requires identifying and analyzing risk and protective factors at the levels of the child, the child's family, and the broader society. This analytic scheme is also consistent with recent disability studies that have identified a *social model of disability*, which distinguishes between individual impairment and disability. *Impairment* is an individual's biological condition, whereas *disability* is what accrues to an individual when society's attitudes, expectations, and built environments do not accommodate a full range of human difference. Davis (2000) succinctly described the relationship between disability and impairment:

> Disability is not so much the lack of a sense or the presence of a physical or mental impairment as it is the reception and construction of that difference. . . . An impairment is a physical fact, but a disability is a social construction. For example, lack of mobility is an impairment, but an environment without ramps turns that impairment into a disability. (p. 56)

This social model of disability is entirely consistent with an emancipatory and empowerment perspective. The goal of this chapter, then, is not to understand how individual impairments place children at risk but to evaluate how the larger environment—and especially society's response to impairment, as codified in public policy—increases the risk of adverse development or, alternatively, promotes the optimal development of children with disabilities. We turn first to the risk and protective factors associated with childhood disabilities.

Risk and Protective Factors for Problems Experienced by Children With Disabilities

Risk Factors

In addition to living in poverty, a number of important risk factors are associated with childhood disability, including likelihood of experiencing abuse, social isolation, and ostracism from peers and the larger society; difficulty accessing needed supportive services, and problems obtaining medical care when it is needed.

Poverty and childhood disability status are compellingly related. About 28% of children with disabilities live in households with incomes below the federal poverty level, which is a dramatically higher rate than the 16% of nondisabled children who live in poverty (Fujiura & Yamaki, 2000). In general, child poverty rates tend to be highest among African American and Hispanic children, and households of any race or ethnicity that are headed by a single parent are much more likely to live in poverty than households headed by married parents (DeNavas-Walt, Proctor, & Smith, 2009).

The elevated risk of living in poverty for children with disabilities is a phenomenon that has been widely described by researchers and policy analysts, but it is not well understood. Even more disturbing, evidence shows the prevalence of disability increased between the early 1980s and the mid-1990s among families living in poverty or those headed by a single mother (Fujiura & Yamaki, 2000). Causal ambiguity precludes understanding the direction of effects, and further research is needed to determine the nature of the causal relationship between poverty and disability. A case for effects in both directions can be made. Low-income families are less likely to have access to sufficient food, adequate prenatal and other medical care, and decent safe housing, all of which are factors that can be implicated in increasing the risk of childhood disability.

However, the extensive care needs of children with disabilities are likely to prohibit their parents from obtaining or maintaining sufficient employment necessary to bring the household out of poverty (Emerson, 2007).

Regardless of the direction of the relationship between poverty and disability, the fact that so many children with disabilities live in poverty has serious implications for their well-being. For children generally, living in poverty is associated with a host of negative consequences, including poor physical health, increased emotional and behavioral problems, diminished cognitive abilities, and reduced educational attainment (Brooks-Gunn & Duncan, 1997). However, concern is mounting that poverty is likely to have more deleterious effects for children with disabilities than it does for typically developing children (Park, Turnbull, & Turnbull, 2002). This is because children with disabilities require greater care and stimulation to achieve proper development, prevent regression, and avert the development of secondary conditions.

Costs of disability. Research into how poverty influences child development is still in its infancy, and it will likely take some time before risk-inducing relationships and their applicability to children with disabilities are clear. We do know the disability-related costs of raising a child are extremely high in the United States (General Accounting Office, 1999; Parish, Seltzer, Greenberg, & Floyd, 2004). Families of children with disabilities face unique financial burdens, such as increased therapy costs and home adaptations (Newacheck & Kim, 2005; Parish & Cloud, 2006). These increased costs are particularly burdensome for lower income families (Lukemeyer, Meyers, & Smeeding, 2000; Parish, Shattuck, & Rose, 2009). Mothers of children with disabilities often have to reduce the number of hours they work or quit work outside the home completely to provide adequate care for their children with special needs (Parish et al., 2004). This phenomenon is subsequently associated with reduced income and lower asset accumulation over time (Parish et al., 2004).

Public income transfer and insurance programs do not cover most disability-related expenses (General Accounting Office, 1999). Impoverished families of children with disabilities have few choices or resources for meeting their child's impairment-related needs (Scorgie, Wilgosh, & McDonald, 1998). Inadequate financial resources are associated with diminished parental ability to cope with the extra health and daily care needs of children with disabilities (Yau & Li-Tsang, 1999). Moreover, evidence suggests that families raising children with disabilities often experience significant hardships (e.g., food insecurity, housing instability, foregone medical care).

These hardships and deprivation extend well into the middle-class stratum of families raising children with disabilities; this finding is important because this pattern of hardship is not found among families of nondisabled children (Parish, Rose, Andrews, Grinstein-Weiss, & Richman, 2008).

Generally, poverty has a direct negative influence on maternal behavior and on the quality of parenting (Brooks-Gunn, Klebanov, & Liaw, 1995). We would expect to find similar relationships in the behavior of low-income mothers of children with disabilities; however, this issue has not been studied directly. High rates of abuse and neglect also place children with disabilities at risk. Child abuse is widely recognized as placing victimized children at considerable risk for adverse social, developmental, educational, and behavioral outcomes. Although it is difficult to determine the rates of abuse for the general population (See Chapter 3; Pagelow, 1984), it is even more problematic to ascertain abuse rates for children with disabilities because their impairments in cognitive and language skills make detection of abuse substantially more difficult (Sobsey, 1994). Rates of physical, sexual, and emotional abuse for children with disabilities are significantly higher than those for nondisabled children, with one conservative estimate suggesting that children with disabilities are maltreated at twice the rate of children without disabilities (National Center on Child Abuse and Neglect, 1993). However, many in the field have argued that this estimate is quite low (Sobsey), and one study found abuse rates for children with disabilities were 4 to 10 times the rates for nondisabled children (Ammerman & Baladerian, 1993).

Serious risks to emotional well-being are associated with the social isolation of children with disabilities, as well as their encounters with ostracism from peers and the larger society. The history of discriminatory and prejudicial treatment of people with disabilities of all ages is a dismal and pervasive aspect of Western history (Braddock & Parish, 2001). Unfortunately, contemporary reports of children with disabilities have indicated these attitudes have not materially diminished. There is long-standing evidence that children interact differently with rejected and ignored classmates (Chazan, Laing, Jones, Harper, & Bolton, 1983; Dodge, 1983). Given these different patterns of interactions, children with disabilities, and particularly those with severe impairments, often have limited opportunities for friendships and integration with their peers.

Social isolation—having few friendships, limited reciprocal relationships, and minimal peer interactions—follows children with disabilities from early childhood into adolescence and adulthood (Keogh & Bernheimer, 1987; Keogh, Bernheimer, & Guthrie, 2004). Although the long-term effects of this isolation have not been widely studied in children with disabilities, in general, children's social skills, networks, and relationships predict later adjustment (Kupersmidt, Coie, & Dodge, 1990; Meyer, Cole, McQuarter, & Reichle, 1990). In addition, childhood disability is associated with negative personal and employment outcomes (Edgar & Levine, 1987; Sitlington, Frank, & Carson, 1992; Whitney-Thomas & Moloney, 2001). Moreover, adolescents and children with disabilities express great dissatisfaction related to their lack of friends and social integration (Keogh et al., 2004).

Evidence has converged to indicate that parents encounter ongoing stress and family disruption over the life course of caring for their children with disabilities (e.g., Farber, 1960; Turnbull, Brotherson, & Summers, 1986). These stresses may result from the child's behavior problems, nighttime disturbance caused by the child's care needs, social isolation, family chaos, multiple child impairments, chronic ill health, and financial concerns (Singer & Irvin, 1989). However, compelling evidence also exists that parents who cope well with their child's needs enhance the child's cognitive and social adjustment and minimize further family disruption and distress (Crnic, Friedrich, & Greenberg, 1983; Landesman, Jaccard, & Gunderson, 1989; Summers, Behr, & Turnbull, 1989). Successful parental adaptation and coping contributes to what is arguably the most critical protective factor related to childhood disability: strong parental support.

Parental support for children with disabilities takes a number of forms across childhood and often into adulthood. Because of the nature and organization of disability policy in the United States, parents are compelled to serve both as their child's advocate and as the child's case manager. When parents aggressively champion their child's needs, the child is much more likely to receive the services and supports to which he or she is entitled. Parental support also bolsters the child's self-esteem, creating resilience to the rejection most children with disabilities encounter from peers and society.

A closely related protective factor is the competence and mastery parents develop as their child ages; these capacities are gained through surmounting the adversity they face in securing services for their child and in coming to terms with their child's impairment. For parents of young children with disabilities, a common developmental trajectory begins at the point of diagnosis with mourning for the nondisabled child they had anticipated. After this mourning period, most parents report increasing levels of satisfaction with their caregiving abilities and identify their caregiving role as a positive part of their self-identity. However, over the course of their child's development, parents might revisit grief and depression during transition periods (e.g., entry into kindergarten, high school graduation). For some parents, these transition points represent jarring reminders that the child's impairment has altered his or her developmental trajectory. Even so, parents also overwhelmingly report that their children with disabilities contribute emotionally, socially, and intellectually to the richness of family life (Summers et al., 1989).

Protective Factors

Research on protective and promotive factors associated with childhood disability is far more limited. The most likely explanation for this deficit is that the medical model of disability that prevailed for much of the 20th century still informs policy and services for children with disabilities. The most important protective factors associated with childhood disability are those which emerge from the family and community context: parental competence as advocates, case managers, and caregivers for their children; supportive networks of peers, extended families, and communities; inclusion in activities of daily life and community life; and adequate and available medical, educational, and financial resources to enable parents to provide appropriate care for their children.

Extrafamilial protective factors include supportive schools, faith-based organizations such as churches or synagogues, and communities, as well as adequate levels of family support services, including support from disability and advocacy organizations that address the needs of children with disabilities and their families. Having sufficient and appropriate supports available is a critical factor in helping parents positively adapt to their child's disability (Singer & Irvin, 1989). The policies that structure such supports are discussed in the next section. However, little research has been conducted investigating the mechanisms by which these risk and protective factors directly affect children with disabilities and their families. Although limited, some evidence supports our hypothesis that these protective factors (parental and other supports, responsive public policies, nurturing communities) are directly involved in building resilience among children with disabilities (Singer & Irvin; Summers et al., 1989).

In summary, the life circumstances and development of children with disabilities are shaped by risk and protective factors that emerge from the environments in which these children live. These environmental factors emerge from within the family, the community, and the larger society and are manifested in the public policies that contribute to different facets of child and family life. Table 7.1 summarizes these significant factors.

Table 7.1   Risk and Protective Factors for Problems Experienced by Children With Disabilities

Risk Factors	Protective Factors
Poverty	Parental competence as advocates, case managers, and caregivers
Increased abuse and neglect	Supportive peer networks, extended families, and communities
Social isolation	Inclusion in community life and activities
Difficulty obtaining supportive services and medical care	Adequate medical, financial, and educational resources to enable parents to meet their children's needs
Ostracism by community and peers	

Risk, Resilience, and Protection in Policies for Children With Disabilities

Over the course of the last century, extraordinary changes occurred in policies for children with disabilities. At the outset of the 20th century, policy was organized at the state level and provided limited custodial care in segregated institutions to the exclusion of nearly all other services. Beginning in the 1930s, small-scale experimental programs in extra-institutional long-term care were implemented in New York and Ohio, but this approach did not take hold nationally. In response to the lack of services for children with disabilities, parents began organizing their own educational systems for their special needs children, and by the early 1940s, fledgling parent advocacy groups had been established. Parent advocacy had a lasting impact on the service system and ultimately exerted greater influence than any other force over the shape of services for children with disabilities (Braddock & Parish, 2001).

Over the past four decades, assertive and effective advocacy by parents of children with disabilities has precipitated the development of policies that support services tailored to the individual needs of the child with disabilities and meet the needs of the entire family (Braddock & Parish, 2001). In addition, in the decades since the 1970s, parent advocacy culminated in the closure of hundreds of custodial institutions across the United States and led to the 1975 passage of legislation mandating education for children with disabilities. As parents emerged as champions for their children with disabilities, adult activists with disabilities also began to demand their civil rights, following the trail blazed by African American leaders in the civil rights movement.

These enormous changes resulted in two significant transformations. First, the service system, particularly in education and long-term care, began to reject the prevailing medical model, which held that individuals with disabilities were inherently defective and in need of professional cures. As noted previously, supporters of the social model of disability argued for the thorough inclusion of people with disabilities in all aspects of society, one that accommodates the full range of human differences. Advocacy by those with disabilities and their allies ultimately contributed to the successful passage of the Americans with Disabilities Act of 1990, which prohibits discrimination in public settings and requires employers to accommodate people with disabilities (Braddock & Parish, 2001).

A second major transformation was the federal government's entry into the service and policy arena for children with disabilities, which began on a large scale in the 1970s. Even when the Social Security Act of 1935 was passed, the federal government's role was minimal and limited to funding supports or services for people with disabilities (i.e., money allocated through Title X of the act provided limited income transfers to the blind). The only exceptions to federal noninvolvement were income transfer and vocational rehabilitation provisions for veterans. For children with disabilities, the federal government continued its role of noninvolvement through much of the 20th century. However, the federal role changed in the 1970s when Medicaid was amended to allow federal reimbursement for medical and long-term care services for children and adults with mental retardation; federal law mandated education of children with disabilities, and the disability income transfer program (Supplemental Security Income [SSI]) was expanded to cover children.

These policy transformations evolved concurrently with practice changes. Consistent with the medical model of disability, which was strongly followed at the beginning of the 20th century, people with disabilities were considered deviants, and social policy responded with segregation and sterilization to prevent a perceived group of undesirables from procreating. Through most of that century, negative attitudes toward people with disabilities prevailed, and practice models encouraged parents to institutionalize young children with disabilities, surrendering them to warehouse-like facilities that provided rudimentary care (Braddock & Parish, 2001). As attitudes toward people with disabilities shifted, a civil and human rights perspective emerged, and practices began shifting to focus on supporting parents in providing at home care for their children with disabilities (Braddock & Parish).

At the outset of the 21st century, a number of disparate public policies influenced children with disabilities and their families. We describe key federal policies that address income support, education and early intervention, maternal and child health services, and family support. Medical care, which is also critically important for children with disabilities, is discussed in Chapter 6 of this volume.

Income Transfers

Children with disabilities and their families can receive income transfer payments through several different programs: initiatives designed specifically for people with disabilities, and initiatives designed for low-income people in general. The two major disability income transfer programs in the United States are Social Security Disability Insurance and Supplemental Security Income (SSI). The disability insurance program targets workers who become disabled (and their dependents), and the program is not a major source of income for children with disabilities. In contrast, SSI stipulates provision of assistance specifically for children with disabilities. Generally, the largest cash assistance program for low-income families is the Temporary Assistance to Needy Families (TANF) program, the nation's welfare program, which states administer and jointly fund with the federal government.

SSI is a means-tested, monthly income program for the elderly and people with disabilities. The program is federally financed and administered, although some states supplement federal payments and a few states administer their own programs directly. Children with disabilities have received SSI since the program's inception in 1972 (Social Security Administration [SSA], 2000). Eligibility is based on the child's functional limitations,and parental income and assets relative to family size. For example, in 2009, a single child with disabilities living in a two-parent home could receive SSI payments if parental household income did not exceed $3,495 per month.

A total of 1.1 million children with disabilities younger than age 18 years old received SSI benefits in December 2007, the latest year for which data are available (SSA, 2009). For 2007, the average monthly SSI benefit payment for children was $541 (SSA, 2009), which translates to an annual rate of $6,492. In 2007, the federal poverty threshold was $10,210 for one person (U.S. Department of Health and Human Services, 2007). Therefore, the SSI payment level for one individual was 36% below the federal poverty level. Although nearly 26% of children receiving SSI still live below the federal poverty level (Grad, 2000), the SSI program plays a vital role in reducing the extent of poverty experienced by these children. Two thirds of SSI beneficiaries receive at least half of their total income from SSI; Social Security benefits are responsible for reducing the poverty gap for SSI recipients by an average of 60% (Grad). Although the level of support provided by SSI is limited, reduced poverty for many children with disabilities and their families is an important protective factor.

However, the protective benefits of SSI have been eroded by the Personal Responsibility and Work Opportunity Reconciliation Act (PRWORA) of 1996. PRWORA catalyzed important changes in SSI for children with disabilities by constricting child SSI eligibility rules. Following new guidelines for eligibility, SSI retrenchment associated with PRWORA had dire consequences for children with disabilities and their families. Between 1996 and 2000, the number of child SSI beneficiaries with mental retardation declined by nearly 22% (or 76,000 individuals) and declined by 12% for children with all other disabilities (Parish, 2003). To compensate for the loss of their children's SSI income, some parents entered the workforce or increased their work hours (Inkelas, Rowe, Karoly, & Rogowski, 1999). However, increased work activity did not prevent total income from declining for most families, some of whom had to seek other forms of public assistance to compensate for the loss of SSI benefits (Davies, Iams, & Rupp, 2000; Inkelas et al., 1999).

Low-income families of children with disabilities can also receive income transfers through TANF, which was reauthorized by the Deficit Reduction Act of 2005. TANF, which replaced the earlier welfare program, Aid to Families with Dependent Children (AFDC), represented a major policy shift in public assistance. Under AFDC, parents raising children with disabilities were generally exempted from work requirements, whereas TANF requires participants to be involved in either work or job training; TANF also limits receipt of cash benefits to a lifetime maximum of 60 months (Thompson, Holcomb, Loprest, & Brennan, 1998).

When Congress was debating the PRWORA legislation, the National Commission on Childhood Disability (1995) recommended exempting one parent of a child with disabilities from mandatory work requirements, excluding parents from being removed from welfare for 2 years following a child's termination from SSI, and prohibiting states from counting children's SSI benefits when assessing families' welfare eligibility. However, these recommendations were rejected in the final version of PRWORA. Current TANF policies allow states to exempt a parent caring for a family member with a disability from working if the person with a disability is living at home and is not a full-time student; however, states also have the discretion to establish more strict work participation rules than those set by the federal legislation (Parrott et al., 2007). Recent analyses have found that TANF has had a limited effect on low-income mothers of children with disabilities. Although TANF's stated purposes included increasing marriage and employment to reduce welfare reliance, evaluation of the program's effects show limited employment gains, no marriage increases, and no reduction in overall welfare use among low-income mothers of children with disabilities (Parish, Rose, & Andrews, 2010).

A real and urgent need exists for policies that accommodate the responsibilities of parents caring for children with disabilities. First, these parents face many barriers to maintaining employment, including children's ongoing and episodic needs for affordable and appropriate care (Rosman, McCarthy, & Woolverton, 2001; Shearn & Todd, 2000). In addition, low-income families, which are overrepresented among those raising children with disabilities, pay for most child care out-of-pocket; child care for children with disabilities is more expensive than routine child care, and the burden of these costs contributes substantially to the poverty of these families (Lukemeyer et al., 2000; Meyers, Han, Waldfogel, & Garfinkel, 2001; Meyers & Heintze, 1999). The elevated care needs of children with disabilities and the extraordinary caregiving responsibilities assumed by their parents place these parents at elevated risk of unemployment and underemployment, both of which are directly associated with family poverty (Parish et al., 2004; Lichter & Eggebeen, 1994).

The system of income transfers in the United States provides critical support to children with disabilities and their families. These programs directly address the increased risk of living in poverty for children with disabilities and attempt, albeit in a limited way, to ameliorate the high costs of raising children with disabilities. Although SSI alone does not provide sufficient resources to raise family income above the federal poverty level, its provisions are important protective factors for the thousands of families who receive it.

Education and Early Intervention

The Individuals with Disabilities Education Act (IDEA) began as the Education for All Handicapped Children Act of 1975 (PL 94–142) and gave all children with disabilities the right to a free and appropriate public education. This watershed civil rights law resulted from sustained advocacy by parents of children with disabilities. IDEA was reauthorized in 2004 under the Individuals with Disabilities Education Improvement Act (IDEIA).

Special education has been shaped by the six core principles that formed the nucleus of the Education for All Handicapped Children Act:

1. Zero reject means schools cannot exclude any children with disabilities from instruction.

2. Nondiscriminatory evaluation guarantees every child an individualized, culturally and linguistically appropriate evaluation before being placed in special education.

3. Individualized Education Plans (IEPs) delineate current performance, progress on past objectives, goals and services for the school year, and evaluation of outcomes.

4. Least restrictive environment describes the goal that children with disabilities are educated to the extent possible in settings with children without disabilities.

5. Due process codifies the legal steps to ensure school fairness and accountability in meeting a child's needs and how parents can obtain relief via a hearing or second opinions.

6. Parental participation gives parents the right to access their child's education records and participate in IEP planning. (adapted from Kirk, Gallagher, & Anastasiow, 1993, pp. 51–52)

These principles have remained fixtures of the act since its initial passage in 1975. However, the act has also changed over the years in response to litigation and reauthorizing statutes. We will describe least restrictive environment, IEPs, and some of the issues that have emerged, including school district responsibility to fund and provide needed services, procedures to plan for a child's transition out of school, and reliance on parents to serve as advocates for their children.

Least Restrictive Environment

The notion of least restrictive environment exists to ensure that children are served in inclusive and integrated settings and are not segregated from typically developing peers. However, because this is a recommendation and not a requirement of IDEA, there is great variability among school districts in the proportion of children with disabilities who are educated in inclusive settings. Furthermore, parents and teachers have reported mixed feelings about mainstreaming children with disabilities into least restrictive environments. Although regular education teachers generally support mainstreaming, their endorsement appears to deteriorate when they address their own willingness to include children with disabilities in their classrooms (Scruggs & Mastropieri, 1996). Moreover, teachers often are ill equipped or unwilling to adequately include children with special needs in classroom activities. Concerns about mainstreaming are common to parents whether raising children with or without disabilities. Some parents of typically developing children fear mainstreaming will mean that time will be taken away from their children's learning experiences, and some parents of children with disabilities fear their children will not receive the level of attention available in segregated classes (Rallis & Anderson, 1994). Despite this controversy, many agree that mainstreaming is critical for children with disabilities because it allows them to develop interpersonal and life skills and concurrently allows children without disabilities to learn to accept those with disabilities (Osborne & Dimattia, 1994).

Individualized Education Plans

The IEP is a legal document developed for each student with a disability. The IEP is developed by a multidisciplinary team, including the student, his or her parents, teachers, social workers, speech and physical therapists, psychologists, and other support people as necessary given the child's needs. The IEP is intended to ensure that the child receives an appropriate education in the least restrictive environment.

It is a malleable document that is supposed to be revised annually, or more often if the child's needs change. IEPs address current educational performance levels, goals, services to support mainstreaming, and other considerations warranted by the child's particular abilities and needs (Sopko, 2003). Although IEPs were mandated by IDEIA and its IDEA forerunner, parents and teachers recognize numerous barriers in developing appropriate IEPs for children with disabilities. For example, IEPs take considerable time and skill to develop and involve varying perceptions and attitudes about interpretations of inclusion and the responsibilities of educators (Sopko).

Since 1997, IEPs have been required to include plans for the transition from school to adult life. This mandate was passed in response to overwhelming evidence of negative outcomes for children with disabilities who left high school. The goal of transition planning is to enable children with disabilities to become active and productive citizens by helping them bridge the distance between closely supervised, sheltered educational settings and the less-structured adult world. School districts can begin including transition planning in a child's IEP as early as age 14 years. Transition plans should address instruction, community involvement, employment, and other adult life objectives and should incorporate the child's individual interests and preferences (Sopko, 2003).

Although IDEIA guarantees children with disabilities the right to a free appropriate public education, there is frequent disagreement between parents and professionals regarding what constitutes an appropriate education. Schools often contest the education and support services requested by parents, and challenges are more common when school districts are asked to provide related services such as transportation, assistive technology, and medical services to assist children in obtaining an education (Katsiyannis & Yell, 2000).

Expensive health services for students with chronic health problems are often among the most controversial issues. The U.S. Supreme Court ruling in *Cedar Rapids Community School District v. Garret F.* (1999) required the school district to provide a specially trained nurse as part of a child's special education plan when having the nurse available was necessary for the child's participation in school (Katsiyannis & Yell, 2000). This ruling was an important victory for children whose impairments necessitate ongoing medical care. For all children with disabilities, this ruling represents a clear statement from the Supreme Court that schools are responsible for the provision of needed ancillary and supportive services.

Extensive litigation surrounding IDEIA and ongoing challenges by schools to the rights of children with disabilities has created a system in which parents must be assertive advocates. The burden parents undertake in being their child's advocates and the level of sophistication and resources they must bring to bear to secure their child's education are considerable. Part of the parental role in IEP planning is to safeguard their child's educational rights, which engenders an inherently adversarial relationship between parents and schools. Parents must be active decision makers and are expected to fulfill the role of teacher within in the home (Turnbull & Turnbull, 1982). Although this expectation that parents will be vigorous advocate for their children has produced important outcomes such as the *Garret F.* decision, it is unrealistic and unreasonable to expect all parents to be effective advocates. Many parents, and particularly low-income parents, lack the educational and financial resources to effectively champion their children's needs. Children with disabilities who lack a resourceful parent-advocate may be denied their right to an education.

The second part of IDEIA that is critically important for children with disabilities is early intervention, which aims to provide prevention and treatment services to improve cognitive, social, and emotional development of children younger than 3 years old. Children may receive early intervention services if they are considered either at risk for delayed development or have been identified as having a developmental disability (Ramey & Ramey, 1998). Early intervention services have long been recognized as important for helping children with disabilities achieve their developmental potential. Best practices for early intervention programs involve a range of family-centered services that focus on meeting the needs of the child within the context of his or her family and larger environment. For example, in the course of early intervention, parents may be referred to job assistance or adult education and may receive assistance in obtaining housing and health care.

The philosophy undergirding early intervention is grounded in the concepts of protective and promotive factors. Ideally, early intervention services promote well-being and optimal development by providing comprehensive community-based support services to help improve developmental outcomes. Even young children with disabilities are at risk of developing further complications that may exacerbate their impairments or cause secondary conditions (Zipper & Simeonsson, 2004). Early intervention in the United States has been structured by a federal mandate since 1986, when Part H (now Part C) was added to the Education for All Handicapped Children Act, mandating the provision of early intervention services (PL 99–457). The act's early intervention mandate is to provide comprehensive services to families of children from birth to age 3 (Richmond & Ayoub, 1993).

When possible, early intervention services should be provided in the most appropriate natural setting, which includes the home or other community setting. The emphasis on community-based intervention is intended to promote children's integration and inclusion in their home communities (Graham & Bryant, 1993). Between 2003 and 2004, about 80% of early intervention programs were provided in children's homes (U.S. Department of Education, 2009). Broad-based early intervention services are essential for the cognitive, social, and emotional development of young children (e.g., Graham & Bryant, 1993).

Multidisciplinary supports and programs scaffold the early intervention system, including audiology services, nutrition, family training and counseling, social work, physical and occupational therapy, and services providing assistive technology devices. At a minimum, states must identify infants and toddlers deemed to be at risk for or with identified developmental delays. Among other requirements, states are required to obtain Individualized Family Service Plans and provide data collection methods and evaluation procedures. When a child enters early intervention, assessments are conducted of child and family strengths and risk factors (Ramey & Ramey, 1998). Parents and professionals collaboratively develop the Individualized Family Service Plan, which addresses the child and family as a unit (Ramey & Ramey, 1998). This collaborative effort is important for adequately assessing risk and protective factors within the family structure and larger social environment.

Despite higher rates of disability and poverty among African American and Hispanic children, non-Hispanic White children are more likely to receive early intervention services than their peers (U.S. Department of Education, 2009). The disparity represents problems minority families face in accessing early intervention services and are not indicative of decreased need. After age 6, the likelihood that an African American child is enrolled in services increases as the child moves from early intervention into special education. However, Hispanic children remain less likely to receive needed services than children from other racial/ethnic groups (U.S. Department of Education, 2009). The reasons for this trend are not fully understood and warrant further investigation.

Title V of the Social Security Act: Maternal and Child Health

Title V of the Social Security Act, also known as the Maternal and Child Health Services Block Grant, is a federal–state partnership program that is aimed at improving the health of all mothers and children. Title V is not an entitlement program, and eligibility criteria and how and what programs are funded vary widely across states (Beers et al., 2003; Maternal and Child Health Bureau, n.d.; Rosenbaum, Proser, Schneder, & Sonosky, 2002). Title V provides funds to states as block grants that allow the states autonomy to determine how to spend funds within general guidelines and goals. For every $4 in federal funds for the program, states are expected to spend $3 in matching funds. In general, states allocate funds to four levels of services:

- direct health care services, such as health services for children with special health care needs;
- enabling services, such as transportation, respite care, and health education;
- population-based services, such as newborn screening and immunization; and
- infrastructure building services, such as policy development, training, and applied research. (U.S. Department of Health and Human Services, 2008)

In fiscal year 2009, the total budget for the Federal–State Partnership Block Grant exceeded $5 billion. Of that money, almost 50% was earmarked for children with special health care needs, which includes children with disabilities. However, there was a great deal of variation among states in spending their Title V budgets on children with special health care needs, ranging from 6% in Illinois to 83% in California. States also varied in what level of service they chose to fund. For example, Tennessee allocated more than 72% of its total budget to direct health services, whereas Missouri allocated only 4% of its budget for such services (Maternal and Child Health Bureau, n.d.).

Family Support

Families bear the greatest responsibility for caring for children with disabilities, and parents constitute the largest group of care providers (Hogan & Msall, 2002). Family support services are often provided over a child's life course and include respite care, environmental adaptations,

assistive devices, personal assistance, mental health, and crisis intervention. These supports enable families to care for their children with disabilities at home rather than seek out-of-home care (Bruns & Burchard, 2000;
Curran et al., 2001). In addition, these supports play a significant role in
reducing the burden and stress associated with caring for children with
disabilities at home (Floyd & Gallagher, 1997; Freedman & Boyer, 2000;
Haveman, van Berkum, Reijinder, & Heller, 1997), and they help families
obtain services for unmet needs (Heller, Miller, & Hsieh, 1999).

Despite the extent of care that families provide for their children with
disabilities, none of the states provide any more than a meager level of
family support. For example, spending for family support services to
serve both children and adults with developmental disabilities and their
families totaled just less than $2 billion in 2004; this was far short of the
$39 billion spent for the entire developmental disabilities service system
in all the states (Rizzolo, Hemp, & Braddock, 2006). Family support services across the United States are usually jointly financed by the federal
and state governments, often using Medicaid resources that are typically
administered by state or county governments. Not surprisingly, given
that departments of social services vary greatly among the states, so do
the levels of funding dedicated for family support and the types of services available (Parish, Pomeranz, & Braddock., 2003).

Even families that receive support services encounter difficulty in
obtaining all the services they need to care for children with disabilities.
Freedman and Boyer (2000) found supports, such as respite care, demon-
strably enhanced family well-being and were critically important to
families. However, barriers to securing needed support services have
been found consistently, such as a lack of flexibility in the types and frequency of services families received, and critical access difficulties, such
as services being unavailable when they were most needed (Freedman &
Boyer, 2000).

We have reviewed the major public policies that influence the lives of
children with disabilities and their families in the United States: income
transfers, education, early intervention, and family supports. Considerable
variation exists in the extent to which knowledge of risk and resilience has
informed the development of these policies. However, despite contention
about their effectiveness, these policies are significant in the lives of
children with disabilities and their families. The policies are contributing—
although not yet optimally—to promoting child development and the successful adjustment of children with disabilities. Table 7.2 provides an
overview of these policies and their features.

Table 7.2   Major Policy Approaches Related to Children and Youth With Disabilities

	Income Transfers	Education	Early Intervention	Family Support	Maternal and Child Health (Title V)
Policy Authority	Temporary Assistance to Needy Families (TANF); Personal Responsibility and Work Opportunity Reconciliation Act of 1996 (federal); Supplemental Security Income benefits: Social Security Act, amended 1972 (federal)	Education for All Handicapped Children Act of 1975; replaced by Individuals with Disabilities Education Act (IDEA)	Part H added to Education for All Handicapped Children Act in 1986; replaced by Part C	Varies by state; federal Medicaid funds available to states through Home and Community Based Services Waiver (authorized by the Omnibus Budget Reconciliation Act of 1981)	Social Security Act of 1935; converted to a federal Maternal and Child Health block grant through the Omnibus Budget Reconciliation Act of 1981
Funding	TANF: State and federal; SSI: federal	Local and state; limited federal funding	Local and state; limited federal funding	State; Medicaid programs financed jointly by federal and state	State and federal
Core Features	TANF: time-limited cash assistance to low-income families; work requirements for parents; SSI: monthly payments to	Children with disabilities entitled to free, appropriate public education in least restrictive	Children with disabilities and possible developmental delays eligible to receive services to	Varies by state; some states offer cash to families; others offer services like respite, parent	Aims to improve health of all mothers and children; services and eligibility vary by state; major

(Continued)

Table 7.2 (Continued)

	Income Transfers	Education	Early Intervention	Family Support	Maternal and Child Health (Title V)
	to low-income children; eligibility based on child disability and family income	environment; Individualized Education Plan (IEP) guides child's education; parents serve as advocates	promote their development; Individualized Family Service Plan guides services to entire family	support groups, etc.; eligibility requirements and breadth/depth of services vary by state	services funded include direct health, enabling, population-based, and infrastructure building services

Using Knowledge of Risk, Protection, and Resilience to Achieve Service Integration in Disabilities Policy

Two features define policies related to children with disabilities: (1) the reliance on parents to be advocates, case managers, and caregivers for their children; and (2) the fragmentation of policy across service domains. Parents are expected to have a central role in providing care for their children from the point of diagnosis to entry into early intervention, to obtaining support services, enrolling in the education system, and through transition planning and beyond. In some policies, this parental role is explicit: early intervention programs have for decades embraced collaboration between parents and professionals, and the partnership has long been regarded as a best practice for infants, toddlers, and preschoolers with disabilities (Blue-Banning, Summers, Frankland, Nelson, & Beegle, 2004).

However, many parents lack the time, knowledge, and financial and emotional resources required to be full or effective partners in this endeavor. Within the formal education system, IDEIA has established ground rules through which parents can enter an adversarial role with their children's schools to obtain needed services. Parents speak poignantly of their advocacy at every step of their child's development to ensure needed services are secured. Although over time sustained advocacy often helps parents become masters in navigating bureaucracies and securing services, such efforts are by no means the optimal way for children with disabilities to obtain what they need. Parents face enough stress in meeting their children's physical and emotional care needs and should not also have to fulfill roles as advocates and case managers.

Fragmentation of services remains an ongoing challenge for children with disabilities. Often, to obtain the services their children need, parents must navigate numerous different bureaucracies, with separate institutions governing income transfers, early intervention and education, family support, and medical care. All of these programs have different eligibility criteria, paperwork requirements, definitions of disability, revenue sources, and administrative entities. Despite considerable redundancy requiring parents to "prove" that their child has an impairment, streamlined applications or coordination across providers typically does not exist.

Juanita: A Case Example

To further illustrate the fragmentation and parental advocacy that are hallmarks of disability policy, we considered the experiences of a young girl, Juanita, who has cerebral palsy and intellectual disabilities. Cerebral palsy is a nonprogressive group of chronic conditions that results from a brain injury, which affects muscle coordination and motor development. Cerebral palsy was formerly included in the category of mental retardation, although cerebral palsy does not always include intellectual disabilities. Intellectual disabilities are characterized as below-average intelligence.

Juanita

Juanita is a 9-year-old who lives with her mother. Juanita's father has not had contact with the family since the girl's diagnosis with cerebral palsy at 20 months of age. Their extended family lives out of state. Juanita was slower than other young children to reach developmental milestones, and her pediatrician's referral to a neurologist established the diagnosis for cerebral palsy. Juanita was in a center-based early intervention program until she entered public school. Juanita is in a self-contained classroom with other children with disabilities,

(Continued)

(Continued)

but her mother would prefer for her to be mainstreamed into a regular education classroom. Juanita walks with crutches, has difficulty grasping objects, and has limited speech that is difficult to understand. She is incontinent. She is very friendly and outgoing and is well liked by her teacher, classmates, and other children in her neighborhood. She has a great sense of humor and likes to tell jokes. Juanita's mother has a close relationship with one neighbor, but this neighbor is not comfortable providing child care for Juanita. Juanita's mother has had to limit her work to part-time employment because she cannot find afterschool care for Juanita, and she must drive and accompany Juanita to frequent medical appointments. Juanita's father does not pay child support, and because her mother's income is low, Juanita qualifies for monthly SSI payments and Medicaid. Over the past few years, when her mother's income temporarily increased because of work bonuses, Juanita's SSI benefits were reevaluated and terminated. Although her mother appealed those termination decisions, the appeals process took several weeks in each case. The appeals process is confusing, and Juanita's mother was not aware that she could ask for aid pending the outcome of the appeals.

Juanita's current IEP recommends only one specialized service, which is speech therapy that she receives in a group setting with several other classmates. Juanita's earlier IEP had also recommended physical therapy, but those services were discontinued 2 years ago when her IEP team, with the exception of her mother, decided the therapy was no longer necessary because she had made limited progress. Since that time, Juanita's physical functioning has deteriorated, but the IEP team rejected her mother's initial appeal to have the physical therapy put back into her IEP. Her mother wants to pursue this appeal further but needs to learn how to initiate further appeals.

During her early childhood, Juanita had a number of orthopedic surgeries to increase her physical functioning. Although she has Medicaid, the only health care providers in the region who accept Medicaid are in a county clinic. Because of the practice structure of the county clinic, Juanita and her mother always have lengthy waits for care, and she usually sees different providers at each visit. Juanita needs adaptive devices to help her manipulate tools and independently complete activities of daily living (e.g., feeding, personal hygiene). To give Juanita greater independence in self-care, her mother has applied through the clinic's pediatrician for a number of these devices. Medicaid has denied these applications, but her mother is appealing those decisions. Medicaid does not cover the cost of Juanita's diapers, which are expensive. The mother has also applied for a cash subsidy to cover the cost of purchasing the adaptive devices Juanita needs, but she was told that she is ineligible because the household income is too high.

Juanita's mother contacted the regional office of the state's developmental disabilities department to request respite services. She would like to use the respite services for Juanita's afterschool care so she could work more hours. Although she has completed the application, it cannot be submitted until the clinic pediatrician finalizes the paperwork certifying Juanita's disability. Even if the application is approved, Juanita will be placed on the waiting list. The regional office told the mother the wait for respite services averages 18 months, and once services are available, she will be eligible to receive a maximum of 10 hours respite care a month. After receiving respite services for 1 year, she will again be wait-listed so that other families can receive the respite service. Given the long wait, Juanita's mother is anxious to get the application submitted. However, over the past 2 months, she has called the clinic weekly to check on the pediatrician's progress with this paperwork, but it has not yet been completed. No one has given her a reason for the delay.

Juanita and her mother's situation, like so many others, illustrates the complexity involved in navigating a fragmented and unresponsive service delivery system.

Policy Recommendations

Children with disabilities and their families are protected by policies that are designed to enhance family functioning and to provide services and therapies that maximize independence and inclusion in society. At present, family support and early intervention are based on principles of risk and protective factors. Special education was developed within a civil rights framework: Children with disabilities were entitled to the same educational opportunities as their nondisabled peers. Like SSI payments for children, special education offers some protective benefits, but such benefits are limited in scope. On balance, the accrued benefits do not mitigate the risks associated with childhood disability.

The limited availability of family support services across the United States translates into few benefits for most families. The model of early intervention, in which service provision is driven by collaborative parent–professional partnerships, has much to offer the broader arena of disability policy for children. In this model, the focus is the whole family rather than just the child with disabilities, and the goal is to meet the needs of the whole family across a spectrum of domains. Compelled by a single Individualized Family Support Plan (IFSP), care and services are typically coordinated to meet the full constellation of family needs. Our central policy recommendation is related to using an IFSP model to integrate and coordinate services across all service and support domains. Expanding the rubric of the IFSP to include family support services from all funding sources, including income transfers and Medicaid, would minimize the avenues and channels parents must navigate to obtain the services a child needs and to which he or she may be entitled. A "one-stop shopping" approach would also reduce the fragmentation in services and create a cohesive service structure. If the IFSP model were incorporated in children's education plans, a holistic framework of serving children with disabilities within the context of their families would replace the current fractured focus on child deficits and skills.

Summary

We have described five of the major policies that influence the well-being of children with disabilities and their families: (1) income transfers, (2) education, (3) early intervention, (4) Title V Maternal and Child Health Services, and (5) family support services. We have shown that these policies place a burden on parents to function as advocates and case managers, and, more broadly, that the services produced by these policies function in similar ways but have inherent differences.

Understanding and accessing programs is difficult because of the lack of communication between systems, different eligibility criteria, and an array of separate (and competing) revenue sources. Although concepts of risk and protective factors are fundamental in early intervention and family support policies, they are applied in very limited ways to education and income transfer policies. In addition, family support is so inadequately funded that it has little meaning or impact for most families raising children with disabilities. Therefore, our final recommendations stem from a desire to enable families to meet the care needs of their children, at a minimum. To accomplish this objective, early intervention must be fully funded, and funding for family support and income transfers should be increased to meet the true needs of low-income families.

QUESTIONS FOR DISCUSSION

1. What are the implications of categorically based eligibility criteria for efforts to integrate policies for children with developmental disabilities with other child and family policies?

2. What policy changes would you recommend to better provide an integrated service delivery system for children and youth with developmental disabilities and their families?

3. How will the transition away from a medical model of disability to a social model of disability influence the delivery of services for children and youth with developmental disabilities and their families in the coming decades?

References

Abelson, A. G. (1999). Respite care needs of parents of children with developmental disabilities. *Focus on Autism & Other Developmental Disabilities, 14,* 96–101. doi:10.1177/108835769901400204

Ammerman, R.T., & Baladerian, N. J. (1993). *Maltreatment of children with disabilities.* Chicago: National Committee to Prevent Child Abuse.

Beers, N., Kemeny, A., Sherritt, L., & Palfrey, J. (2003). Variations in state-level definitions: Children with special health care needs. *Public Health Reports, 118,* 434–447.

Blue-Banning, M., Summers, J. A., Frankland, H. C., Nelson, L. L., & Beegle, G. (2004). Dimensions of family and professional partnerships: Constructive guidelines for collaboration. *Exceptional Children, 70,* 167–184.

Braddock, D., & Parish, S. (2001). Disability history from antiquity to the Americans with Disabilities Act. In G. L. Albrecht, K. D. Seelman, & M. Bury (Eds.), *Handbook of disability studies* (pp. 11–68). Thousand Oaks, CA: Sage.

Bronfenbrenner, U. (1979). *The ecology of human development: Experiments by nature and design.* Cambridge, MA: Harvard University Press.

Bronfenbrenner, U. (1986). Ecology of the family as a context to human development: Research perspectives. *Development Psychology, 22,* 723–742. doi:10.1037/0012–1649.22.6.723

Brooks-Gunn, J., & Duncan, G. J. (1997). The effects of poverty on children. *Future of Children, 7,* 55–71. doi:10.2307/1602387

Brooks-Gunn, J., Klebanov, P. K, & Liaw, F. (1995). The learning, physical, and emotional environment of the home in the context of poverty: The Infant Health and Development program. *Children and Youth Services Review, 17,* 251–276. doi:10.1016/0190–7409(95)00011-Z

Bruns, E. J., & Burchard, J. D. (2000). Impact of respite care services for families with children experiencing emotional and behavioral problems. *Children's Services: Social Policy, Research, & Practice, 3,* 39–61. doi:10.1207/S15326918CS0301_3

Cedar Rapids Community School District v. Garret F., 526 U.S. 66 (1999). Retrieved from http://supreme.justia.com/us/526/66/

Chazan, M., Laing, A., Jones, J., Harper, G., & Bolton, J. (1983). The management of behavior problems in your children. *Early Childhood Development and Care, 11,* 227–244. doi:10.1080/0300443830110302

Creasy, R. K., & Resnik, R. (1999). *Maternal-fetal medicine* (4th ed.). Philadelphia: Saunders.

Crnic, K. A., Friedrich, W. N., & Greenberg, M. T. (1983). Adaptation of families with mentally retarded children. *American Journal of Mental Deficiency, 88,* 125–138.

Curran, A. L., Sharples, P. M., White, C., & Knapp, M. (2001). Time costs of caring for children with severe disabilities compared with caring for children without disabilities. *Developmental Medicine & Child Neurology, 43,* 529–533. doi:10.1017/S0012162201000962

Davies, P., Iams, H., & Rupp, K. (2000). The effect of welfare reform on SSA's disability programs: Design of policy evaluation and early evidence. *Social Security Bulletin, 63,* 3–11.

Davis, L. (2000). Dr. Johnson, Amelia, and the discourse of disability in the eighteenth century. In H. Deutsch & F. Nussbaum (Eds.), *"Defects": Engendering the modern body* (pp. 54–74). Ann Arbor: University of Michigan Press.

DeNavas-Walt, C., Proctor, B., & Smith, J. (2009). *Income, poverty, and health insurance coverage in the United States: 2008* (P60–236RV). Washington, DC: U.S. Census Bureau.

Developmental Disabilities Assistance and Bill of Rights Act of 2000, Pub. L. 106–402. Retrieved from http://www.acf.hhs.gov/programs/add/ddact/DDACT2.html

Dodge, K. A. (1983). Behavioral antecedents of peer social status. *Child Development, 54,* 1386–1399.

Edgar, E., & Levine, P. (1987). *A longitudinal follow-along study of graduates of special education.* Seattle: University of Washington Child Development and Mental Retardation Center.

Emerson, E. (2007). Poverty and people with disabilities. *Mental Retardation and Developmental Disabilities Research Reviews, 13,* 107–113. doi:10.1002/mrdd.20144

Farber, B. (1960). Family organization and crisis: Maintenance of integration in families with a severely retarded child. *Monographs of the Society for Research in Child Development, 25,* 1–95. doi:10.2307/1165524

Floyd, F. J., & Gallagher, E. M. (1997). Parental stress, care demands, and use of support services for school-age children with disabilities and behavior problems. *Family Relations, 46,* 359–371. doi:10.2307/585096

Fraser, M. W., Kirby, L. D., & Smokowski, P. (2004). Risk and resilience in childhood. In M. W. Fraser (Ed.), *Risk and resilience in childhood: An ecological perspective* (pp. 13–66). Washington, DC: NASW Press.

Freedman, R. I., & Boyer, N. C. (2000). The power to choose: Supports for families caring for individuals with developmental disabilities. *Health & Social Work, 25,* 59–68.

Fujiura, G. T., & Yamaki, K. (2000). Trends in demography of childhood poverty and disability. *Exceptional Children, 66,* 187–199.

General Accounting Office. (1999, June). *SSI children: Multiple factors affect families' costs for disability-related services* (GAO/HEHS-99-99). Washington, DC: Author.

Grad, S. (2000, December 15). *The role of disability benefits in the economic well-being of beneficiaries.* Paper presented at the National Academy of Social Insurance

Conference, Disability Income Policy: Opportunities and Challenges in the Next Decade, Washington, DC.

Graham, M., & Bryant, D. (1993). Characteristics of quality, effective service delivery systems for children with special needs. In D. Bryant & M. Graham (Eds.), *Implementing early intervention: From research to effective practice* (pp. 233–254). New York: Guilford Press.

Haveman, M., van Berkum, G., Reijinder, R., & Heller, T. (1997). Differences in service needs, time demands, and caregiving burden among parents of persons with mental retardation across the life cycle. *Family Relations, 46,* 417–425. doi:10.2307/585101

Heller, T., Miller, A. B., & Hsieh, K. (1999). Impact of a consumer-directed family support program on adults with developmental disabilities and their family caregivers. *Family Relations, 48,* 419–427. doi:10.2307/585250

Hogan, D. P., & Msall, M. E. (2002). Family structure and resources and the parenting of children with disabilities and functional limitations. In J. G. Borkowski, S. L. Ramey, & M. Bristol-Power (Eds.), *Parenting and the child's world: Influences on academic, intellectual, and social-emotional development* (pp. 311–328). Mahwah, NJ: Lawrence Erlbaum.

Hogan, D. P., Msall, M. E., Rogers, M. L., & Avery, R. C. (1997). Improved disability population estimates of functional limitation among children 5–17. *Maternal and Child Health Journal, 1,* 203–216. doi:10.1023/A:1022354126797

Inkelas, M., Rowe, M., Karoly, L., & Rogowski, J. (1999). *Policy evaluation of the effects of the 1996 welfare reform legislation on SSI benefits for disabled children: First round case study findings.* Santa Monica, CA: Rand.

Katsiyannis, A., & Yell, M. L. (2000). The Supreme Court and school health services: *Cedar Rapids v. Garret F. Exceptional Children, 66,* 317–326.

Keogh, B. K., & Bernheimer, L. P. (1987). Developmental delays in preschool children: Assessment over time. *European Journal of Special Needs Education, 2,* 211–220. doi:10.1080/0885625870020401

Keogh, B. K., Bernheimer, L. P., & Guthrie, D. (2004). Children with developmental delays twenty years later: Where are they? How are they? *American Journal on Mental Retardation, 109,* 219–230. doi:10.1352/0895–8017(2004)109<219:CWD-DTY>2.0.CO;2

Kirk, S., Gallagher, J., & Asastasiow, N. (1993). *Educating exceptional children* (7th ed). Boston: Houghton Mifflin.

Kupersmidt, J. B., Coie, J. D., & Dodge, K. A. (1990). The role of peer relationships in the development of disorder. In S. R. Asher & J. D. Coie (Eds.), *Peer rejections in childhood* (pp. 17–59). New York: Cambridge University Press.

Landesman, S., Jaccard, J., & Gunderson, V. (1989). The family environment: The combined influences of family behavior, goals, strategies, resources, and individual experiences. In M. Lewis & S. Feinman (Eds.), *Social influences on development* (pp. 63–96). New York: Plenum Press.

Lichter, D. T., & Eggebeen, D. J. (1994). The effect of parental employment on child poverty. *Journal of Marriage and the Family, 56,* 633–645. doi:10.2307/352874

Lukemeyer, A., Meyers, M. K., & Smeeding, T. (2000). Expensive kids in poor families: Out of pocket expenditures for the care of disabled and chronically ill children and welfare reform. *Journal of Marriage and the Family, 62,* 399–415. doi:10.1111/j.1741-3737.2000.00399.x

Maternal and Child Health Bureau. (n.d.). *Title V information system.* Retrieved from https://perfdata.hrsa.gov/mchb/TVISReports/Default.aspx

Meyer, L., Cole, D. A., McQuarter, R., & Reichle, J. (1990). Validation of the assessment of social competence for children and young adults with developmental disabilities. *Journal of the Association for Persons with Severe Handicaps, 15,* 57–68.

Meyers, M. K., Han, W. J., Waldfogel, J., & Garfinkel, I. (2001). Child care in the wake of welfare reform: The impact of government subsidies on the economic well-being of single-mother families. *Social Service Review, 75,* 29–59. doi:10.1086/591881

Meyers, M. K., & Heintze, T. (1999). The child care subsidy shortfall: Is the subsidy system working? *Social Service Review, 73,* 37–64. doi:10.1086/515796

National Center on Child Abuse and Neglect. (1993). *A report on the maltreatment of children with disabilities.* Washington, DC: U.S. Department of Health and Human Services, Administration on Children, Youth, and Families.

National Commission on Childhood Disability. (1995, October). *Supplemental Security Income for children with disabilities: Report to Congress.* Washington, DC: Author.

Newacheck, P. W., & Kim, S. E. (2005). A national profile of healthcare utilization and expenditures for children with special health care needs. *Archives of Pediatric and Adolescent Medicine, 159,* 10–17. doi:10.1001/archpedi.159.1.10

Newacheck, P. W., Stein, R. K., Bauman, L., & Hung, Y. (2003). Disparities in the prevalence of disability between Black and White children. *Archives of Pediatric & Adolescent Medicine, 157,* 244–248.

Osborne, A. G., & Dimattia, P. (1994). The IDEA's least restrictive environment mandate: Legal implications. *Exceptional Children, 61,* 6–14.

Pagelow, M. D. (1984). *Family violence.* New York: Praeger.

Parish, S. L. (2003). Mental retardation and federal income transfers: The political and economic context. *Mental Retardation, 41,* 446–459. doi:10.1352/0047-6765(2003)41<446:FIPAMR>2.0.CO;2

Parish, S. L., & Cloud, J. M. (2006). Financial well-being of young children with disabilities and their families. *Social Work, 51,* 223–232.

Parish, S. L., Pomeranz, A. E., & Braddock, D. (2003). Family support in the United States: Financing trends and emerging initiatives. *Mental Retardation, 41,* 174–187. doi:10.1352/0047-6765(2003)41<174:FSITUS>2.0.CO;2

Parish, S. L., Rose, R. A., & Andrews, M. E. (2010). TANF and the employment, marriage, and welfare use of low-income mothers raising children with disabilities. *Exceptional Children, 76,* 234-253.

Parish, S. L., Rose, R. A., Andrews, M. E., Grinstein-Weiss, M., & Richman, E. L. (2008). Material hardship among U.S. families raising children with disabilities. *Exceptional Children, 75,* 71–92.

Parish, S. L., Seltzer, M. M., Greenberg, J. S., & Floyd, F. J. (2004). Economic implications of caregiving at midlife: Comparing parents of children with developmental disabilities to other parents. *Mental Retardation, 42,* 413–426.

Parish, S. L., Shattuck, P. T., & Rose, R. A. (2009). A multi-level analysis of state Medicaid and financial burden of raising children with special health care needs. *Pediatrics, 124,* Supplement 6, S435-S442. doi:10.1542/peds.2009–1255P

Park, J., Turnbull, A. P., & Turnbull, H. R. (2002). Impacts of poverty on quality of life in families of children with disabilities. *Exceptional Children, 68,* 151–170.

Parrott, S., Schott, L., Sweeney, E., Baider, A., Ganzglass, E., Greenberg, M., . . . Turetsky, V. (2007). *Implementing the TANF changes in the Deficit Reduction Act: "Win-win" solutions for families and states* (2nd ed.). Washington, DC: Center on Budget and Policy Priorities and Center for Law and Social Policy. Retrieved from http://www.cbpp.org/cms/?fa=view&id=1176

Perrin, J. M. (2002). Health services research for children with disabilities. *The Milbank Quarterly, 80,* 303–324. doi:10.1111/1468–0009.t01–1-00005

Rallis, S. F., & Anderson, G. (1994). *Building inclusive schools: Places where all children can learn* (Occasional Paper Series, Vol. 9, No. 2). Andover, MA: Regional Laboratory for Educational Improvement of the Northeast & Islands.

Ramey, C. T., & Ramey, S. L. (1998). Early intervention and early experience. *American Psychologist, 53,* 109–120. doi:10.1037/0003–066X.53.2.109

Richmond, J., & Ayoub, C.C. (1993). Evolution of early intervention philosophy. In D. M. Bryant & M. A. Graham (Eds.), *Implementing early intervention: From research to effective practice* (pp. 1–17). New York: Guilford Press.

Rizzolo, M. C., Hemp, R., & Braddock, D. (2006). Family support services in the United States. *Policy Research Brief, 17*(1), Minneapolis: University of Minnesota.

Rosenbaum, S., Proser, M., Schneider, A., & Sonosky, C. (2002). *Using the Title V Maternal and Child Health Services Block Grant to support child development services.* Washington, DC: The Commonwealth Fund. Retrieved from http://www.commonwealthfund.org/usr_doc/rosenbaum_titlev_481.pdf

Rosman, E., McCarthy, J., & Woolverton, M. (2001). *Child care: Adults with mental health needs and children with special needs.* Washington, DC: Georgetown University Child Development Center.

Scorgie, K., Wilgosh, L., & McDonald, L. (1998). Stress and coping in families of children with disabilities: An examination of recent literature. *Developmental Disabilities Bulletin, 26,* 22–42.

Scruggs, T. E., & Mastropieri, M. (1996). Teacher perceptions of mainstreaming/ inclusion, 1958–1995: A research synthesis. *Exceptional Children, 63,* 59–74.

Shearn, J., & Todd, S. (2000). Maternal employment and family responsibilities: The perspectives of mothers of children with learning disabilities. *Journal of Applied Research in Intellectual Disabilities, 13,* 109–131.

Singer, G. H., & Irvin, L. K. (1989). Family caregiving, stress, and support. In G. H. Singer & L. K. Irvin (Eds.), *Support for caregiving families: Enabling positive adaptation to disability* (pp. 207–219). Baltimore, MD: Brookes.

Sitlington, P., Frank, A., & Carson, R. (1992). Adult adjustment among high school graduates with mild disabilities. *Exceptional Children, 59,* 221–233.

Sobsey, D. (1994). *Violence and abuse in the lives of people with disabilities: The end of silent acceptance?* Baltimore, MD: Brookes.

Social Security Administration. (2000, September 11). Supplemental Security Income: Determining disability for a child under 18. Final rules. *Federal Register, 65,* 54747–54790.Retrieved from http://frwebgate.access.gpo.gov/cgi-bin/getdoc .cgi?dbname=2000_register&docid=00–22753-filed.pdf

Social Security Administration. (2009). *Annual statistical supplement to the Social Security Bulletin, 2008* (13–11700). Washington, DC: Author.

Sopko, K. M. (2003). *The IEP: A synthesis of current literature since 1997.* Alexandria, VA: National Association of State Directors of Special Education.

Summers, J. A., Behr, S. K., & Turnbull, A. P. (1989). Positive adaptation and coping strengths of families who have children with disabilities. In G. H. S. Singer & L. K. Irvin (Eds.), *Support for caregiving families* (pp. 27–40). Baltimore, MD: Brookes.

Thompson, T. S., Holcomb, P. A., Loprest, P., & Brennan, K. (1998). *State welfare-to-work policies for people with disabilities.* Washington, DC: Urban Institute.

Turnbull, A. P., Brotherson, M. J., & Summers, J. A. (1986). Family lifecycle: Theoretical and empirical implications and future directions for families with mentally retarded members. In J. J. Gallagher & P. M. Vietze (Eds.), *Families of handicapped persons: Research, programs and policy issues* (pp. 45–66). Baltimore, MD: Brookes.

Turnbull, A. P., & Turnbull, H. R. (1982). Parent involvement in the education of handicapped children: A critique. *Mental Retardation, 20,* 115–122.

U.S. Department of Education. (2009). *Twenty-eighth annual report to Congress on the implementation of the Individuals with Disabilities Education Act, 2006.* Washington, DC: Author.

U.S. Department of Health and Human Services. (2007, January 24). Annual update of the HHS poverty guidelines. *Federal Register, 72,* 3147–3148.

U.S. Department of Health and Human Services. (2008). *State Medicaid-MCH coordination: A review of Title V and Title XIX interagency agreements* (2nd ed.). Washington DC: Author.

Whitney-Thomas, J., & Moloney, M. (2001). "Who I am and what I want": Adolescents' self-definition and struggles. *Exceptional Children, 67*, 375–389.

Yau, M. K., & Li-Tsang, C. W. (1999). Adjustment and adaptation in parents of children with developmental disabilities in two-parent families: A review of the characteristics ancillary attributes. *British Journal of Developmental Disability, 45*, 38–51.

Yeargin-Allsopp, M., Rice, C., Karapurkar, T., Doernberg, N., Boyle, C., & Murphy, C. (2003). Prevalence of autism in a US metropolitan area. *Journal of the American Medical Association, 289*, 49–55. doi:10.1001/jama.289.1.49

Zipper, I., & Simeonsson, R. J. (2004). Promoting the development and well-being of young children with disabilities. In M. Fraser (Ed.), *Risk and resilience in childhood: An ecological perspective* (pp. 244-264). Washington, DC: NASW Press.

Additional Reading

Cryer, D., & Clifford, R. M. (2003). *Early childhood education and care in the USA.* Baltimore: Brookes.

Pianta, R. C., & Kraft-Sayre, M. (2003). *Successful kindergarten transition: Your guide to connecting children, families, and schools.* Baltimore: Brookes.

Barnes, C., Barton, L., & Oliver, M. (2002). *Disability studies today.* Cambridge, UK: Polity Books.

Web-Based Resources

Institute for Community Inclusion, http://www.communityinclusion.org/
Kids Together, Inc., http://www.kidstogether.org/
The Arc, http://www.thearc.org/
Tash, Equal Opportunity and Inclusion for People with Disabilities, http://www.tash.org/
Family Voices, http://www.familyvoices.org/
Bazelon Center for Mental Health Law, http://www.bazelon.org/
Children's Defense Fund, http://www.childrensdefense.org/

8

Policies and Programs for Adolescent Substance Abuse

Jeffrey M. Jenson

Elizabeth K. Anthony

Matthew O. Howard

Adolescent substance abuse has been the subject of frequent discussion in local, state, and federal policy circles since the 1960s. Substance abuse among children and youth has also attracted the attention of the American public. A recent opinion poll conducted by the Gallup Organization revealed that 68% of Americans viewed drug use as one of the most serious problems facing teenagers (Gallup Organization, 2009). About 53% of respondents believe that the federal government has made little or no progress in preventing drug use in the past several years.

The visible and often devastating effects of substance use on individuals—coupled with the societal and economic costs associated with abuse—have been the targets of repeated social intervention in

270

the past century. Demands for policy and program reform have come from a range of constituents and organizations. A report published at the beginning of the past decade by Physician Leadership on National Drug Policy (2002) outlined the need for more policy directives aimed at preventing adolescent substance abuse in the United States. Recent reports from the National Institute on Drug Abuse (NIDA) and the Substance Abuse and Mental Health Services Administration (SAMHSA) place considerable emphasis on informing practitioners about efficacious ways to prevent and treat adolescent substance abuse (NIDA, 2009; SAMHSA, 2010). It is significant that researchers and policy officials are working together to apply knowledge about the risk and protective factors associated with the onset and use of alcohol and illicit drugs to social interventions and policies for children and families (Hawkins, 2006; Liddle & Rowe, 2006; Scheier, 2010; Woolf, 2008).

In this chapter, we describe risk and protective factors related to substance use and abuse. In addition, we review past and current policy and program responses to treating and preventing substance abuse in adolescence. The utility of a public health framework that emphasizes risk, protection, and resilience for the development of innovative policy and programs is examined. We begin with a brief discussion of recent trends in adolescent substance use.

Trends in Adolescent Substance Use

Adolescent substance use exists on a continuum that includes no use, nonproblematic use, abuse, and dependence. Substance abuse and dependence represent the most serious concerns to practitioners and policymakers. However, even low levels of drug use by children and youth can be problematic, given the many developmental tasks they encounter at school and in the community. Our review of trends in substance use, therefore, includes reports of experimental and regular use.

The nation's most accurate prevalence estimates for adolescent substance use come from the Monitoring the Future (MTF) study (Johnston, O'Malley, Bachman, & Schulenberg, 2009), sponsored by NIDA and the University of Michigan. MTF is an annual assessment of alcohol and drug use in a random sample of about 16,000 public and private high school students. In-school surveys with nationally representative samples of high school seniors have been conducted since 1975. Eighth- and 10th-grade students have been surveyed since 1991.

There have been several notable trends in adolescent substance use since the 1970s. Lifetime illicit drug use—marijuana, hallucinogen, cocaine, heroin, and other opiate use as well as use of stimulants, barbiturates, or tranquilizers that are not under a doctor's order—peaked among seniors in 1981. About 66% of 12th graders in 1981 used an illicit drug at least once in their lives; 43% used an illicit drug other than marijuana. Lifetime use of illicit drugs reached its lowest point in 1992; only 41% of seniors used any illicit drug, and 25% used an illicit drug other than marijuana. In 1993, seniors reversed a decade-long pattern of declining illicit drug use.

Rates of illicit drug use rose for 6 consecutive years, and by 1999, 55% of seniors reported using illicit drugs. A 10-year trend of declining rates of illicit drug use among high school seniors began in 2000. By 2009, only 47% of seniors reported illicit drug use in their lifetime.

Lifetime alcohol and tobacco use by seniors reached their highest levels in the late 1970s and early 1980s. About 93% of seniors reported lifetime alcohol use between 1977 and 1985. In 2009, 73% of seniors reported lifetime alcohol use. Interestingly, lifetime cigarette smoking among young people peaked in 1977. About 76% of seniors smoked cigarettes in 1977, compared to 44% in 2009.

Substance use among younger adolescents is of particular concern to policymakers and practitioners because early initiation is positively related to later problem use. The number of eighth-grade students reporting lifetime use of any illicit drug decreased from a high of 31% in 1996 to 20% in 2009. About 36% of 10th grade students used illicit drugs in 2009.

Males continue to use most drugs at higher rates than females. However, recent MTF results show a decrease with regard to gender differences in drug use. In 2009, the difference in annual illicit drug use between boys and girls in the 12th grade was only 3 percentage points; 49% of boys, compared with 46% of girls, reported annual illicit drug use in 2009. MTF results indicate that alcohol and drug use are more prevalent among White students than among African American or Hispanic students (Johnston et al., 2009). In 2009, annual prevalence of illicit drug use among 12th graders was 49% for White, 46% for Hispanic, and 41% for African American students.

MTF results provide a fairly accurate picture of substance use among American youth. However, it is important to acknowledge that the MTF study may underestimate the magnitude of substance use among youth in the United States because it does not include school dropouts (an estimated 15% to 20% of students in this age group), a group at high risk for alcohol and drug use. Estimates of drug and alcohol use among minority groups may be particularly affected because more American Indian and Hispanic high school seniors drop out of school than African American, Asian American, or White seniors (Johnston et al., 2009).

Trends in adolescent substance use point to the need for a continuum of policy and practice responses. Prevention strategies are needed to delay initiation and to interrupt the progression of substance use that often begins with alcohol or tobacco and culminates with more serious drug use. Conversely, treatment options are necessary for individuals exhibiting symptoms of abuse or dependence. In recent years, policy and program approaches aimed at preventing and treating adolescent substance abuse have been based on etiological models that emphasize principles of risk, protection, and resilience.

The Etiology of Adolescent Substance Abuse: Principles of Risk, Protection, and Resilience

Knowledge generated by investigations examining the relationship among risk and protective factors and adolescent substance use has led to significant advancements in the etiology, assessment, and prevention of drug abuse (for a review of such investigations, see Belcher & Shinitzky, 1998; Brook, Brook, & Pahl, 2006; Hawkins, Catalano, & Miller, 1992; Jenson, 2004; Kim, 2009; Schinke, Fang, & Cole, 2008). Yet, definitions and policy applications underlying concepts of risk and protection are clouded with controversy. Most researchers, practitioners, and public health specialists agree that risk factors for adolescent substance use can be empirically identified. As noted in Chapter 1, there is considerably less agreement about the concept and definition of protection. Some authors (Luthar, 2003) assert that risk and protective factors act as polar opposites of one another. Other investigators (Fraser, 2004; Rossa, 2002; Rutter, 2000) argue that protective factors are characteristics and conditions that moderate or mediate levels of risk for problem behaviors like substance abuse. The following discussion of protective factors, consistent with the interpretation presented in Chapter 1, is based on the view that protective factors are traits, conditions, and characteristics that influence or modify risk for substance abuse.

Risk Factors

Risk factors for adolescent substance abuse occur at environmental, interpersonal, social, and individual levels. These factors are summarized next and in Table 8.1.

Table 8.1   Risk Factors for Adolescent Substance Abuse

Environmental Factors

  Low taxation and weak regulation of alcohol and drugs
  Permissive cultural and social norms about substance use
  Availability of alcohol and drugs
  Poverty
  Limited economic opportunity
  Neighborhood disorganization
  Low neighborhood attachment
  High rates of residential mobility
  High rates of adult criminality
  High population density

Interpersonal and Social Factors

  Family conflict
  Poor family management practices
  Dysfunctional family communication patterns
  Parent and sibling substance use
  Poor parent–child bonding
  School failure
  Low commitment to school
  Rejection by conforming peer groups
  Association with drug-using friends

Individual Factors

  Family history of alcoholism
  Sensation-seeking orientation
  Poor impulse control
  Attention deficits
  Hyperactivity

SOURCE: Table adapted from Jenson (2004).

Environmental Risk Factors

Community laws and norms favorable to drug use, such as low legal drinking ages and low taxes on alcoholic beverages, increase the risk of substance use during adolescence (Joksch, 1988). Studies examining the relationship between legal age for drinking and adolescent drinking and driving have shown that lowering the drinking age increases underage drinking and teen traffic fatalities (Saffer & Grossman, 1987). Laws and norms that express intolerance for use of alcohol and illicit drugs by adolescents are associated with a lower prevalence of alcohol and drug use (Johnston, 1991).

In 2008, nearly 18% of children under the age of 18 lived in conditions of poverty (Annie E. Casey Foundation, 2010). Poverty is associated with many adverse adolescent outcomes, including conduct problems, delinquency, and unwanted pregnancy (Cauce, Stewart, Rodriguez, Cochran, & Ginzler, 2003; Hannon, 2003). Poverty may also have an indirect effect on adolescent substance use. Family income is associated with many other risk factors for drug use (e.g., parenting practices and academic difficulties); low family income may affect drug use indirectly through such risk factors.

Low neighborhood attachment, school transitions, and residential mobility are associated with drug and alcohol abuse (Murray, 1983). Neighborhoods with high population density and high rates of adult crime also have high rates of adolescent crime and drug use (Simcha-Fagan & Schwartz, 1986). Neighborhood disorganization may also indirectly affect risk for drug abuse by eroding the ability of parents to supervise and control their children.

Interpersonal and Social Risk Factors

Interpersonal and social risk factors for adolescent substance abuse occur in family, school, and peer settings. Children whose parents or siblings engage in serious alcohol or illicit drug use are themselves at greater risk for these behaviors (Biederman, Faraone, Monuteaux, & Feighner, 2000). Children raised in families with lax supervision, excessively severe or inconsistent disciplinary practices, and little communication and involvement between parents and children are also at high risk for later substance abuse (Hill, Shen, Lowers, & Locke, 2000). Similarly, studies have shown that parental conflict is related to subsequent alcohol or drug use by adolescent family members (Brook, Whiteman, Gordon, & Brook, 1988).

School failure, low degree of commitment to education, and lack of attachment to school are school-related factors that increase the risk of substance abuse during adolescence (Holmberg, 1985). Adolescent drug users are more likely to skip classes, be absent from school, and perform poorly than non-drug users (Gottfredson, 1981).

Association with friends who use drugs is among the strongest predictors of adolescent substance abuse (Fergusson & Horwood, 1999; Reinherz, Giaconia, Hauf, Wasserman, & Paradis, 2000). Peer rejection in elementary grades is associated with school problems and delinquency (Coie, 1990; Kupersmidt, Coie, & Dodge, 1990), which are also risk factors for drug abuse. Some investigators hypothesize that rejected children form friendships with other rejected children and that such groups become delinquent or engage in drug use during adolescence (Patterson, 2002; Patterson, Reid, & Eddy, 2002).

Individual Risk Factors

Psychosocial and biological factors are related to drug and alcohol abuse during adolescence. For example, evidence from adoption, twin, and half-sibling studies supports the notion that alcoholism is an inherited disorder (Cadoret, Cain, & Grove, 1980). Several studies have found that a sensation-seeking orientation predicts initiation and continued use of alcohol and other drugs (Cicchetti & Rogosch, 1999; Cloninger, Sigvardsson, & Bohman, 1988). Research also indicates that attention deficit disorders, hyperactivity, and poor impulse control before the age of 12 predict the age of onset of drinking and drug use (Shedler & Block, 1990).

Jenson and Potter (2003) found three distinct patterns of co-occurring mental health and substance use patterns in a longitudinal investigation of 154 detained youths. Adolescents who were most likely to abuse alcohol and other drugs also had high levels of self-reported depression, paranoia, hostility, and suicidal ideation. This and other investigations (Loeber, Farrington, Stouthamer-Loeber, & van Kammen, 1998; Vaughn, Freedenthal, Jenson, & Howard, 2007; Vaughn, Wallace, Davis, Fernandes, & Howard, 2008) suggest that mental health problems may play an important role in a youth's decision to experiment with and to persistently use alcohol or other drugs.

Protective Factors

Many adolescents develop healthy relationships and succeed in school and the community despite being exposed to multiple risk factors. Empirical research devoted to identifying individual and environmental characteristics that protect youth from substance abuse has lagged behind similar efforts aimed at identifying risk factors for drug use. However, an increasing number of investigators have begun to examine the relationship between protective factors and substance use in recent years (Brook et al., 2006; Jenson, 2004). When identified in children and adolescents, protective factors can be established or enhanced to reduce risks for substance abuse. Protective factors for alcohol and other drug use are summarized next and in Table 8.2.

Environmental, Interpersonal, and Social Protective Factors

Environmental, interpersonal, and social protective factors are attributes that buffer community, neighborhood, family, school, and peer risk factors. The most comprehensive study of protective factors among

Table 8.2 Protective Factors Against Adolescent Substance Abuse

Environmental, Interpersonal, and Social Factors

Being a firstborn child

Being raised in a small family

Low parental conflict

Caring relationships with siblings

Caring relationships with extended family members

Attachment to parents

Social support from nonfamily members

Commitment to school

Involvement in conventional activities

Belief in pro-social norms

Individual Factors

Social and problem-solving skills

Positive attitude

Positive temperament

High intelligence

Low childhood stress

SOURCE: Table adapted from Jenson (2004).

children has been conducted by Werner and colleagues. Werner and Smith (1989) began following a cohort of high-risk children in Kauai, Hawaii, in 1955. Analysis of the children's outcomes as adolescents and adults has contributed to knowledge about factors that prevent youth from abusing alcohol and other drugs.

Werner (1994) found that being raised in a family with four or fewer children, experiencing low parental conflict, and being a firstborn child reduce the effects of poverty and other risk factors for substance abuse. Children who abstained from drug use during adolescence and early adulthood had positive parent–child relationships in early childhood and caring relationships with siblings and grandparents. Children abstaining from alcohol and other drugs also received social support and frequent counsel from teachers, ministers, and neighbors (Werner, 1994).

A positive family milieu and community supports are protective factors for drug abuse among children exposed to multiple risk factors. Garmezy (1985) found low childhood stress among high-risk children living in supportive family environments and in adolescents who had strong external support systems. Because stress increases risk for drug use in later adolescence and early adulthood (Rutter, 2000), such findings have implications for preventing childhood and early adolescent drug abuse.

Strong social bonds to parents, teachers, and pro-social peers are significant factors in children's resistance to drug use (Berrueta-Clement, Schweinhart, Barnett, Epstein, & Weikhard, 1984). Four elements of the social bond have been found to be inversely related to adolescent drug abuse: (1) strong attachments to parents (Brook et al., 2006), (2) commitment to school (Friedman, 1983), (3) involvement in pro-social activities such as church or community organizations (Miller, Davies, & Grenwald, 2000), and (4) belief in the generalized norms and values of society (Jenson & Howard, 1999).

Understanding the processes by which strong social bonds develop is necessary to develop strategies that increase healthy bonding in high-risk youth. Social learning (Bandura, 1989) and social development (Catalano & Hawkins, 1996) theorists indicate that three conditions are critical to the formation of strong social bonds: (1) opportunities for involvement in pro-social activities, (2) possession of the requisite behavioral and cognitive skills necessary to achieve success in such activities, and (3) rewards or recognition for positive behaviors. To promote healthy bonds, policies should support intervention strategies that provide opportunities, enhance skills, and offer rewards to high-risk youth.

Individual Protective Factors

Individual protective factors are psychosocial and biomedical characteristics that inhibit drug use. Competence in social and problem-solving situations is associated with abstinence and reductions in teenage drug use and delinquency. In a sample of high-risk urban children, Rutter (2000) found that problem-solving skills and strong self-efficacy were associated with successful adolescent outcomes. Youth who possessed adequate problem-solving skills and the ability to use skills were less likely to engage in drug use and delinquency. Jenson, Wells, Plotnick, Hawkins, and Catalano (1993) found that strong self-efficacy decreased the likelihood of drug use 6 months following drug treatment among adjudicated delinquents. These findings suggest that social and problem-solving skills moderate the effects of multiple risk factors for drug abuse and other adolescent outcomes.

Attitude and temperament are protective factors for substance abuse. Positive social orientation and positive temperament reduce the likelihood of adolescent drug abuse in several studies of high-risk youth (e.g., Jenson & Howard, 1999). Low intelligence (Werner, 1994) is also related to drug use.

Resilience

In Chapter 1 of this volume, Jenson and Fraser note the importance of resilience—an individual's ability to succeed in the face of adverse life circumstances—in the prevention of adolescent problem behaviors such as substance abuse. Anecdotal accounts detailing a person's ability to overcome substance abuse and addiction are common in American popular literature (Burroughs, 2003; Hamill, 1994; Knapp, 1996). However, the concept of resilience as an empirical construct in the explanation, prevention, or treatment of adolescent substance use remains a relatively new area of investigation (Luthar, 2003; Meschke & Patterson, 2003).

Studies indicate that some children and adolescents display high levels of functioning despite being surrounded by adverse familial or environmental influences (Fergusson & Horwood, 2003; Zucker, Wong, Puttler, & Fitzgerald, 2003). Zucker et al. (2003) examined the relationship between levels of resilience and subsequent childhood and adolescent outcomes among sons of alcoholic fathers and found that resilient youth were significantly more likely than nonresilient youth to resist substance use and other antisocial behaviors. Other studies have focused on the role of resilience in overcoming conditions of poverty (Cauce et al., 2003) and exposure to violence (Gorman-Smith & Tolan, 2003). Additional research is needed to better understand the direct and indirect effects of resilience on substance use.

Summary

Risk factors for substance use have been shown to be relatively stable over the past several decades. The factors summarized earlier consistently predict alcohol and drug use even though social norms about the acceptability of substance use have changed several times during this period. This suggests that policies and programs should encourage the development of strategies that target risk factors at multiple levels, including differential vulnerability, poor child-rearing practices, school achievement, social influences, social learning, and broad social norms.

Protection and resilience hold great promise in understanding, preventing, and treating substance abuse. Knowledge gained from studies examining the complex relationships among risk, protection, and resilience should be considered in policy and program design.

Risk, Protection, and Resilience in Substance Abuse Policy

The Evolution of Drug Policy: A Brief Overview

Drug policy in the United States reflects cultural beliefs about the risks associated with substance use and the role of governmental regulation in people's personal and social lives. Cultural beliefs about substance use and opinions about the best way to prevent or treat substance abuse are in turn affected by a host of social, political, and economic conditions (DuPont & Voth, 1995). The evolving nature of these beliefs may best be seen in the underlying tension that is evident between policy approaches favoring control and regulation and those favoring prevention and treatment. The relative emphasis placed on control strategies versus prevention and treatment alternatives has a significant impact on the nature of policies, programs, and services for children and adolescents available at any given point in time (McBride, VanderWaal, & Terry-McElrath, 2001; Musto, 1996). The good news for prevention and treatment advocates may be that increases in federal funding for adolescent health have led to a greater array of substance abuse prevention and treatment alternatives for children and youth (Dougherty, 1993; Irwin, Burg, & Cart, 2002). In the current economic climate, however, there is considerable competition for funds, and efforts to reduce substance abuse among youth must demonstrate evidence of effectiveness. Major American drug policies of the past century are reviewed next and are shown in Table 8.3.

Table 8.3   Major Federal Substance Abuse Policies for Children and Families, 1990 to Present

Legislation	Purpose
1906 Pure Food and Drug Act	Required the patent medicine industry to list product ingredients
1914 Harrison Narcotics Act	Prohibited the manufacture, sale, and possession of narcotics
1919 Volstead Act and Eighteenth Amendment to the Constitution	Prohibited the sale of alcohol
1937 Marijuana Tax Act	Prohibited the nonmedical use of marijuana
1966 Narcotic Addict Rehabilitation Act	Established civil commitment system (treatment) for federal offenders rather than prosecution
1970 Comprehensive Drug Abuse Prevention and Control Act	Consolidated previous drug laws and reduced penalties for marijuana possession; included the Controlled Substances Act, which established five schedules for regulating drugs based on medicinal value and potential for addiction or abuse
1986 and 1988 Anti-Drug Abuse Acts	Emphasized law enforcement in general, with the 1988 act also attending to treatment and prevention; created the Office of National Drug Control Policy (ONDCP) and the Substance Abuse and Mental Health Services Administration (SAMHSA)
1997 Title XXI (SSA), State Child Health Insurance (SCHIP) established	Expanded health insurance coverage for children and allowed flexibility in resource distribution
2008 Mental Health Parity and Addiction Equity Act (MHPAE)	Requires equity with all medical/surgical benefits for financial requirements and treatment limitations for mental health or substance use disorder benefits

Early Drug Policy

American drug policy emerged at the turn of the century with the passage of several important acts. The Pure Food and Drug Act of 1906 required labeling of all drugs sold in the country. The Harrison Narcotics Act of 1914 and the 1919 Volstead Act prohibited the sale of narcotics and alcohol (DuPont & Voth, 1995). Prohibition against illicit drugs was used as a public policy approach well into the 1950s, when the federal government implemented drug trafficking laws and enacted strict penalties for drug violations.

1960–1980

The "drug revolution" of the 1960s and 1970s created an increase in demand for illicit drugs that was unparalleled in prior years. Changing social norms reflecting greater tolerance for experimental drug use led to a shift from the predominantly punitive stance that was common before 1960 to an interest in decriminalizing marijuana and other less serious drugs. As "recreational" and experimental drug use became more common, increased public awareness of the health risks associated with substance use coincided with the development of prevention and treatment strategies for illicit drug abuse (McBride et al., 2001). Passage of the Narcotic Addict Rehabilitation Act of 1966 reflected society's desire to help individuals suffering from addiction. And, in 1967, the American Medical Association endorsed the disease theory as the predominant explanation of alcohol addiction, a change that was to have a profound effect on American social policy (Freeman, 2001).

The 1970s witnessed several key pieces of drug-related legislation. Predating President Richard Nixon's declaration calling for a "war on drugs" by just 1 year, Congress passed the Comprehensive Drug Abuse Prevention and Control Act in 1970. The act consolidated several previous federal laws and categorized addictive drugs for purposes of control and regulation. While reducing the penalties for certain types of possession offenses, the act also strengthened law enforcement efforts. The emphasis on rehabilitation, however, remained an important part of the 1970 legislation.

1980–Present

An increase in drug use among the nation's youth at the end of the 1970s marked a reversal in public opinion about the nature of substance use policy. "Get-tough" approaches began to replace policies favoring community-based treatment, and the subsequent passage of the Anti-Drug Abuse Acts of 1986 and 1988 reinforced a return to policies favoring law enforcement and control (McBride et al., 2001). The federal Office of National Drug Control Policy (ONDCP) was created in 1988 to better coordinate drug policy across states and international borders. By the late 1980s, all states raised the legal drinking age to 21 in response to growing concerns about the dangers and consequences of adolescent alcohol abuse. Arrest, conviction, and incarceration rates for drug-related offenses—particularly among poor and minority youth—increased following tougher policy provisions passed in the 1980s (Snyder, 1990).

Some policy experts have noted an apparent return to drug policies favoring prevention and rehabilitation in the past decade (Physician Leadership, 2002). As one important example, treatment parity with other health conditions from an insurance perspective has long been sought by mental health and substance-related disorder advocates. When the Mental Health Parity Act was first introduced in 1996, it provided parity for mental health benefits in terms of aggregate lifetime and annual dollar limits, when compared to medical/surgical benefits. Substance abuse or chemical dependency was excluded, however. When the Mental Health Parity and Addiction Equity Act was passed in 2008, it required equity for mental health and substance use disorder benefits. Specifically, the financial requirements such as co-pays or deductibles and limitations set on treatment must be "no more restrictive" than the limitations set for all medical/surgical benefits (U.S. Department of Labor, 2010).

This change coincides with a newfound interest in viewing adolescent substance abuse as a public health problem and applying principles of risk and protection to substance policy and programs. Next, we discuss specific federal policies across the domains of law enforcement, prevention, and treatment. These selected policies highlight major trends in policy approaches aimed at adolescent substance abuse.

Law Enforcement

Law enforcement has always been a critical component of American drug policy (Morin & Collins, 2000; Physician Leadership, 2002). Funding for law enforcement efforts aimed at combating adolescent substance abuse has increased substantially each year since 1980. Federal spending for the control of illicit drugs alone increased from $1.5 billion in 1981 to $17.9 billion in 1999 (Robert Wood Johnson Foundation, 2001). More than 75% of federal funds distributed to state and local communities for illicit drug use control are devoted to law enforcement activities (Kleiman, 1998).

The 2009 National Drug Control Strategy earmarked 65% of the nearly $15 billion drug control budget for the supply reduction strategies of interdiction and law enforcement. The remaining 35% of the overall budget was allocated to prevention and treatment (ONDCP, 2009). As Figure 8.1 demonstrates, federal spending for supply reduction has increased and remains disproportionate to spending levels for prevention and treatment (ONDCP, 2009).

Domestic and international law enforcement and interdiction policies constitute what is known as a *supply reduction strategy*. Intended to disrupt the drug trade market and to limit access to drugs, supply reduction relies on practices such as taxation and law enforcement to control alcohol and illicit drug use. Initiatives to dismantle illicit drug trafficking networks are also included in supply reduction strategies. The federal drug control budget provides funding through various initiatives to increase the capacity of organizations such as the Drug Enforcement Administration, Federal Bureau of Investigation, U.S. Customs Service, Border Patrol, and Coast Guard to implement these approaches. Federal initiatives to disrupt international illegal markets, particularly through partnerships with Colombian and Mexican governments, were major goals of the Bush administration (ONCDP, 2009).

Figure 8.1   Federal Spending for Substance Abuse Policy and Programs: The National Drug Control Budget (in Millions), 2007–2009

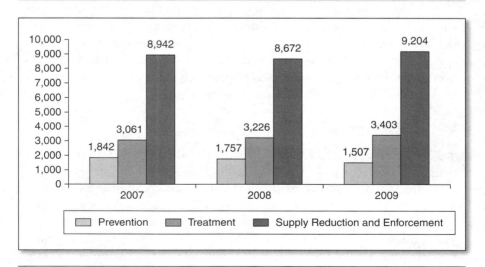

NOTE: This figure is adapted from the *National Drug Control Strategy, FY 2009 Budget Summary,* by ONDCP, 2009, Washington, DC: The White House.

The effectiveness of law enforcement and drug interdiction can be evaluated by assessing the cost of illicit drugs and by monitoring rates of adolescent substance use. Based on these outcome measures, the results of law enforcement and drug interdiction efforts have achieved limited success. Although the United States has spent more than $18 billion a year on international law enforcement and interdiction, evidence suggests that the relative price of many "hard drugs" has actually decreased in recent years (Bach & Lantos, 1999; Kleiman, 1998) and that access to illicit drugs has not diminished (Robert Wood Johnson Foundation, 2001). In 2009, about 47% of adolescents had tried an illicit substance by the time they graduated from 12th grade (Johnston et al., 2009), a finding that offers at least cursory evidence to suggest that law enforcement and interdiction efforts alone are not effective in reducing adolescent substance use.

Supply reduction strategies restricting access and increasing taxes for alcohol and other drugs appear to have produced greater success in reducing substance abuse. For example, an increase in the minimum drinking age is associated with a decline in alcohol consumption and in alcohol-related auto fatalities (Cook & Tauchen, 1984). Furthermore, federal taxes on alcohol and tobacco have generated government revenue that has been used to fund efficacious prevention and treatment services in many states (Robert Wood Johnson Foundation, 2001).

Many experts assert that policy debates about the merits of supply reduction strategies do not lie in the specific findings regarding the effectiveness of law enforcement, interdiction, taxation, and restrictive access strategies (Caulkins, Reuter, Iguchi, & Chiesa, 2005; Kleiman, 1998; Morin & Collins, 2000). Rather, the primary concern of many policy officials is the disproportionate allocation of federal funding, which has historically relegated prevention and treatment alternatives to a secondary priority. Continuing to increase funding for law enforcement and interdiction during periods of limited funding for prevention and treatment illustrates this source of major policy contention. Given the enormous cost of interdiction and enforcement and the ongoing increases necessary to reduce the illicit drug trade, many public health officials are advocating higher levels of funding for prevention and treatment.

Prevention

The history of adolescent substance abuse prevention efforts dates to at least the 1960s. Early prevention efforts educated children and youth about different types of drugs and informed young people about the physical effects of using alcohol and other substances. These "information only" programs fell short of providing interactive experiences to young people and relied on didactic learning approaches to educate them about substance abuse. Other programs employed "scared-straight" tactics to warn adolescents about the adverse individual and social consequences of alcohol and illicit drugs. Perhaps not surprisingly, programs relaying only information about alcohol and other drugs or exposing youth to the risks of drug use produced few positive results (Hawkins, 2006; Jenson, in press).

The evolution of substance abuse prevention advanced slowly following the early 1970s. It was not until the mid-1980s that an emerging group of prevention researchers began to introduce and test school-based curricula as a new approach to prevent substance abuse (Botvin, 2004; Catalano, 2007). These curricula were based on known correlates of substance abuse and relied on interactive and structured activities that involved children in the concept of prevention. Subsequent longitudinal studies of these interventions revealed that well-designed prevention curricula could effectively prevent the initiation of drug use among young people (e.g., Hansen, 1992). The common thread among the programs was the use of a risk and protective factor framework as a guiding source of program design.

Policies and programs supporting substance abuse prevention have increased significantly since the initial program evaluations of the mid-1980s. It is widely agreed that the adoption of the risk-based prevention paradigm is largely responsible for the increase in attention paid to prevention policy and to prevention research (Robertson, David, & Rao, 2003). NIDA, SAMHSA, and governmental entities such as the Office of Juvenile Justice and Delinquency Prevention (OJJDP) all recognize the utility of a public health prevention framework and have taken efforts to implement principles of risk, protection, and resilience in their program and policy initiatives (Howell, 2003; Robertson et al., 2003; Schinke, Brounstein, & Gardner, 2002). Programs targeting factors that increase and guard against risk for substance abuse now represent the most commonly used prevention strategy in the United States (American Academy of Pediatrics, 2001; Centers for Disease Control and Prevention, 2008; Jenson, in press). The results from a number of longitudinal investigations of risk-based prevention programs implemented in school, family, and community settings reveal positive outcomes with regard to substance use (for reviews, see Biglan & Smolkowski, 2002; Foxcroft, Ireland, Lister-Sharp, Lowe, & Breen, 2003; Pentz, 2010).

Federal Policy Initiatives

Several important federal policy directives support the use of a public health framework for substance abuse prevention. The Drug-Free Communities Program initiated in 1997 supports community and anti-drug coalitions that create collaborative efforts among prevention agencies and organizations (ONDCP, 2010). The Department of Education and SAMHSA provide funds for school- and community-based prevention programs under this initiative.

Changing social norms about substance use is a primary objective of several media campaigns and education programs that have received generous federal support. In 1998, the National Youth Anti-Drug Media Campaign received $195 million in federal funding and $2 billion in public and private funds to combat media images promoting substance use (Kelder, Maibach, Worden, Biglan, & Levitt, 2000).

In collaboration with the Ad Council and Partnership for a Drug-Free America, the media campaign is one of the most visible and widespread prevention strategies in the country. The program's primary objective is to educate children, youth, and parents about drug use and to promote young people's ability to reject illegal drugs through personal and social skill development (ONDCP, 2004). The campaign aims to change social norms about drug use by communicating messages about youth who do not use substances, discussing the negative effects of drugs, and portraying the positive aspects of a drug-free lifestyle (ONDCP, 1997). An evaluation of the campaign revealed that nearly 80% of youth and 70% of parents who were polled about the campaign recalled seeing at least one message delivered through media sources each week (Westat & the Annenberg School for Communication, 2003). However, like the information-only effort before it, the media campaign in this format produced little direct evidence of reducing substance use. Despite this result, the campaign is scheduled to continue; however, some modifications were made to the overall strategy in 2005. The "Above the Influence" (http://www.abovetheinfluence.com/) teen-targeted campaign is based on commercial advertising and marketing principles. The ad and campaign messages are developed and tracked through research and testing phases. Preliminary tracking evidence suggests the campaign has a positive impact on anti-drug beliefs and intentions among youth, and ONDCP (2010) is currently soliciting a national external outcome evaluation of this initiative.

Public schools have been a primary location of substance abuse prevention activities. Funding for school-based drug education formally began in the 1980s, when Congress allocated about $500 million a year for prevention activities (Burke, 2002; Wyrick, Wyrick, Bibeau, & Fearnow-Kenney 2001). Federal government involvement in substance abuse prevention, however, has had an uneven history. In the late 1980s and early 1990s, significant amounts of government dollars were devoted to a drug abuse resistance education program called Project D.A.R.E. The popular program brought police officers and law enforcement officials to school classrooms. Officers warned children about the dangers of alcohol and other drug use and worked to reduce negative stereotypes of law enforcement. Evaluations of Project D.A.R.E. revealed that the program was no more effective than routine prevention approaches being used in the nation's schools and classrooms to prevent substance use (Lynam et al., 1999). To their credit, the developers of D.A.R.E. used these findings to retool the program to include more interactive and skills-based teaching strategies in the curriculum. Still, the enormous sum of money allocated to an ineffective program has been a stark lesson to policymakers about the risk of funding untested prevention approaches.

In 1997, the U.S. Department of Education's Safe and Drug-Free School and Communities Program took an important step in prevention policy by requiring all programs that receive federal funds to select and implement interventions that had demonstrated some degree of effectiveness in preventing substance use. Efforts to increase the number of empirically supported interventions in prevention settings have positively affected the quality and outcomes of school-based prevention programs since 1997 (Burke, 2002). NIDA supports considerable substance abuse prevention research and has developed specific action steps for school and community-based programs that are based on principles of risk and protection (Robertson et al., 2003).

Prevention research continues to advance what is known about effective ways to delay or prevent substance use initiation. Efforts are now under way to implement efficacious programs on a larger scale across school districts and communities. No matter how effective such efforts become, the need for treatment services for children and youth experiencing more serious substance use problems must also be an important part of a policy and program continuum.

Treatment

Several public health organizations, including Physician Leadership on Drug Policy and the American Academy of Pediatrics (2000) are at the forefront of advocacy efforts aimed at increasing funding for substance abuse treatment. A position paper on adolescent drug policy published by Physician Leadership (2002) called for the use of evidence-based interventions in drug treatment. The group also suggested that levels of substance abuse funding should be similar to funds provided for diseases such as diabetes and heart disease. Physician Leadership continues to argue that the long-standing federal emphasis on law enforcement policy has mitigated the potential of treatment as a means of reducing substance abuse problems.

There is currently no national standard of care for treating adolescent substance abusers in the United States. Substance abuse treatment varies by region, state, and locality and is generally considered to be poorly funded and difficult to access. Recent estimates from SAMHSA's National Survey on Drug Use and Health reveal that about 1.5 million young people require treatment for alcohol abuse annually; an estimated 1.4 million youth require treatment for illicit drug use (Office of Applied Studies, 2005). Other reports indicate that as few as 1 in every 10 adolescents who need substance abuse treatment actually receive it and that only 25% of those participating in treatment receive the appropriate type and level of assistance (Center for Substance Abuse Treatment, 2002; NIDA, 2008). Access to care appears to be strongly related to inadequate health insurance coverage and to complicated managed-care regulations that limit time allotted for treatment (American Academy of Pediatrics, 2001).

A major concern affecting access to care for many children and adolescents is the fragmented nature of substance abuse treatment. Policies and programs supporting adolescent substance abuse treatment come from such disparate domains as education, juvenile justice, child welfare, labor, and health. Each system has its own eligibility criteria, and each operates independently from the other. The result is a fragmented system of care (SOC) in which many youth may be shuffled from program to program with little coordination across service sectors.

Youth with substance abuse problems are also more likely to experience other mental health problems. In many cases, treatment facilities in one system are not equipped to handle multiple problems. For example, estimates indicate that 60% to 80% of youth involved in the juvenile justice system also have a substance use disorder (Washburn et al., 2008). Few resources currently exist to treat youth with multiple problems.

Public sources provide funding for alcohol and drug treatment through a combination of Medicaid and state and local funds. Funds for public substance abuse treatment are limited, and restrictions placed on the type of eligible service often prevent integration across systems of care (Physician Leadership, 2002). The Medicaid program provides health insurance coverage for more than 16.4 million children. However, Medicaid programs display considerable variation in the services they fund, ranging from comprehensive treatment benefits in some states to only inpatient detoxification in other states (Gehshan, 1999). Medicaid reimbursement rates are also typically quite low, which has led to less incentive to provide treatment services (American Academy of Pediatrics, 2001).

Expansion of health care coverage for low-income children was included as a provision in a 1997 bill that created the State Children's Health Insurance Program (SCHIP). This program allows states to access federal funds for children who are not eligible for other coverage. Funds are provided via the Medicaid program or through a separate program established specifically for SCHIP participants. Although coverage still varies considerably by state, all states using SCHIP generally pay for detoxification and for some types of outpatient substance abuse treatment (Gehshan, 1999).

Medicaid and SCHIP are required to implement the Early and Periodic Screening, Diagnosis, and Treatment Program (EPSDT). Many experts believe that EPSDT could be an effective way to increase substance abuse treatment services for troubled youth (Rosenbaum, Johnson, Snonsky, Markus, & DeGraw, 1998). However, a general lack of awareness about EPSDT in the professional community has led to underutilization. Weak coordination between Medicaid and SCHIP has also limited use of EPSDT as a referral source for substance abuse treatment.

Federal block grants provide resources that seek to improve access to substance abuse treatment services. These grants typically provide funds that are channeled through federal and state agencies. For example, prevention services funded by the Substance Abuse Prevention and Treatment Block Grant are administered by the Center for Substance

Abuse Prevention. Corresponding treatment services are funded and administered by the Center for Substance Abuse Treatment, SAMHSA, and the U.S. Department of Health and Human Services. With many states rolling block-grant money into specialty "carve-out" arrangements, one policy concern is that substance abuse services may be inappropriately offered by mental health providers rather than by trained substance abuse treatment specialists.

Finally, financial barriers to substance abuse treatment exist. The Mental Health Parity and Addiction Equity Act now requires the same financial requirements and treatment limitations for mental health and substance abuse benefits in group health plans of 50 or more employees, however, access to services and availability of developmentally appropriate services is still a concern. The act does not mandate that a health plan cover mental health and substance abuse services, only that if it does, it must do so in the same manner as medical and surgical benefits. Insurance companies are still able to deny or limit coverage in circumstances in which care is not deemed medically necessary. Several public health organizations have recently made policy recommendations calling for a more thoughtful and integrated continuum of care in adolescent substance abuse prevention and treatment (American Academy of Pediatrics, 2010; Robert Wood Johnson Foundation, 2010). We explore these and other ideas more fully in the next section.

Using Knowledge of Risk, Protection, and Resilience to Achieve Service Integration

Principles of risk, protection, and resilience are key components of effective substance abuse intervention. The potential of these principles for public policy has yet to be fully realized. To be effective, knowledge of risk, protection, and resilience should undergird policy and programs in all systems of care for children and youth.

A Continuum of Substance Abuse Policy

Substance use disorders are prevalent among children and youth in nearly all public sectors of care in the United States. Aarons Brown, Hough, Garland, and Wood (2001) examined prevalence rates for substance use disorders among adolescents who were receiving care in five service systems in San Diego County. Prevalence estimates ranged from 19% for youth in the child welfare system to 41% and 62% for adolescents in the mental health and juvenile justice systems, respectively. More recent estimates reveal that as many as 49% of children in foster care (Vaughn, Ollie, McMillen, Scott, & Munson, 2007), 80% of youth in the juvenile justice system (Washburn et al., 2008), and 50% of youth with serious mental health problems use alcohol and illicit drugs (James, 2007). The high prevalence of substance abuse across systems of care points to the need for better integration and coordination of prevention and treatment policy and programs.

Policies aimed at adolescent substance abuse, like policies targeting other childhood and adolescent problems, have largely been incremental and fragmented. That is, programs and interventions tend to develop as a result of localized conditions that fail to consider national trends vis-à-vis substance abuse or empirical evidence regarding the relative effectiveness of prevention and treatment approaches. To confound matters, service sectors for high-risk youth develop responses to problems that tend to be very similar to one another. Creating an integrated continuum of care must begin with assessment and screening policies and practices.

Assessment and Screening Policies

An integrated SOC for children and youth must first acknowledge the need to assess and screen youth for a variety of problem behaviors, including substance abuse. Once appropriate assessment data are collected, appropriate placements and sanctions can be more easily determined. Policies are needed to create centralized assessment centers that serve diagnostic and referral needs across major service systems for children and adolescents. Provisions of these policies should include standardized diagnostic tools that offer interpretative guidelines for juvenile justice, mental health, child welfare, and substance abuse practitioners. Standardized assessment procedures might also lead to more systematic placement criteria and decision making and would allow cross-system comparisons of risk and protective factors found to be prevalent among youth and their family members. Knowledge of these factors, in turn, could be used to inform the direction of prevention and treatment programs.

Prevention Policies

Perhaps the single greatest policy need in substance abuse prevention lies in funding. Prevention has historically been underfunded when compared with competing demands made by treatment providers and law enforcement

(Catalano, 2007). In recent years, longitudinal studies have indicated that some prevention programs are effective in preventing and reducing substance abuse and are more cost-effective than treatment and law enforcement approaches (Aos, Lieb, Mayfield, Miller, & Pennucci, 2004). The availability of effective programs through the dissemination efforts of entities such as SAMHSA's National Registry of Effective Programs, the Center for the Study and Prevention of Violence, and interdisciplinary groups dedicated to advancing evidence-based practice such as the Cochrane Collaboration and the Campbell Collaboration is further argument for the adoption of prevention policy as a national priority for children and families.

A Prevention Case Example

Bishopville, a (fictitious) suburban community on the East Coast, has recently become alarmed about increases in adolescent substance abuse. Anecdotal reports about all-night drug parties (i.e., raves) involving alcohol, marijuana, and hallucinogens have surfaced in local schools and neighborhoods. A recent party led to the arrest of six teenagers and alerted officials that action steps were necessary.

Officials chose the Communities That Care (CTC) model (Hawkins, Catalano, & Associates, 1992) as a means of better understanding and addressing the problem of adolescent substance abuse in Bishopville. Using the model, Bishopville employed the following action steps that led to the creation of a citywide prevention policy:

Step 1: *Organizing and mobilizing.* Leaders of Bishopville selected key individuals to guide the prevention planning process. These included the mayor, educators, business representatives, and other elected officials. The group subsequently formed a community prevention board that was charged with organizing and mobilizing other community advocates and constituency groups.

Step 2: *Developing a community profile of strengths, resources, and challenges.* Risk and protective factors for adolescent substance use were assessed using a CTC survey with a random sample of children and adolescents in Grades 6 to 12. Survey results were used to rank the most common risk and protective factors found among children and youth in Bishopville. A community needs assessment aimed at identifying existing and needed services for children and youth was also conducted in this phase.

(Continued)

(Continued)

Step 3: *Creating a strategic prevention plan.* In this phase, the Bishopville Community Prevention Board reviewed and selected several efficacious prevention strategies that will be implemented in their local schools and neighborhoods. A school-based curriculum that targets early onset of substance use and a community-level media campaign were among the strategies selected for implementation.

Step 4: *Evaluating and monitoring the plan.* Steps were identified to monitor and evaluate the prevention strategies selected by the board. Outcome measures and other methodological decisions were made in consultation with local and national experts to ensure a rigorous evaluation process.

Please see Hawkins, Catalano, and Associates (1992) and Hawkins et al. (2008) for a more detailed description of using the CTC model in a community setting.

To reach more children and families, prevention policy must bring effective programs to scale at the school, neighborhood, and community levels. One method of increasing the use of effective programs in community settings is found in the Communities that Care (CTC) intervention. In the CTC model, coalitions are formed to engage in systematic prevention planning that requires communities to identify prevalent risk and protective factors for adolescent problems in their localities. Following the assessment of such factors, communities are encouraged to select, implement, and evaluate prevention strategies on the basis of available empirical evidence. Recent findings from a longitudinal study called the Community Youth Development Study, a randomized trial that uses principles of CTC, have revealed significantly lower rates of delinquency and drug use among students in experimental communities compared to control communities (Hawkins et al., 2008). These promising results have led the Center for Substance Abuse Prevention (2010) to recommend CTC as a key component in its overall prevention strategy.

Treatment Policies

Historically, treatment for young people has mirrored that provided to adults; 12-step and self-help interventions based on a disease model of addiction have dominated the field (Liddle & Rowe, 2006). Reviews of adolescent substance abuse treatment report relatively few controlled trials in the past two decades (Deas & Thomas, 2001; Jenson, Howard, & Vaughn, 2004; Vaughn & Howard, 2004). Meta-analytic studies assessing treatment outcomes for young drug abusers suggest that cognitive-behavioral interventions promoting skill development and family-based therapeutic approaches are among the most effective treatment strategies for adolescents (Vaughn & Howard). Additional controlled studies of adolescent substance use treatment are needed to create the knowledge base necessary to recommend and disseminate efficacious programs to the practice community. Only limited empirical evidence is available to form the basis of a policy continuum reflecting different levels of treatment for adolescent substance abuse. Standards of care for treatment connected to evidence-based interventions also need to be made available to professionals in the treatment community.

A Treatment Case Example

A case history. Johnny is a 16-year-old boy who is currently under the jurisdiction and supervision of the juvenile justice system. He has a history of property offending dating back some 6 years to when he was arrested for stealing. In recent years, Johnny's behavior escalated to more serious offenses including assault. He first experimented with alcohol and marijuana at age 12 and now admits to using marijuana, cocaine, and hallucinogens "whenever and wherever" they are available. Johnny was placed in the juvenile justice system for assaulting a boy in his neighborhood. He reports that he had been drinking and was high on cocaine at the time of the incident.

Johnny's family life had been unstable. His father left home when Johnny was 5 years old; the family has had relatively little contact with him since that time. Johnny has heard from other relatives that his father frequently uses alcohol and that he has been incarcerated on several occasions. Johnny's mother has worked a series of low-paying jobs but has no history of substance abuse. Two years ago, his mother invited her boyfriend into the family home. Johnny was initially resentful of this decision and has adapted to the situation by largely ignoring the boyfriend. Johnny has two sisters, both of whom are younger in age. Johnny's mother reports that Johnny tends to be withdrawn and sad much of the time. He spends long periods of time alone in his room and has recently stopped seeing many of his friends.

(Continued)

(Continued)

System response. Johnny's case represents a profile that is common among youth in the juvenile justice system. Perhaps what is most typical is the presence of multiple and overlapping behavior problems. Johnny's problems include antisocial conduct, substance abuse, and undiagnosed symptoms of depression.

Theoretically, the presence of these problems could logically lead to placement in the juvenile justice system for antisocial conduct, the substance abuse treatment network for drug-using behaviors, or the mental health system for symptoms of depression. The challenge for treating Johnny—and the thousands of young people like him—lies in integrating system responses and treatments in a manner that addresses Johnny's multiple problems. In Johnny's case, policies that create and support a centralized assessment process might best lead to a coordinated response across multiple service systems.

Years of anecdotal evidence suggest that a lack of communication between drug treatment agencies and poor coordination across service systems have interacted to create a mix of programs that have not adequately met the needs of adolescent substance abusers like the case shown here. Several treatment initiatives show promise with regard to improving the disjointed treatment system. Drug courts, an initiative funded by the federal government under the National Drug Control Strategy (ONDCP, 2009) are one alternative for juvenile offenders with substance abuse problems. As part of the program, youth may be referred to treatment and receive mandatory drug sanctions in lieu of traditional case processing. The Tribal Youth program administered by OJJDP (2000) emerged in response to the problem of violent crime and co-occurring substance use disorders among American Indian youth. The departments of Health and Human Services, Education, Interior, and Justice collaborated to design the program. Program objectives include providing a range of assessment and treatment prevention strategies aimed at addressing the unique needs of substance-abusing American Indian youth. The Tribal Youth initiative represents the type of cross-system coordination needed to implement integrated policies and service for troubled youth.

These initiatives represent only the surface of adolescent substance abuse treatment needs in the United States. Efficacy trials of treatment approaches, community advocacy efforts, and standards of care are needed to inform the direction of substance abuse treatment. Coordination across agencies and the development of SOCs should be a top priority in treatment policy discussions.

Summary

Principles of risk, protection, and resilience hold great promise for substance abuse programs and policies. A prevention and treatment continuum based on risk and protective factors offers a cogent solution to legislators and policy officials charged with developing effective ways to prevent and reduce adolescent substance abuse. A public health model that incorporates risk and protection as guiding principles is also consistent with the current evidence-based practice movement.

Efforts toward integrating substance abuse policy might benefit by examining overlapping initiatives in juvenile justice and mental health. Co-occurring drug use and mental health problems are well documented among young people. Many youth with concomitant problems are subsequently placed in the nation's juvenile justice and mental health systems. Efforts to improve coordination must also include the array of treatment providers who contract for services with public agencies. Community-based programs that offer outpatient care, day treatment, and residential care must be added to policy discussions across the multiple service systems for children, youth, and families. A public health approach emphasizing risk, protection, and resilience may provide a common language and effective organizing framework for adolescent substance programs and policies.

QUESTIONS FOR DISCUSSION

1. What have been the dominant public policy approaches to adolescent substance abuse in the past four decades? Which strategy has received the greatest percentage of funding?

2. What are the financial and organizational implications of a shift to a public health approach to substance abuse prevention and treatment?

3. What are the challenges in integrating service systems for the delivery of adolescent substance abuse treatment and prevention?

4. What policy recommendations would you make to address the disjointed delivery system?

References

Aarons, G. A., Brown, S. A., Hough, R. L., Garland, A. F., & Wood, P. A. (2001). Prevalence of adolescent substance use across five sectors of care. *Journal of the American Academy of Child & Adolescent Psychiatry, 40*, 419–426.

American Academic of Pediatrics. (2010). About us. Retrieved from http://www .aap.org/visit/cmte35.htm

American Academy of Pediatrics. (2000). Insurance coverage of mental health and substance abuse services for children and adolescents: A consensus statement. *Pediatrics, 106*, 860–862.

American Academy of Pediatrics. (2001). Improving substance abuse prevention, assessment, and treatment financing for children and adolescents. *Pediatrics, 108*, 1025–1029.

Annie E. Casey Foundation. (2010). *Kids count.* Retrieved from http://www .kidscount.org/datacenter/

Aos, S., Lieb, R., Mayfield, J., Miller, M., & Pennucci, A. (2004). *Benefits and costs of prevention and early intervention programs for youth.* Olympia: Washington State Institute for Public Policy.

Bach, P. B., & Lantos, J. (1999). Methadone dosing, heroin affordability and the severity of addiction. *American Journal of Public Health, 89*, 662–665.

Bandura, A. (1989). Human agency in social cognitive theory. *American Psychologist, 14*, 1175–1184.

Belcher, H. M., & Shinitzky, H. E. (1998). Substance abuse in children: Prediction, protection, and prevention. *Archives of Pediatrics and Adolescent Medicine, 152*, 952–960.

Berrueta-Clement, J. R., Schweinhart, L. J., Barnett, W. S., Epstein, A. S., & Weikhard, D. P. (1984). *Changed lives: The effects of the Perry Preschool Program on youths through age 19.* Ypsilanti, MI: High/Scope Press.

Biederman, J., Faraone, S. V., Monuteaux, M. C., & Feighner, J. A. (2000). Patterns of alcohol and drug use in adolescents can be predicted by parental substance use disorders. *Pediatrics, 106*, 792–797.

Biglan, A., & Smolkowski, K. (2002). Intervention effects on adolescent drug use and critical influences on the development of problem behavior. In D. B. Kandel (Ed.). *Stages and pathways of drug involvement: Examining the gateway hypothesis* (pp. 158–183). New York: Cambridge University Press.

Botvin, G. J. (2004). Advancing prevention science and practice: Challenges, critical issues, and future directions. *Prevention Science, 5*, 69–72.

Brook, J. S., Brook, D. W., & Pahl, K. (2006). The developmental context for adolescent substance abuse intervention. In H. A. Liddle & C. L. Rowe (Eds.), *Adolescent substance abuse: Research and clinical advances* (pp. 25–51). New York: Cambridge University Press.

Brook, J. S., Whiteman, M., Gordon, A. S., & Brook, D. W. (1988). The role of older brothers in younger brothers' drug use viewed in the context of parent and peer influences. *Journal of Genetic Psychology, 151,* 59–75.

Buck, J. A., & Umland, B. (1997). Covering mental health and substance abuse services. *Health Affairs (Millwood), 16,* 120–126.

Burke, M. R. (2002). School-based substance abuse prevention: Political finger-pointing does not work. *Federal Probation, 66,* 66–71.

Burroughs, A. (2003). *Dry: A memoir.* New York: St. Martin's Press.

Cadoret, R. J., Cain, C. A., & Grove, W. M. (1980). Development of alcoholism in adoptees raised apart from alcoholic biologic relatives. *Archives of General Psychiatry, 37,* 561–563.

Catalano, R. F. (2007). Prevention is a sound public and private investment. *Criminology and Public Policy, 6,* 377–398. doi: 10.1111/j.1745-9133.2007.00443.x

Catalano, R. F., & Hawkins, J. D. (1996). The social development model: A theory of antisocial behavior. In J. D. Hawkins (Ed.), *Delinquency and crime: Current theories* (pp. 149–197). New York: Cambridge University Press.

Cauce, A. M., Stewart, A., Rodriguez, M. D., Cochran, B., & Ginzler, J. (2003). Overcoming the odds? Adolescent development in the context of urban poverty. In S. S. Luthar (Ed.), *Resilience and vulnerability: Adaptation in the context of childhood adversities* (pp. 343–363). Cambridge, UK: Cambridge University Press.

Caulkins, J. P., Reuter, P., Iguchi, M. Y., & Chiesa, J. (2005). *How goes the "war on drugs"? An assessment of U.S. drug problems and policy.* Santa Monica, CA: RAND Corporation.

Center for Substance Abuse Prevention. (2010). *Communities That Care® community planning system.* Rockville, MD: Author.

Center for Substance Abuse Treatment. (2002). *Treatment episode data set, 2002.* Retrieved from www.icpsr.umich.edu/SAMHDA/das.html.

Centers for Disease Control and Prevention. (2008). *Understanding youth violence: Fact sheet.* Atlanta: Author.

Cicchetti, D., & Rogosch, F. A. (1999). Psychopathology as risk for adolescent substance use disorders: A developmental psychopathology perspective. *Journal of Clinical Child Psychology, 28,* 355–365.

Cloninger, C. R., Sigvardsson, S., & Bohman, M. (1988). Childhood personality predicts alcohol abuse in young adults. *Alcoholism: Clinical and Experimental Research, 12,* 494–503.

Coie, J. D. (1990). Towards a theory of peer rejection. In S. R. Asher & J. D. Coie (Eds.), *Peer rejection in childhood* (pp. 365–398). New York: Cambridge University Press.

Cook, P. J., & Tauchen, G. (1984). The effect of minimum drinking age legislation on youthful auto fatalities, 1970–1977. *Journal of Legal Studies, 13,* 169–190.

Deas, D., & Thomas, S. E. (2001). An overview of controlled studies of adolescent substance abuse treatment. *The American Journal on Addictions, 10*, 178–189.

Dougherty, D. M. (1993). Adolescent health: Reflections on a report to the U.S. Congress. *American Psychologist, 48*, 193–201.

DuPont, R. L., & Voth, E. A. (1995). Drug legalization, harm reduction, and drug policy. *Annals of Internal Medicine, 123*, 461–465.

Fergusson, D. M., & Horwood, L. J. (1999). Prospective childhood predictors of deviant peer affiliations in adolescence. *Journal of Child Psychology and Psychiatry and Allied Disciplines, 40*, 581–592.

Fergusson, D. M., & Horwood, L. J. (2003). Resilience in childhood adversity: Results of a 21-year study. In S. S. Luthar (Ed.), *Resilience and vulnerability: Adaptation in the context of childhood adversities* (pp. 130–155). New York: Cambridge University Press.

Foxcroft, D. R., Ireland, D., Lister-Sharp, D. J., Lowe, G., & Breen, R. (2003). Longer term primary prevention for alcohol misuse in young people: A systematic review. *Addiction, 98*, 397–411.

Fraser, M. W. (Ed.). (2004). *Risk and resilience in childhood: An ecological perspective* (2nd ed.). Washington, DC: NASW.

Freeman, E. M. (2001). *Substance abuse intervention, prevention, rehabilitation, and systems change strategies: Helping individuals, families, and groups to empower themselves.* New York: Columbia University Press.

Friedman, A. S. (1983). *Clinical research notes.* Rockville, MD: National Institute on Drug Abuse.

Gallup Organization. (2009). *Illegal drugs.* Retrieved from http://www.gallup.com/poll/1657/illegal-drugsw.aspx

Garmezy, N. (1985). Stress-resistant children: The search for protective factors. In J. E. Stevenson (Ed.), *Recent research in developmental psychology* (pp. 213–233). Oxford, UK: Pergamon Press.

Gehshan, S. (1999). *Substance abuse treatment in state children's health insurance programs.* Washington, DC: National Conference of State Legislatures.

Gorman-Smith, D., & Tolan, P. H. (2003). Positive adaptation among youth exposed to community violence. In S. S. Luthar (Ed.), *Resilience and vulnerability: Adaptation in the context of childhood adversities* (pp. 392–413). New York: Cambridge University Press.

Gottfredson, G. D. (1981). Schooling and delinquency. In S. E. Martin, L. B. Sechrest, & R. Redner (Eds.), *New directions in the rehabilitation of criminal offenders* (pp. 424–469). Washington, DC: National Academy Press.

Hamill, P. (1994). *A drinking life: A memoir.* Boston: Little, Brown.

Hannon, L. (2003). Poverty, delinquency, and educational attainment: Cumulative disadvantage or disadvantage saturation? *Sociological Inquiry, 73*, 576–594.

Hansen, W. B. (1992). School-based substance abuse prevention: A review of the state of the art in curriculum: 1980–1990. *Health Education Research, 7*, 403–430.

Hawkins, J. D. (2006). Science, social work, prevention: Finding the intersections. *Social Work Research, 137*–152.

Hawkins, J. D., Brown, E. C., Oesterle, S., Arthur, M. W., Abbot, R. D., & Catalano, R. F. (2008). Early effects of Communities that Care on targeted risks and initiation of delinquent behavior and substance use. *Journal of Adolescent Health, 43,* 15–22.

Hawkins, J. D., Catalano, R. F., & Associates. (1992). *Communities That Care: Action for drug abuse prevention.* San Francisco: Jossey-Bass.

Hawkins, J. D., Catalano, R. F., & Miller, J. Y. (1992). Risk and protective factors for alcohol and other drug problems in adolescence and early adulthood: Implications for substance abuse prevention. *Psychological Bulletin, 112,* 64–105.

Hill, S. Y., Shen, S., Lowers, L., & Locke, J. (2000). Factors predicting the onset of adolescent drinking in families at high risk for developing alcoholism. *Biological Psychiatry, 48,* 265–275.

Holmberg, M. B. (1985). Longitudinal studies of drug abuse in a fifteen-year-old population. I. Drug career. *Acta Psychiatrica Scandinavia, 71,* 67–79.

Howell, J. C. (2003). *Preventing and reducing juvenile delinquency: A comprehensive framework.* Thousand Oaks, CA: Sage.

Irwin, C. E., Burg, S. J., Cart, C. U. (2002). America's adolescents: Where have we been, where are we going? *Journal of Adolescent Health, 31,* 91–121.

James, A. (2007). Mental health in childhood and adolescence. *The Lancet, 369,* 1251–1252.

Jenson, J. M. (2004). Risk and protective factors for alcohol and other drug use in childhood and adolescence. In M. W. Fraser (Ed.), *Risk and resilience in childhood: An ecological perspective* (2nd ed., pp. 183–208). Washington, DC: NASW.

Jenson, J. M. (in press). Advances in preventing childhood and adolescent problem behavior. *Research on Social Work Practice.*

Jenson, J. M., & Howard, M. O. (1999). Hallucinogen use among juvenile probationers: Prevalence and characteristics. *Criminal Justice and Behavior, 26,* 357–372.

Jenson, J. M., Howard, M. O., & Vaughn, M. G. (2004). Assessing social work's contribution to controlled studies of adolescent substance abuse treatment. *Journal of Social Work in the Addictions, 4,* 54–66.

Jenson, J. M., & Potter, C. C. (2003). The effects of cross-system collaboration on mental health and substance abuse problems of detained youth. *Research on Social Work Practice, 13,* 588–607.

Jenson, J. M., Wells, E. A., Plotnick, R. D., Hawkins, J. D., & Catalano, R. F. (1993). The effects of skills and intentions to use drugs on posttreatment drug use of adolescents. *American Journal of Drug and Alcohol Abuse, 19,* 1–17.

Johnston, L. D. (1991). Toward a theory of drug epidemics. In L. Donohew, H. E. Sypher, & W. J. Bukoski (Eds.), *Pervasive communication and drug abuse prevention* (pp. 93–131). Hillsdale, NJ: Lawrence Erlbaum.

Johnston, L. D., O'Malley, P. M., Bachman, J. G., & Schulenberg, J. E. (2009). *Monitoring the Future. National survey results on drug use, 1975–2008*. Bethesda, MD: National Institute of Drug Abuse.

Joksch, H. C. (1988). *The impact of severe penalties on drinking and driving*. Washington, DC: AAA Foundation for Traffic Safety.

Kelder, S. H., Maibach, E., Worden, J. K., Biglan, A., & Levitt, A. (2000). Planning and initiation of the ONDCP National Youth Anti-Drug Media Campaign. *Journal of Public Health Management Practice, 6*, 14–26.

Kim, K. J. (2009). Risk and protective factors for drug use among American youth. In J. A. Mancini & K. A. Roberto (Eds.), *Pathways of human development: Explorations of change* (pp. 113–126). Lanham, MD: Lexington Books.

Kleiman, M. A. (1998). Drugs and drug policy: The case for a slow fix. *Issues in Science and Technology, 15*, 45–52.

Knapp, C. (1996). *Drinking: A love story*. New York: Delta.

Kupersmidt, J. B., Coie, J. D., & Dodge, K. A. (1990). The role of poor peer relationships in the development of disorder. In S. R. Asher & J. D. Coie (Eds.), *Peer rejection in childhood* (pp. 274–305). New York: Cambridge University Press.

Liddle, H. A., & Rowe, C. L. (Eds.). (2006). *Adolescent substance abuse: Research and clinical advances*. New York: Cambridge University Press.

Loeber, R., Farrington, D. P., Stouthamer-Loeber, M., & van Kammen, W. B. (1998). *Antisocial behavior and mental health problems: Explanatory factors in childhood and adolescence*. Mahwah, NJ: Lawrence Erlbaum.

Luthar, S. S. (Ed.). (2003). *Resilience and vulnerability: Adaptation in the context of childhood adversities*. Cambridge, UK: Cambridge University Press.

Lynam, D. R., Milich, R., Zimmerman, R., Novak, S. P., Logan, T. K., Martin, C., & Leukefeld, C., & Clayton, R. (1999). Project DARE: No effects at 10-year follow-up. *Journal of Consulting and Clinical Psychology, 67*, 590–593.

McBride, D. C., VanderWaal, C. J., & Terry-McElrath, Y. M. (2001). *The drug-crime wars: Past, present and future directions in theory, policy and program interventions* (Research Paper Series 14). Washington, DC: The National Institute of Justice.

Meschke, L. L., & Patterson, J. M. (2003). Resilience as a theoretical base for substance abuse prevention. *The Journal of Primary Prevention, 23*, 483–514.

Miller, L., Davies, M., & Greenwald, S. (2000). Religiosity and substance use and abuse among adolescents in the National Comorbidity Survey. *Journal of the American Academy of Child and Adolescent Psychiatry, 39*, 1190–1197.

Morin, S. F., & Collins, C. (2000). Substance abuse prevention: Moving from science to policy. *Addictive Behaviors, 25*, 975–983.

Murray, C. A. (1983). The physical environment and community control of crime. In J. Q. Wilson (Ed.), *Crime and public policy* (pp. 67–91). San Francisco: Institute for Contemporary Studies.

Musto, D. F. (1996). Alcohol in American history. *Scientific American, 274*, 78–82.

National Institute on Drug Abuse. (2009). *Principles of drug addiction treatment: A research-based guide* (2nd ed., NIH Publication No. 09–4180). Washington, DC: U.S. Department of Health and Human Services.

Office of Applied Studies. (2005). *Results from the 2004 National Survey on Drug Use and Health: National findings* (DHHS Publication No. SMA 05–4062, NSDUH Series H-28). Rockville, MD: Substance Abuse and Mental Health Services Administration.

Office of Juvenile Justice and Delinquency Prevention. (2000). *Tribal youth program.* Washington, DC: U.S. Department of Justice, Office of Justice Programs, Office of Juvenile Justice and Delinquency Prevention.

Office of National Drug Control Policy. (1997). *The national youth anti-drug media campaign: Communication strategy statement.* Washington, DC: Author.

Office of National Drug Control Policy. (2009). *The president's national drug control strategy, 2009.* Washington, DC: Executive Office of the President.

Office of National Drug Control Policy. (2010). *National youth anti-drug media campaign.* Retrieved from http://www.mediacampaign.org/about.html

Office of National Drug Control Policy. (2010). *Drug free communities support program.* Retrieved from http://www.whitehousedrugpolicy.gov/dfc/overview.html

Patterson, G. R. (2002). The early development of coercive family process. In J. B. Reid, G. R. Patterson, & J. Snyder (Eds.), *Antisocial behavior in children and adolescents: A developmental analysis and model for intervention* (pp. 25–44). Washington, DC: American Psychological Association.

Patterson, G. R., Reid, J. B., & Eddy, J. M. (2002). A brief history of the Oregon model. In J. B. Reid, G. R. Patterson, & J. Snyder (Eds.), *Antisocial behavior in children and adolescents: A developmental analysis and model for intervention* (pp. 3–24). Washington, DC: American Psychological Association.

Pentz, M. A. (2010). Translating research into practice and practice into research for drug use prevention. In L. Scheier (Ed.). *Handbook of drug use etiology: Theory, methods, and empirical findings* (pp. 581–596). Washington, DC: American Psychological Association.

Physician Leadership on National Drug Policy. (2002). *Adolescent substance abuse: A public health priority: An evidence-based, comprehensive, and integrative approach.* Providence, RI: Brown University, Center for Alcohol and Addiction Studies.

Reinherz, H. Z., Giaconia, R. M., Hauf, A. M., Wasserman, M. S., & Paradis, A. D. (2000). General and specific childhood risk factors for depression and drug disorders by early childhood. *Journal of the American Academy of Child and Adolescent Psychiatry, 39,* 223–231.

Robertson, E. B., David, S. L., & Rao, S. A. (2003). *Preventing drug use among children and adolescents: A research-based guide for parents, educators, and community leaders* (2nd ed.). Bethesda, MD: U.S. Department of Health and Human Services.

Robert Wood Johnson Foundation. (2001). *Substance abuse: The nation's number one health problem. Key indicators for policy.* Princeton, NJ: Author.

Robert Wood Johnson Foundation. (2010). *Publications and research: Addictions.* Retrieved from http://www.rwjf.org/pr/topic.jsp?topicid=1006

Rosenbaum, S., Johnson, K., Snonsky, C., Markus, A., & DeGraw, C. (1998). The children's hour: The state of children's health insurance program. *Health Affairs, 17,* 75–89.

Rossa, M. W. (2002). Some thoughts about resilience versus positive development, main effects, versus interaction effects and the value of resilience. *Child Development, 71,* 567–569.

Rutter, M. (2000). Psychosocial influences: Critiques, findings, and research needs. *Development and Psychopathology, 12,* 375–405.

Saffer, H., & Grossman, M. (1987). Beer taxes, the legal drinking age, and youth motor vehicle fatalities. *Journal of Legal Studies, 16,* 351–374.

Scheier, L. (Ed.). (2010). *Handbook of drug use etiology: Theory, methods, and empirical findings.* Washington, DC: American Psychological Association.

Schinke, S., Brounstein, P., & Gardner, S. (2002). *Science-based prevention programs and principles, 2002* (DHHS Pub No. SMA 03–3764). Rockville, MD: Substance Abuse and Mental Health Services Administration.

Schinke, S. P., Fang, L., & Cole, K. C. A. (2008). Substance use among early adolescent girls: Risk and protective factors. *Journal of Adolescent Health, 43,* 191–194.

Shedler, J., & Block, J. (1990). Adolescent drug use and psychological health: A longitudinal inquiry. *American Psychologist, 45,* 612–630.

Simcha-Fagan, O., & Schwartz, J. E. (1986). Neighborhood and delinquency: An assessment of contextual effects. *Criminology, 24,* 667–703.

Snyder, H. (1990). *Growth in minority detentions attributed to drug law violators.* Washington, DC: Office of Juvenile Justice and Delinquency Prevention.

Substance Abuse and Mental Health Administration. (2010). *National registry of effective programs.* Retrieved from http://www.nrepp.samhsa.gov/

U.S. Department of Labor. (2010). *Frequently asked questions about the Mental Health Parity Act.* Retrieved from http://www.dol.gov/ebsa/faqs/faq_consumer_mentalhealthparity.html

Vaughn, M. G., Freedenthal, S., Jenson, J. M., & Howard, M. O. (2007). Psychiatric symptoms and substance use among juvenile offenders. *Criminal Justice and Behavior, 34,* 1296–1312.

Vaughn, M. O., & Howard, M. O. (2004). Adolescent substance abuse treatment: A synthesis of controlled evaluations. *Research on Social Work Practice, 14,* 325–335.

Vaughn, M. G., Ollie, M. T., McMillen, J. C., Scott, L., & Munson, M. (2007). Substance use and abuse among older youth in foster care. *Addictive Behaviors, 32,* 1929–1935.

Vaughn, M. G., Wallace, J. M., Davis, L., Fernandes, G. T., & Howard, M. O. (2008). Variations in mental health problems, substance use, and delinquency between African American and Caucasian juvenile offenders. *International Journal of Offender Therapy and Comparative Criminology, 52,* 311–329.

Washburn, J. J., Teplin, L. A., Voss, L. S., Simon, C. D., Abram, K. M., & McCelland, G. M. (2008). Pyschiatric disorders among detained youths: A comparison of youths processed in juvenile court and adult criminal court. *Psychiatric Services, 59,* 965–973.

Werner, E. E. (1994). Overcoming the odds. *Developmental and Behavioral Pediatrics, 15,* 131–136.

Werner, E. E., & Smith, R. S. (1989). *Vulnerable but invincible: A longitudinal study of resilient children and youth.* New York: Adams, Bannister, and Cox.

Westat & the Annenberg School for Communication. (2003). *Evaluation of the National Youth Anti-Drug Media Campaign: 2003 report of findings executive summary* (Contract No: N01DA-8–5063). Washington, DC: National Institute on Drug Abuse.

Woolf, S. H. (2008). The power of prevention and what it requires. *Journal of the American Medical Association, 299,* 2437–2439.

Wyrick, D., Wyrick, C. H., Bibeau, D. L., & Fearnow-Kenney, M. (2001). Coverage of adolescent substance use prevention in state frameworks for health education. *Journal of School Health, 71,* 437–442.

Zucker, R. A., Wong, M. M., Puttler, L. I., & Fitzgerald, H. E. (2003). Resilience and vulnerability among sons of alcoholics: Relationship to developmental outcomes between early childhood and adolescence. In S. S. Luthar (Ed.), *Resilience and vulnerability: Adaptation in the context of childhood adversities* (pp. 76–103). New York: Cambridge University Press.

Additional Reading

Liddle, H. A., & Rowe, C. L. (Eds.). (2006). *Adolescent substance abuse: Research and clinical advances.* New York: Cambridge University Press.

Scheier, L. (Ed.). (2010). *Handbook of drug use etiology: Theory, methods, and empirical findings.* Washington, DC: American Psychological Association.

Springer, D. W., & Rubin, A. (Eds.). (2009). *Substance abuse treatment for youth and adults.* Hoboken, NJ: John Wiley.

Tolan, P., Szapocznik, J., & Sambrano, S. (Eds.). (2007). *Preventing youth substance abuse: Science-based programs for children and adolescents.* Washington, DC: American Psychological Association.

Web-Based Resources

The Campbell Collaboration, www.campbellcollaboration.org
The Cochrane Collaboration, www.cochrane.org
Monitoring the Future, www.monitoringthefuture.org
National Institute on Drug Abuse, www.nida.nih.gov
Physician Leadership on National Drug Policy, www.PLNDP.org
Robert Wood Johnson Foundation, www.impacteen.org
Social Development Research Group, www.sdrg.u.washington.edu
Substance Abuse and Mental Health Services Administration, www.samhsa.gov

9

Juvenile Justice
Policies and Programs

William H. Barton

J uvenile justice policy and practices are greatly influenced by knowledge, events, and values that are viable at any given point in time. After decades of "getting tough" with young offenders and flirting with the treatment model du jour, the juvenile justice system now finds itself at a policy and programmatic crossroad. Recent advances in theory, research, and practice that are based on principles of risk, protection, and resilience hold promise for a more rational, comprehensive set of juvenile justice policies and practices. Nevertheless, such optimism must be tempered by the inevitable role played by societal values, politics, and public perceptions and by limitations in the knowledge base itself.

This chapter provides an outline of this conceptual advance in juvenile justice policy, places it in a historical context, and suggests ways it can be used to improve current and future policies and practices. The first section presents an overview of the goals and stakeholders involved in juvenile justice policy. The second section reviews what is known about the prevalence and incidence of delinquency. The third section outlines the risk and protective factors associated with delinquent behavior. The fourth section traces the history of juvenile justice policies, noting the extent to which presumed risk and protective factors have exerted an influence. The final section applies what we have learned about risk, protection, and resilience to juvenile justice policies and practices and concludes that this knowledge base can provide a foundation for more effective and efficient ways to address delinquency through the promotion of positive youth development.

Purpose and Overview of Juvenile Justice Policy

Prior to the 20th century, the United States did not have a juvenile justice policy per se. Although age was considered a factor in mitigating punishment, children who committed crimes were under the jurisdiction of the adult court. The first juvenile court was established in Chicago in 1899, and by 1925, all but two states had followed suit (Bernard, 1992). The juvenile court was the expression of the first formal juvenile justice policy, which held that juveniles were distinct from adults and that the system should act in the best interests of the child. Specialized juvenile probation services emerged to monitor juveniles who were under the jurisdiction of the court (National Center for Juvenile Justice, 1991).

This two-tiered court system created a tension between the goals of rehabilitation and punishment that continues to this day. As described later in this chapter, the parade of policy reforms during the 20th century has reflected alternating emphases on these two primary goals. Historically, relatively lenient policies favoring treatment have been followed by "get tough" policies mandating punishment. Table 9.1 summarizes events that have shaped juvenile justice policy since the founding of the first juvenile court.

To whom do juvenile justice policies apply? The juvenile court has jurisdiction over young people who meet the definition of a juvenile in a given state and against whom a petition is filed alleging a delinquent act (which would be a crime if committed by an adult) or a status offense (behavior, e.g., school truancy or running away from home, which would not be considered criminal if committed by an adult). Once a petition is filed, the juvenile probation department prepares a predisposition report summarizing the facts and context of the case and containing recommendations to the judge for corrective action. Should the judge *adjudicate* the child as delinquent, which is analogous to a determination of guilt in adult criminal court, dispositional options might include probation supervision, placement in a nonresidential program, or residential placements of varying restrictiveness.

The definition of a juvenile, that is, those who come under the jurisdiction of the juvenile court, varies from state to state. In most states, the upper age limit of juvenile court jurisdiction is 17 years, but in New York and North Carolina, that limit is 15 years; in 10 other states, including Georgia, Massachusetts, Michigan, and Texas, it is 16 years; and Connecticut recently raised the age limit from 15 to 18 years (Total Criminal Defense, 2010). Further complicating the definition of a juvenile, policies in some states extend juvenile court jurisdiction to age 20 years for status offenses, and most states allow extended juvenile court supervision of placements of delinquents until 20 years old (24 years old in a few states, including California; Sickmund, 2003).

Table 9.1   Chronology of Events Affecting U.S. Juvenile Justice Policy

Date	Event	Comments
<1899		Children treated the same as adults under the law
1899	First juvenile court established in Cook County, Illinois	*Parents patriae* philosophy—juvenile court was to act in the best interests of the child
1900–1950	All states establish juvenile courts	
1960s–1980s	Interest in delinquency prevention, diversion, and deinstitutionalization programs	Community organization approaches (e.g., Mobilization for Youth), diversion, and deinstitutionalization are implemented (see 1974 JJDPA below)
1966	*Kent v. United States*	Courts must provide the "essentials of due process" in transferring juveniles to the adult system
1967	*In re* Gault	In hearings that could result in commitment to an institution, juveniles have four basic constitutional rights (notice, counsel, questioning witnesses, protection against self-incrimination)
1968	Juvenile Delinquency Prevention and Control Act	Children charged with status offenses were to be handled outside the court system

Date	Event	Comments
1970	*In re* Winship	In delinquency matters, the state must prove its case beyond a reasonable doubt
1971	*McKeiver v. Pennsylvania*	Jury trials are not constitutionally required in juvenile court hearings
1974	Juvenile Justice and Delinquency Prevention Act (JJDPA)	Deinstitutionalization of status offenders; separation of juvenile and adult offenders
1975	Lipton, Martinson, & Wilks report	Results misinterpreted by most as indicating that "nothing works" in juvenile corrections
1975	*Breed v. Jones*	Waiver to criminal court following adjudication in juvenile court constitutes double jeopardy
1977–1979	*Oklahoma Publishing Co. v. District Court / Smith v. Daily Mail*	The press may report juvenile court proceedings under certain circumstances
1980	Amendment to the JJDPA	Juveniles removed from adult jails and lockups
1982	*Eddings v. Oklahoma*	Reversed the death sentence of a 16-year-old tried in adult court; ruled that a defendant's young age should be considered a mitigating factor
1984	*Schall v. Martin*	Preventive "pretrial" detention of juveniles is allowable under certain circumstances
1988	Maloney, Romig, & Armstrong introduce the "balanced approach"	Some juvenile justice jurisdictions adopt the three goals of public safety protection, accountability, and competency development
1988	*Thompson v. Oklahoma*	Ruled that the Eighth Amendment prohibited the death penalty for persons younger than 16 years old
1989	*Stanford v. Kentucky*	Ruled that the Eighth Amendment does not prohibit the death penalty for crimes committed at age 16 or 17 years
1980s–1990s	Several highly publicized violent acts by juveniles; states "toughen" juvenile codes	More juveniles are transferred to the adult system; many states adopt mandatory sentences; juvenile court confidentiality provisions are weakened; special programs target serious juvenile offenders; "Scared-Straight" and boot camp programs proliferate

(Continued)

Table 9.1 (Continued)

Date	Event	Comments
1990s	Many states adopt blended sentencing policies	Extends sanctions beyond upper age of juvenile court jurisdiction; creates a middle ground between juvenile and adult sanctions
1990s	Many schools adopt "zero-tolerance" policies	More youths excluded from school; often end up in the juvenile justice system
1993	Office of Juvenile Justice and Delinquency Prevention (OJJDP) introduces its "comprehensive strategy"	Approach favors prevention, risk assessment and classification, and adoption of evidence-based treatment programs; adopted by several states
1995	OJJDP launches "balanced & restorative justice" project	Restorative justice philosophy begins to appear in some jurisdictions (e.g., victim–offender mediation, family group conferences, teen courts)
1995–2010	The rate of juvenile crime declines; Annie E. Casey Foundation's Juvenile Detention Alternatives Initiative spreads; "What Works" initiative is marketed to jurisdictions to encourage use of evidence-based interventions; major federal re-entry initiatives launched (Serious and Violent Offender Re-entry Initiative)	Despite juvenile crime reductions, formal court processing continues to increase and "get tough" policies remain; use of secure detention and post-adjudication incarceration decrease slightly; some jurisdictions adopt evidence-based interventions
2005	*Roper v. Simmons*	U.S. Supreme Court ruled that the Eighth Amendment prohibits imposing the death penalty on all juveniles under the age of 18
2010	*Graham v. Florida*	U.S. Supreme Court ruled that the Eighth Amendment does not allow a juvenile offender to be sentenced to life in prison without parole for a non-homicide offense

SOURCES: Bazemore and Umbreit (1995); Bernard (1992); Latessa (2004); Lattimore et al. (2004); McNeese (1998); Skiba et al. (2003); Snyder and Sickmund (1999, 2006); Stanfield (1999); Wilson and Howell (1993).

States have long been able to use judicial waiver to transfer young offenders to adult court jurisdiction under certain conditions. In the 1990s, many states modified their juvenile codes to redefine young people who commit certain crimes as adults, even though their age would otherwise define them as juveniles. For example, in many states, 14- or 15-year-olds charged with murder or certain other serious crimes can be processed automatically in adult court. In addition, most states have other mechanisms of transferring jurisdiction from juvenile to adult court by judicial waiver, prosecutorial discretion, or both.

Juvenile justice policies affect many other stakeholders, including the family members of young offenders, the neighborhoods in which they live, the broader community, and the public and private service providers who administer juvenile justice programs. Thus, as juvenile justice policies shift emphases among the system's goals, there are ongoing implications for family stability, neighborhood social capital, and the economy. Taxpayers pay for the majority of juvenile justice services. In recent years, the cost of such services has been rapidly increasing, led by treatments that are more intensive, settings that are most restrictive (i.e., requiring greater security measures), and services that are of greater duration.

Delinquency and Delinquents: Prevalence and Trends

As noted earlier, the term *delinquency* technically refers to acts committed by juveniles that would be crimes if committed by adults. However, delinquency is often used colloquially to refer to the full range of problem behaviors exhibited by young people that could result in their appearance in juvenile court. A complication emerges when we realize that what is thought of as delinquent behavior changes over time. Indeed, some behaviors that are currently not considered as delinquency may have once fit the definition, whereas some contemporary constructions of delinquent behavior might not have been labeled as problematic in other times. For example, in earlier eras, delinquency included simply being seen near an unsavory establishment or being poor and congregating in public with other poor children (Bernard, 1992). More recently, some altercations among youth that previously would have been ignored or handled informally by parents, neighbors, or schools now lead to formal charges. Delinquency is a concept defined through a combination of behavioral indicators and societal definitions and responses, and these definitions and responses tend to change over time. The dynamic nature of the concept poses some problems for a discussion of risk and protective factors because there is at least an implicit assumption that the outcome being "predicted" is at the individual level.

Despite the preceding caveat, describing the current prevalence and distribution of delinquency provides a sense of its scope. There are two ways to approach this task. First, given the focus of this chapter on juvenile justice policies and how they apply to those who become involved with the juvenile justice system, we summarize recent data on juvenile arrests and court processing. Then, because not all delinquent behavior is detected or formally processed but is, at least in large part, presumably related to the same etiological factors, we summarize what is known from self-report delinquency studies.

In 2008, the most recent year for which data are available, 2.11 million people younger than age 18 years were arrested in the United States, accounting for 26% of all arrests for property crimes and 16% of all violent crime arrests (Puzzanchera, 2009). Most U.S. crimes are committed by people between the ages of 10 and 49 years old, 20% of whom were between 10 and 17 years old in 2008 (U.S. Census Bureau, 2008). Thus, juveniles are overrepresented in arrests for such crimes as arson (47%), vandalism (39%), burglary (27%), larceny-theft (26%), robbery (27%), and motor vehicle theft (25%) but underrepresented in arrests for such crimes as murder (10%), aggravated assault (13%), and forcible rape (15%) (Puzzanchera, 2009). In 2008, females were involved in about one third (30%) of juvenile arrests (Puzzanchera). Although African Americans make up just 16% of the U.S. population between the ages of 10 and 17 years old, African American youth accounted for much higher percentages of juvenile arrests for nearly all offense categories (e.g., violent crimes, 52%; property crimes, 33%; drug abuse violations, 27%) (Puzzanchera). Similar arrest data are not available for Hispanic youth. However, there is evidence that Hispanic youth are overrepresented at other points in the juvenile justice system. In 2006, only 18% of the U.S. population between 10 and 17 years old was Hispanic, yet in a 1-day census, Hispanic youth accounted for 23% of those detained and 20% of those in residential juvenile correctional placement (Sickmund, Sladky, & Kang, 2008).

Another way to look at juvenile offense patterns is to consider the proportion of juvenile arrests accounted for by various crimes. Of the 2.11 million juvenile arrests in 2008, 5% were for violent index offenses (e.g., murder, non-negligent manslaughter, forcible rape, robbery, aggravated assault);

21% were for property crime index offenses (e.g., burglary, larceny-theft, motor vehicle theft, arson); 11% for other assaults; 9% for drug offenses; 9% for disorderly conduct; 7% for alcohol offenses; 5% for vandalism; 12% for running away, curfew violations, or loitering; and the remaining 23% for other nonindex offenses (based on Puzzanchera, 2009). Considering all juveniles 10 to 17 years old in 2008, about 6% were arrested, with about 1% arrested for property index crimes and about 0.3% arrested for a violent index crime (Puzzanchera, Sladky, & Kang, 2009). Juvenile arrest rates for nearly all crimes have decreased noticeably since a high point in the mid-1990s, with an overall decline of 16% from 1999 to 2008 (Puzzanchera, 2009). Although the decline was even more pronounced for African American youth than for White youth, the violent crime index arrest rate for African American juveniles has recently trended upward (Puzzanchera).

The official record data described above reflect the volume of delinquency processed by law enforcement and the courts. However, juvenile arrest data do not give a good estimate of the overall incidence or prevalence of delinquent behavior. Much delinquent activity goes undetected or unprocessed by the system. Moreover, arrests are case specific rather than person specific or crime specific. That is, the same juvenile may account for several arrests, a single arrest may result from several crimes committed by an individual, and a single crime may result in the arrest of multiple individuals (Puzzanchera, 2009). Therefore, studies of self-reported delinquency can be a useful supplement to official data.

Self-report delinquency studies have a long history in criminology research, with the consensus being that youths' self-reports of delinquent activity are reasonably reliable and valid when collected under appropriate conditions of anonymity or confidentiality (Elliott & Ageton, 1980; Farrington, Loeber, Stouthamer-Loeber, Van Kammen, & Schmidt, 1996; Hindelang, Hirschi, & Weis, 1981; O'Malley, Bachman, & Johnston, 1983). Studies based on samples of general school populations have consistently found that about 80% of adolescents report having engaged in behavior that could have gotten them in trouble with the law if detected. A relatively high number of adolescents report use of alcohol and illegal substances, truancy, and minor fights (Elliott, Huizinga, & Ageton, 1985; Farrington et al., 1996). A smaller number of adolescents report involvement in serious offenses against people or property. Relatively few adolescents report frequently committing such offenses, and most do not go on to commit crimes as adults (Elliott et al., 1985; Farrington et al., 1996; Moffitt & Caspi, 2001). Thus, although a large majority of youth engages in some misconduct, relatively few—only 6% to 8%—are the chronic, serious juvenile offenders who account for most of the serious juvenile crime (Hamparian, 1978; Wolfgang, Figlio, & Sellin, 1972; Wolfgang, Thornberry, & Figlio, 1987). Risk and protective factors for delinquent conduct are described next.

Risk and Protective Factors for Delinquency

The risk and protection framework for understanding delinquency has evolved from separate lines of research and theory. Some researchers have adopted an epidemiological approach to the study of youth problem behaviors, such as psychopathology, substance abuse (Hawkins, Catalano, & Miller, 1992), delinquency (Dryfoos, 1990; Elliott, 1994; Thornberry, Huizinga, & Loeber, 1995; Tremblay & Craig, 1995), school dropout (Wehlage, Rutter, Smith, Lesko, & Fernandez, 1989), and teenage pregnancy (Dryfoos, 1990; Franklin, Grant, Corcoran, O'Dell, & Bultman, 1995). From a different perspective, other researchers have attempted to understand why some individuals achieve positive developmental outcomes despite resembling those at highest risk for failure (Anthony, 1987; Rutter, 1985; Werner & Smith, 2001). In recent decades, these streams of research and theory have converged to identify a common set of risk and protective factors associated with various developmental outcomes.

Risk factors have been defined by Fraser, Kirby, and Smokowski (2004) as "any influences that increase the chances for harm or, more specifically, influences that increase the probability of onset, digression to a more serious state, or maintenance of a problem condition" (p. 14). *Protective factors* operate in the presence of risk to mediate or buffer the effect of risk, thus enhancing positive adaptation (Garmezy, 1985; Masten, 1994; Rutter, 1985). Some scholars suggest using the term *promotive factors* for those influences associated with positive developmental outcomes for all people, reserving the term *protective factors* for those that operate only or more strongly in the presence of risk (Fraser et al., 2004; Fraser & Terzian, 2005; Sameroff, 1999). Risk, promotive, and protective factors each may operate in either domain-specific (i.e., related to specific developmental outcomes) or general ways.

Several recent reviews summarized the research regarding risk factors, protective factors, and resilience in general (Durlak, 1998; Fraser et al., 2004; Werner & Smith, 2001) and for delinquency and violence in particular (Hawkins et al., 2000; Howell, 2003; Lipsey & Derzon, 1998; Office of the Surgeon General, 2001; Stouthamer-Loeber, Loeber, Wei, Farrington, & Wikström, 2002; Williams, Ayers, Van Dorn, & Arthur, 2004). Table 9.2 lists risk, protective, and promotive factors identified at various ecological levels in those reviews.

Table 9.2 Risk, Protective, and Promotive Factors for Juvenile Delinquency

Level	Risk Factors	Protective/Promotive Factors
Individual: Biological and Genetic	Gender (male)[bcde] Absence of MAOA gene[b] Neuropsychological defects[h] Cognitive defects—low IQ[cdegh] Difficult temperament[dh] Hyperactivity/ADHD[ceh] Perinatal trauma[gh] Neurotoxins[h] Maternal alcohol or drug use in pregnancy[h]	Gender (female)[h] High IQ[befg] Easy temperament[bgh]
Individual: Psychological and Behavioral	Aggression[cde] Beliefs favorable to deviance[ce] Alienation[edh] Rebelliousness[h] Impulsiveness[d] Risk taking[cd]	Assertiveness[g] Pro-social beliefs[hef] Social problem-solving skills[agh] Self-efficacy[ab] Self-esteem[b] Internal locus of control[g]
Family	Family management problems[bcdeh] Family conflict[bdeh] Lack of parental involvement[cdeh] Low level of parental education[g] Child maltreatment[bcdeg] Family history of crime[cdeh] Parental antisocial personality[h] Parental psychopathology[bg] Parental attitudes favoring deviance[c] Parent–child separation[cdeg] Divorce[edgh] Large family size[d]	Positive discipline techniques[bh] Supportive relationships[abfgh] Monitoring and supervision[h] Parent with high school education or more[g] Good communication[f] Family advocacy[h] Achievement orientation[h] Strong spiritual values[h] Racial pride[h] Extended family bonds[h] Fewer siblings[g]
Other Adults		Presence of caring adult[bg]
Peers	Antisocial peers[cdeh] Delinquent siblings[c] Gang membership[ce]	Pro-social peer group[afgh]

(Continued)

Table 9.2 (Continued)

Level	Risk Factors	Protective/Promotive Factors
School	Early academic failure[cdegh] Low school commitment[cdeh] Aggressive behavior in school[h] Poor-quality schools[d] Truancy[cd] Frequent school transitions[c]	Academic success[bfgh] Positive bonding to school[efgh] High-quality schools[a]
Neighborhood	High population density[h] High population mobility[h] Physical deterioration[dh] High crime rates[ceh] Availability of drugs/weapons[ch] Lack of social cohesion[h] Low resident attachment[h]	Collective efficacy[b] Non-disadvantaged neighborhood[f] Low neighborhood crime[f]
Society/ Community	Antisocial community norms/laws[h] Exposure to violence[c] Racial prejudice and discrimination[bc] Few education/employment opportunities[b] Poverty[bcdegh]	Pro-social community norms/ laws[ah] Support[h] Empowerment[h] Many education/employment opportunities[b] Boundaries and expectations[h] Constructive use of time[h] Regular church involvement[g]

a. Durlak (1998).

b. Fraser, Kirby, and Smokowski (2004).

c. Hawkins et al. (2000).

d. Lipsey and Derzon (1998).

e. Office of the Surgeon General (2001).

f. Stouthamer-Loeber et al. (2002).

g. Werner and Smith (2001).

h. Williams et al. (2004).

Individual Level

Some risk and protective factors are biological or genetic in origin. For example, males are at higher risk than females for antisocial behavior (e.g., Patterson, Reid, & Dishion, 1992). Recent work suggests that the absence of the genetically controlled monoamine oxidase (MAOA) enzyme is associated with aggressive behavior (Rowe, 2001). The role of temperament in resilience has been identified by several researchers, who noted that, from an early age, children with an "easy" temperament fared better than did those with a "difficult" temperament (Moffitt & Caspi, 2001; Werner & Smith, 2001). Presumably, the child's natural temperament elicits responses in kind from parents and others. Hyperactivity in young children is associated with later behavioral problems and delinquency (Loeber, Farrington, & Petechuk, 2003). Intelligence, as measured by IQ tests, can be seen as a protective factor when high (Masten, 1994) and a risk factor when low (Loeber, Farrington, Stouthamer-Loeber, & van Kammen, 1998). Hawkins, Catalano, and Miller (1992) reported a relationship between a mother's alcohol and drug use during pregnancy and a child's later delinquency.

Other factors at the individual level are psychological or behavioral. Risk factors include early aggressive behavior (Farrington, 1991; Hawkins et al., 2000), rebelliousness, and alienation (Williams et al., 2004). Attitudes and beliefs favorable to deviance are a risk factor (Hawkins et al., 2000), whereas prosocial attitudes act as a protective factor (Office of the Surgeon General, 2001; Williams et al., 2004). High levels of internal locus of control and assertiveness (Werner & Smith, 2001), social problem-solving skills (Durlak, 1998; Werner & Smith, 2001; Williams et al., 2004), self-efficacy, and self-esteem (Fraser et al., 2004) have been identified as protective or promotive factors.

Family Level

The family represents the most salient social context for children; therefore, it is not surprising that the literature identifies a number of important risk and protective or promotive factors within the family. A relatively consistent picture emerges. Through attachment and modeling, the family exerts a profound effect on children's behavior. Nearly all reviews have noted inconsistent or harsh discipline practices, parental criminality, child maltreatment, lack of parental involvement, and divorce as risk factors and concurrently mentioned warm relationships with prosocial parents who are involved in their children's lives and who provide consistent monitoring and discipline as perhaps the strongest protective or promotive factor (Durlak, 1998; Fraser et al., 2004; Hawkins et al., 2000; Lipsey & Derzon, 1998; Office of the Surgeon General, 2001; Stouthamer-Loeber et al., 2002; Werner & Smith, 2001; Williams et al., 2004). Werner and Smith (2001) noted the role of parental education in preventing antisocial conduct and found that parents with a high school education represented the line tipping the scale from a risk factor to a protective factor. However, a more recent study by Theokas and Lerner (2006) has suggested that the strongest family factor protecting against adolescent risk behaviors is not parental education but rather "collective activity," such as eating dinner together. Williams et al. (2004) mentioned several protective factors that appear to apply specifically to African American families, including a strong achievement orientation, presence of strong spiritual values, racial pride, and bonds to extended family members.

Peers

Association with delinquent peers is a frequently cited and relatively strong predictor of delinquency, which appears to apply more to adolescents than to younger children (Hawkins et al., 2000; Moffitt, 1993; Office of the Surgeon General, 2001). On the other hand, association with prosocial peers may provide protection from this risk (Durlak, 1998; Stouthamer-Loeber et al., 2002; Werner & Smith, 2001).

Other Adults

A relationship with a caring adult outside of the immediate family is an important protective factor or asset (Eccles & Gootman, 2002; Fraser et al., 2004; Scales & Leffert, 1999; Werner & Smith, 2001). Such a relationship may emerge naturally with an extended family member, a neighbor, or teacher. Alternatively, this relationship may be arranged in formal mentoring programs, such as the Big Brothers and Big Sisters program. This program has been successful in reducing recidivism among young offenders (Tierney, Grossman, & Resch, 1995).

Schools

Next to the family, schools are the most important social arena for children and adolescents. The literature consistently indicates that school commitment and academic performance are linked to developmental outcomes. Low commitment and poor performance are consistently identified as risk factors, and strong commitment and good performance identified as protective factors (Fraser et al., 2004; Hawkins et al., 2000; Lipsey & Derzon, 1998; Mann & Reynolds, 2006; Office of the Surgeon General, 2001; Richart, Brooks, & Soler, 2003; Stouthamer-Loeber et al.,

2002; Werner & Smith, 2001; Williams et al., 2004). Moreover, there is evidence that the quality of the school environment plays an important role in the onset and prevention of delinquency (Durlak, 1998; Gottfredson, 2000; Lipsey & Derzon, 1998).

Neighborhood and Community

Poverty is one of the most frequently cited correlates of delinquency (Fraser et al., 2004; Hawkins, Catalano, & Miller, 1992; Hawkins et al., 2000; Lipsey & Derzon, 1998; Office of the Surgeon General, 2001; Werner & Smith, 2001). The availability of drugs and weapons, exposure to violence, and neighborhood disorganization in general (e.g., high population mobility, physical deterioration, high crime rates, and lack of social cohesion) are risk factors for delinquency (Aisenberg & Herrenkohl, 2008; Hawkins et al., 2000; Nash & Bowen, 1999; Sampson, Raudenbush, & Earls, 1997; Williams et al., 2004). On the other hand, communities and neighborhoods with high collective efficacy are presumed to exert informal social control that helps protect against delinquency (Fraser et al., 2004; Nash & Bowen, 1999; Sampson et al., 1997).

Community norms broadly affect delinquency through formal laws and policies as well as informal means (Durlak, 1998; Hawkins, Catalano, & Miller, 1992; Williams et al., 2004). For example, a community that vigorously pursues enforcement of age limits for the purchase of alcohol might be expected to have lower delinquency rates. Fraser et al. (2004) noted that limited opportunities for education and employment and the presence of racial discrimination are risk factors for delinquency, whereas the presence of opportunities for education and employment provides protection from delinquency.

Gender Differences

A recent meta-analysis of predictors of delinquency among girls documented important gender differences in risk and needs profiles (Hubbard & Pratt, 2002). The results indicated that even though many of the strong predictors were the same as those for boys (e.g., prior history of antisocial behavior, antisocial peers, antisocial attitudes, and antisocial personality), the role of other predictors was more pronounced among girls. These gender-dependent factors included IQ, family dysfunction, trauma and sexual abuse, mental health and substance abuse problems, high-risk sexual behaviors, and school problems (Hubbard & Pratt, 2002). These findings were consistent with those of a recent study of 672 girls in detention, which determined that most had experienced trauma (84%), met criteria for mental health problems (78%), reported having a parent or close friend with criminal justice system involvement (61%), and had been sexually active (76%; Lederman, Dakof, Larrea, & Li, 2004). In another study, detained girls were significantly more likely than were detained boys to exhibit risks and needs related to family and parenting, mental health, traumatic events, physical health, psychopathy, accountability, and peer relationships (Gavazzi, Yarcheck, & Chesney-Lind, 2006).

Although these differences suggest the need for gender-specific programming, the evidence supporting the effectiveness of gender-specific programming is not yet compelling. A recent systematic review of evaluations conducted of gender-specific programs and gender-neutral programs reported evaluation results by gender, concluding that (a) there were very few strong studies available, (b) there was no evidence that gender-specific programs were more effective than other programs in reducing recidivism, and (c) there was evidence that programs with a strong history of success with boys also worked well for girls (Zahn, Day, Mihalic, & Tichavsky, 2009). However, the review noted that gender-specific programs showed positive results on measures related to empowerment and quality of life including education, employment, relationships, self-esteem and self-efficacy (Zahn et al., 2009).

Summary

In addition to illustrating the ecological nature of risk and protection, several key themes emerge from this review:

- Many risk, promotive, and protective factors are malleable (e.g., the presence of social support, the development of social skills, parenting skills); others are not subject to change (e.g., IQ, temperament, gender).
- The effect of risk factors is not linear; that is, the presence of multiple risk factors increases the probability of undesirable outcomes exponentially (Pollard, Hawkins, & Arthur, 1999; Rutter, 2001).
- There is both overlap—among the risk, protective, and promotive factors— and co-occurrence—among adolescent problem behaviors—with a set of common risk and protective factors associated with a range of problems (Dryfoos, 1990; Hawkins, Catalano, & Miller, 1992; Huizinga, Loeber, Thornberry, & Cothern, 2000).
- The effect of some risk and protective factors is developmentally specific (Hawkins et al., 2000; Office of the Surgeon General, 2001).

- Risk and protective factors appear to operate similarly across cultural and ethnic groups (Elliott, Huizinga, & Menard, 1989; Hawkins, Laub, & Lauritsen, 1998; Williams, Ayers, Abbott, Hawkins, & Catalano, 1999); however, there are gender differences as noted above.
- Risk factors can combine either simultaneously or cumulatively over time and, in either case, increase the probability of undesirable outcomes.
- In general, risk factors and protective factors are inversely distributed across social strata; that is, those at highest risk generally have fewer natural protections than those at lower risk (Pollard et al., 1999).

A useful theoretical framework for summarizing knowledge of risk, protection, resilience, and developmental outcomes comes from the social development model (Catalano & Hawkins, 1996), which is a synthesis of social control theory, social learning theory, and differential association theory. Although developed as an explanation for antisocial behavior, the social developmental model is more broadly applicable to developmental outcomes. Catalano and Hawkins (1996) outlined the four purported socialization processes affecting children that comprise the heart of the model:

(1) perceived opportunities for involvement in activities and interactions with others, (2) the degree of involvement and interaction, (3) the skills to participate in these involvements and interactions, and (4) the reinforcement they perceive as forthcoming from performance in activities and interactions. (p. 156)

Through these processes, the child develops a social bond with the socializing unit, with its strength dependent on the consistency of the socializing processes. Bonding, which consists of attachment, commitment, and beliefs, then influences the child's subsequent behavior as he or she seeks to maintain the connection. Antisocial behavior results from (a) a weakening of the bond with pro-social socialization agents; (b) a situation in which, even in the presence of a pro-social bond, the situational inducements to deviance are sufficiently compelling; or (c) a situation in which the child develops a strong bond to anti-social socialization agents, including parents or peers. Finally, the social developmental model contains developmentally specific submodels that reflect changes in the child's salient socialization agents at different ages (e.g., the progression from family to school). From this model, it can be seen that behavior emerges from the ecological interplay of individual characteristics, social interactions, and environmental supports/constraints; the direction of the developmental trajectory (pro-social or antisocial) is dependent on the array of risk, protective, and promotive factors.

Notwithstanding the substantial advances in research and theory regarding risk and resilience, no one should assume that knowledge of risk and protective profiles can predict long-term developmental outcomes with pinpoint accuracy. For example, attempts to quantify the effect sizes of various risk factors have shown that the predictive power of even the most powerful risk factors is modest (Hawkins et al., 2000; Office of the Surgeon General, 2001). Evidence from longitudinal studies suggests that turning points, such as military service and, especially, marriage, can have a profound effect on positively redirecting developmental trajectories (Laub & Sampson, 2003; Werner & Smith, 2001). The error variance in predictive models may be due to incomplete specification of the predictors, or it may indicate that chance, personal agency, and individuals' interpretation of the immediate context play major roles in eliciting behavior. As Lösel and Bender (2003) noted, "errors in prediction of antisociality in childhood and adolescence should not just be viewed as a technical deficit. They are also indicators of the general phenomena of multifinality and equifinality in development" (p. 131). In sum, although the growing knowledge base of the risk and resilience framework may have great relevance for policies and practices, that knowledge must be applied cautiously and with recognition of its limits.

Risk, Protection, and Resilience in Juvenile Justice Policy

Until recently, knowledge of risk, protection, and resilience had not influenced juvenile justice policies and programs in profound ways. This lack of influence in itself is not surprising because this knowledge base has emerged only within the last few decades. Instead, policies and practices appear to have primarily reflected concepts such as deterrence, incapacitation, and retribution, with an occasional dose of developmental psychology. Juvenile justice policies and programs have sought to protect the community and to reform offenders by teaching offenders that delinquency leads to unpleasant consequences. This lesson has been implemented by either closely supervising offenders' behavior or placing offenders in restrictive settings, keeping them off the streets for some time.

In the century since the founding of the juvenile court, juvenile justice policies have evolved amid the dialectic between the goals of punishment and rehabilitation of young offenders. Bernard (1992) has captured this fluctuating history well, describing the "cycle of juvenile justice" as beginning with the observation that delinquency is a serious and escalating problem, blaming the problem on the current tenor of policies (either "get tough" or lenient), advocating reforms moving to the other pole, discovering that the problem remains unsolved, blaming the then-current tenor of policies, switching to the other pole again, and so on.

Juvenile courts were meant to function in the best interests of the child, and early juvenile correctional programs were supposed to be treatment programs rather than prisons. However, when high rates of delinquency and recidivism concerns continued, the juvenile court and juvenile correctional practices became tougher. Specifically, the court's discretionary powers, which were intended to reduce the punitiveness of the adult courts, became suspect because juveniles lacked many due process protections. A series of U.S. Supreme Court challenges gradually brought many of those due process protections into the juvenile court by the latter part of the 20th century (Bernard, 1992; Snyder & Sickmund, 1999). However, the increasing formality of the juvenile court system has rendered it more like the adult system and perhaps paved the way for policies such as "three strikes," mandatory sentences for some offenses, and the increasing use of transfer to the adult system via judicial waiver, prosecutorial direct file, or statutory exclusion.

Juvenile Justice System Involvement and Incarceration as Risk Factors

Throughout its checkered history, the juvenile justice system has continually relied on secure, residential placements, both before adjudication (detention) and after adjudication (training schools and private secure residential facilities). In recent years, a number of studies have documented major problems with the use of such facilities. Specifically:

1. Secure facilities are overused; many youths in secure residential facilities are not serious or chronic offenders and could be placed in less restrictive settings (Snyder & Sickmund, 1999, 2006).

2. Many secure residential facilities house youths in poor conditions characterized by overcrowding (Livesy, Sickmund, & Sladky, 2009), sexual abuse (Beck, Harrison, & Guerino, 2010), or otherwise unsafe environments (Lerner, 1986; Parent et al., 1994).

3. Secure residential facilities are relatively ineffective; that is, gains made while incarcerated, if any, tend to dissipate when youths return to the community, and recidivism outcomes are often no better—or even worse—than would be found in less restrictive, community-based settings (Gatti, Tremblay, & Vitaro, 2009; Holman & Ziedenberg, 2006; Lipsey, 1992; Loeber & Farrington, 1998; Loughran et al., 2009).

Treatment programming in juvenile corrections has used behavioral contingencies and, more recently, cognitive-behavioral approaches to modify behavior and thinking patterns that are presumed to lead to offending behavior. Within the field, there has been some recognition of the importance of peer influences on adolescents, as expressed in treatment models such as *guided group interaction* (McCorkle, Elias, & Bixby, 1958) and *positive peer culture* (Vorath & Brendtro, 1974). However, whatever the treatment modality, recidivism has remained high, with studies finding that between 50% and 90% of youths are reincarcerated in juvenile or adult facilities within 1 to 3 years of their release from juvenile correctional facilities (Howell, 2003; Minor, Wells, & Angel, 2008; Trulson, Marquart, Mullings, & Caeti, 2005).

Considerable evidence has accumulated to suggest that juvenile justice system involvement is itself a risk factor for poor developmental outcomes. The iatrogenic effects (i.e., unintentional detrimental or harmful effects) of involvement with the juvenile justice system include, but are not limited to, future offending. For example, even after controlling for offense-related and demographic factors, both the use of secure detention and the decision to formally process a case have been linked to more restrictive dispositions and higher levels of recidivism (Feld, 1991; Frazier & Bishop, 1985; Frazier & Cochran, 1986). Similarly, the research cited above about the iatrogenic effects of incarceration is compelling (Gatti et al., 2009; Holman & Ziedenberg, 2006; Lipsey, 1992; Loeber & Farrington, 1998; Loughran et al., 2009). Social learning theory (Akers, 1985) provides one theoretical explanation for these relationships; exposure to other delinquent peers occurs in most juvenile justice interventions, especially incarceration, and it results in peer-deviancy training (Dishion, McCord, & Poulin, 1999; Dishion, Spracklen, & Patterson, 1996; Dodge, Dishion, & Lansford, 2006). Alternatively, labeling theory (Becker, 1963; Bernburg, Krohn, & Rivera, 2006; Lemert, 1951) suggests that others respond to the label of *delinquent* by expecting the youth to behave accordingly, and youth labeled delinquent might also internalize that label. In addition to being a risk factor for recidivism, juvenile justice system involvement during adolescence is associated with limited educational, employment, and financial outcomes as well as adult mental health disorders and substance abuse (Fagan & Freeman, 1999; Moffitt, Caspi, Harrington, & Milne, 2002). For a recent review of the evidence regarding the deleterious social, developmental, and fiscal consequences of incarcerating juveniles, see a recent report from the Justice Policy Institute (Petteruti, Walsh, & Velázquez, 2009).

Risk, Resilience, and Recent Reform Efforts

Despite the "get tough" climate of juvenile justice policies initiated since the latter part of the 20th century, some policy officials have recognized the ineffectiveness and expense of relying on incarceration to reform offenders. Therefore, some policymakers have advocated for greater use of community-based programs at all stages of the juvenile justice system. In many instances, community-based responses have served to divert youths from formal processing through the system. In other instances, community-based resources have served as integral parts of the formal system (e.g., probation) or as complementary components (e.g., community-based treatment programs). For a review of community-based programs in juvenile justice, see Barton (2002).

In an attempt to move beyond the punishment–rehabilitation dialectic, Maloney, Romig, and Armstrong (1988) provided a major advance in conceptualizing juvenile justice goals by articulating the "balanced approach" to probation. According to this approach, juvenile justice policymakers must consciously balance concern for three system goals: (1) public safety protection, (2) accountability (of the juvenile and the system), and (3) competency development. In other words, every decision point in the system must consider and account for these three goals. Several states subsequently adopted the balanced approach in their juvenile codes or agency mission statements.

More recently, advocates of restorative justice (e.g., Bazemore & Terry, 1997; Bazemore & Umbreit, 1995) have sought to replace the traditional retributive paradigm of juvenile justice, which views crimes as offenses committed against society, with a new paradigm that views crimes as upsetting the balance of rights and obligations, with victims and offenders seeking a mediated restoration of that balance. Although the restorative justice paradigm has not been adopted fully in most places, elements of restorative justice have increasingly appeared, usually targeting minor or first-time offenders, including such practices as family-group conferences (McGarrell, Olivares, Crawford, & Kroovand, 2000) and teen courts (Butts, Buck, & Coggeshall, 2002). In many ways, the restorative justice approach is consistent with the principles of risk, protection, and resilience.

Since the mid-1990s, knowledge about risk and protective factors has found its way into mainstream juvenile justice policy discussions and has been heavily promoted by the Office of Juvenile Justice and Delinquency Prevention in its comprehensive strategy (Howell, 1995; Wilson & Howell, 1993). This strategy combines an emphasis on prevention strategies, which attempt to reduce community risk factors and enhance protective factors, with the application of community-based interventions (and less use of incarceration) and evidence-based treatment models in the juvenile justice system. Although not limited to jurisdictions adopting the comprehensive strategy, an increasingly common application of risk principles (albeit not resilience) to juvenile justice has been the use of structured risk-assessment instruments (Howell, 2003; Wiebush, Baird, Krisberg, & Onek, 1995). Many jurisdictions now use such instruments at various points in the juvenile justice system to guide decisions regarding placement in secure detention, probation supervision levels, dispositional placement restrictiveness, and aftercare planning (Wiebush et al., 1995).

Risk, protection, and resilience are explicitly ecological concepts; however, the tendency is to apply them primarily at the individual level. Thus, we see the contemporary extension of the typological enterprise, with an emphasis on developing risk and need profiles of individual youths and making juvenile justice system decisions (e.g., detention placements, treatment plans) at least partly based on these assessments. This approach may or may not be much of an improvement. The evidence suggests that although risk and protective factors have some explanatory power at the aggregate level, these factors do not do a very good job of predicting individual level outcomes (Laub & Sampson, 2003; Office of the Surgeon General, 2001; White, Moffitt, Earls, Robins, & Silva, 1990). The use of risk profiles represents an improvement over pure chance predictions, but the rate of false-positive and false-negative predictions is high. False-positive predictions are characterized by individuals with high-risk profiles who do not go on to commit more offenses. Conversely, false-negative predictions involve youths with low-risk profiles who do go on to commit crimes. In some sense, the advances in risk and protective factor research may have provided juvenile justice policymakers and practitioners with an exaggerated sense of confidence that their decisions are evidence-based decisions.

Risk, Resilience, and Evidence-Based Programs

A burgeoning literature on "what works" in juvenile justice has emerged in recent decades as a counter to the now infamously misinterpreted "nothing works" mantra of the 1970s (Lipton, Martinson, & Wilks, 1975). Major reviews and meta-analyses of juvenile correctional treatment programs have indicated that many approaches, if implemented correctly and targeted toward the appropriate youths, can reduce recidivism (Andrews et al., 1990; Lipsey, 1992; Lipsey & Wilson, 1998). Several websites list prevention and intervention programs with research-based evidence of effectiveness. For example, The Blueprints for Violence Prevention (Center for the Study and Prevention of Violence, 2010) considers model programs to be those that meet the following criteria: evidence of a deterrent effect with a strong research design, sustained effect, and multiple site replications. Promising programs meet only the first criterion. As of this writing, the Blueprints website lists 12 model programs and 20 promising programs.

The financial burden of programs is also an important consideration. The Washington State Institute for Public Policy (WSIPP) has applied a sophisticated cost–benefit analysis based on meta-analyses of a wide range of crime prevention and intervention programs for juveniles and adults (Drake, Aos, & Miller, 2009). The WSIPP analysis found that many prevention and intervention programs are cost-effective, whereas others are not. Table 9.3 presents a listing of several juvenile programs and indicates whether they are Blueprint model programs and whether the program has been determined as cost-effective by the WSIPP.

In the WSIPP model, benefits are estimated per participant and reflect the combined savings to taxpayers from reduced criminal justice processing costs (if any) and the value of crime victim benefits based on the program's estimated effect on preventing future crimes, net of program

Table 9.3   Model and/or Cost-Effective Prevention/Intervention Programs

Program	Model Program[a]	Cost-Effective[b]
Functional Family Therapy	Yes	Yes
Life Skills Training	Yes	Yes
Multisystemic Therapy	Yes	Yes
Nurse-Family Partnership	Yes	Yes
Multidimensional Treatment Foster Care	Yes	Yes
Olweus Bullying Prevention Program	Yes	
Promoting Alternative Thinking Strategies (PATHS)	Yes	
The Incredible Years: Parent, Teacher and Child Training Series	Yes	
Project Towards No Drug Abuse	Yes	
Big Brothers Big Sisters of America	Yes	
Midwestern Prevention Project	Yes	
Aggression Replacement Therapy		Yes
Restorative Justice for low risk offenders		Yes
Teen Courts		Yes
Family Integrated Transitions		Yes
Adolescent diversion project		Yes
Interagency coordination programs		Yes
Pre-K Education for low-income 3- and 4-year-olds		Yes

a. Center for the Study and Prevention of Violence (2010).

b. Drake, Aos, and Miller (2009).

costs (Drake et al., 2009). Programs with poor economic returns include "Scared Straight" programs, wilderness challenge programs, intensive probation or parole programs, and boot camps, none of which is even remotely informed by the risk and resilience framework. In contrast, prevention programs that strengthen families, provide mentoring, and foster school success and social skills, along with intervention programs that are either explicitly ecological or target key risk factors, were found to be highly cost effective (Drake et al., 2009). Examples of highly cost-effective programs included Multisystemic Therapy, Functional Family Therapy, and coordinated services (i.e., comprehensive, coordinated services also called *wraparound* services). Drake and colleagues (2009) reported that these programs offered combined benefits (see above for how benefits were calculated) per participant ranging from about $15,000 to as much as $88,000. It is no accident that these cost-effective approaches are either informed by or consistent with the risk and resilience framework.

Although much of the research base on risk and protection uses the presence or absence of delinquency as the primary dependent variable, merely preventing delinquent or antisocial behavior may not be the only positive goal of risk- and resilience-based interventions. The resilience literature and positive youth development literature remind us that being "problem-free isn't fully prepared" (Pittman & Irby, 1996, p. 3). The juvenile justice system is primarily concerned with preventing the recurrence of delinquency. However, that system might be more successful if it were to embrace the universal goals of positive youth development, which focus on promoting competence, character, connections, confidence, and contribution (Hamilton, Hamilton, & Pittman, 2004). In this way, communities would have the opportunity not only to prevent youth problem behaviors but also to promote long-term, healthy development.

Clearly, formal juvenile justice system involvement, particularly incarceration, interrupts the normal course of adolescent development. It disrupts adolescents' ability to complete developmental tasks by removing them from the supports and opportunities available in the community to their nondelinquent peers (Altschuler, 2005; Chung, Little, & Steinberg, 2005). Although the risk and resilience framework has increasingly informed juvenile justice policies and programs, its full potential has yet to be realized. It can provide a foundation for more fundamental changes in juvenile justice policies and practices. These changes would incorporate the truly ecological nature of risk and resilience, broaden the system goals from merely controlling delinquent behavior to promoting positive youth development, and rely on and further promote coordination among the various service systems that affect the lives of adolescents, as advocated by Jenson and Fraser (2006). The next section explores what some of those changes might look like and highlights some efforts currently under way.

Using Knowledge of Risk, Protection, and Resilience to Enhance Juvenile Justice Policy and Practices

Based on the risk and resilience framework, Fraser and Terzian (2005) outlined three basic practice principles: (1) strengthen protection and reduce risk (both must be addressed); (2) understand the effect of the social and developmental context on protection and risk; and (3) identify and disrupt risk mechanisms, that is, the "sequencing of events that elevate risk" (p. 20). The Blueprint model programs and the cost-effective programs identified by WSIPP, along with the following discussion of additional ways to incorporate the risk and resilience framework into juvenile justice, are congruent with these practice principles.

Changing the Culture of Juvenile Justice

Thorough application of the risk and resilience framework would require a change in the prevailing juvenile justice culture, and that traditional culture is deeply entrenched. It is difficult for justice system actors to transcend long-standing beliefs in the effectiveness of deterrence and punishment, despite evidence to the contrary. It is also difficult for those working in the current juvenile justice system to take an ecological view when confronted with a steady stream of individuals. The culture of many juvenile justice agencies is "passive-defensive," with routinized procedures, resistance to innovation, and "climates characterized by depersonalization, emotional exhaustion, role overload, and role conflict" (Hemmelgarn, Glisson, & James, 2006, pp. 76–77). The effects of this culture and climate include low morale, high rates of staff turnover, and cookie-cutter approaches to case planning and interventions. The poor outcomes have been documented previously in this chapter.

In the last few years, interest in incorporating positive youth development principles into juvenile justice has grown, albeit not without recognition of the challenges facing such a transformation (Barton, 2004; Butts, Bazemore, & Meroe, 2010; Butts, Mayer, & Ruth, 2005; Frabutt, Di Luca, & Graves, 2008; Schwartz, 2001; Torbet & Thomas, 2005). There are some juvenile justice settings in which the positive youth development perspective has taken root, and although strong evidence of effectiveness is not yet available, these settings tend to produce more positive climates, less staff turnover, and much lower rates of recidivism (Barton & Butts, 2008; Barton, Mackin, & Fields, 2008; Kurtz & Linnemann, 2006). The comments of an administrator who shepherded such a transformation are provided in Box 1.

Comments of a County Juvenile Probation Administrator About Changing the Culture

I would say that, . . . commonly in our field, there are two different mindsets. One is that these kids are doing things that are harmful to other people, to society, and that's true. And so people who have that view of these kids—harmful to society— they often have a lot of compassion for victims, and they take a point of view that the only way to approach that is to control that, to contain that, and that might mean removing kids from the community or restricting [kids]; this whole restrictive-punitive notion of how you deal with that. And then there are the other people who [think that] these are kids who you need to support, develop, and help. And I think that the most significant realization that we can come to is that they are not mutu-ally exclusive, incompatible approaches, and that there is another way—which acknowledges that the kids have hurt society and have created victims and hurt people—but at the same time acknowledges that they have the capabilities and strengths and capacities that haven't been tapped; and that the approach is that you can do all of these things at one time. . . . Just because you have identified a kid's strengths doesn't mean that you . . . say, "We accept the things you've done." And I think it's the same thing for parents or running any organization. There are certain things that are not acceptable—and you have to be very clear about what those are—but at the same time you acknowledge that there are a lot of things in each individual that are very strong, and you point those to success. So I think that it's that bifocal frame of reference that you have to overcome: it's not either or.

I think the only way you can overcome it—[because] you *don't* go into a big room of 400 people or your big staff and tell them that, you *don't* preach it. I could probably say better what you *don't* do; I know what you don't do—What you do is first of all [have] patience and recognize that organizational change takes years, and that you need to [be] very explicit. . . . I approach things [with] fairly long-range plans, long-range vision and constantly communicate that vision. [I am] very clear about what that [vision] is; it's not very complicated. It can be very simple, and you pretty much keep saying the same things over and over again. You can see it here; we are pretty clear about what our values are. We defined what they are, we make decisions of hiring based on those values, we incorporate them at every level. You model them, and then you see change over the course of the years.

SOURCE: [Name withheld], from interview transcript with this author, October 11, 2006. This county department had adopted a strength-based, positive youth development approach in 2001. By 2004, its rate of delinquency petitions was substantially lower than that of the other large coun-ties in its state. Its recidivism rate of 25% was lower than the state average, and had fallen faster than that in the rest of the state.

Several factors appear to promote the successful transformation of an agency's culture:

- A hospitable community culture—the values in relatively progressive communities are more likely to be congruent with positive youth development principles;
- The commitment of leadership—establishing and championing a vision, facilitating and empowering staff to adopt innovation, and staying the course;
- Adopting the strengths perspective as the practice model;
- Encouraging early adopters to serve as role models and peer trainers;
- Thorough training, followed by periodic "booster" trainings;
- Intentional hiring—bringing on staff already familiar with positive youth development principles and/or strength-based practice, or at least those who do not have to "unlearn" the traditional approaches;
- Integration into bureaucratic processing—make the paperwork reflect the goals and practice principles (more details on this point appear below);
- Consistent reinforcement through regular staff supervision;
- Collaboration with other agencies in the community—organizational permeability helps to prevent a return to the isolated correctional culture;
- Using feedback from data on youth outcomes for continuous quality improvement, and to help "sell" the new approach. (Barton & Butts, 2008, pp. 43–45)

The integration of positive youth development principles and the strengths perspective into the bureaucratic processing of juvenile justice agencies is especially critical. This integration can be, and should be, completed at two levels: individual practice and program accountability. Integration at the level of individual practice requires the adoption of a structured strengths assessment. Some of the risk assessment instruments mentioned previously include some coverage of strengths but typically address strengths as an afterthought, and seldom do the strengths inform case planning in any meaningful way. There are instruments that staff can use to assess strengths, including the Behavioral and Emotional Rating Scale (Epstein & Sharma, 1998), Child and Adolescent Needs and Strengths (Lyons, Griffin, Fazio, & Lyons, 1999), and the Youth Competency Assessment (Mackin, Weller, Tarte, & Nissen, 2005; Nissen, Mackin, Weller, & Tarte, 2005). These instruments encourage staff to create truly individualized intervention plans, and the process of administering the assessment also enables staff to develop stronger relationships with the youths, and such relationships are at the heart of producing positive change (Barton & Butts, 2008).

To promote program accountability congruent with the risk-resilience and positive youth development frameworks, program design and evaluation should be based on explicit program theory, which highlights the role of the positive youth development principles as both intermediate and longer term outcomes. An evaluation of an out-of-school-time program provides an example of the application of such a logic model (Anthony, Alter, & Jenson, 2009). This model begins with the identification of risks at multiple ecological levels and then designs interventions to provide protections intended to build resilience and produce intermediate outcomes related to positive youth development (competence, confidence, character, and connection), which, in turn, are expected to produce long-term outcomes including not only reduced antisocial behavior but milestones of positive development (educational achievement and economic self-sufficiency; Anthony et al., 2009, p. 49). Making explicit the linkages between risk, resilience, positive youth development, and long-term promotion of positive developmental outcomes (and reduction of the probability of negative developmental outcomes), models such as this encourage program stakeholders to focus rationally on those strategies that risk and resilience theory and research suggest will be most effective.

Juvenile Justice Interventions

As noted previously, efforts within the core of the juvenile justice system to incorporate knowledge of risk, protection, and resilience in policy and practice have been limited. Nevertheless, there are some promising ways that the risk and resilience perspective can inform juvenile justice policies and practices. Chief among these is the use of truly individualized, collaborative case coordination in system of care (SOC; Duchnowski, Kutash, & Friedman, 2002; Stroul & Friedman, 1986) or wraparound service models (Burchard, Bruns, & Burchard, 2002; Goldman, 1999; VanDenBerg & Grealish, 1996). The wraparound approach explicitly values culturally competent, strengths-based assessment and practice (Saleebey, 2006); involves youths, parents, informal sources of support, and professionals as partners in service planning; and operates through a formal collaboration among provider agencies that span traditional service arenas and use blended funding streams (Goldman, 1999). A growing body of evidence supports the promise of wraparound services (Burchard et al., 2002) and indicates that this approach is cost-effective (Aos, Phipps, Barnoski, & Lieb, 2001).

Models of individualized wraparound service can be applied to juvenile justice (Kendziora & Osher, 2004). Wraparound programs such as Wraparound Milwaukee (Kamradt, 2000) and the Dawn Project in Indianapolis (Choices, 2010) serve youth with mental health or substance abuse needs who enter the juvenile justice system. These programs have reported promising results in terms of reduced residential placements and lowered recidivism (Choices, 2010; Kamradt, 2000). Most, if not all, cases currently entering the juvenile justice system or transitioning from residential placements could benefit from wraparound services. The intensity of services could vary based on the assessed needs and strengths of the individuals, their families, and contexts. Not all would require lengthy and expensive services, and the use of and length of stay in costly residential placements would likely decrease.

The Annie E. Casey Foundation's Juvenile Detention Alternatives Initiative (JDAI) is another vehicle that has triggered culture shifts in several jurisdictions. Using a detailed blueprint to guide detention reform, JDAI encourages stakeholders to adopt values consistent with the risk and resilience framework to reshape their understanding of detention and, by extension, the broader juvenile justice system. Formally launched in five sites in 1993, JDAI had been adopted in more than 100 sites in 25 states by 2009, covering more than one third of the nation's youths (Mendel, 2009). Although the initiative has not been successful or sustained in all sites, a recent evaluation documented dramatic reductions in the use of secure detention (50% or more) in many sites, with no concomitant increases in juvenile crime or failures to appear for court hearings (Mendel, 2009). Moreover, the JDAI approach has been credited with other system improvements beyond reductions in secure detention use, including reduced disproportionate minority contact, fewer commitments to state juvenile correctional institutions, enhancements to community-based intervention alternatives, and greater collaboration among system stakeholders (Mendel, 2007). From personal experience with several JDAI sites, I have been struck by changes in the way JDAI site stakeholders view and talk about youth, including greater recognition of the applicability of a strengths-based, positive youth development lens that focuses as much on enhancing protective factors as on controlling risk factors.

A more radical way of embracing the risk and resilience framework might be to divorce the juvenile justice system from treatment programming altogether. Others have advocated splitting the legal and social welfare programming aspects of the court (e.g., Feld, 1999), but for slightly different reasons. Recall the three goals of juvenile justice articulated in the balanced approach as described earlier (Maloney et al., 1988). Perhaps the juvenile justice system should concentrate on what it could do best—public safety protection and accountability enforcement from a *just deserts* framework, transferring responsibility for competency development to community service providers more aligned with the risk and resilience framework. That is, there would still be juvenile court proceedings, probation oversight, and enforcement of the terms of accountability. However, probation would work in partnership with community service providers and other community stakeholders, who would both participate in the development of dispositional recommendations to the court and provide the individualized case management services.

Prevention

Knowledge of risk, protection, and resilience may be most useful for juvenile justice at the periphery of the system, where the corrosive influence of the traditional juvenile justice culture is either absent or minimal. The best example is prevention, where this knowledge can inform efforts to lower the risks and increase the protection in entire communities or focus efforts on targeting risks and strengthening protection in the more specific contexts of schools or families. The *Communities That Care* (CTC) approach of Hawkins, Catalano, and Associates (1992) is an example of community-wide prevention that is developed in considerable detail. CTC components include a framework for community mobilization, local assessment of risk and protective factors, and a menu of evidence-based programs that can be tailored to meet specific communities' needs. An evaluation of CTC in several Pennsylvania communities showed CTC counties with modestly reduced delinquency rates even though implementation was inconsistent (Greenberg & Feinberg, 2002). More recently, a CTC evaluation that used a randomized, county-level design in several states showed promising early results in terms of reductions in targeted risk factors and delayed onset of delinquent behavior among youth in CTC sites (Hawkins et al., 2008).

There is evidence that school-based prevention programs targeting risk factors can be effective (Hawkins & Herrenkohl, 2003). These programs address the major school-based risks, including early aggressive behavior, academic failure, and low commitment to school. The promising approaches that Hawkins and Herrenkohl reviewed included attempts to improve organizational climate and classroom management, to engage families in supporting academic achievement, to increase opportunities for school bonding, to teach emotional skills for self-control and social interaction, and to promote pro-social norms.

Similarly, Tremblay and Japel (2003) reviewed a number of programs that appeared effective in preventing delinquency by improving parents' skills and supports, addressing children's cognitive skills, and reducing early disruptive behavior among children. Tremblay and Japel's review showed that several perinatal and preschool programs effectively changed parenting behavior in at-risk families (e.g., communication, attitudes, discipline techniques) in ways that would appear to reduce risks and strengthen protection. Another group of studies included in Tremblay and Japel's review supported the notion that very early interventions with at-risk families, including parent training, environmental stimulation, and parent support could improve children's cognitive functioning and reduce early disruptive behaviors. Tremblay and Japel (2003) concluded, "The general impression from the review of the twenty-eight prevention experiments is that early childhood interventions can have a positive impact on the three most important risk factors for juvenile delinquency: disruptive behavior, cognitive skills, and parenting" (p. 237).

Aftercare

Another key opportunity for incorporating the risk and resilience framework at the periphery of juvenile justice is aftercare, as best exemplified by the Intensive Aftercare Program model (IAP) developed by Altschuler and Armstrong (1991, 1998). IAP includes the following key components:

- case management services:
- a collaborative network of community services;
- services that are "backed in" to the residential facility (i.e., the case manager meets with the youth, conducts an assessment, develops a release plan, and arranges for relevant community-based service providers to visit the youth in the facility prior to release);
- a "step-down" process, in which youths move first into a transition phase, gradually experiencing more community interaction during the last weeks of incarceration, and then go on to closely supervised release, and finally to decreased supervision; and
- a system of graduated sanctions to help control behavior during aftercare. (Altschuler & Armstrong, 1998; Altschuler, Armstrong, & MacKenzie, 1999)

The Boys & Girls Clubs of America has recently attempted to blend IAP and strengths-based principles in juvenile aftercare programs in several sites (Barton, 2006). A case example illustrating ways to incorporate strengths into aftercare programming is discussed in Box 2.

Incorporating Strengths in Juvenile Aftercare

When Raymond was a 12-year-old, he was committed for possession of a firearm on school property. He was sent to one of two maximum security facilities for boys in the state. He struggled with the program at the facility and spent 2 years at the facility before he was released on 6 months parole and allowed to live with his mother. Just after he completed his parole, while staying with his father in a nearby county, he was arrested on a battery charge. He was placed back with his mother and ordered to serve home detention for 3 months. The day after he was released from home detention, he left the house without permission. He used drugs he stole from his aunt, who also lived in the house, and his mother reported him to the police. He resisted arrest and was committed back to the state, sent to the second maximum security facility as a 15-year-old.

This time, he completed the treatment program at the state facility with few problems. Although he could have been released after 10 months, there were concerns about him living with either parent. The mother lived in a trailer with four children and a husband. The father owned a strip club and was at work every night for the entire night. Consequently, Raymond would have been without supervision in his father's home. Raymond preferred to live with his father; his mother resented this and acted to prevent it. Their relationship was very strained as a result, and they broke off all contact. Raymond no longer knows how to get in touch with his mother. Finally, arrangements were made for Raymond to be released to a group home. He spent 7 days at the group home before he was arrested for shoplifting. He was recommitted to the secure care facility. He is now 17-years-old and expects to be released this fall.

He currently has access to an aftercare program that began working with him in the facility. In addition to many risk factors (early involvement with the system, aggression, broken home, strained relationship with his mother, negative peer involvement), his aftercare worker has identified several strengths in Raymond. He is strong academically; is a skilled athlete; is competent in using assertiveness to avoid peer pressure; is eager to please adults and people in authority; is developing skills in decision making and problem solving; and is able to reflect critically on his own thinking, choices, and behavior. He has demonstrated good insights into his relationships with his family, expressed that he wants to work with a mentor, and has been open to asking for assistance. He enjoys working on service projects and willingly takes a leadership role, if allowed.

(Continued)

(Continued)

Raymond and his father have a good relationship, and each cares about the other. His father is planning to remarry soon. A placement with his father may be possible this time, if the father's new wife is willing and able to help with evening supervision. Raymond expects to complete his GED while in the facility and wants to go to college. His aftercare worker will help him apply to the local technical college. Other components of his re-entry plan include providing Raymond with an opportunity to participate in Youth as Resources service projects with other prosocial youth and perhaps to work at a Boys & Girls Club, where he can combine his athletic interests with his leadership skills. He will be referred for counseling to help him deal with his feelings about his relationship with his mother. An important aspect of this aftercare program is the continuity of the mentoring relationship with the aftercare worker begun in the facility and continuing into the community.

SOURCE: Adapted from Dr. Roger Jarjoura, director, Aftercare for Indiana Through Mentoring, personal communication, June 10, 2004. Used with permission.

Evidence for the effectiveness of juvenile aftercare programs is mixed. The National Council on Crime and Delinquency (NCCD) evaluated three IAP pilot sites over a 5-year period, using an experimental design that included random assignment to IAP and a control group in each site (Wiebush, Wagner, McNulty, Wang, & Le, 2005). The study concluded that recidivism rates were high for both the IAP and control groups. These disappointing results were tempered somewhat by cautions related to small sample sizes and by the observation that many youths in the control groups may have received enhanced parole services as well. Finally, there was some evidence that among the IAP participants, those who received higher levels of services both pre- and postrelease showed lower rates of recidivism (Wiebush et al., 2005). A more recent evaluation of the Boys & Girls Clubs of America's juvenile re-entry programs, which are also based on the IAP model, produced findings similar to those of the NCCD study (Barton, Jarjoura, & Rosay, 2008). The authors attributed the lack of strong evidence for effectiveness to many daunting implementation challenges faced by the sites. However, Aos (2004) found promising results in a quasi-experimental evaluation of Washington State's Family Integrated Transitions (FIT) program. Although not identical to the IAP model, the FIT program shares many important elements, including family involvement, a collaborative team approach to case management, and continuity between prerelease and postrelease phases.

Summary

Juvenile justice policies and practices are society's way of confronting and dealing with behavior beyond the social norms, that is, juvenile delinquency. The United States historically has vacillated between an emphasis on punishment and treatment of juvenile delinquents, with neither approach proving very effective. The juvenile court was established in 1899 to formally recognize that children were distinct from adults. However, in the last century, the vacillation between punishment and treatment emphases has intensified. To illustrate, the juvenile court has taken on more of the trappings of the adult system, and the end of the 20th century produced a wave of "get tough" policies such as zero tolerance and the increased use of transfers to the adult court, despite a decline in juvenile crime rates since the late 1990s.

An examination of juvenile justice policy and practice trends reveals little explicit connection to the research and theory that has grown from the risk and resilience perspective until very recently, and to date, its impact has been limited. The risk and resilience framework evolved from two initially separate streams of research: developmental psychopathology, using epidemiological methods to identify the causes of youth problem behaviors, and longitudinal studies of resilience seeking to understand why some people attain positive developmental outcomes in the face of high risk or adversity. A reasonable consensus has emerged regarding an array of risk and protective or promotive factors at various ecological levels—the individual, family, peers, neighborhood, community, and society—that influence the probability of delinquency and other youth problems.

It is logical to assume that this knowledge can help the juvenile justice system develop policies and practices that, by reducing risk and enhancing protection, prevent delinquency or its recurrence. At present, the most common application of this framework has been the proliferation of risk-assessment instruments to guide placement or treatment decisions at various points in the juvenile justice process. This chapter has argued that despite the impressive aggregate claims of the risk and resilience research, this risk-assessment approach, although perhaps an improvement over purely discretionary, clinical judgment, has limitations because it primarily presumes a degree of predictive accuracy at the individual level that does not exist.

This chapter has presented several promising strategies for incorporating risk and resilience into the juvenile justice system, including community-wide prevention initiatives, targeted prevention in schools or with families, and interventions such as individualized wraparound services and after-care programs that aim to work across system boundaries. Truly meaning-ful change in juvenile justice policies and practices requires a culture shift in the way system actors view youth and the goals of the system. This shift should be based on the ecological risk and resilience framework, pursue positive youth development goals in addition to the prevention and control of delinquency, and incorporate a strengths-based, collaborative approach to practice. This chapter highlighted some recent attempts to transform the juvenile justice culture, including the explicit adoption of a strength-based, positive youth development approach in some jurisdictions and the Annie E. Casey Foundation's JDAI. All of these strategies include making the bound-aries of the juvenile justice system more permeable through formal collabo-rations with other community entities. In this way, the partnering agencies and stakeholders can reinforce the application of the risk and resilience framework, thereby enhancing the juvenile justice system's ability to achieve all three of its goals: public safety protection, accountability, *and* competency development.

QUESTIONS FOR DISCUSSION

1. What are the main obstacles to incorporating the principles of risk, protection, and resilience into juvenile justice policies and practices?

2. In what ways is the strengths perspective compatible with the principles of risk, protection, and resilience?

3. What are major factors leading to reforms or modifications of juvenile justice policies and practices? Which, if any, are most apt to lead to sustained changes? Why?

4. How do risk and protective factors for juvenile delinquency compare to those identified for other youth problems, such as substance abuse or poor school adjustment?

References

Aisenberg, E., & Herrenkohl, T. (2008). Community violence in context: Risk and resilience in children and families. *Journal of Interpersonal Violence, 23,* 296–315. doi:10.1177/0886260507312287

Akers, R. L. (1985). *Deviant behavior: A social learning approach* (3rd ed.). Belmont, CA: Wadsworth.

Altschuler, D. M. (2005). Policy and program perspectives on the transition to adulthood for adolescents in the juvenile justice system. In D. W. Osgood, E. M. Foster, C. Flanagan & G. R. Ruth (Eds.), *On your own without a net:*

The transition to adulthood for vulnerable populations (pp. 92–113). Chicago: University of Chicago Press.

Altschuler, D. M., & Armstrong, T. L. (1991). *Intensive community-based aftercare prototype: Policies and procedures.* Baltimore: The Johns Hopkins University, Institute for Policy Studies.

Altschuler, D. M., & Armstrong, T. L. (1998). Recent developments in juvenile aftercare: Assessment, findings, and promising programs. In A. R. Roberts (Ed.), *Juvenile justice: Policies, programs, and services* (2nd ed., pp. 448–472). Chicago: Nelson-Hall.

Altschuler, D. M., Armstrong, T. L., & MacKenzie, D. L. (1999). *Reintegration, supervised release, and intensive aftercare* (NCJ 175715). Washington, DC: U.S. Department of Justice, Office of Juvenile Justice and Delinquency Prevention.

Andrews, D. A., Zinger, I., Hoge, R. D., Bonta, J., Gendreau, P., & Cullen, F. T. (1990). Does correctional treatment work? A clinically relevant and psychologically informed meta-analysis. *Criminology, 28,* 369–404. doi:10.1111/j.1745–9125.1990.tb01330.x

Anthony, E. J. (1987). Children at high risk for psychosis growing up successfully. In E. J. Anthony & B. J. Cohler (Eds.). *The invulnerable child* (pp. 147–184). New York: Guilford Press.

Anthony, E. K., Alter, C. F., & Jenson, J. M. (2009). Development of a risk and resilience-based out-of-school time program for children and youths. *Social Work, 54,* 45–55.

Aos, S. (2004). *Washington State's Family Integrated Transitions program for juvenile offenders: Outcome evaluation and benefit-cost analysis.* Olympia: Washington State Institute for Public Policy. Retrieved from http://www.wsipp.wa.gov/rptfiles/04–12–1201.pdf

Aos, S., Phipps, P., Barnoski, R., & Lieb, R. (2001). *The comparative costs and benefits of programs to reduce crime: Version 4.0.* Olympia: Washington State Institute for Public Policy.

Barton, W. H. (2002). Juvenile justice: Community treatment. In J. Dressler (Ed.-in-chief), *Encyclopedia of crime and justice* (2nd ed., pp. 917–927). New York: Macmillan Reference.

Barton, W. H. (2004). Bridging juvenile justice and positive youth development. In S. F. Hamilton & M. A. Hamilton (Eds.), *The youth development handbook: Coming of age in American communities* (pp. 77–102). Thousand Oaks, CA: Sage.

Barton, W. H. (2006). Incorporating the strengths perspective into intensive juvenile aftercare. *Western Criminology Review, 7*(2), 48–61.

Barton, W. H., & Butts, J. A. (2008). *Building on strength: Positive youth development in juvenile justice programs.* Chicago: Chapin Hall Center for Children at the University of Chicago. Retrieved from http://www.chapinhall.org/article_abstract.aspx?ar=1471

Barton, W. H., Jarjoura, G. R., & Rosay, A. B. (2008). *Evaluation of the Boys and Girls Clubs of America targeted re-entry initiative. Final report.* Unpublished manuscript.

Barton, W. H., Mackin, J. R., & Fields, J. (2008). Assessing youth strengths in a residential juvenile correctional program. *Residential Treatment for Children & Youth, 23*(3/4), 11–36.

Bazemore, G., & Terry, W. C. (1997). Developing delinquent youths: A reintegrative model for rehabilitation and a new role for the juvenile justice system. *Child Welfare, 76,* 665–716.

Bazemore, G., & Umbreit, M. (1995). *Balanced and restorative justice: Program summary* (NCJ 149727). Washington, DC: U.S. Department of Justice, Office of Juvenile Justice and Delinquency Prevention.

Beck, A. J., Harrison, P. M., & Guerino, P. (2010). Sexual victimization in juvenile facilities reported by youth, 2008–09. *Bureau of Justice Statistics Special Report.* Washington, DC: U.S. Department of Justice, Office of Justice Programs, Bureau of Justice Statistics. Retrieved from http://bjs.ojp.usdoj.gov/index.cfm?ty=pbdetail&iid=2113

Becker, H. S. (1963). *Outsiders: Studies in the sociology of deviance.* New York: Free Press.

Bernard, T. J. (1992). *The cycle of juvenile justice.* New York: Oxford University Press.

Bernburg, J. G., Krohn, M., & Rivera, C. J. (2006). Official labeling, criminal embeddedness, and subsequent delinquency: A longitudinal test of labeling theory. *Journal of Research in Crime and Delinquency, 43,* 67–88. doi:10.1177/0022427805280068

Burchard, J. D., Bruns, E. J., & Burchard, S. N. (2002). The wraparound approach. In B. J. Burns & K. Hoagwood (Eds.), *Community treatment for youth: Evidence-based interventions for severe emotional and behavioral disorders* (pp. 69–90). New York: Oxford University Press.

Butts, J. A., Bazemore, G., & Meroe, A. S. (2010). *Positive youth justice: Framing justice interventions using the concepts of positive youth development.* Washington, DC: Coalition for Juvenile Justice.

Butts, J. A., Buck, J., & Coggeshall, M. B. (2002). *The impact of teen court on young offenders.* Washington, DC: Urban Institute, Justice Policy Center.

Butts, J., Mayer, S., & Ruth, G. (2005). *Focusing juvenile justice on positive youth development.* Chicago: Chapin Hall Center for Children at the University of Chicago.

Catalano, R. F., & Hawkins, J. D. (1996). The social development model: A theory of antisocial behavior. In J. D. Hawkins (Ed.), *Delinquency and crime: Current theories* (pp. 149–197). Cambridge, UK: Cambridge University Press.

Center for the Study and Prevention of Violence. (2010). *Blueprints for violence prevention.* Boulder: University of Colorado, Center for the Study and Prevention of Violence. Retrieved from http://www.colorado.edu/cspv/blueprints/

Choices, Inc. (2010). *The Dawn Project.* Indianapolis, IN: Author. Retrieved from http://www.choicesteam.org/dawn.html

Chung, H. L., Little, M., & Steinberg, L. (2005). The transition to adulthood for adolescents in the juvenile justice system: A developmental perspective. In D. W. Osgood, E. M. Foster, C. Flanagan & G. R. Ruth (Eds.), *On your own without a net: The transition to adulthood for vulnerable populations* (pp. 68–91). Chicago: University of Chicago Press.

Dishion, T. J., McCord, J., & Poulin, F. (1999). When interventions harm. Peer groups and problem behavior. *American Psychologist, 34,* 755–764. doi:10.1037/0003–066X.54.9.755

Dishion, T. J., Spracklen, K. M., & Patterson, G. R. (1996). Deviancy training in male adolescent friendships. *Behavior Therapy, 27,* 373–390. doi:10.1016/S0005–7894(96)80023–2

Dodge, K. A., Dishion, T. J., & Lansford, J. E. (2006). Deviant peer influences in intervention and public policy for youth. *Social Policy Report, 20*(1), Retrieved from http://www.srcd.org/index.php?option=com_content&task=view&id=232&Itemid=550

Drake, E. K., Aos, S., & Miller, M. G. (2009). Evidence-based public policy options to reduce crime and criminal justice costs: Implications for Washington State. *Victims and Offenders, 4,* 170–196. doi:10.1080/15564880802612615

Dryfoos, J. G. (1990). *Adolescents at risk: Prevalence and prevention.* New York: Oxford University Press.

Duchnowski, A. J., Kutash, K., & Friedman, R. M. (2002). Community-based interventions in a system of care and outcomes framework. In B. J. Burns & K. Hoagwood (Eds.), *Community treatment for youth: Evidence-based interventions for severe emotional and behavioral disorders* (pp. 16–37). New York: Oxford University Press.

Durlak, J. A. (1998). Common risk and protective factors in successful prevention programs. *American Journal of Orthopsychiatry, 68,* 512–520. doi:10.1037/h0080360

Eccles, J., & Gootman, J. A. (Eds.). (2002). *Community programs to promote youth development.* Washington, DC: National Academy Press.

Elliott, D. S. (1994). Serious violent offenders: Onset, developmental course, and termination—The American Society of Criminology 1993 presidential address. *Criminology, 32,* 1–21. doi:10.1111/j.1745–9125.1994.tb01144.x

Elliott, D. S., & Ageton, S. (1980). Reconciling race and class differences in self-reported and official estimates of delinquency. *American Sociological Review, 45,* 95–100. doi:10.2307/2095245

Elliott, D. S., Huizinga, D., & Ageton, S. (1985). *Explaining delinquency and drug use.* Beverly Hills, CA: Sage.

Elliott, D. S., Huizinga, D., & Menard, S. (1989). *Multiple problem youth: Delinquency, substance use and mental health problems.* New York: Springer-Verlag.

Epstein, M. H., & Sharma, J. M. (1998). *Behavioral and Emotional Rating Scale (BERS).* Austin, TX: PRO-ED.

Fagan, J., F., & Freeman, R. B. (1999). Crime and work. In M. Tonry (Ed.), *Crime and justice: A review of research* (pp. 225–290). Chicago: University of Chicago Press.

Farrington, D. P. (1991). Childhood aggression and adult violence. In D. Pepler & K. H. Rubin (Eds.), *The development and treatment of childhood aggression* (pp. 2–29). Hillsdale, NJ: Lawrence Erlbaum.

Farrington, D. P., Loeber, R., Stouthamer-Loeber, M., Van Kammen, W. B., & Schmidt, L. (1996). Self-reported delinquency and a combined delinquency seriousness scale based on boys, mothers, and teachers: Concurrent and predictive validity for African-Americans and Caucasians. *Criminology, 34,* 493–517. doi:10.1111/j.1745–9125.1996.tb01217.x

Feld, B. C. (1991). Justice by geography: Urban, suburban, and rural variations in juvenile justice administration. *Journal of Criminal Law and Criminology, 82*(1), 156–210. doi:10.2307/1143795

Feld, B. C. (1999). *Bad kids: Race and the transformation of the juvenile court.* New York: Oxford University Press.

Frabutt, J. M., Di Luca, K. L., & Graves, K. N. (2008). Envisioning a juvenile justice system that supports positive youth development. *Notre Dame Journal of Law, Ethics & Public Policy, 22,* 107–125.

Franklin, C., Grant, D., Corcoran, J., O'Dell, P., & Bultman, L. (1995). *Effectiveness of prevention programs for adolescent pregnancy: A meta-analysis.* Austin: University of Texas at Austin, School of Social Work.

Fraser, M. W., Kirby, L. D., & Smokowski, P. R. (2004). Risk and resilience in childhood. In M. W. Fraser (Ed.), *Risk and resilience in childhood: An ecological perspective* (2nd ed., pp. 13–66). Washington, DC: NASW Press.

Fraser, M. W., & Terzian, M. A. (2005). Risk and resilience in child development: Principles and strategies of practice. In G. P. Mallon & P. McCartt Hess (Eds.), *Child welfare for the twenty-first century: A handbook of practices, policies, and programs* (pp. 55–71). New York: Columbia University Press.

Frazier, C. E., & Bishop, D. M. (1985). The pretrial detention of juveniles and its impact on case dispositions. *Journal of Criminal Law and Criminology, 76*(4), 1132–1152. doi:10.2307/1143504

Frazier, C. E., & Cochran, J. C. (1986). Detention of juveniles: Its effects on subsequent juvenile court processing decisions. *Youth and Society, 17,* 286–305. doi:10.1177/0044118X86017003005

Garmezy, N. (1985). Stress-resistant children: The search for protective factors. In J. E. Stevenson (Ed.), *Recent research in developmental psychopathology* (pp. 213–233). New York: Pergamon Press.

Gatti, U., Tremblay, R. E., & Vitaro, F. (2009). Iatrogenic effect of juvenile justice. *Journal of Child Psychology and Psychiatry, 50,* 991–998. doi:10.1111/j.1469–7610.2008.02057.x

Gavazzi, S. M., Yarcheck, C. M., & Chesney-Lind, M. (2006). Global risk indicators and the role of gender in a juvenile detention sample. *Criminal Justice and Behavior, 33,* 597–612. doi:10.1177/0093854806288184

Goldman, S. K. (1999). The conceptual framework for wraparound: Definition, values, essential elements, and requirements for practice. In B. J. Burns & S. K. Goldman (Eds.), *Systems of care: Promising practices in children's mental health, 1998 Series* (Vol. 4, pp. 27–34). Washington, DC: Center for Effective Collaboration and Practice, American Institutes for Research.

Gottfredson, D. C. (2000). *Schools and delinquency.* New York: Cambridge University Press.

Greenberg, M., & Feinberg, M. (2002). *An evaluation of PCCD's Communities That Care delinquency prevention initiative: Final report* (NCJ 281283). Harrisburg: Pennsylvania State University, College of Human Development.

Hamilton, S. F., Hamilton, M. A., & Pittman, K. (2004). Principles for youth development. In S. F. Hamilton & M. A. Hamilton (Eds.), *The youth development handbook: Coming of age in American communities* (pp. 3–22). Thousand Oaks, CA: Sage.

Hamparian, D. (1978). *The violent few: A study of dangerous juvenile offenders.* Lexington MA: Lexington Books.

Hawkins, D. F., Laub, J. H., & Lauritsen, J. L. (1998). Race, ethnicity, and serious juvenile offending. In R. Loeber & D. P. Farrington (Eds.), *Serious and violent juvenile offenders: Risk factors and successful interventions* (pp. 30–47). Thousand Oaks, CA: Sage.

Hawkins, J. D., Brown, E. C., Oesterle, S., Arthur, M. W., Abbott, R. D., & Catalano, R. F. (2008). Early effects of Communities That Care on targeted risks and initiation of delinquent behavior and substance use. *Journal of Adolescent Health, 43,* 15–22. doi:10.1016/j.jadohealth.2008.01.022

Hawkins, J. D., Catalano, R. F., & Associates. (1992). *Communities That Care: Action for drug abuse prevention.* San Francisco: Jossey-Bass.

Hawkins, J. D., Catalano, R. F., & Miller, J. Y. (1992). Risk and protective factors for alcohol and other drug problems in adolescence and early adulthood: Implications for substance abuse prevention. *Psychological Bulletin, 112,* 64–105. doi:10.1037/0033–2909.112.1.64

Hawkins, J. D., & Herrenkohl, T. I. (2003). Prevention in the school years. In D. P. Farrington & J. W. Coid (Eds.), *Early prevention of adult antisocial behaviour* (pp. 265–291). Cambridge, UK: Cambridge University Press. doi:10.1017/CB09780511489259.009

Hawkins, J. D., Herrenkohl, T. I., Farrington, D. P., Brewer, D., Catalano, R. F., Harachi, T. W., & Cothern, L. (2000). *Predictors of youth violence* (NCJ 179065). Washington, DC: U.S. Department of Justice, Office of Juvenile Justice and Delinquency Prevention.

Hemmelgarn, A. L., Glisson, C., & James, L. R. (2006). Organizational culture and climate: Implications for services and interventions research. *Clinical Psychology: Science and Practice, 13,* 73–89. doi:10.1111/j.1468–2850.2006.00008.x

Hindelang, M. J., Hirschi, T., & Weis, J. G. (1981). *Measuring delinquency.* Beverly Hills, CA: Sage.

Holman, B., & Ziedenberg, J. (2006). *The dangers of detention: The impact of incarcerating youth in detention and other secure facilities.* Washington, DC: Justice Policy Institute. Retrieved from http://www.justicepolicy.org/images/upload/06–11_REP_DangersOfDetention_JJ.pdf

Howell, J. C. (Ed.). (1995). *Guide for implementing the comprehensive strategy for serious, violent, and chronic offenders* (NCJ 153681). Washington, DC: U.S. Department of Justice, Office of Juvenile Justice and Delinquency Prevention.

Howell, J. C. (2003). *Preventing and reducing juvenile delinquency: A comprehensive framework.* Thousand Oaks, CA: Sage.

Hubbard, D. J., & Pratt, T. C. (2002). A meta-analysis of the predictors of delinquency among girls. *Journal of Offender Rehabilitation, 34*(3), 1–13. doi:10.1300/J076v34n03_01

Huizinga, D., Loeber, R., Thornberry, T. P., & Cothern, L. (2000). *Co-occurrence of delinquency and other problem behaviors* (NCJ 182211). Washington, DC: U.S. Department of Justice, Office of Juvenile Justice and Delinquency Prevention.

Jenson, J. M., & Fraser, M. W. (2006). Toward the integration of child, youth, and family policy: Applying principles of risk, resilience, and ecological theory. In J. M. Jenson & M. W. Fraser (Eds.), *Social policy for children and families: A risk and resilience perspective* (pp. 265–279). Thousand Oaks, CA: Sage.

Kamradt, B. (2000). Wraparound Milwaukee: Aiding youth with mental health needs. *Juvenile Justice Journal, 7.* Retrieved from http://www.ncjrs.org/html/ojjdp/jjjnl_2000_4/wrap.html

Kendziora, K. T., & Osher, D. M. (2004). Fostering resilience among youth in the juvenile justice system. In C. S. Clauss-Ehlers & M. D. Wiest (Eds.), *Community planning to foster resilience in children* (pp. 177–195). New York: Kluwer Academic.

Kurtz, D., & Linnemann, T. (2006). Improving probation through client strengths: Evaluating strength based treatments for at-risk youth. *Western Criminology Review, 7*(1), 9–19.

Latessa, E. J. (2004). The challenge of change: Correctional programs and evidence-based practices. *Criminology and Public Policy, 3,* 547–559.

Lattimore, P. K., Brumbaugh, S., Visher, C., Lindquist, C. H., Winterfield, L., Salas, M., & Zweig, J. (2004). *National Portrait of the Serious and Violent Offender Reentry Initiative* (RTI Report 8805). Research Triangle Park, NC: Research Triangle Institute. Retrieved from http://www.svori-evaluation.org/index.cfm?fuseaction=nationalportrait

Laub, J. H., & Sampson, R. J. (2003). *Shared beginnings, divergent lives.* Cambridge, MA: Harvard University Press.

Lederman, C. S., Dakof, G. A., Larrea, M. A., & Li, H. (2004). Characteristics of adolescent females in juvenile detention. *International Journal of Law and Psychiatry, 27,* 321–337. doi:10.1016/j.ijlp.2004.03.009

Lemert, E. M. (1951). *Social pathology.* New York: McGraw-Hill.

Lerner, S. (1986). *Bodily harm: The pattern of fear and violence at the California Youth Authority.* Bolinas, CA: Common Knowledge Press.

Lipsey, M. (1992). Juvenile delinquency treatment: A meta-analytic inquiry into the variability of effects. In T. D. Cook, H. Cooper, D. S. Cordray, H. Hartman,

L. V. Hedges, R. J. Light, & F. Mosteller (Eds.), *Meta-analysis for explanation: A casebook* (pp. 83–127). New York: Russell Sage Foundation.

Lipsey, M. W., & Derzon, J. H. (1998). Predictors of violent and serious delinquency in adolescence and early adulthood: A synthesis of longitudinal research. In R. Loeber & D. P. Farrington (Eds.), *Serious and violent juvenile offenders: Risk factors and successful interventions* (pp. 86–105). Thousand Oaks, CA: Sage.

Lipsey, M. W., & Wilson, D. B. (1998). Effective intervention for serious juvenile offenders: A synthesis of research. In R. Loeber & D. P. Farrington (Eds.), *Serious and violent juvenile offenders: Risk factors and successful interventions* (pp. 313–345). Thousand Oaks, CA: Sage.

Lipton, D., Martinson, R., & Wilks, J. (1975). *The effectiveness of correctional treatment: A survey of treatment evaluation studies.* New York: Praeger.

Livesy, S., Sickmund, M., & Sladky, A. (2009). *Juvenile residential facility census, 2004: Selected findings* (NCJ 222721). Washington, DC: U.S. Department of Justice, Office of Justice Programs, Office of Juvenile Justice and Delinquency Prevention.

Loeber, R., & Farrington, D. P. (Eds.). (1998). *Serious & violent juvenile offenders: Risk factors and successful interventions.* Thousand Oaks, CA: Sage.

Loeber, R., Farrington, D. P., & Petechuk, D. (2003). *Child delinquency: Early intervention and prevention* (NCJ 186162). Washington, DC: Office of Juvenile Justice and Delinquency Prevention. Retrieved May 19, 2004, from http://www .ncjrs.org/pdffiles1/ojjdp/186162.pdf

Loeber, R., Farrington, D. P., Stouthamer-Loeber, M., & van Kammen, W. B. (1998). *Antisocial behavior and mental health problems: Explanatory factors in childhood and adolescence.* Mahwah, NJ: Lawrence Erlbaum.

Lösel, F., & Bender, D. (2003). Protective factors and resilience. In D. P. Farrington & J. W. Coid (Eds.), *Early prevention of adult antisocial behaviour* (pp. 130–204). Cambridge, UK: Cambridge University Press. doi:10.1017/CBO9780511489259.006

Loughran, T. A., Mulvey, E. P., Schubert, C. A., Fagan, J., Piquero, A. R., & Losoya, S. H. (2009). Estimating a dose–response relationship between length of stay and future recidivism in serious juvenile offenders. *Criminology, 47,* 699–740. doi:10.1111/j.1745–9125.2009.00165.x

Lyons, J. S., Griffin, E., Fazio, M., & Lyons, M. B. (1999). *Child and adolescent needs and strengths: An information integration tool for children and adolescents with mental health challenges (CANS-MH). Manual.* Chicago: Buddin Praed Foundation.

Mackin, J. R., Weller, J. M, Tarte, J. M., & Nissen, L. B. (2005). Breaking new ground in juvenile justice settings: Assessing for competencies in juvenile offenders. *Juvenile and Family Court Journal,* 25–37. doi:10.1111/j.1755–6988.2005.tb00104.x

Maloney, D., Romig, D., & Armstrong, T. (1988). Juvenile probation: The balanced approach. *Juvenile and Family Court Journal, 39,* 1–62. doi:10.1111/j.1755–6988.1988.tb00623.x

Mann, E. A., & Reynolds, A. J. (2006). Early intervention and juvenile delinquency prevention: Evidence from the Chicago Longitudinal Study. *Social Work Research, 30,* 153–167.

Masten, A. S. (1994). Resilience in individual development: Successful adaptation despite risk and adversity. In M. C. Wang & E. W. Gordon (Eds.), *Educational resilience in inner-city America: Challenges and opportunities* (pp. 3–25). Hillsdale, NJ: Lawrence Erlbaum.

McCorkle, L. W., Elias, A., & Bixby, F. L. (1958). *The Highfields story: A unique experiment in the treatment of juvenile delinquents.* New York: Holt.

McGarrell, E. F., Olivares, K., Crawford, K., & Kroovand, N. (2000). *Returning justice to the community: The Indianapolis restorative justice experiment.* Indianapolis, IN: Hudson Institute, Crime Control Policy Center.

McNeese, C. A. (1998). Juvenile justice policy: Current trends and twenty-first century issues. In A. R. Roberts (Ed.), *Juvenile justice: Policies, programs, and services* (2nd ed., pp. 21–39). Chicago: Nelson-Hall.

Mendel, R. A. (2007). Beyond detention: System transformation through juvenile detention reform. *Pathways to Juvenile Detention Reform* (Vol. 14). Baltimore, MD: Annie E. Casey Foundation.

Mendel, R. A. (2009). *Two decades of JDAI: From demonstration project to national standard. A progress report.* Baltimore: Annie E. Casey Foundation.

Minor, K. I., Wells, J. B., & Angel, E. (2008). Recidivism among juvenile offenders following release from residential placements: Multivariate predictors and gender differences. *Journal of Offender Rehabilitation, 46,* 171–188. doi:10.1080/10509670802143474

Moffit, T. E. (1993). Adolescence-limited and lift-course-persistent antisocial behavior: A developmental taxonomy. *Psychological Review, 100,* 674–701. doi:10.1037/0033–295X.100.4.674

Moffit, T. E., & Caspi, A. (2001). Childhood predictors differentiate life-course persistent and adolescence-limited antisocial pathways among males and females. *Development and Psychopathology, 132,* 355–375. doi:10.1017/S0954579401002097

Moffitt, T. E., Caspi, A., Harrington, H., & Milne, B. J. (2002). Males on the life-course-persistent and adolescence-limited antisocial pathways: Follow-up at 26 years. *Development and Psychopathology, 14,* 179–207. doi:10.1017/S0954579402001104

Nash, J. K., & Bowen, G. L., (1999). Perceived crime and informal social control in the neighborhood as a context for adolescent behavior: A risk and resilience perspective. *Social Work Research, 23,* 171–186.

National Center for Juvenile Justice. (1991). *Desktop guide to good juvenile probation practice.* Washington, DC: U.S. Department of Justice, Office of Juvenile Justice and Delinquency Prevention.

Nissen, L. B., Mackin, J. R., Weller, J. M., & Tarte, J. M. (2005). Identifying strengths as fuel for change: A conceptual and theoretical framework for the Youth Competency Assessment. *Juvenile and Family Court Journal,* 1–15. doi:10.1111/j.1755–6988.2005.tb00099.x

Office of the Surgeon General. (2001). *Youth violence: A report of the Surgeon General.* Washington, DC: U.S. Department of Health and Human Services. Retrieved from http://www.surgeongeneral.gov/library/youthviolence/

O'Malley, P. M., Bachman, J. G., & Johnston, L. D. (1983). Reliability and consistency in self reports of drug use. *International Journal of Addictions, 18,* 805–824.

Parent, D. G., Leiter, V., Kennedy, S., Levins, L., Wentworth, D., & Wilcox, S. (1994). *Conditions of confinement: Juvenile detention and corrections facilities. Research summary* (NCJ 145793). Washington, DC: U.S. Department of Justice, Office of Juvenile Justice and Delinquency Prevention.

Patterson, G. R., Reid, J. B., & Dishion, T. J. (1992). *Antisocial boys.* Eugene, OR: Castalia.

Petteruti, A., Walsh, N., & Velázquez, T. (2009). *The cost of confinement: Why good juvenile justice policies make good fiscal sense.* Washington, DC: Justice Policy Institute. Retrieved from http://www.justicepolicy.org/images/upload/09_05_REP_CostsOfConfinement_JJ_PS.pdf

Pittman, K., & Irby, M. (1996). *Preventing problems or promoting development: Competing priorities or inseparable goals?* Baltimore: International Youth Foundation.

Pollard, J. A., Hawkins, J. D., & Arthur, M. W. (1999). Risk and protection: Are both necessary to understand diverse behavioral outcomes in adolescence? *Social Work Research, 23,* 145–158.

Puzzanchera, C. (2009). *Juvenile arrests 2008* (NCJ 228479). Washington, DC: Office of Juvenile Justice and Delinquency Prevention. Retrieved from http://www.ncjrs.gov/pdffiles1/ojjdp/228479.pdf

Puzzanchera, C., Sladky, A., & Kang, W. (2009). *Easy access to juvenile populations: 1990–2008.* Retrieved from http://www.ojjdp.ncjrs.gov/ojstatbb/ezapop/

Richart, D., Brooks, K., & Soler, M. (2003). *Unintended consequences: The impact of zero tolerance and other exclusionary polices on Kentucky students.* Washington, DC: Building Blocks for Youth. Retrieved from http://www.buildingblocksforyouth.org/kentucky/kentucky.pdf

Rowe, D. C. (2001). *Biology and crime.* Los Angeles: Roxbury Press.

Rutter, M. (1985). Resilience in the face of adversity: Protective factors and resistance to psychiatric disorders. *British Journal of Psychiatry, 147,* 598–611. doi:10.1192/bjp.147.6.598

Rutter, M. (2001). Psychosocial adversity: Risk, resilience and recovery. In J. M. Richman & M. W. Fraser (Eds.), *The context of youth violence: Resilience, risk, and protection* (pp. 13–41). Westport, CT: Praeger.

Saleebey, D. (Ed.). (2006). *The strengths perspective in social work practice* (4th ed.). Boston: Pearson Education, Allyn & Bacon.

Sameroff, A. J. (1999). Ecological perspectives on developmental risk. In J. D. Osofsky & H. E. Fitzgerald (Eds.), *WAIMH handbook of infant mental health: Vol. 4. Infant mental health groups at high risk* (pp. 223–248). New York: Wiley.

Sampson, R. J., Raudenbush, S. W., & Earls, R. (1997). Neighborhoods and violent crime: A multilevel study of collective efficacy. *Science, 277,* 918–924.

Scales, P. C., & Leffert, N. (1999). *Developmental assets: A synthesis of scientific research on adolescent development.* Minneapolis, MN: Search Institute.

Schwartz, R. G. (2001). Juvenile justice and positive youth development. In P. L. Benson & K. Pittman (Eds.), *Trends in youth development: Visions, realities and challenges* (pp. 231–268). Boston: Kluwer Academic.

Sickmund, M. (2003). *Juveniles in court* (NCJ 195420). Washington, DC: Office of Juvenile Justice and Delinquency Prevention. Retrieved from http://www.ncjrs.org/pdffiles1/ojjdp/195420.pdf

Sickmund, M., Sladky, T. J., & Kang, W. (2008). *Census of juveniles in residential placement databook.* Retrieved from http://www.ojjdp.ncjrs.gov/ojstatbb/cjrp/

Skiba, R., Simmons, A., Staudinger L., Rausch, M., Dow, G., & Feggins, R. (2003, May). *Consistent removal: Contributions of school discipline to the school-prison pipeline.* Paper presented at the School to Prison Pipeline Conference, Harvard Civil Rights Project, Cambridge, MA.

Snyder, H. N., & Sickmund, M. (1999). *Juvenile offenders and victims: 1999 national report.* Pittsburgh, PA: National Center for Juvenile Justice.

Snyder, H. N., & Sickmund, M. (2006). *Juvenile offenders and victims: 2006 national report* (NCJ 212906). Washington, DC: U.S. Department of Justice, Office of Justice Programs, Office of Juvenile Justice and Delinquency Prevention.

Stanfield, R. (1999). The JDAI story: Building a better juvenile detention system. In *Pathways to Juvenile Detention Reform, Overview.* Baltimore, MD: Annie E. Casey Foundation.

Stouthamer-Loeber, M., Loeber, R., Wei, E., Farrington, D. P., & Wikström, P. H. (2002). Risk and promotive effects in the explanation of persistent serious delinquency in boys. *Journal of Consulting and Clinical Psychology, 70,* 111–123. doi:10.1037/0022-006X.70.1.111

Stroul, B. A., & Friedman, R. M. (1986). *A system of care for seriously emotionally disturbed children and youth.* Washington, DC: CASSP Technical Assistance Center, Georgetown University Child Development Center.

Theokas, C., & Lerner, R. M. (2006). Observed ecological assets in families, schools, and neighborhoods: Conceptualization, measurement, and relations with positive and negative developmental outcomes. *Applied Developmental Science, 10,* 61–74. doi:10.1207/s1532480xads1002_2

Thornberry, T. P., Huizinga, D., & Loeber, R. (1995). The prevention of serious delinquency and violence: Implications from the program of research on the causes and correlates of delinquency. In J. C. Howell, B. Krisberg, J. D. Hawkins, & J. J. Wilson (Eds.), *Serious, violent, and chronic juvenile offenders: A sourcebook* (pp. 213–237). Thousand Oaks, CA: Sage.

Tierney, J., Grossman, J., & Resch, N. (1995). *Making a difference: An impact study of Big Brothers/Big Sisters.* Philadelphia: Public/Private Ventures.

Torbet, P., & Thomas, D. (2005). *Advancing competency development: A white paper for Pennsylvania.* Pittsburgh, PA: National Center for Juvenile Justice.

Total Criminal Defense. (2010). *Juvenile court jurisdiction.* Retrieved from http://www.totalcriminaldefense.com/juvenile-crime/who-is-a-juvenile.aspx

Tremblay, R. E., & Craig, W. M. (1995). Developmental crime prevention. In M. Tonry & D. P. Farrington (Eds.), *Building a safer society: Strategic approaches to crime prevention* (pp. 151–236). Chicago: University of Chicago Press.

Tremblay, R. E., & Japel, C. (2003). Prevention during pregnancy, infancy, and the preschool years. In D. P. Farrington & J. W. Coid (Eds.), *Early prevention of adult antisocial behaviour* (pp. 205–264). Cambridge, UK: Cambridge University Press. doi:10.1017/CB09780511489259.007

Trulson, C. R., Marquart. J. W., Mullings, J. L., & Caeti, T. J. (2005). In between adolescence and adulthood. Recidivism outcomes of a cohort of state delinquents. *Youth Violence and Juvenile Justice, 3,* 355–387. doi:10.1177/1541204005278802

U.S. Census Bureau. (2008). *U.S. interim projections by age, sex, race, and Hispanic origin: 2000–2050.* Washington, DC: Author. Retrieved from http://www.census.gov/population/www/projections/usinterimproj/

VanDenBerg, J. E., & Grealish, M. E. (1996). Individualized services and supports through the wraparound process: Philosophy and procedures. *Journal of Child and Family Studies, 5,* 7–21. doi:10.1007/BF02234675

Vorath, H., & Brendtro, L. K. (1974). *Positive peer culture.* Chicago: Aldine.

Wehlage, G., Rutter, R. A., Smith, G. A., Lesko, N., & Fernandez, R. R. (1989). *Reducing the risk: Schools as communities of support.* London: Falmer Press.

Werner, E. E., & Smith, R. S. (2001). *Journeys from childhood to midlife: Risk, resilience, and recovery.* Ithaca, NY: Cornell University Press.

White, J. L., Moffitt, T. E., Earls, F., Robins, L. N., & Silva, P. A. (1990). How early can we tell? Predictors of childhood conduct disorder and adolescent delinquency. *Criminology, 29,* 507–533. doi:10.1111/j.1745–9125.1990.tb01337.x

Wiebush, R. G., Baird, C., Krisberg, B., & Onek, D. (1995). Risk assessment and classification for serious, violent, and chronic juvenile offenders. In J. C. Howell, B. Krisberg, J. D. Hawkins, & J. J. Wilson (Eds.), *Serious, violent, & chronic juvenile offenders: A sourcebook* (pp. 171–212). Thousand Oaks, CA: Sage.

Wiebush, R. G., Wagner, D., McNulty, B., Wang, Y., & Le, T. N. (2005). *Implementation and outcome evaluation of the Intensive Aftercare Program: Final report* (NCJ 206177). Washington, DC: U.S. Department of Justice, Office of Juvenile Justice and Delinquency Prevention.

Williams, J. H., Ayers, C. D., Abbott, R. D., Hawkins, J. D., & Catalano, R. F. (1999). Racial differences in risk factors for delinquency and substance use among adolescents. *Social Work Research, 23,* 241–256.

Williams, J. H., Ayers, C. D., Van Dorn, R. A., & Arthur, M. W. (2004). Risk and protective factors in the development of delinquency and conduct disorder.

In M. W. Fraser (Ed.), *Risk and resilience in childhood: An ecological perspective* (2nd ed., pp. 209–249). Washington, DC: NASW Press.

Wilson, J. J., & Howell, J. C. (1993). *A comprehensive strategy for serious, violent, and chronic juvenile offenders: Program summary* (NCJ 143453). Washington, DC: U.S. Department of Justice, Office of Juvenile Justice and Delinquency Prevention.

Wolfgang, M. E., Figlio, R. M., & Sellin, T. (1972). *Delinquency in a birth cohort.* Chicago: University of Chicago Press.

Wolfgang, M., Thornberry, T. P., & Figlio, R. M. (1987). *From boy to man, from delinquency to crime: Follow up to the Philadelphia birth cohort of 1945.* Chicago: University of Chicago Press.

Zahn, M. A., Day, J. C., Mihalic, S. F., & Tichavsky, L. (2009). Determining what works for girls in the juvenile justice system: A summary of evaluation evidence. *Crime & Delinquency, 55,* 266–293. doi:10.1177/0011128708330649

Additional Reading

Bazemore, G., & Walgrave, L. (Eds.). (1999). *Restorative juvenile justice: Repairing the harm of youth crime.* Monsey, NY: Criminal Justice Press.

Bernard, T. J. (1992). *The cycle of juvenile justice.* New York: Oxford University Press.

Hamilton, S. F., Hamilton, M. A., & Pittman, K. (2004). Principles for youth development. In S. F. Hamilton & M. A. Hamilton (Eds.), *The youth development handbook: Coming of age in American communities* (pp. 3–22). Thousand Oaks, CA: Sage.

Howell, J. C. (2003). *Preventing and reducing juvenile delinquency: A comprehensive framework.* Thousand Oaks, CA: Sage.

Mendel, R. A. (2000). *Less hype, more help: Reducing juvenile crime, what works–and what doesn't.* Washington, DC: American Youth Policy Forum. Retrieved from http://www.aypf.org/publications/mendel/index.htmll

Web-Based Resources

Annie E. Casey Foundation, http://www.aecf.org/

Building Blocks for Youth, http://www.buildingblocksforyouth.org/

Center for the Study and Prevention of Violence (Blueprints), http://www.colorado.edu/cspv/index.html

Office of Juvenile Justice and Delinquency Prevention (OJJDP), http://ojjdp.ncjrs.gov/

OJJDP: Model Programs Guide, http://www2.dsgonline.com/mpg/

OJJDP: Statistical Briefing Book, http://ojjdp.ncjrs.gov/ojstatbb/default.asp

Washington State Institute for Public Policy, http://www.wsipp.wa.gov/intro.asp

10

Toward the Integration of Child, Youth, and Family Policy

Applying Principles of Risk, Resilience, and Ecological Theory

Jeffrey M. Jenson

Mark W. Fraser

The chapters in this book describe policies and programs aimed at pressing problems facing American children and their families. These policies—and the services they have generated—represent a complex array of legislative, administrative, and judicial responses to social and health problems affecting children. Identifying and analyzing major policy responses to the challenges confronted by children and their families is a difficult undertaking for legislators, governmental officials, judges, scholars and other experts. Imagine, then, the confusion experienced by a child, adolescent, or parent receiving assistance in one or more of the service systems reviewed in this book. Unfortunately, no road map exists to guide family members through the labyrinth of programs and agencies that provide services for children and youth. For many families, what we call the "service system" is not a system. Rather, it is a maze of programs and procedures with varying eligibility requirements and service definitions. In their complexity, these systems too often wind up compromising the good intentions of advocates, policymakers, and practitioners.

To try to make sense of public policies in terms of their historical development and current dimensions, chapter authors have applied a risk and resilience framework that is grounded in ecological theory. In the following section, we summarize their findings using the constructs of risk and protection. The second section outlines a developmental process to guide the creation and implementation of a logical continuum of policies and programs for children, youth, and families.

Policies and Programs Across Service Systems

This book has traced the origins and evolution of public policies that define major American service systems for children, youth, and families. Chapter authors have used the principles of risk and resilience to describe and assess policy responses to a range of child and adolescent problems and conditions. Each chapter began with a review of risk and protective factors that were relevant to problem behaviors or to conditions within particular policy domains, such as child welfare and mental health.

Services in the areas of income maintenance, child welfare, developmental disabilities, education, health, juvenile justice, mental health, and substance abuse are usually developed vertically with separate funding streams and administrative structures; however, the reader is likely to have been struck by the similarity of risk and protective factors across substantive domains. Prior reviews of risk and protection have also noted the overlap of risk and protective factors across problem domains (Fraser, Kirby, & Smokowski, 2004; Hawkins, Catalano, & Miller, 1992). The similarity of factors related to different service systems is a clue both to the complexity of public responses to issues confronting children and families and to the potential for reform. In Chapter 1, we identified common risk and protective factors for childhood and adolescent problems at the environmental, interpersonal, social, and individual levels of influence. These characteristics and conditions are ubiquitous across all the policy domains discussed in the book.

The presence of common risk and protective factors for different childhood and adolescent behaviors and conditions affords a special opportunity to think systemically about creating policies that address the root causes of problem behaviors. For example, the authors in this volume have indicated that a number of common environmental factors, such as poverty, poor parenting, and community disorganization, are associated with juvenile delinquency, substance abuse, and child maltreatment. It follows, then, that these risk factors should become the targets of coordinated and integrated policy and program responses in the juvenile justice, substance abuse, and child welfare systems.

A parallel theme that emerged from each chapter concerned the lack of attention in policy development that has been afforded to the underlying correlates of child and adolescent problems. On balance, chapters described an incremental and reactive approach to the creation of policies that collect over time to form the basis for programs in public service systems for children, youth, and families. Policies tend to be the product of reform cycles that stem from changes in the nature and prevalence of social and health problems. For example, the rubella epidemic of the mid-1960s increased the number of children with severe auditory and visual disabilities. The sudden increase in the population with specials needs contributed to the reform of special education policies; through the Education for All Handicapped Children Act (P.L. 94–142) in 1975, public schools were provided with resources to serve children with disabling conditions that had once been considered so severe that only institutional care was thought appropriate. When incidence and prevalence rates increase dramatically, the attention of the public and policymakers is diverted to particular service systems or programs. When the prevalence of problems increases, policy reforms tend to be introduced at a fast pace, but often without adequate consideration of unintended consequences or long-term effects.

This pattern of hurried, inadequately considered policy is common. In Chapter 9, Barton noted the cyclical nature of juvenile justice policy, which is characterized by a shifting emphasis on rehabilitation and punishment. This revolving cycle of policy has defined a myriad of reforms ranging from the creation of probation in the first juvenile courts of the early 1900s to recent judicial waiver procedures that permit juvenile offenders to be tried in criminal courts and exposed to adult sanctions. Barton noted correctly that officials in the juvenile justice system are currently debating the merits of policy changes made in the mid-1990s, which led to a greater emphasis on punishing young offenders. Similarly, Fraser (Chapter 5) identified fluctuations in mental health policy based on evolving beliefs about the appropriate role of institutional and community-based care for those with serious mental illnesses. In addition, Pecora and Harrison-Jackson (Chapter 3) traced the evolution of child welfare policy through periods that saw dramatic changes in social norms regarding child abuse and neglect. Examples of the cyclical and reformist nature of social policy for children and families are numerous.

Only the naive would not recognize the important contribution of social norms and public perceptions to public policy. After all, legislation is largely a result of the public's reaction to social conditions and behavioral patterns. The discussion of the No Child Left Behind Act (P.L. 107–110) provided by Frey, Walker, and Perry in Chapter 4 illustrated the power of public perception in reshaping education. Public outcry for school reform and accountability in the latter part of the 1990s was reflected in many provisions of the act. Similar examples can be drawn from the evolution of public policies in the antipoverty (Williams Shanks and Danziger's Chapter 2) and developmental disabilities (Parish, Whisnant, and Swain's Chapter 7) fields.

The recent passage of the national Patient Protection and Affordable Care Act (P. L. 11–148) demonstrates clearly the complexities inherent in balancing incremental change and public perception. Following 18 months of deliberation, the U.S. Senate and House of Representatives passed significant health care legislation in March 2010. Legislative deliberations highlighted the tension between legislators who favored comprehensive reform and legislators who favored incremental change in health care policy. Sentiment for comprehensive or incremental reform was also expressed in public actions taken by members of the medical profession, health insurance companies, and public interest groups. The final bill was the product of a long and contentious debate that led to a series of compromises between officials who held competing views on comprehensive and incremental change. Key provisions of the legislation are designed to make health care more affordable and accountable. The bill bans insurance companies from discriminating against individuals with pre-existing health conditions and provides a means for uninsured people to obtain health care. Specific provisions of the bill will be implemented in defined phases during the next several years. However, the effects of what many public officials perceive to be a comprehensive and radical change in health care policy will likely be debated for many years.

The confluence of public concern and substantive knowledge should be the source of policy. However, the urgency created by public perception and pressure sometimes precipitates changes that produce reforms with unintended and negative side effects. When pressured to respond to real or apparent changes in the nature of a child or adolescent problem behavior, officials frequently turn to convenient policy solutions that address symptoms but fail to address the underlying risk and protective factors associated with that problem (Jenson & Howard, 1998). The result of this process is ineffective, fragmented, and short-lived programs that sometimes do more harm than good. Arguably the greatest and most damaging effect is that such programs add to bureaucratic inertia, making systems more complicated, slower to respond with true reform, and less fertile for creating innovations.

Few service systems for children, youth, and families have developed a deliberate or effective continuum of care. Nearly all chapter authors noted that primary care systems tend to offer a patchwork assortment of programs and services that are seldom delivered to children and families in a sequential or rational fashion. One exception might be the comprehensive strategy for the prevention, treatment, and control of juvenile delinquency, which was adopted by the juvenile justice system in the late 1990s. This strategy, developed by the Office of Juvenile Justice and Delinquency Prevention (Howell, 2003; Zavlek, 2005), outlines a continuum of care and graduated sanctions (i.e., punishments related to the seriousness of offenses) that many states are now using as a framework for handling young offenders. The strategy emphasizes a continuum of service that matches the individual's needs, which are often identified through systematic risk assessment, and the individual's history of offending to appropriate interventions and sanctions. If this strategy continues to be implemented and is shown to be effective, the approach may provide valuable lessons for other service systems.

Finally, careful historical analysis reveals that untested and ineffective policies and programs are repeated over time. One example is the reoccurring use of media campaigns as a way to increase awareness about the dangers of substance use. Jenson, Anthony, and Howard note in Chapter 8 that this strategy had little effect on reducing substance use in the 1970s and early 1980s. However, recent public awareness of increasing drug use among adolescents has rekindled interest in media and information campaigns that alert young people and their parents to the dangers of alcohol and other illicit drug use. As Jenson and colleagues discussed, this interest is reflected in the large allocation of federal funds to a national media campaign in recent years.

Perhaps the most salient point in each author's historical review of public policy is the absence of a uniform underlying framework to guide policy development. No common model or framework for policy development could be found across the eight service systems reviewed by authors. We believe that principles of risk and resilience—grounded in ecological theory—offer a useful framework for considering the conditions that affect children, and that by applying a risk and protective factor perspective we can better design social programs to address these conditions. Next, we offer some thoughts on how these principles might be used to develop policy for children, youth, and families.

Risk and Resilience: An Ecological Perspective for Developing Child, Youth, and Family Policy

Rooted in ecological theory, principles of risk, protection, and resilience have been successfully applied to prevention and treatment with children and adolescents in varied settings. In particular, substance abuse and delinquency prevention programs have been based on risk and protective factors occurring at levels of influence (e.g., environmental, interpersonal and individual) that are compatible with ecological theory (Germain, 1991). However, the full utility of risk, protection, and ecological theory for policy development remains untapped.

Using a risk- and protection-based approach to creating policies for children, youth, and families requires a step-by-step approach. These steps are outlined next and summarized in the developmental policy process shown in Figure 10.1.

Step 1: Evaluate Risk and Protective Factors

Policy making begins with developing an understanding of the risk and protective factors associated with a targeted child or adolescent problem behavior. Consistent with ecological theory, factors should be assessed or summarized at environmental, interpersonal, social, and individual levels. Chapter authors have reviewed risk and protective factors associated with each of the problem behaviors and conditions discussed in this book. Because common risk and protective factors have been identified for many social and health problems, it may not always be necessary for policymakers to conduct basic risk or protective factor assessments. In many fields, research studies already specify predominant risk and protective factors (e.g., Fraser, 2004; Hawkins, 2006; Herrenkohl, Chung, & Catalano, 2004; Woolf, 2008). However, differences in local environmental conditions may necessitate new assessments in some circumstances. For example, an urban center may be concerned about the disproportionate nature of poverty or the needs of racial/ethnic groups in certain geographic areas. The ways risk and protective factors vary by region, gender, and culture is the subject of much current research. Although some risk and protective factors are common, risk factors also clearly vary from the tribal lands of the mountain and plains states to the urban centers of the East and West coasts. These differences complicate risk assessment and pose a major challenge for policymakers.

Thinking about policy from a risk and protection perspective offers two advantages. First, the perspective allows for the use of a common language across policy domains. This gives policymakers, advocates, practitioners, and researchers a uniform vocabulary to use in describing related behaviors, setting program objectives, and assessing program outcomes. Second, because the concepts of risk and protection emerged from research in child development and prevention science, we can build on scientific knowledge. This rapidly expanding knowledge base holds the potential—as demonstrated in juvenile justice—to reform service systems across the country.

Step 2: Assign Policy Responsibility in Ways That Promote Service Integration Across Systems

Policies based on empirical evidence about the risk and protective factors associated with child and youth problems should be developed and implemented across the policy arenas addressed in this book. Integrating key programs and services identified or implied by policies across and within systems of care should be a priority. Critical questions that should be considered in the policy development and integration processes include the following:

1. Which service systems have primary responsibility for the programs and services defined or implied by the policy?

2. Where does fiscal accountability lie for the programs and services defined or implied by the stated policy?

3. Does the stated policy explicitly develop links between and within the major service systems for children, youth, and families?

4. Do adequate implementation resources exist within or across the primary systems to achieve service integration?

5. How can service systems share existing or new program resources, including staff, physical locations, training curricula, and evaluation tools and methods?

Figure 10.1 A Developmental Process of Child, Youth, and Family Policy

Implement, Monitor, and Evaluate
- Child, Youth, and Family Outcomes
- Costs and Benefits

Determine Social Interventions
- Prevention
- Control
- Treatment

Develop Policy Responses
- Evidence-Based Practice
- Risk and Protection

Assessment and Feedback

Targeted Behavior

Evaluate Risk and Protective Factors
- Environmental
- Individual
- Social
- Interpersonal

Assign to Service Delivery Systems

Developmental Disabilities · Education · Child Welfare · Juvenile Justice · Mental Health · Substance Abuse · Health · Income & Assets

Locating and integrating program components defined by social policies within and across service systems are challenging undertakings. Collaborative partnerships between researchers, policy experts, and administrators are necessary to achieve the more fluid delivery and integration of policies aimed at children, youth, and families. Collaboration between service systems to prevent early and unwanted teen pregnancy illustrates policy and program efforts aimed at integration. See the accompanying box.[1]

The Value of Collaboration and Integration

The Case of Early and Unwanted Teen Pregnancy

Early and unwanted adolescent pregnancy rates fell by 24% between 1996 and 2001 (Centers for Disease Control and Prevention, 2002). The decline, although likely influenced by a host of factors, was partially attributed to improvements in the coordination of policies and programs between the nation's health care and educational systems. This collaborative effort included:

- The systematic dissemination of information by public health departments, government agencies, and schools aimed at educating and creating awareness among the public about the high rates of adolescent pregnancy in the United States.
- The implementation of school-based prevention efforts aimed at delaying the onset of adolescents' sexual activity and educating students about the risks associated with unprotected sex.
- The creation of school-based health clinics to reach adolescents who might not have access to medical care and thus were likely to be at highest risk for early and unwanted pregnancy.
- The allocation of targeted federal, state, and local funds to establish community-based health clinics that educate young men and women at risk for early, unwanted pregnancy and offer treatment for young families.

The decline in adolescent pregnancy rates came at a time of increased collaboration between the nation's health care and educational systems. This successful collaboration demonstrated the potential of policy and program integration for reducing child and adolescent problems.

A similar example illustrating the positive effects that system collaboration and integration can have on adolescent behavior is found in efforts to treat co-occurring substance abuse and mental health problems. Jenson and Potter (2003) tested an experimental intervention created to fill the mandate of legislation passed by the Colorado State Legislature. A legislative note mandated the mental health and juvenile justice systems to find innovative ways to treat co-occurring substance use and mental health problems among young offenders. The state systems responded by assessing risk and protective factors for adolescent substance abuse and mental health problems. An intervention was designed to place mental health case managers in juvenile justice facilities. Jenson and Potter conducted a longitudinal investigation of the program and found that the youth who received the intervention reported significant reductions in their levels of depression, anxiety, and substance use. This type of cross-system integration holds promise for reducing child and adolescent problem behaviors. Studies reporting positive outcomes from coordinated interventions involving systems from mental health, health, juvenile justice, and substance abuse domains illustrate the potential of social policies supporting programs that cross traditional boundaries (Finkelstein & Markoff, 2004; Graves, Frabutt, & Shelton, 2007; Kaufman et al., 2006). These findings are encouraging because they indicate that we are beginning to recognize the benefits of policies, programs, and services that use coordinated and collaborative efforts.

Step 3: Use Evidence to Create Public Policy Responses

Empirical evidence gained from studies of risk and protective factors should be used to create child, youth, and family public policies. Developing evidence-based policy, or at least evidence-informed policy, will require the dissemination of aggregate-level information about the etiology of child and adolescent problems to policymakers during the deliberation processes that lead to the creation of public policy. A critical step in dissemination is translating the empirical evidence in a manner that is immediately useable and practical for legislators and policy experts.

Recent developments in evidence-based practice (EBP) offer an opportunity to advance the notion of creating policies for children and families from an empirical framework. In the 1990s, EBP evolved in the medical profession from a concept to a movement to a professional imperative aimed at helping physicians select effective treatments for their patients. Definitions and perceptions of what EBP is—and what it is not—vary widely. In what is arguably the most accepted definition of EBP, Sackett and colleagues (Sackett, Straus, Richardson, Rosenberg, & Haynes, 2000) stated that EBP is "the integration of best research evidence with clinical expertise and [client] values" (p. 1). This definition implies that EBP is a process, characterized by specific steps and actions that require practitioners to locate, select, and implement the best available interventions for a targeted group or population.

An important parallel exists between the essential steps of EBP and the policy-making process as illustrated in Figure 10.1. In both processes, the identification of risk and protective factors associated with specific problems lead to the design, selection, and testing of individual and social interventions. In an ideal setting, the best available interventions—meaning those with strong research evidence supporting their effectiveness—are then translated to broad-based social policies aimed at improving the lives of children and families.

Unfortunately, relatively few effective interventions manage to navigate the difficult path from implementation to policy. One recent exception is the Nurse-Family Partnership Program developed by David Olds and his colleagues (Olds, Henderson, Tatelbaum, & Chamberlin, 1986). Aimed at guiding low-income mothers and their firstborn children toward successful futures, the program offers intensive home visitation services during a woman's pregnancy and for 2 years after the birth of a first child. Controlled trials of the intervention have demonstrated positive effects in preventing child maltreatment and reducing maternal arrests (Olds, 2008; Olds, Sadler, & Kitzman, 2007). In addition, other evaluation studies have reported reductions in child and adolescent conduct problems (Olds et al., 2009). More important, the program has recently been adopted by Colorado, among several other states, as part of a required set of interventions aimed at helping vulnerable young women and their families. The successful translation of evidence gained from intervention trials of the Nurse-Family Partnership to specific child and family policy may provide a template for other systems of care discussed in this book.

Step 4: Determine the Course of Specific Individual and Social Interventions

To determine the course of individual and social interventions, policy officials should consider evidence that identifies evidence-based programs and services for children and adolescents. Policy creation that integrates principles of risk, resilience, and EBP requires a comprehensive review of empirical evidence about the efficacy of alternative intervention approaches. In essence, determining the appropriate course of social intervention begs the old question, "What works best for whom under what conditions?"

Several outlets have surfaced as sources for obtaining information about effective interventions for children and youth. In Chapter 1, we noted the work of the University of Colorado's Center for the Study and Prevention of Violence. The center has identified a number of efficacious prevention programs that can be selected as the basis for a community or state's violence prevention efforts (Center for the Study and Prevention of Violence, 2010). Similarly, the Substance Abuse and Mental Health Services Administration (2010) maintains the National Registry of Evidence-Based Programs and Practice, a comprehensive list of effective substance abuse and mental health programs. The Coalition for Evidence-Based Policy (2010) has compiled a compendium of early childhood, educational, and youth development programs that have been found effective in preventing violence and other childhood and adolescent problems. In addition, interdisciplinary groups such as the international Campbell and Cochrane Collaborations have provided public worldwide access to systematic reviews of the literature on treatment outcomes across a range of adolescent problems. These reviews offer a rich source of information for policy officials who are engaged in the process of recommending or selecting interventions for public systems of care (Campbell Collaboration Library, 2010; Cochrane Collaboration, 2010).

Decision makers are beginning to consider both program and cost-effectiveness when selecting interventions and creating policies for children and families. Historically, practitioners and policy officials have had little credible empirical evidence regarding the costs and benefits of social interventions to guide their decisions about which programs to select or to fund. Fortunately, this situation is changing through work conducted by numerous research teams, such as Aos and colleagues at the Washington State Institute for Public Policy (Aos, Lieb, Mayfield, Miller, & Pennucci, 2004). These researchers reviewed the benefits and costs of a wide range of prevention programs aimed at problems such as aggression, delinquency, school failure, and substance abuse. All of the programs included in their review had been previously tested in research using either an experimental design or a well-constructed quasi-experimental design. Findings from the study showed that some prevention programs yielded cost savings and effectively prevented or delayed the onset of problem behaviors. Equally important, Aos and associates produced tangible evidence in the form of a *benefit-per-dollar cost figure* for early childhood, prenatal and infant home visitation, youth development, mentoring, substance abuse, teen pregnancy, and juvenile offender programs. Benefits were greatest for juvenile offender programs. In these programs, the cost savings ranged from $1,900 to more than $31,000 per participant. Substantial benefits were also found among prenatal and infant home visitation programs, ranging from $6,200 to $17,200 in savings per individual youth. In addition, early childhood education programs and selected youth development programs were shown to produce significant benefits. The cost-saving figures generated by the Aos team point both to the importance of investing in effective programs and to the danger of funding ineffective programs. Policymakers and other decision makers are well advised to consider the findings and to implement the recommendations consistent with the growing evidence base. To make better use of the research literature on the effectiveness of interventions for children and adolescents (for a review, see Allen-Meares & Fraser, 2004) and to implement the kind of collaborative programs the authors have described in every chapter will require state and local officials to find ways of breaking down organizational barriers. In addition, policymakers will need to break through institutional isomorphism and exert leadership in overcoming the turf issues that have confounded previous reform efforts (e.g., the implementation of the Children's and Community Mental Health Services Improvement Act of 1992, which attempted to create systems of care within mental health). Unfortunately, many of the nation's educational systems, human services agencies, and state and community organizations fail to consider, select, or implement tested or effective programs. There continues to be a significant gap between what we know to be effective in preventing and treating childhood and family problems and what programs are actually implemented; this gap must be narrowed (Fixsen, Naoom, Blasé, Friedman, & Wallace, 2005). Policymakers should be encouraged to pay greater attention to the benefits gained by implementing proven and tested programs. Perceived barriers associated with replicating and implementing effective program strategies must be eliminated.

Step 5: Implement, Monitor, and Evaluate Policies and Interventions

The development of collaborative systems of care will also require greater emphasis on monitoring and evaluating the interventions. The energy and enthusiasm associated with reforms must be converted into systemic procedures that monitor the implementation of new programs, provide feedback, and articulate consequences for failed or inconsistent implementation. This level of accountability implies using fidelity checks to ensure that interventions are being implemented as intended, conducting cost–benefit analyses to assess the economic consequences of programs and policies, and assessing child, youth, and parent outcomes. Monitoring and evaluation allow legislators and others to determine the outcomes of policies and programs; effective efforts can be re-funded, and ineffective approaches can be redesigned.

Summary

In this book, we have suggested that this country needs a new framework for child, youth, and family policy. Specifically, we have argued that a risk and resilience model, grounded in principles of ecological theory, offers potential for creating policies and programs that will lead to effective interventions for the problems that confront children and families in America.

The time is ripe for a new paradigm that will specifically focus on the developmental processes—both risk and protective—related to the social and health problems that child, youth, and family policies are intended to address. Opinion polls assessing public willingness to fund early intervention and rehabilitation programs for children and youth have shown strong support for collaborative and community-based efforts (National Council on Crime and Delinquency, 2007). Advances in strengths-based practice, assets-oriented programming, and positive youth development have emerged, and they complement the risk, protection, and resilience framework set forth in this volume (Catalano, 2007; Maton, Schellenbach, Leadbeater, & Solarz, 2004). Although more research is needed to better understand the interactive processes inherent in these approaches, the potential of the risk and resilience model for policy development should not be understated. Finally, recent trends in the acceptance of evidence-based practice have brought researchers and policy experts together in ways that were unseen in past years.

The principles of risk and resilience arose from research on developmental psychopathology and prevention science. Major advances have occurred in these fields in the articulation of the developmental trajectories of children who drop out of school, become delinquent, use illicit substances, experience serious emotional disorders, or have other poor developmental outcomes. At the same time, this knowledge has been used to design effective prevention programs, many of which have been described in the previous chapters. These programs attempt to reduce risk and alter developmental trajectories. Findings from these programs are promising (Dodge, 2009).

In the glow of promise from these programs, we ask, "Is it adequate to construct policy on the basis of risk factors alone?" We think risk reduction alone is an insufficient goal for public policy, although achieving risk reduction would be a significant step forward. It is the hope incumbent in the concept of resilience—where children at high risk prevail over adversity—that gives us pause. One driving force behind policy development must clearly be a moral imperative to reduce risk. However, from resilient children, we learn that risk reduction is defined, in part, by strategies that ameliorate or buffer adversities. In studying these protective processes, we often find that what protects children at risk also serves to promote positive developmental outcomes for all children (e.g., Fraser, 2004; Jenson, in press).

From this perspective, public policy for children and youths should be guided by attempts toward reducing risk *while* promoting protection. For all children (including those at risk), public policy should promote competence in social and academic settings, confidence in interpersonal relationship, and a self-efficacy in making life-course decisions. In addition, child policy should seek to foster connections to others who provide support and mentoring, the development of character or moral integrity regarding right and wrong behaviors, and feelings of caring or compassion for others who may be less fortunate (Catalano, Berglund, Ryan, Lonczak, & Hawkins, 2004; Catalano, Hawkins, Berglund, Pollard, & Arthur, 2002; Lerner, Fisher, & Weinberg, 2000). Too often, policy development is influenced by changes in problem rates or by catalyzing events such as epidemics or disasters. Of course, it is important to respond when rates rise or events create great need. However, public policy for children and youth should be proactive rather than reactive. It should promote protective processes that nurture developmental outcomes for all children, but especially those at great risk. In the sense of *Healthy People 2020* (U.S. Department of Health and Human Services, 2010), the intent of public policy for children, youth, and families should extend beyond the prevention of delinquency, substance abuse, or other social and health problems. Rather, the intent of policy should express health-promoting societal goals related to positive developmental outcomes for all children and the creation of widely accessible means for achieving those outcomes. Although highly structured and focused programs may always be needed to help children who have special needs (e.g., children who are victimized by individual disadvantage or tragic events), public policy for children should be rooted in core commitments that strengthen families, improve schools, and reinvigorate neighborhoods.

Much remains to be done to solve the fragmented nature of child, youth, and family policy in the United States. Individual service systems employ skilled practitioners, and each system can point to exemplary programs and innovative service delivery patterns. Despite those examples, child, youth, and family policies continue to suffer from the lack of an underlying and unifying framework that integrates services across problem domains and creates fully articulated systems of care. A risk and resilience perspective, coupled with ecological theory, holds promise as an organizing framework for future public policy efforts directed at the nation's young people. It is their future and our challenge.

Note

1. Biglan, Brennan, Foster, and Holder (2004) used a similar format with a different example to demonstrate the importance of collaboration in developing strategies for working with high-risk youth.

References

Allen-Meares, P., & Fraser, M. W. (Eds.). (2004). *Intervention with children and adolescents: An interdisciplinary perspective*. Needham Heights, MA: Allyn & Bacon.

Aos, S., Lieb, R., Mayfield, J., Miller, M., & Pennucci, A. (2004). *Benefits and costs of prevention and early intervention programs for youth*. Olympia: Washington State Institute for Public Policy.

Biglan, A., Brennan, P. A., Foster, S. L., & Holder, H. D. (2004). *Helping adolescents at risk. Prevention of multiple problems*. New York: Guilford Press

Campbell Collaboration Library. (2010). *The Campbell Collaboration Library of systematic reviews*. Retrieved from http://www.campbellcollaboration.org/library.php

Catalano, R. F. (2007). Prevention is a sound public and private investment. *Criminology and Public Policy, 6,* 377–398. doi: 10.1111/j.1745-9133.2007.00443.x

Catalano, R. F., Berglund, M. L., Ryan, J. A. M., Lonczak, H. S., & Hawkins, J. D. (2004). Positive youth development in the United States: Research findings on evaluations of positive youth development programs. *Annals of the American Academy of Political and Social Science, 591,* 98–124. doi:10.1177/0002716203260102

Catalano, R.F., Hawkins, J.D., Berglund, L., Pollard, J. A., & Arthur, M. W. (2002). Prevention science and positive youth development: Competitive or cooperative frameworks? *Journal of Adolescent Health, 31,* 230–239. doi:10.1016/S1054-139X(02)00496-2

Center for the Study and Prevention of Violence. (2010). *Blueprints for violence prevention*. Retrieved from: http://www.colorado.edu/cspv/

Centers for Disease Control and Prevention. (2002). *Special tabulations of first births from the 1997–2002 natality data sets* (Nos. 9–16, Series 21). Retrieved from http://wonder.cdc.gov/wonder/help/Natality.html

Coalition for Evidence-Based Practice. (2010). *Increasing government effectiveness through rigorous evidence about "what works."* Retrieved from http://coalition4evidence.org/wordpress/

Cochrane Collaboration. (2010). *Cochrane reviews*. Retrieved from http://www.cochrane.org/cochrane-reviews

Dodge, K. A. (2009). Community intervention and public policy in the prevention of antisocial behavior. *Journal of Child Psychology and Psychiatry, 50,* 194–200. doi:10.1111/j.1469–7610.2008.01985.x

Finkelstein, N., & Markoff, L. S. (2004). The Women Embracing Life and Living (WELL) Project: Using the relational model to develop integrated systems of care for women with alcohol/drug use and mental health disorders with histories of violence. *Alcoholism Treatment Quarterly, 22,* 63–80. doi:10.1300/J020v22n03_04

Fixsen, D. L., Naoom, S. F., Blasé, K. A., Friedman, R. M., & Wallace, F. (2005). *Implementation research: A synthesis of the literature* (FHMI Publication #231). Tampa: University of South Florida, Louis de la Parre Florida Mental Health Institute, National Implementation Research Network.

Fraser, M. W. (Ed.). (2004). *Risk and resilience in childhood: An ecological perspective* (2nd ed.). Washington, DC: NASW Press.

Fraser, M. W., Kirby, L. D., & Smokowski, P. R. (2004). Risk and resilience in childhood. In M. W. Fraser (Ed.), *Risk and resilience in childhood: An ecological perspective* (2nd ed., pp. 13–66). Washington, DC: NASW Press.

Germain, C. B. (1991). *Human behavior in the social environment: An ecological view.* New York: Columbia University Press.

Graves, K. N., Frabutt, J. M., & Shelton, T. L. (2007). Factors associated with mental health and juvenile justice involvement among children with severe emotional disturbance. *Youth Violence and Juvenile Justice, 5,* 147–167. doi:10.1177/1541204006292870

Hawkins, J. D. (2006). Science, social work, prevention: Finding the intersections. *Social Work Research,* 137–152.

Hawkins, J. D., Catalano, R. F., & Miller, J. Y. (1992). Risk and protective factors for alcohol and other drug problems in adolescence and early adulthood: Implications for substance abuse prevention. *Psychological Bulletin, 112,* 64–105. doi:10.1037/0033–2909.112.1.64

Herrenkohl, T. I., Chung, I. J., & Catalano, R. F. (2004). Review of research on predictors of youth violence and school-based and community-based prevention approaches. In P. Allen-Meares & M. W. Fraser (Eds.), *Intervention with children and adolescents: An interdisciplinary perspective* (pp. 449–476). Boston: Pearson Education.

Howell, J. C. (2003). *Preventing and reducing juvenile delinquency: A comprehensive framework.* Thousand Oaks, CA: Sage.

Jenson, J. M. (in press). Advances and challenges in preventing childhood and adolescent problem behavior. *Research on Social Work Practice.*

Jenson, J. M., & Howard, M. O. (1998). Youth crime, public policy, and practice in the juvenile justice system: Recent trends and needed reforms. *Social Work, 43,* 324–334.

Jenson, J. M., & Potter, C. A. (2003). The effects of cross-system collaboration on mental health and substance abuse problems of detained youth. *Research on Social Work Practice, 13,* 588–607. doi:10.1177/1049731503253405

Kaufman, J. S., Crusto, C. A., Quan, M., Ross, E., Friedman, S. R., O'Rielly, K., & Call, S. (2006). Utilizing program evaluation as a strategy to promote community change: Evaluation of a comprehensive, community-based, family violence initiative. *American Journal of Community Psychology, 38,* 191–200. doi:10.1007/s10464–006–9086–8

Lerner, R. M., Fisher, C. B., & Weinberg, R. A. (2000). Toward a science for and of the people: Promoting civil society through the application of developmental science. *Child Development, 71,* 11–20. doi:10.1111/1467–8624.00113

Maton, K. I., Schellenbach, C. J., Leadbeater, B. J., & Solarz, A. L. (2004). *Investing in children, youth, families, and communities. Strengths-based research and policy.* Washington, DC: American Psychological Association. doi:10.1037/10660–000

National Council on Crime and Delinquency. (2007). *New NCCD poll shows public strongly favors youth rehabilitation and treatment.* Retrieved from http://www.nccd-crc.org/nccd/pubs/zogbyPR0207.pdf.

Olds, D. L. (2008). Preventing child maltreatment and crime with prenatal and infancy support of parents: The nurse–family partnership. *Journal of Scandinavian Studies in Criminology and Crime Prevention, 9,* 2–24. doi:10.1080/14043850802450096

Olds, D. L, Eckenrode, J., Henderson, C., Kitzman, H., Cole, R., Luckey, D., Holmberg, J., & Baca, P. (2009). Preventing child abuse and neglect with home visiting by nurses. In K. A. Dodge & D. L. Coleman (Eds.), *Preventing child maltreatment: Community approaches* (pp. 29–54). New York: Guilford Press.

Old, D. L., Hendeson, C. R., Tatelbaum, R., & Chamberlin, R. (1986). Improving the prenatal care and outcomes of pregnancy: A randomized trial of nurse home visitation, *Pediatrics, 77,* 16–28.

Olds, D. L., Sadler, L., & Kitzman, H. (2007). Programs for parents of infants and toddlers: Recent evidence from randomized trials. *Journal of Child Psychology and Psychiatry, 48,* 355–391. doi:10.1111/j.1469–7610.2006.01702.x

Sackett, D. L., Straus, S. E., Richardson, W. S., Rosenberg, W., & Haynes, R. B. (2000). *Evidence-based medicine: How to practice and teach EBM* (2nd ed.). New York: Churchill Livingstone.

Substance Abuse and Mental Health Services Administration. (2010). *NREPP: SAMHSA's national registry of evidence-based programs and practices.* Retrieved from http://www.nrepp.samhsa.gov/

U.S. Department of Health and Human Services. (2010). *Healthy people 2020: The road ahead.* Washington, DC: Government Printing Office.

Woolf, S. H. (2008). The power of prevention and what it requires. *Journal of the American Medical Association, 299,* 2437–2439. doi:10.1001/jama.299.20.2437

Zavlek, S. (2005). *Promoting community-based facilities for violent juvenile offenders as part of a system of graduated sanctions* (NCJ 209326; Juvenile Justice Practice Series). Washington, DC: U.S. Department of Justice, Office of Justice Programs, Office of Juvenile Justice and Delinquency Prevention.

Index

Abandoned Infants Assistance Act, 83
Abuse. *See* Adolescent substance abuse;
    Alcohol abuse; Child
    abuse/neglect; Emotional abuse;
    Sexual abuse; Substance abuse
Academic achievement:
    children with disabilities and, 238
    delinquency and, 318
    home environment and, 33
    juvenile justice policies/programs
        and, 335
    poverty and, 25
    race/ethnicity/protective factors
        and, 79
    risk factors and, 115–116
    standards to assess, 129
    welfare reform and, 43
Academic failure, 7
    promotive/protective factors and,
        118 (table)
    risk factors and, 117 (table)
    student-specific risk factors and,
        114–115
Achievement gap, 131, 134
Acquired Immunodeficiency Syndrome
    (AIDS):
    African American youths and, 73
    health care for children/youth and,
        205, 207, 209
    infants and, 83
    risk/protection/resilience and, 15
Ad Council and Partnership for a
    Drug-Free America, 287
Addiction Equity Act, 283

Administration for Children and
    Families, 131
Adolescent substance abuse,
    270–271, 280
    prevention policies for, 292–294
    protective factors and, 276–279,
        277 (table)
    resilience and, 279–280
    risk factors and, 273–276, 274 (table)
    treatment of, 279, 280, 281 (table),
        289–291
    treatment policies for, 294–297
    trends in, 272
    See also Substance abuse
Adoption:
    child welfare and, 63
    child welfare legislation and, 83
    increase of, 58, 60
    policies/programs and, 93
Adoption and Foster Care Analysis and
    Reporting System (AFCARS),
    100n. 2
Adoption and Safe Families Act of 1997,
    65, 83
Adoption Assistance and Child Welfare
    Act of 1980, 65, 82
Adoption assistance programs, 84
Adoption Incentive Program, 83
Adoption Promotion Act of 2003, 83
Adoption Reform Act of 1978, 83
Advocacy groups, 245–246, 259
African American issues:
    adolescent substance abuse and, 272
    anti-poverty policies and, 49

371

About the Editors

Jeffrey M. Jenson, Ph.D., is the Philip D. and Eleanor G. Winn Professor for Children and Youth at Risk and Associate Dean for Research in the Graduate School of Social Work, University of Denver. Dr. Jenson's teaching and research interests address the etiology and prevention of childhood and adolescent problems of bullying, aggression, school dropout, and juvenile delinquency. His research focuses on the application of a risk and resilience approach to preventing childhood and adolescent health and behavior problems and on the evaluation of prevention strategies aimed at promoting positive youth development. Dr. Jenson has published four books and numerous articles on the topic of adolescent problem behavior. He is currently principal investigator of the Bridge Project Afterschool Initiative, a longitudinal investigation aimed at improving academic and behavioral outcomes among children and youth residing in four Denver public housing communities. Dr. Jenson has received several awards for his scholarship, including the Aaron Rosen Award from the Society for Social Work and Research. He was awarded the University of Denver Distinguished Scholar Award in 2003 and the University Lecturer Award in 2007. He was Editor-in-Chief of the journal *Social Work Research* from 2004 to 2008.

Mark W. Fraser, Ph.D., holds the Tate Distinguished Professorship at the School of Social Work, University of North Carolina, where he serves as Associate Dean for Research. He has won numerous awards for research and teaching, including the Distinguished Achievement Award from the Society for Social Work and Research. His work focuses on risk and resilience, child behavior, child and family services, and research methods. He has published widely and is the co-author or editor of nine books. These include *Families in Crisis*, a study of intensive family-centered services, and *Evaluating Family-Based Services*, a text on methods for family research. In *Risk and Resilience in Childhood*, he and his colleagues describe resilience-based perspectives for child maltreatment, substance abuse, and other social problems. In *Making Choices,* Dr. Fraser and his co-authors outline a program to help children build social relationships with peers and adults. In *The Context of Youth Violence,* he explores violence from the perspective of resilience, risk, and protection, and in *Intervention with Children and Adolescents,* Dr. Fraser and his colleagues review advances in intervention knowledge for social and health problems. An award-winning text, *Social Policy for Children and Families,* reviews the bases for public policy in income support, child welfare, juvenile justice, mental health, developmental disabilities, and health. *Intervention Research: Developing Social Programs* describes the design and development of social programs. His most recent book is *Propensity Score Analysis: Statistical Methods and Applications.* Dr. Fraser is a member of the American Academy of Social Work and Social Welfare.

About the Contributors

Elizabeth K. Anthony, Ph.D., is an Assistant Professor in the School of Social Work at Arizona State University, where she teaches courses in applied research and clinical practice with children and adolescents. Dr. Anthony's research and publications focus on resilience and interventions to promote healthy outcomes among youth living in poverty. Prior to coming to Arizona State University, she served as Research Director at the University of Denver for a longitudinal study in Denver Public Housing neighborhoods and was a postdoctoral fellow at the University of California, Berkeley.

William H. Barton, Ph.D., is a Professor in the Indiana University School of Social Work at Indiana University-Purdue University in Indianapolis, where he teaches courses in juvenile justice policy, research methods, leadership, and the philosophy of science. Dr. Barton's research interests include juvenile justice, delinquency prevention, youth development, and community practice. For more than 30 years, he has conducted evaluations of juvenile justice programs and policies throughout the United States. Dr. Barton has published numerous journal articles and book chapters. He has co-authored two books, and he is a frequent presenter at national conferences.

Sandra K. Danziger, Ph.D., is a Professor of Social Work, School of Social Work, and Research Professor of Public Policy, Gerald R. Ford School of Public Policy, at the University of Michigan. Her primary research interests and publications examine the effects of public anti-poverty and social service programs and policies on the well-being of disadvantaged families, particularly single mothers and their children. Professor Danziger was a 2009 Scholar in Residence at the Rockefeller Foundation Bellagio Center, Bellagio, Italy. She received the 2006 Society for Social Work Research Excellence in Research Award. She was a Visiting Scholar at the Russell Sage Foundation, New York, in 2002 to 2003 and, in 1994, Visiting Research Scientist, Office of the Secretary,

398 SOCIAL POLICY FOR CHILDREN AND FAMILIES

Assistant Secretary for Planning and Evaluation, U.S. Department of Health and Human Services, Washington, DC.

Mary E. Fraser, D.S.W., has worked as a program and policy consultant to mental health departments in three states. Dr. Fraser wrote the Child and Adolescent Service System Program grant for the state of Utah in the early 1990s and served as that office's first director. She worked in the capacity of executive staff member to the North Carolina Legislative Oversight Committee on Mental Health Reform in 2000. Dr. Fraser's numerous publications focus on mental health policy and practice for children and families. She was previously a clinical adjunct professor in social work and psychiatry at the University of North Carolina at Chapel Hill.

Andy J. Frey, Ph.D., is an Associate Professor and the Chair of the school social work specialization in the Kent School of Social Work at the University of Louisville. Dr. Frey's research interests and publications address the provision of school-based mental health and school social work services and prevention and intervention for young children with disruptive behavior. Prior to his appointment at the University of Louisville, he was a school social worker and behavioral consultant in Douglas County, Colorado.

Markell Harrison-Jackson, Ph.D., serves as an Educational and Child Welfare Consultant for the Transitional Foster Care Alliance, where he has developed programs for domestic and international child welfare and foster care systems. He also teaches independent living skills to foster care youth and provides individual and group counseling to at-risk students in a variety of social service and custodial protective services agencies. Dr. Markell-Jackson was formerly a Special Education Specialist with Pinal County Education Service Agency in Florence, Arizona. He has 13 years of experience in teaching and leadership capacities in the urban K through 12 special education continuum of services.

Matthew O. Howard, Ph.D., is the Frank A. Daniels, Jr. Distinguished Professor of Human Services Policy Information in the School of Social Work and Faculty Research Fellow in the Cecil G. Sheps Center for Health Services Research at the University of North Carolina at Chapel Hill. Dr. Howard has published numerous articles in the field of substance abuse and is the recipient of several research grants from the National Institutes of Health aimed at understanding the natural history of inhalant abuse. Dr. Howard is the current Editor-in-Chief of the journal *Social Work Research*.

Guadalupe V. Huitron, B.A., is completing a dual degree program in social work and public health at the University of North Carolina at Chapel Hill. She is a fellow in the Public Health Social Work Leadership Program at North Carolina and serves on the board of directors of El Centro Hispano of Durham, North Carolina.

Thomas C. Ormsby, B.A., is a graduate of the dual degree program in social work and public health at the University of North Carolina at Chapel Hill. He is currently Associate Director of Business Development in the Thailand Office of Family Health International.

Susan L. Parish, Ph.D., M.S.W., is the Nancy Lurie Marks Professor of Disability Policy and Director, Lurie Institute for Disability Policy, at The Heller School for Social Policy and Management, Brandeis University. Her research examines the health and well-being of children and adults with disabilities and their caregiving families. She teaches courses in social policy and research methods.

Peter J. Pecora, Ph.D., is the Managing Director of Research Services for Casey Family Programs and Professor in the School of Social Work at the University of Washington. Dr. Pecora has worked with state departments of social services in the United States and in other countries to refine foster care programs, develop evaluation strategies, and implement intensive home-based services and risk assessment systems for child protective services. His co-authored books and articles focus on child welfare program design, administration, and research. In 2009, he was elected to the American Academy of Social Work and Social Welfare as a fellow and inaugural board member.

Armon R. Perry, Ph.D., is an Assistant Professor in the Kent School of Social Work at the University of Louisville. Dr. Perry's research interests include fathers' involvement with their children and social welfare policy. Prior to his appointment at the University of Louisville, Dr. Perry was a child protective services social worker in Montgomery, Alabama.

Kathleen A. Rounds, Ph.D., is a Professor in the School of Social Work at the University of North Carolina at Chapel Hill. She is the Director of the Maternal and Child Health Public Health Social Work Leadership Program and Co-Chair of the dual degree program in social work and public health. Dr. Rounds's research has included evaluations of services for people with HIV, services for pregnant and postpartum women using substances, adolescent parenting programs, and interdisciplinary leadership and workforce development in maternal and child health.

Alison W. Saville, M.S.W, M.S.P.H., is the Project Manager for the Children's Outcomes Research Program (COR) at University of Colorado-Denver. She currently manages an investigation funded by the National Institutes of Health entitled Population versus Practice-based Interventions to Increase Immunizations.

Jamie G. Swaine, M.S.W., is a Clinical Instructor in the Developmental Disabilities Training Institute at the School of Social Work, University of North Carolina at Chapel Hill. She currently manages a project funded by the U.S. Department of Education that is testing the effectiveness of a community-based intervention to improve cervical and breast cancer screening rates for women with intellectual disabilities.

Hill M. Walker, Ph.D., is a Professor of Special Education, Co-Director of the Institute on Violence and Destructive Behavior, and Research Director of the Center on Human Development in the College of Education at the University of Oregon. He has a long-standing interest in behavioral assessment and in the development of effective intervention procedures for use in school settings with a range of behavior disorders. Dr. Walker's research interests include social skills assessment, curriculum development and intervention, longitudinal studies of aggression and antisocial behavior, and the development of early screening procedures for detecting students who are at-risk for social-behavioral adjustment problems and/or later school dropout.

Trina R. Williams Shanks, Ph.D., is an Assistant Professor in the School of Social Work at the University of Michigan. She is Co-Principal Investigator on the SEED impact assessment survey, a quasi-experimental study of children's savings accounts among preschool families. Her interests include asset-building policy and practice across the life cycle, the impact of poverty and wealth on child development outcomes, and community and economic development in urban areas.